Care of Collections

Leicester Readers in Museum Studies
Series editor: Professor Susan M. Pearce

Care of Collections
Simon Knell

Collections Management
Anne Fahy

The Educational Role of the Museum
Eilean Hooper-Greenhill

Interpreting Objects and Collections
Susan M. Pearce

Museum Management
Kevin Moore

Museum Provision and Professionalism
Gaynor Kavanagh

Care of Collections

Edited by Simon Knell

London and New York

First published 1994
by Routledge
11 New Fetter Lane, London EC4P 4EE

Simultaneously published in the USA and Canada
by Routledge
29 West 35th Street, New York, NY 10001

Typeset in Sabon by Florencetype Ltd, Stoodleigh, Devon
Printed and bound in Great Britain by TJ Press Ltd,
Padstow, Cornwall

British Library Cataloguing in Publication Data
A catalogue record for this book is available from the British Library

Library of Congress Cataloging in Publication Data
A catalog record for this book has been requested

ISBN 0–415–11284–2 (hbk)
ISBN 0–415–11285–0 (pbk)

Contents

List of figures		viii
List of tables		ix
Series preface		x
Preface to this volume		xi
Acknowledgements		xii

Introduction: the context of collection's care   1
Simon Knell

1   The ethics of conservation   11
    Jonathan Ashley-Smith

2   Cleaning and meaning: *The Ravished Image* reviewed   21
    Gerry Hedley

3   Solvent abuse   30
    Michael Daley

4   Working exhibits and the destruction of evidence in the   35
    Science Museum
    Peter R. Mann

5   The role of the scholar-curator in conservation   47
    Peter Cannon-Brookes

6   Do objects have a finite lifetime?   51
    Susan M. Bradley

7   Audits of care: a framework for collections condition surveys   60
    Suzanne Keene

8   Preventive conservation   83
    Getty Conservation Institute

9   Paintings: the (show) case for passive climate control   88
    Emil Bosshard

10   Silica gel and related RH buffering materials, conditioning   93
    and regeneration techniques
    Nathan Stolow

11 Conservation in the computer age   101
    Richard Hall

12 Museums tune in to radio   105
    Graham Martin and David Ford

13 Fresh-air climate conditioning at the Arthur M. Sackler Museum   107
    Michael Williams

14 Light and environmental measurement and control in
    National Trust houses   117
    Sarah Staniforth

15 The Clore Gallery for the Turner collection at the Tate Gallery:
    lighting strategy and practice   123
    Peter Wilson

16 Construction materials for storage and exhibition   129
    Ann Brooke Craddock

17 Indoor air pollution: effects on cultural and historic materials   135
    Norbert S. Baer and Paul N. Banks

18 Managing museum space   147
    U. Vincent Wilcox

19 Museum collections storage   155
    John D. Hilberry and Susan K. Weinberg

20 Here's what to consider in selecting high-density storage   176
    Abigail Terrones

21 A policy for collections access   179
    Jeanette A. Richoux, Jill Serota-Braden and Nancy Demyttenaere

22 Visible storage for the small museum   187
    Paul C. Thistle

23 Curators' closet   197
    Carrie Rebora

24 Rules for handling works of art   202
    Eric B. Rowlison

25 Rentokil bubble: results of test   212
    R. M. Entwistle and J. Pearson

26 Carpet beetle: a pilot study in detection and control   217
    Lynda Hillyer and Valerie Blyth

27 Pest control in museums: the use of chemicals and associated
    health problems   234
    Martyn J. Linnie

28 Experiencing loss   240
    Barclay G. Jones

29 Museum disaster preparedness planning   246
    John E. Hunter

30 Emergency treatment of materials   262
    M. S. Upton and C. Pearson

31 Protecting museums from threat of fire   276
    H. L. Lein

Further reading   280
Index   281

Figures

7.1   The uses of collections condition surveys   64
7.2   An example of a survey form   74
7.3   The hierarchical nature of museum collections data   76
9.1   Schematic cross-section of a climate-controlled case as used by the
      Thyssen-Bornemisza Collection   90
9.2   Empirical RH test in Lugano 1989   92
10.1 Isotherms of 'Art Sorb' silica gel, Kaken Gel (Nikka Pellets),
      Montmorillonite and standard silica gel   94
10.2 Conditioning technique using a fan over a tray of silica gel to speed
      up the process   96
10.3 Conditioning technique using an evaporative-type humidifier
      (revolving drum) with hygrostat control with a tent-like enclosure   96
10.4 Conditioning technique using saturated salt solutions   97
13.1 Standard reheat VAV system   110
13.2 Fresh-air climate conditioning system   114
24.1 Right and wrong way to stack paintings and other framed works   206
24.2 In stacking, crisscross framed works back to back and face to face,
      vertically and horizontally   206
24.3 Stacking large or heavy works   206
24.4 Stack works with ornate frames on padded blocks   206
24.5 Placing a large painting on a dolly for transport   207
24.6 Taping glass on works of art for protection during transit   208
24.7 Right and wrong way to remove tape from glass   208
26.1 Life-cycle of the woolly bear carpet beetle   230
26.2 Larval moult of the woolly bear carpet beetle   231
27.1 Pesticides used to protect collections   238
27.2 Medical complaints associated with pesticide usage   238

Tables

7.1	The objectives of collections surveys	66
7.2	Broad damage types	68
7.3	Information to be derived from pilot surveys	73
7.4	Checklist of topics for survey reports	77
17.1	Indoor air pollution damage to materials	137
17.2	Measured indoor–outdoor pollution levels for archives, libraries and museums	139
17.3	Air quality criteria for archives, libraries and museums	143

Series preface

Museums are established institutions, but they exist in a changing world. The modern notion of a museum and its collections runs back into the sixteenth or even fifteenth centuries, and the origins of the earliest surviving museums belong to the period soon after. Museums have subsequently been and continue to be founded along these well-understood lines. But the end of the second millennium AD and the advent of the third point up the new needs and preoccupations of contemporary society. These are many, but some can be picked out as particularly significant here. Access is crucially important: access to information, the decision-making process and resources like gallery space, and access by children, ethnic minorities, women and the disadvantaged and underprivileged. Similarly, the nature of museum work itself needs to be examined, so that we can come to a clearer idea of the nature of the institution and its material, of what museum professionalism means, and how the issues of management and collection management affect outcomes. Running across all these debates is the recurrent theme of the relationship between theory and practice in what is, in the final analysis, an important area of work.

New needs require fresh efforts at information-gathering and understanding, and the best possible access to important literature for teaching and study. It is this need which the Leicester Readers in Museum Studies series addresses. The series as a whole breaks new ground by bringing together, for the first time, an important body of published work, much of it very recent, much of it taken from journals which few libraries carry, and all of it representing fresh approaches to the study of the museum operation.

The series has been divided into six volumes, each of which covers a significant aspect of museum studies. These six topics bear a generic relationship to the modular arrangement of the Leicester Department of Museum Studies postgraduate course in Museum Studies, but, more fundamentally, they reflect current thinking about museums and their study. Within each volume, each editor has been responsible for his or her choice of papers. Each volume reflects the approach of its own editor, and the different feel of the various traditions and discourses upon which it draws. The range of individual emphases and the diversity of points of view is as important as the overarching theme in which each volume finds its place.

It is our intention to produce a new edition of the volumes in the series every three years, so that the selection of papers for inclusion is a continuing process and the contemporary stance of the series is maintained. All the editors of the series are happy to receive suggestions for inclusions (or exclusions), and details of newly published material.

Preface to this volume

The articles in this volume cover those aspects of collections management concerned with the care of collections (i.e. conservation issues, light, relative humidity, pollutants, pests, storage, disaster planning, packing, handling and transport). A companion volume covers matters of policy, standards, documentation, security and insurance. In selecting articles for inclusion in this reader, I have intentionally chosen those which provide information of practical use to the student of collections management. I have not chosen works simply because they are benchmarks in the development of the subject or necessarily focused on subjects which are particularly fashionable in the mid-1990s. I have also avoided overly technical or scientific works simply because the majority of museum studies students do not have a science background. There are also a number of books on the subject which need to be read in their entirety and cannot be dissected for inclusion here. Many of the articles here are the best short statements on these subjects available, but I welcome comments and suggestions from readers.

Thanks are due to Margaret Knell for her assistance with proofreading and indexing.

Acknowledgements

The publishers and editors would like to thank the following people and organizations for permission to reproduce copyright material:

Jonathan Ashley-Smith, 'The ethics of conservation', reproduced from *The Conservator* 6 (1982), pp. 1–5, by permission of the United Kingdom Institute for the Conservation of Historic and Artistic Works of Art. Gerry Hedley, 'Cleaning and meaning: *The Ravished Image* reviewed', reproduced from *The Conservator* 10 (1986), pp. 2–6, by permission of the United Kingdom Institute for the Conservation of Historic and Artistic Works of Art. Michael Daley, 'Solvent abuse', reproduced from *The Spectator*, 30 January 1993, pp. 55–8, by permission of *The Spectator*. Peter R. Mann, 'Working exhibits and the destruction of evidence in the Science Museum'. This article was first published in *Museum Management and Curatorship*, Volume 8 (1989), pp. 369–87, and is reproduced here with the permission of Butterworth-Heinemann, Oxford, UK, and the author. Peter Cannon-Brooks, 'The role of scholar-curator in conservation'. This article was first published in *Museum Management and Curatorship*, Volume 7 (1988), pp. 323–5, and is reproduced here with the permission of Butterworth-Heinemann, Oxford, UK, and the author. Susan M. Bradley, 'Do objects have a finite lifetime?' reproduced from S. Keene (ed.) (1990) *Managing Conservation*, pp. 24–7, by permission of the United Kingdom Institute for Conservation of Historic and Artistic Works of Art. Suzanne Keene, 'Audits of care: a framework for collections condition surveys, reproduced from M. Norman and V. Todd (1991) *Storage* (preprints for the UKIC conference, 'Restoration '91'), pp. 6–14, by permission of the United Kingdom Institute for Conservation of Historic and Artistic Works of Art. Getty Conservation Institute, 'Preventive conservation' (1992), reprinted from *Conservation, the GCI Newsletter*, Vol. 7, No. 1, pp. 4–7, with permission of the Getty Conservation Institute 1992. Emil Bosshard, 'Paintings: the (show) case for passive climate control' (1992), pp. 46–50, reproduced from *Museum* No. 173, © UNESCO 1992. Nathan Stolow, 'Silica gel and related RH buffering materials, conditioning and regeneration techniques', reproduced by permission of the author, Dr Nathan Stolow, Conservation Consultant, Williamsburg, VA, USA, originally from the book, *Conservation and Exhibitions* (1987), pp. 241–6, published by Butterworth-Heinemann, Ltd. Richard Hall, 'Conservation in the computer age'. This article was first published in *Museum Management and Curatorship*, Volume 6 (1987), pp. 291–4, and is reproduced here with the permission of Butterworth-Heinemann, Oxford, UK. Graham Martin and David Ford, 'Museums tune in to radio' reproduced from *Museum Development* (November 1992), pp. 15–16, by permission of The Museum Development Company and the Victoria and Albert Museum Conservation Journal. Michael Williams, 'Fresh-air climate conditioning at the Arthur M. Sackler Museum'. This article was first published in *Museum Management and Curatorship*, Volume 5, Number 4 (1986), pp. 329–36, and is reproduced here with the permission of Butterworth-Heinemann, Oxford, UK, and the author. Sarah Staniforth, 'Light and environmental measurement and control in National Trust houses', reproduced from J. Black (ed.) (1987) *Recent Advances in the Conservation and Analysis of Artifacts*, University College London Press. Peter Wilson, 'The Clore Gallery for the Turner collection at the Tate Gallery: lighting strategy and practice'. This article was first published in *Museum Management and Curatorship*, Volume 6, Number 1 (March 1987), pp. 37–42, and is reproduced here with the permission of Butterworth-Heinemann, Oxford, UK. Ann Brooke Craddock, 'Construction materials for storage and exhibition', reproduced from Konstanze Bachmann (ed.) (1992) *Conservation Concerns: A Guide for Collectors and Curators* (Washington DC: Smithsonian Institution Press), pp. 23–8. Copyright 1992 Smithsonian Institution. Norbert S. Baer and Paul N. Banks, 'Indoor air pollution: effects on cultural and historic materials'. This article was first published in *Museum Management and Curatorship*, Volume 4, Number 1 (March 1985), pp. 9–20, and is reproduced here with the permission of Butterworth-Heinemann, Oxford, UK. U. Vincent Wilcox, 'Managing museum space', in Suzanne Keene (ed.) (1990) *Managing Conservation*, pp. 7–10 by permission of the United Kingdom Institute for Conservation of Historic and Artistic Works of Art. John D. Hilberry and Susan K. Weinberg, 'Museum collections storage'. Reprinted, with permission, from *Museum News* (March/April, pp. 7–21, May/June, pp. 5–23, July/ August, pp. 49–60, 1981). Copyright 1981 the American Association of Museums. Abigail Terrones, 'Here's what to consider in selecting high-density storage'. Reprinted, with permission, from *Museum News* (March/April 1989), pp. 80–1. Copyright 1989 the American Association of Museums. Jeanette A. Richoux, Jill Serota-Braden and Nancy Demyttenaere, 'A policy for collections access'. Reprinted from *Museum News* (July/August 1981), pp. 43–7. Copyright 1981 the American Association of Museums. Paul C. Thistle, 'Visible storage for the small museum', *Curator* 33(1) (1990), pp. 49–62. Copyright © the American Museum of Natural History 1990. Carrie Rebora, 'Curators' closet'. Reprinted, with permission, from *Museum News* (July/ August 1991), pp. 50–4. Copyright 1991 the American Association of Museums. Eric B. Rowlison, 'Rules for handling works of art' reproduced from D. H. Dudley and I. B. Wilkinson (eds) (1979) *Museum Registration Methods*, pp. 355–66, by permission of the American Association of Museums, Washington. R. M. Entwhistle and J. Pearson, 'Rentokil bubble: results of test' reproduced from *Conservation News* 38 (1989), pp. 7–9, by permission of the United Kingdom Institute for Conservation of Historic and Artistic Works of Art. Lynda Hillyer and Valerie Blyth, 'Carpet beetle – a pilot study in detection and control' reproduced from *The Conservator* 16 (1992), pp. 65–77, by permission of the United Kingdom Institute for Conservation. Martyn J. Linnie, 'Pest control in museums – the use of chemicals and associated health problems'. This article was first published in *Museum Management and Curatorship*, Volume 9, Number 4 (December 1990), pp. 419–23, and is reproduced here with the permission of Butterworth-Heinemann, Oxford, UK. Barclay G. Jones, 'Experiencing loss' in B. G. Jones, *Protecting Historic Architecture and Museum Collections from Natural Disasters*, Oxford: Butterworth-Heinemann, 1986, pp. 3–13. John E. Hunter, 'Museum disaster preparedness planning' in B. G. Jones, *Protecting Historic Architecture and Museum Collections from Natural Disasters*, Oxford: Butterworth-Heinemann, 1986, pp. 211–30. M. S. Upton and C. Pearson, 'Emergency treatment of materials', in *Disaster Planning and Emergency Treatments in Museums, Art Galleries, Libraries, Archives and Allied Institutions*, Institute for the Conservation of Cultural Material, Inc., Canberra, 1978. H. L. Lein, 'Protecting museums from threat of fire', reproduced from *Curator* 25(2) (1982), pp. 91–6. Copyright © the American Museum of Natural History 1982.

Every attempt has been made to obtain permission to reproduce copyright material. If any proper acknowledgement has not been made, we would invite copyright holders to inform us of the oversight.

Introduction: the context of collections care

Simon Knell

Museums exist to assemble and exploit collections. Collections fuel all museum activity: research, exhibitions, publication, outreach and education. Primarily a limited and non-renewable resource, they have much in common with the resource concerns of the ecology movement in requiring careful management and conservation. The 'green' ethos which embodies the principles of resource conservation remained largely in the ownership of 'alternative' society for more than thirty years and was only given widespread governmental approval towards the end of the 1980s. Similarly, within the last decade, a new consciousness has emerged within museums, and with it an increased determination to protect our historic, scientific and artistic inheritance. To appreciate why this has happened we must understand something of the origins of existing collections and museums, and their more recent history.

The collections manager cannot consider the care of collections in isolation; it is neither an end in itself nor can it be divorced from the socio-political circumstances which determine its provision. Museums have rarely developed from national or regional plans. They are invariably the relics of a local decision made by a previous generation in response to the perceived needs of their time. The majority of museums can trace their origins to the collections of 'great' men and women, or those of the various learned societies which became fashionable particularly during the nineteenth century. Thus museums as a phenomenon have their own historical dimension, and it is this which often impedes a logical pattern of collection acquisition and care. In both the nature of the material now preserved and the resources currently dedicated to its preservation, the influence of history can be profound. Collections derived from a popular pursuit of the 1850s may be considered to have lost their original purpose, abandoned by progress and change in research, leisure, education and communication. The financial pressures of the 1990s mean that objects must have a purpose; they cannot be kept simply because they already exist in the museum's collections. Some collections, but particularly those in the universities, have with the passing decades become increasingly estranged from the intellectual activities of their parent bodies – objects and collections no longer form the backbone of most pioneering research. As a consequence collections of international importance can find themselves foundering on a shrinking budget as the universities themselves struggle to maximize the research and training potential of their own diminishing resources. Elsewhere lesser collections may be well supported by institutions which are either more enlightened or more committed to objects.

The museums we establish today, despite our passion for plans and mission statements, still do not fall within a national or co-ordinated strategy. Just like those we have

1

inherited, they reflect local interests and will present their own legacy of problems for the next generation. But we, as collections managers, are not principally concerned with new museums as their collections are minuscule when compared to those of the large number of museums created in the eighteenth, nineteenth and early twentieth centuries.

Much collections management activity today attempts to counter the inconsistencies of provision derived from the diverse origins and funding base of museums. A widespread response has been to develop policies and plans which regulate and standardize previously haphazard practice. Museums in every country are now developing statements on collecting, access, documentation, collection care and so on. The process includes a fundamental review of museum operation – not only do museums more fully understand their purpose but also how this relates to regional or national provision, and the resources and strategies required to achieve their goal.

Museums can only achieve their objectives by working effectively within the existing economic and political framework but this presents the collection care function of the museum with its stiffest challenge. The museum's mission, as regards collections care, is simply located in a temporal dimension which bears no relation to the political and economic world in which museums operate. While curators rarely seem to think of the life expectancy of objects in finite terms, few of the accountants or politicians who fund their activities have plans which extend beyond five years. Museums are charged with the long-term duty of preserving and presenting the patrimony of a nation, culture or community, but must achieve this within a system which fosters financial insecurity, political and professional inconsistency and crisis management. However, museums are a product of this economic system and must live or die by it. The challenge facing museums, and indeed libraries and archives, in attempting to carry their cultural baggage into the next century, is not how to beat the system but how to work more effectively within it. Long-term political and financial security could guarantee effective collections care but, as neither is likely, the primary concern of museum managers must be to establish strategies and structures which counter the impact of fluctuating support.

Unfortunately, museums are most often seen by those outside the profession as display and interpretation centres – the cultural guardianship role of the museum is usually overlooked. But if museums are not given the resources to care for the material evidence of society, what is the alternative? A nation's heritage filtering through salesrooms, auction houses and private collections? Museums are all too conscious of how their mission differs from that of the art market but politicians often seem less aware. The primary concern of the museum is to protect the intellectual integrity of collections and objects; the private collector and auction house are more interested in protecting capital investment and simple aesthetics. Museums today attempt to create a documented resource; private collectors will ultimately preserve the valuable, beautiful, rare and curious. In terms of object care there are also differences. As Ashley-Smith points out (chapter 1), many of the restorers supporting the art and antiques market are without the scruples of museum conservators. In the United States there has been some recognition of the importance of material in private collections and the need for its proper care. Museums must communicate their unique role as collectors, and protectors, of material culture more effectively. In times of economic constraint museums always answer their critics by proclaiming the importance of the education, exhibition and outreach services they provide. As a result, when money is in short supply, there is increased pressure to divert funds away from collections care and into these services; the guardianship of collections should be seen not simply as a support to these services but as a service in its own right.

That museums might not be particularly effective in this guardianship role became apparent in the 1980s. For museums in Britain, this was a decade of self-exploration. In nearly every academic discipline collections were examined and assessed in terms of what had survived and the care it was currently receiving. A succession of reports was compiled by various bodies on collections relating to biology, geology, industrial and social history, medicine and, most recently, musical instruments. Every report seemed to restate the conclusions of its predecessor – each produced the same depressing picture of neglect and mismanagement. The early reports were met with shock and astonishment; museums were failing in their primary duty of protecting the inheritance. Users of collections felt betrayed. But why were the results of these surveys so unpredictable? Most curators were aware of the deficiencies of their own collections. But until the 1980s there was little intelligence concerning the whereabouts or quantity of material in these subject areas, or how general were local concerns regarding its care. Equally, these surveys showed that not only were these collections not properly cared for but that the process of neglect had also robbed them of much of their associated information. The reports did not allocate blame to individuals or institutions – it was the profession which was deemed to have failed. As depressing as this admission of failure was, these reports have had a very positive effect on the subsequent development of collection care. They also awakened a new sense of responsibility within the profession with regard to collections and a greater honesty about the state and status of material in museum care.

One result has been the pulling together of specialist professional interests, within both the traditional academic disciplines and the newer professional specialisms associated with collections management. The establishment of specialist groups and associations has created new communities of professionals and new channels for communicating concerns and solutions. Costume specialists, for example, now had a forum for exchanging information and ideas which allowed them to place their work in a wider context.

Another response has been the development of standards of care. In Britain, the Museums and Galleries Commission Registration Scheme established a baseline standard for collections management and museum operation. Despite the very basic requirements of the scheme, many museums will need to expend considerable effort if they hope to realize this standard. As Registration standards are reviewed, developed and implemented in successive phases, the scheme has the potential progressively and profoundly to affect collection care. Most importantly it has teeth and the financial implications of not reaching the required standard can be considerable.

A further, though non-compulsory, stage in the development of standards has more recently been developed by the Museums and Galleries Commission and embodied in a series of publications entitled *Standards in the Museum Care of . . . .* These give a more detailed framework by which curators can monitor quality of performance and raise standards above the baseline provided by Registration. Discipline-specific, they have been developed in direct response to the reports of the 1980s. Archaeological collections formed the starting point for these new standards, as standards had already been in existence in this area for many years. Geology, biology and industrial collections, the other front-runners in this scheme, had each been the subject of damning reports. Based on a consensus of opinion drawn widely from specialists working in these fields, the standards are not definitive statements but might be seen as the first step on the road towards defining good practice.

Any welcome for new standards of care must, however, be tempered by the current realities of museum work. Much of the world remains in deep recession – a recession which has produced a worldwide cut in museum staff, and museum closures. Many museums are currently having difficulty in raising sufficient local funds to match grants available for improvements in collection care. In Britain, local government – a principal funder of museums – is again being reorganized, placing more uncertainty over collections and museums.

Not only are museum managers being asked to achieve higher standards with fewer staff but they are also having to consider meeting long-term objectives with temporary employees. The allocation of sufficient staff time to collections management is a problem for all museums. The traditional perception of collections management within the profession is that it is a worthy backroom occupation involving rather mundane tasks which are best undertaken by relatively junior members of staff. The plurality of the curatorial task means that basic collections management is often allocated to spare moments and not undertaken proactively as a principal function of the museum. Since it is largely work that is unseen, its neglect will also go unobserved. And as museums have yet to publicize effectively the relationship between collections and services, collection care is destined to remain a low-profile activity. Overstretched, staff have to focus on high-profile functions while collections management, which demands informed and experienced hands, is often left to those perhaps least equipped to do it. In the past the creation of 'training schemes' for the long-term unemployed has been seen as a possible solution to curatorial backlogs and neglect. Whilst they acted as useful apprenticeships for those who eventually entered the profession, many of these schemes did not produce the desired results. Part of the problem was that hard-pressed staff did not have the time to do the work themselves or to train or supervise a temporary workforce. Collections previously neglected were now also likely to be mismanaged. Many such schemes were very successful but the principle behind them, that collections care is an unsophisticated task which can be undertaken by staff with little knowledge or experience, was entirely erroneous.

A number of the larger museums are tackling the problem of staffing collection care by redefining their organizational structures. They are now establishing collection management divisions containing general collections managers, registrars and conservators. Rather than simply employing curators of relevant academic background, museums are appointing specialists in object management and care. For many of these museums this has meant a radical rethink about how collections are cared for and used. However, it is not a model that has universal applicability. The staffing base of the larger museums facilitates the appointment of collection care specialists, but in smaller organizations this may only be possible at the expense of existing specialists. The multiplicity of objectives entertained by museums requires a flexible and dynamic workforce. In order to collect, care for and interpret material museums have found it necessary to appoint subject specialists. As Peter Cannon-Brookes states (chapter 5), the academic specialist has a vital role to play in object care; there is more to curation than can simply be replaced by the employment of specialists in individual aspects of the curatorial process – conservation, collections management, documentation, and so on. The academic (in the broadest sense) specialist is vital to the success of the museum.

An important element in the development of a workforce able to deal with the requirements of collection care has been the formation of the object conservation profession. Conservators have brought not only science to bear on the problems of object stability and restoration, but also an ethical approach to objects which is affecting all aspects of museum function. The application of science in the museum context is not, however, simply a matter of utilizing off-the-shelf materials or procedures. Research is an integral part of the conservation process and, as is essential in all front-line investigations, this research has a strong international dimension. The profession has been characterized by its keenness to exchange information and an openness about the techniques used. The aim is to share the massive burden of attempting to understand the stability limits of the materials which compose the collections as well as those used in their conservation. An extensive range of materials is available for use in conservation treatments but many of these were not developed specifically for the conservation of museum artefacts. Often their shortcomings become apparent only after years of continued use.

Conservators also need to gain an understanding of the stability of an ever-increasing list of materials entering the collections. New alloys, plastics and synthetic textiles continue to be developed, while artists are choosing to work in ever more exotic and degradable substances which curators then wish to preserve. Fields previously unserved by specialist conservators are now starting to benefit from this expertise. Conservators from art and archaeology collections are now being employed to care for science and history items; some natural science curators and preparators are also beginning to specialize in object conservation.

In establishing themselves, conservators have had to tackle a wide range of ethical issues. This has given the profession credibility and separates it from the activity of many of the restorers and preparators who support commercial activity in science and art objects. As Ashley-Smith explains (chapter 1), these ethical issues extend beyond the reversibility of techniques or the establishment of documentation practices which might prevent accusations of faking. Conservators, and the curators who commission the work, also consider the rights of the user and the intentions of the maker; science alone cannot be allowed to run its own course when other intellectual criteria endow the object with its current museum function and value.

There are no clear-cut solutions to many of these problems. Statements such as 'stabilizing the object' or 'making the object understandable' underpin the minimalist approach adopted by most conservators. However, any treatment, no matter how minimal, obviously has an effect on the object. The conservator is one of very few people permitted to interfere with the object in such a way as to affect its physical or chemical structure. When the techniques applied are perceived as extending beyond what is necessary to ensure the survival of an object, then conservators are liable to criticism. Indeed, as the articles here show, the debate over conservation practice has been raging for many years. It is a debate which seems to undergo cycles of media interest and neglect. Twelve years ago one senior curator complained of the lack of public criticism of cleaning and restoration practices in the larger galleries in London. He suggested that this had, in the past, been one of the greatest safeguards against inappropriate treatments. In the 1990s there are still plenty of people watching, and snapping at the heels of, the conservation profession. Such critics cannot be dismissed as meddlers as they are members of a public that the conservation profession ultimately serves. While remedial conservation, cleaning and restoration will always have a place in museums, openness, and the periodic re-evaluation of techniques and objectives, must remain key elements in the development of the profession.

While it is generally accepted that conservators may alter objects in some way during procedures to enhance their stability, intentionally altering objects through use has less widespread support. Nowhere is this practice more often seen than in science and industry museums. Indeed, so familiar are working exhibits in these museums that these now seem vital to their success. But the use of any object will lead to wear and tear, and the need to replace worn parts. With continued use the object could conceivably be transformed into a replica of itself as all the original parts are replaced. Should this be a subject of concern? It could be argued that this is simply a continuation of the working life of the object. However, as Peter Mann discusses (chapter 4), such a suggestion would appear to contradict the very purpose of adding material to the museum's collections. After all, most of these objects are collected not for demonstration purposes but as material evidence which the museum believes needs to be preserved. Other items collected by museums, such as costume and furniture, also undergo repair during their working lives but few curators would support the notion of continuing to use them once they have been accessioned into the collections. The issues are complex and with the current search for increasingly dynamic displays, and 'interactivity' a buzzword for the 1990s, it is unlikely that working exhibits will disappear. Technology curators are beginning to look at ways in which material evidence can be preserved without compromising the interpretative objectives of the museum. And as the conservation profession develops in this area, it too will influence decisions on how objects are used. Aware of the issues, technical curators probably no longer live in the 'schizophrenic state' Mann suggests.

Given the technical and ethical problems associated with remedial conservation, and an increasing awareness of the factors responsible for object deterioration, conservators are devoting more time to the search for preventative solutions. 'Preventative conservation' is a philosophy which is steadily gaining support as it proves to be the most cost-effective, and ethically sound, solution to the problems of object care. In principle preventative conservation is simply a matter of monitoring and controlling the main agents of destruction: light, inappropriate relative humidity, atmospheric pollutants, handling and transport, pests, poor storage and disasters. Conservators and curators are then able to deal with the care of the whole collection rather than simply responding to the needs of individual objects. Effective preventative measures depend upon reliable information about patterns of object deterioration and the overall condition of the collection. Suzanne Keene (chapter 7) describes a practical method for acquiring an overview of collection condition which can be used to assess the proportion of items requiring laboratory treatment and to prioritize preventative conservation measures. Without such information conservation work can become random or reactionary; knowing the actual and potential problems of the collection allows the development of cost-effective strategies. A realistic overview of collection condition can also influence policies in other areas such as collecting and access. Specimen-specific conservation documentation in the form of object condition reports is vital to understanding the well-being of individual objects but as yet it remains largely an activity undertaken during conservation treatment or for the purposes of loan. It would be more useful if it were included in the preliminary documentation of all objects entering the museum but in most cases it is doubtful if this will ever be a practical proposition.

Of the factors which contribute to object deterioration none have been more intensively studied than those which make up the museum environment. Garry Thomson's book, *The Museum Environment*, forms a cornerstone to its study and is essential reading for all students of museum studies. Thomson suggests standards that might be applied, but his is a pragmatic approach and one which has been developed and extended as conservators, curators and designers have tried to meld object protection with the realities of local climate and new display objectives.

Perhaps the latest manifestation of this pragmatism has been the instigation of environmental surveys as the first step in developing controlled environments. These attempt to gather information on temperature, light, relative humidity and air quality over an annual cycle and relate this to external and internal sources of heat and moisture, and air movements. The findings from these surveys can make the installation of an integrated heating, ventilation and air-conditioning plant inadvisable. Low-cost alternatives, including limited controlled storage, re-routing pipework or further building compartmentalization, may produce better results. As Sarah Staniforth's paper shows (chapter 14), full air-conditioning is not always possible or desirable.

The methods available for monitoring the environment are also changing. Dataloggers, and other electronic sensors able to communicate with computers, are revolutionizing the information-gathering process. Whilst these new devices do not add to the accuracy of earlier measurement techniques, the flexibility and immediacy of the information available is providing new insights into the museum environment. Conditions can now be monitored in previously inaccessible locations – distant sites, the interiors of objects, moving packing cases – and presented and analysed in a variety of ways. These monitors also allow remote or automated control of light, humidity and temperature sources.

The problem with establishing environmental standards is that they can be enforced blindly, without an understanding of the decay mechanisms which underlie the recommended limits. A relative humidity of 50 per cent or 55 per cent is often taken as a good average for the mixed collection as a wide range of materials are stable under these conditions. However, there are many which are not and these will suffer. Also standards which have been developed in Britain cannot necessarily be applied elsewhere as they can lead to the structural deterioration of buildings or require excessive financial investment. Again the need is for a pragmatic solution based on an understanding of the behaviour of materials in the collections. For many types of material emphasis is shifting from maintaining precise levels of relative humidity to the eradication of short-term environmental fluctuations. Whilst this might be achieved through air-conditioning, research is also being undertaken into how building design can contribute to an energy-efficient and stable environment.

In recent years concern over the reliability of mechanical humidity control devices, and an increased understanding of the effects of short-term exposure to extreme relative humidities, have reawakened interest in microenvironments. In their simplest form these consist of sealed enclosures containing a conditioned buffering material, usually silica gel or one of its derivatives. Nathan Stolow's article (chapter 10) discusses how conditioned buffers are created, while Bosshard describes how a very stable and long-lasting environment can be created (chapter 9). There has also been some renewed interest in techniques which predate the introduction of silica gel, most notably the use of saturated salt solutions, although these have more limited application. As oxygen is associated with most deterioration processes, there is also on-going research into oxygen-free microenvironments.

The desire of designers and architects to create lively and pleasant spaces within museums rather than bland viewing areas has reintroduced the debate over the use of natural light in museums. Light is always potentially damaging to objects but is also the most important factor in developing imaginative and exciting displays. Attempting to maintain 200 lux and 50 lux standards can limit the effectiveness of light as a design tool. Peter Wilson (chapter 15) discusses how, by using annual exposure limits, conservation standards could be met during the development of new galleries at the Tate Gallery in London, while the special qualities of natural light are still preserved. Again, recent developments in monitoring and control technologies make this possible. Artificial light sources are also becoming more refined – they are now more energy-efficient and generate considerably less heat for the same level of illuminance. Fibre optic lighting is also finding its way into display areas, particularly for the production of dramatic effects or very low light levels. It has the advantages of not contributing heat or ultraviolet radiation.

Light and relative humidity have been the principal concerns in the attempt to stabilize the museum environment – they are easily measured and controlled. Atmospheric contaminants at the levels found in museums are less easy to detect and eradicate. However, as Baer and Banks's review shows (chapter 17), these are attracting increased attention. Some of these pollutants enter the museum from external sources – most of the world's largest collections are located in city sites where air quality is poor. Objects and the materials we use in storage and display are also responsible for releasing contaminants which adversely affect the collections. The effects of pollutants on materials has been known for centuries. By the middle of the nineteenth century uncontrolled chemical processes in the very towns which were at that time establishing museums had devastating effects on materials: 'metal objects of all kinds, window fittings, locks, gutters, etc. wasted away at an alarming rate. Tools of mechanics were rapidly blunted and window curtains are said to have been destroyed almost as soon as they were hung.' The control of air pollution has been a relatively recent phenomenon; collections in the major centres have suffered prolonged exposure to pollutants such as sulphur dioxide and smoke. Today, while some pollutants occur at levels substantially below those experienced by our predecessors, we are facing increasing pollution from vehicular sources and from new composite materials used in construction. Only full air-conditioning will enable us to reduce the effects of external pollutants on objects, but, as Ann Brooke Craddock explains (chapter 16), much can be done to eradicate internal sources by careful selection of materials.

Space is invariably a limited resource within museums and, perhaps understandably, space for people – offices and public areas – is generally given priority. This can result in conflict. Effective storage must permit collections to be organized and physically protected whilst reserving room for expansion and access. Stores do not necessarily require the same type of accommodation as staff or the public but all three require accessible spaces and it is this that is the root cause of the conflict. A store placed in an accessible location which has potential for public use will not remain a store for long. Part of the reason why stores lose out is because they are viewed not as resource centres but as places where less used, or unused, material is put. The term 'reserve collection' perpetuates this view of objects in store. Inevitably stores are allocated to those areas that remain after the other functions of the museum are catered for. Often these are totally inappropriate – roof spaces, cellars and outbuildings, for example, are popular locations but environmental conditions can be unsuitable. Another popular option is to create storage areas in any spaces left in the galleries – access and organization then become impossible. Collections which become inaccessible are then unused and so starts the spiral of decline which leads to neglect. Vincent Wilcox (chapter 18) argues for a full audit and functional evaluation of museum space before decisions are made on its allocation.

The principles of storage have changed little since Hilberry and Weinberg's paper was published (chapter 19). The procedures are fairly standard but the apparent mundaneness of storage can lead the curator into a false sense of security. Rigorous project management is necessary if a new store is to meet its potential as an effective resource centre which can both supply objects to support the museum function and allow the effective curation of the collections.

A popular solution to the inadequacy of space in the museum has been to create off-site storage and conservation facilities. These can then be constructed with the aim of meeting the requirements of the collection as a first principle. The impact on the management of the collection can be considerable provided adequate provision is made for staffing. However, off-site storage can present new problems such as increased revenue and staffing costs, decreased security, and regular packing and transport of the collections. Collections are also removed from the principal activities of the museum and may become less used. However, given that the majority of museums are in historic buildings intended for other uses, off-site storage may be the only way of creating effective spaces for collections and the operations required to support them.

Objects must be used if they are to justify the expenditure of constructing and maintaining a store. Museums in North America have examined a range of techniques for increasing access to objects. Thistle and Rebora (chapters 22 and 23) discuss the potential of open or visible storage, an option now being applied elsewhere. The principle of allowing greater public access through visible storage would appear to counter one of the principal criticisms of museums – that they place too much material out of public view. Visible storage allows the public to see what is 'in store' but can also be interpreted as poor display. Regardless of how we classify these spaces, visible stores *are* displays and as such they will always compare unfavourably with those based on modern design and communication theory. Thistle discusses some possible solutions to these problems but opinions remain divided as to their value.

Visible storage has been most successful where it has been integrated into discovery centres – galleries where the public can handle and study material. In the majority of these centres objects have been specifically collected for handling, but other items from the main collections may be included in glazed-drawered units. Success here depends largely on the support given by facilitators employed to enable the public to get the most from the available materials. Visible storage tends to be popular with students and others pursuing particular lines of research, but the majority of the visiting public have neither these specific interests nor the research, or investigative, skills, nor the motivation necessary to make effective use of the displays. Interactive technologies may aid the investigative process, and have been used in forming alternative two-dimensional visual databases giving information on objects in the collection. Museums have also started to run themed seminars on collections involving guided tours of the stores. Open days are also a common feature of museums and seek to achieve the same public function. Public access to the collections is vital if museums are to explain their collecting function effectively.

For the majority of the public, access to the collections will simply mean a visual inspection; few will ever be permitted to handle museum objects. Object handling is the most important cause of loss or damage in museums, so the first line of defence is to limit those who are allowed to handle objects. It follows that, as a second line of protection, those who are allowed must be trained. Simple rules, such as those Rowlinson gives here (chapter 24), can provide a framework but this must be supported by practical training which questions our apparent overconfidence in handling objects.

The physical movement of museum objects can also involve packing and long-distance transport. As in many aspects of collections management, much can be learnt from analogous activities in the commercial sector – the science which enables the movement of televisions and computers is the same as that which allows us to ship ancient glass and dinosaur bones. The writings of Nathan Stolow will be particularly familiar to curators concerned with moving objects. His book, *Exhibitions and Conservation*, demonstrates that moving objects means tackling all the preventative conservation issues and not just those specific to objects in transit such as shock and vibration.

Of all the potential problems confronting the collections manager, perhaps none is tackled with less enthusiasm than that of insect infestation. Insect life is not something the majority of curators have much understanding of, and most share a certain timidity when asked to confront an infestation problem. Collections managers don't need to become entomologists in order to deal effectively with actual or potential infestation. The range of damaging insects found in museums is limited, and to a certain extent their behaviour is predictable. Basic monitoring using traps and inspection, good house-keeping and object isolation are the keys to prevention. Rather than wait for an infestation to occur, or use regular fumigation with toxic chemicals as a preventative measure, curators are beginning to adopt a more intelligent approach to the problem. This has two strands: removing likely causes of infestation (food sources and refuges) and monitoring to detect the early signs of a pest problem (sticky traps, insect damage, etc.). Biologists in neighbouring museums are often able to help with identification, and methods of establishing effective strategies are described in books such as David Pinnegar's *Insect Pests in Museums* published by Archetype Books. Hillyer and Blyth's article (chapter 26) describes the development and practical application of a pest control strategy. It also describes an alternative to chemical fumigation. A wide range of options is now being investigated for killing pests infesting collections, including the use of extremely low temperatures, nitrogen and carbon dioxide. A reduction in the use of toxic chemicals in museums must be welcomed and legislation has already cut the type and use of chemical deterrents and fumigants permissible. Linnie's article (chapter 27) describes the harmful effects of these substances, the odour of many of which once characterized the museum environment.

The final area of concern here is disaster planning. The articles by Jones (chapter 28) and Hunter (chapter 29) describe both the impact of disasters on museum collections and a framework for planning to avoid or reduce the loss. Upton and Pearson (chapter 30) discuss some of the methods applied to recovery. Disaster planning is a detailed and complex task which can be expensive in staff time and, once completed, must remain in a state of readiness for years without being used. This means regular training and practice, and the constant maintenance of emergency supplies. Few museums have managed to make available sufficient time to develop a plan but recent disasters in museums and similar heritage attractions have encouraged many museums and grant-giving bodies to think again about disaster planning.

There are many actions which are essential if the objectives of collection survival and access are to be achieved. Training and a proactive approach are vital elements in effective preventative conservation. However, collections management does not operate in a vacuum and its success depends on the widespread recognition of its value to the museum operation.

1

The ethics of conservation
Jonathan Ashley-Smith

Remedial conservation and restoration involve actions which interfere with the structure and materials of the object. In attempting to stabilize or make an object understandable, these processes also pose the greatest threat to its integrity. Jonathan Ashley-Smith's article raises many of the ethical issues which concern the conservation profession. It also embodies a philosophical approach to the object which should be incorporated into the actions of anyone working with real objects.

INTRODUCTION

In the foreword to the preprints of 'Towards a code of ethics in museums' [Museum Professional's Group Symposium, 3 April 1981], Tristram Besterman writes

> Codes of conduct or ethics have become increasingly *de rigueur* for professions in a variety of areas of special competence. Far from being a passing fashion for the attainment of an image of respectability, this trend results both from an increasing concern with 'professionalism' from within the professions and from a fundamental shift of emphasis in the relationship of the professions to society. The change is one of accountability.

At the United Kingdom Institute for Conservation (UKIC) Symposium on Gilding (4 December 1980) Peter Thornton, Keeper of the Furniture and Woodwork collection at the Victoria and Albert Museum, warned that ethics were subject to fashion and that the young people who were adamantly advocating the ethical approach should be made aware of the transient nature of their views.

Here are two warnings. First that a code of ethics may merely be a status symbol to be acquired by a young and aspiring profession and second that whatever ethical stand-point is taken in the 1980s it will not be absolute but will be overtaken by the spirit of the 1990s or of the new millennium.

I have received two helpful pieces of advice from a restorer who is also a member of an experimental philosophy network. First, he writes, 'The one thing that cannot be done is to solve ethical problems. It is largely a matter of knowing what problems are', and in a later letter, 'An institution cannot of course have any ethical problems.'

Despite advice and warnings, the UKIC has formed an Ethics Subcommittee which has recently issued a draft 'Guidelines for conservation practice' to be considered by members of the profession in all disciplines and in both institutions and private practice.

The guidelines are drawn up in a manner that makes no distinction between the many media of which historic or artistic works are made, or between individual works of creative art, mass-manufactured goods or the results of nature. In this article I shall attempt to interpret these general guidelines with particular reference to the specialized field of furniture restoration.

By issuing 'guidelines' the UKIC hopes temporarily to have avoided the issue of professional status. Since there is no mandatory code, there are no sanctions prepared for transgressors. The guidelines are meant to indicate areas where there are ethical problems so that individuals can be made aware of alternative points of view. There is of course the implicit hope that guidelines will result in all people being like-minded in all circumstances. It is hoped that eventually all conservators will automatically argue that one type of conduct is right and one type wrong.

THE RIGHTS OF THE PRACTITIONER

Before the actual wording of the guidelines is discussed, there is still one problem to be resolved. Should conservators be discussing ethics at all? The decisions are not theirs. Surely they are mere technicians? Isn't it the client, the owner, the curator who makes the decisions? Isn't it they who say how much to chop off, how much to paint over and in what colour? Whose body is it anyway?

To deny the actual practitioner the right to an ethical viewpoint is like denying the right of a doctor to withhold or prescribe dangerous drugs or denying the surgeon the right to refuse to undertake an unnecessary cosmetic operation. Knowing that a medical practitioner is guided by ethical principles means that the patient is more willing to accept the doctor's greater experience, professional knowledge and practical skill and temporarily to give up the right to a say in the future of his own body.

THE RIGHTS OF THE OWNER

If the ethical guidelines are sufficiently sensible, then the majority of owners and curators will agree with them and there will never be a conflict. Indeed an owner may wish to impose these guidelines himself. But surely, he who pays the piper calls the tune. Doesn't ownership give absolute rights? There are indications in many other walks of life that ownership gives very few rights at all. I own a cat but I am not allowed to saw its legs off. I own a car but am not allowed to drive it with bald tyres. I own a house and a plot of land but I am not allowed to build minarets on the roof, or keep pigs in the garden or cut down my trees. The owner of a work of art may be prevented from moving it from one country to another.

It is not always easy to decide who the owner is. Parish churches and museums provide two examples of the difficulties of deciding who should take decisions relating to the fate of objects. In both cases the responsible person may be indicated by statute, but in practice decisions are taken (sometimes in good faith) by a range of people and the statutory responsibilities are ignored. In a church, unquestioned action may sometimes be taken by the Parochial Church Council, incumbent, churchwardens, archdeacon, chancellor of a Diocesan Advisory Committee or indeed by the architect responsible for the quinquennial survey. In a museum, decisions may be made, without reference to others, by trustees, director, curator, art historian or conservator.

The person who, rightly or wrongly, assumes ownership will often find himself under pressure from amenity and historical societies to adopt a particular approach. If he needs a grant to fund restoration, he will find himself restricted by the attitude of the grant awarding body, which in turn, may be under pressure from government or professional bodies. Certainly, with historic and important objects that with care will easily outlive several generations of mere humans, the moral and legal privileges afforded by ownership are very small and are open to question.

INDIVIDUAL AND GROUP ACTION

Discussion of ownership may, however, be a red herring if ethical decisions are for the individual. In restoration, the most important individual is the last in the chain, the restorer whose hands will cause actual physical changes in a historic object. He must decide at an individual level whether what he has been requested to do is right or wrong, and then, whether he will do it.

If the restorer individually sticks to an acknowledged code of ethics or set of guidelines, four situations can arise.

A client will arrive with a piece of furniture in need of restoration and will say, 'Do this work, in this fashion.' The restorer will reply, 'Your specification does not offend my ethical principles', he will do the work and both restorer and client will be satisfied.

The client may say, 'Please do what is necessary to restore this piece of furniture' and the restorer will do the job as he sees fit according to his ethical principles and both restorer and client will be satisfied.

The client may say, 'Do this work in this fashion' and the restorer will reply, 'That is unethical but there is an alternative approach.' The client will say, 'I never thought of it that way, but I can see you are right.' The restorer completes the work according to his ethical principles and both he and the client are happy.

Fourth, the client may say, 'Do this work in this fashion' and the restorer will, as before, reply, 'That is unethical but there is an alternative approach', with which the client will strongly disagree and will go, leaving the restorer happy but poor. However, if all the restorers' peers and colleagues, by being members of the British Antique Furniture Restoration Association or UKIC have been guided by the same principles, the client will find there is no point in going anywhere else and the restorer will not lose business. If organizations such as BAFRS, UKIC and the Crafts Council have set out to educate the antiques-owning and antiques-dealing public about the true meaning of conservation and the relevance of ethics of repair, then there should be very little conflict.

THE DEALER

For initiating unethical restoration, the dealers and auction houses are probably the worst culprits, for although the historic object is in their custody for only a short while it often undergoes a dramatic 'improvement' in appearance during this time. The sole reason for the improvement is monetary gain and it follows that the cost of restoration must be kept as a small fraction of the profit margin. The restorer, without the protection of an ethical code, protests that he would like to have done it differently and done a better job. But the dealer wanted it that way and would only pay so much. There must be occasions when a quick cheap job is not in the interests of the object. The real crime is that the purchaser may not now know what it is he is buying. The purchaser no longer has the option of asking for an ethical (possibly more expensive) restoration, since an undocumented renovation has already taken place.

It is worth noting that the 'Code of Ethics and Standards of Practice' of the American Institute for Conservation states: 'Engaging in the business of selling or purchasing for personal profit, or acting as a paid or commissioned agent in the sale of historic and artistic works are activities considered to be inconsistent with the professional integrity of Conservators.' It is about time that the separate professions of dealers and conservators began working with one another professionally in the interests of the object.

THE UKIC GUIDANCE

The American code does carry with it sanctions of some sort; violation can lead to the revocation of a member's fellowship. The American code deals with contracts, fees, punctuality, guarantees, references, advertising and solicitation as well as the conservator's actual work on the object. The United Kingdom Institute has at this early stage avoided all references to professional etiquette and conduct, except where it is likely to have an immediate effect on the integrity of the historic object itself.

In this context the UKIC guidelines have a section on the professional relationship with the owner or custodian: 'It is the responsibility of the conservator, as the person with the necessary technical knowledge, to uphold the best interests of the object and to advise truthfully as to the best course of treatment.'

Similarly, the draft document has a section on professional competence and knowledge advising the restorer to recognize the limitation of his skill and of his workshop facilities, saying: 'Moreover it is the responsibility of the conservator to keep up with current knowledge and to continue to develop skills so as to give the best treatment available.'

On disclosure of knowledge it says: 'There should be no secrecy about any technique or materials used in conservation. The development of new methods of treatment or a new material and the composition and properties of all materials and techniques employed should be fully disclosed.' Continuing with consideration of the object, it states: 'All professional actions of the conservators are governed by total respect for the physical, historic and aesthetic integrity of the object', and also:

> With every object he or she undertakes to conserve regardless of any opinion of its value or quality the conservator should adhere to the highest and most exacting standard of treatment. Although circumstances may limit the extent of treatment the quality should never be lowered.

Apart from these exhortations to the conservator to become a better, more open and honest person, the main message of the draft guidance comes in the sections headed 'The purpose of conservation' and 'The conservator and the object'.

The first defines conservation as 'the means by which the original and true nature of an object is maintained' and explains 'true nature' as including 'evidence of its origins, its original constitution, the materials of which it is composed and information which it may embody as to its maker's intentions and the technology used in its manufacture'.

So although the actions of the conservator may change the appearance of the object, they must not change the true nature. It is irrelevant, for example, that a chest has been converted into a cabinet and later put on a stand and an even later moulding added around the top. As long as the restorer does nothing to hide or destroy the remaining evidence of the original nature of the bits and pieces that the item of furniture is constructed from, he will not be acting unethically. The fact that time and history have destroyed much evidence is not relevant to the conservator's present actions.

In six sentences the guidelines cover all the ethical problems that the restorer faces when confronted with actually having to do something with a real object.

> The conservator should not perform or recommend any treatment which is not appropriate to the preservation of the object.

> The conservator should endeavour only to use techniques and materials which, to the best of current knowledge, will not endanger the true nature of the object, and which will not impede future treatment, or the retrieval of information through scientific examination.

> It is unethical to modify or conceal the original nature of an object through restoration.

> Before carrying out any treatment the conservator should first make an adequate examination of the object, both to record its condition and to establish the causes of its deterioration. A record of methods and materials used should be made. Such records should be kept as a permanent accessible archive.

The conservator is therefore asked not to take antique furniture and upgrade it by adding more intricate ornamentation or converting it into a more sought-after variant. He is asked not to make two new antiques out of one old one, or convert celestial globes into drinks cabinets. These actions endanger the true nature of the object and they modify or conceal its original nature. Similarly, stripping Georgian corner cupboards by immersing them in caustic soda and hosing and wire-brushing would be considered as endangering the true nature of the object. Adding a signature to a clock face modifies its original nature. Many such actions are so stupid, so immoral or even illegal that few readers would do them. The important point is not that they are intrinsically unethical acts but that it would be unethical for a professed conservator to do them.

A treatment not appropriate to the preservation of the object is any one that will shorten the life expectancy of that object. Attempts to prevent movement of wood with changes in humidity are likely to increase the amount of cracking and lead to general collapse. There are many examples of the effect of metal bars screwed under table-tops, supposedly to hold splits together and prevent movement, but in fact causing further splitting. Far better to allow as much movement as the original construction will provide.

REVERSIBILITY

Techniques and materials which will not impede further treatment are generally those which are reversible. Any restoration is bound to be the product of an individual's skills. Not all restorers are highly skilled and there will always be someone who could do it better. All additions, fillings and retouches should be easily removable without damage to the original object.

In a museum or a country house, small *in situ* repairs may have to be done; pieces of veneer become detached, flakes of gesso and gilding become loose, small pieces of carving are knocked off by enthusiastic cleaners. Since these minor repairs will probably have to be undone when the object finally gets into a proper workshop for a complete conservation job, the repair should be made with an easily reversible adhesive.

If a piece of furniture is damaged by bad handling or improper use or inappropriate display, thorough repair may only be possible if the object can be dismantled. If the object has been previously restored using irreversible techniques or techniques less easily reversible than those originally used, proper repair will be impossible.

Any paint medium is bound eventually to discolour and deteriorate. If the retouch, the repaint or the filler discolour at a different rate from that of the original surface, they will soon become unsightly and someone will want to replace them. They should be easily removable.

How reversible any technique is is, of course, a matter of the restorer's skill, and some methods of reversal may not always be applicable. A soluble varnish may only be driven deeper into a porous surface by applying solvent. A skilled restorer can remove veneers and mouldings that were reattached using epoxy resins or contact adhesives.

However, a conservator should not assume a skill greater than he himself possesses. If he couldn't reverse the process without causing damage, he shouldn't employ it.

One irreversible trick that furniture restorers are fond of is deeply scratching numbers on the various parts of a piece of furniture to make sure they put them back where they belong. It is highly desirable not to alter the conformation of a piece of furniture but it must be wrong to mark original parts of an object permanently in this way. Reversible numbering techniques are available and will not confuse future technical scholars. For a conservator deliberately and irreversibly to mark a historic object in this way is no better than carving his initials on the table-top.

SCIENTIFIC EXAMINATION

What actions are likely to 'impede the retrieval of information through scientific examination'? The heating of metal mounts, screws or pins to clean them or to make repairs will destroy metallographic evidence of methods of manufacture or of age.

The deliberate or inadvertent impregnation of wood with adhesives or consolidants may mean that non-original material will be included in samples for carbon-14 dating. Tree-ring dating is only likely to be upset if older or newer wood is included in the restoration and no attempt is made to distinguish it as restoration. Inclusion of incorrectly matched timber might result in wrong attribution and throw doubts on authenticity.

REMOVAL OF ACCRETIONS

The first stage of restoration is often the removal of old accretions and the second stage the replacement of missing parts and addition of new material. Many things can be removed without modifying the original nature of the object. Dirt, grime, accumulations of wax polish (often called patina), decaying or unskilled or speculative restorations can be removed.

In theory nothing original should ever be taken away (removal is nearly always irreversible), but for the greater good, material from the centre of an object is sometimes removed to make way for dowels or other jointing methods that do not distort the surface. There is some logic in that, since the surface is the most important part of any object. This is so because the surface contains all the visual and tactile information – the silhouette, the texture, the reflectivity, the colour and the decoration. Only esoteric and little-sought-for information comes from the centre of a piece of wood, so if a sacrifice has to be made it is the inner unseen parts that have to go and not the precious surface.

Surprisingly, however, surface finishes often seem to be readily sacrificed. Stripping and resurfacing is still considered normal practice. An original surface would have to be in extremely poor condition before removal was justified. In many cases it is doubtful that what is put back is any more truthful or sympathetic to the object than the deteriorated coating that was stripped off.

EVIDENCE TO GUIDE RESTORATION

The replacing of missing parts is a difficult ethical area. The key to the problem is quality of evidence. Most furniture has at least bilateral symmetry. A piece missing from one side will have a pair on the other side from which it can be copied. Inspection of other details should show whether the missing piece should be the mirror image or merely a repeat. In either case the evidence for what is missing is very good and that evidence is part of the object itself. Similar primary evidence can be obtained if the missing piece is part of a repeat pattern, say on a ripple moulding. If an area of veneer is missing, the evidence for what was in that gap is very good and again can be obtained from the object itself. The same is true for areas of plain paint or lacquer and repetitive or symmetrical painted designs.

If carving or decoration is asymmetric then the evidence for missing parts is no longer present in the object itself, except for small gaps or chips where the line of continuation is obvious. If the object is, say, one of a set of six chairs then the others may provide evidence of what the missing piece should look like. This is evidence of a lower grade since in all probability there will be differences in the remaining five since all may have been repaired or restored at some time or, indeed, may never have truly been a set.

Old photographs may provide some evidence but they must definitely be of the particular object in question in its original state. Old engravings are a possible source of information, but the process of recording by engraving involves at least one stage of fallible subjective interpretation and cannot be relied on for accurate detail. Contemporary written accounts suffer from being subjective and in addition have to be reformed by a subjective mind into an objective physical design. Word of mouth and memory are even worse and should be treated as hearsay evidence of very low value.

If a whole passage of asymmetric decoration is missing, say a chinoiserie scene from the door of a lacquer cabinet, and there are no traces of design left, no photographs and no documents, *ethically* there is no way that anything can be put in its place without the risk of modifying or concealing the original nature of the object. Endless studies of many other lacquer cabinets, endless discussions with the most eminent art historians, hours of studying contemporary pattern books will not give evidence of what actually was on that door. In a museum, where there need be no standards but absolute truth (the purpose of a museum being the preservation of truthful information for education), no restoration should be carried out where there is no evidence of what to put back. However, in the 'real' world, where antique furniture may still be in use and functioning as individual decoration or part of a whole decorative scheme, something must be done.

As restoration, the redecoration is potentially unethical so it is a moot point whether an exact copy of one contemporary original is more misleading than a pastiche of several originals. The exact and skilful copy does not introduce erroneous historical information even if it is less readily detectable than the pastiche. All restoration should be detectable, not necessarily immediately visible, not even visible on a more than passing inspection, but *detectable* by an intelligent non-specialist armed with a magnifying glass and allowed five minutes alone with the object.

A restorer who replaces a missing part for which there is no evidence with a skilful copy of another piece and who executes the work such that it is virtually undetectable, may still satisfy his own ethical criteria. He can do this if his work can be reversed (for it may prove necessary to remove it if the piece goes from being a deceitful usable decorative object to being a truthful museum object) and if he makes every attempt to record on the object itself and in the supplementary documentation the fact that he is the author of the new work. This is one reason that the AIC book suggests that dealing and restoration work are incompatible. If the extra profit from the sale of the perfect antique is coming directly to the conservator, the temptation not to record the extent of restoration is very great.

The key to ethical restoration is the quality of the evidence. The best evidence comes from the object itself; symmetry and repetition are obvious but scientific examination of paint fragments, paint cross-sections, tool marks, screw holes and scratches, analysis of stains and varnishes can all provide primary evidence. The opinions of curators and art historians should not be accepted merely because of the eminence of the expert. The restorer is the person making physical alterations to the historic object and the restorer should judge the quality of evidence presented to him. Is the curator's opinion mere subjective whim or can it be backed up by sound rational and relevant fact?

USE OF ORIGINAL MATERIALS AND DISTRESSING

A replacement can either be in the original material or a modern substitute. Ivory can be replaced with white plastic; ormolu can be replaced by cast brass or cold-cast resin. Missing carving can be recarved or replaced by casts from moulds of intact decoration.

It is difficult to decide whether virtually undetectable replacement with original material or misleading substitution by some alien substance is more ethical. Certainly if a synthetic replacement is ugly and easily noticed it has not succeeded as a restoration and should be replaced. Certainly if a synthetic replacement does not last as long as a repair in the original material, then there is little point in putting it in. Often it is more a question of gut reaction about 'the real thing' than a reasoned argument about ethics. The test is to ask the questions: Will it shorten the life of the object? Will it mislead the casual viewer about the original appearance of the piece? Will it mislead a technical scholar about the original constitution of the piece? Will it be difficult to remove without damaging the object? If the answer to any of these is 'yes' then it is unethical to use modern synthetics rather than the original. In many cases the answer to all four questions will be 'no'.

The replacement of missing parts should not involve the removal of original material, or realistically only the very minimum. When a new piece of veneer is being set in, only the smallest margin of crumbling rounded-off material around the edge of the intact area need be cut away. The replacement of missing decoration should not obscure the original so all retouch should be in-painting which will not obscure genuine paint. The original should never be toned in to match the repair.

There is a whole range of tricks of the trade which are designed to mislead. The hand cutting of screws to make them appear to date from before machine-cut threads, the distressing of glue blocks so that they don't look new. Indeed, all aspects of distressing are highly suspect. As the aim of these tricks is to prevent even a determined investigator finding out that restoration has taken place, they must be considered unethical and it is sad that they are still taught even in respected furniture restoration courses.

DOCUMENTATION

The UKIC guidance suggests 'a record of methods and materials used should be made. Such records should be kept as a permanent accessible archive.' The AIC code is more specific, giving details of the information and photographs required. Many private restorers are not convinced of the use of records, saying that when the object leaves the workshop there is no guarantee that the documentation will stay with it. This is often an excuse for laziness or to hide improper behaviour. Many restorers work for museums, area museums services, National Trust properties or churches and in all these cases there is an excellent chance of keeping records and objects together. These days many owners are sufficiently concerned about the history of their possessions that they would be keen to start and keep records of the degree of authenticity and the effects of subsequent alterations.

It is only in the world where people are deliberately making fakes, or making fragments into whole objects and knowingly selling them as genuine, or upgrading poorer objects into unique and priceless antiques, that records are an embarrassment. It is because of the very real value and importance of records and documentation that some so-called restorers want nothing to do with them.

The professional restorer has a role as technical historian; he will never learn anything if all he handles are other restorers' fakes and other restorers' undocumented restorations. He can never hope to teach if there is nothing written down. He can never assess the long-term efficiency of a new material if there is never any record of when that material was first used or if it ever was. There is no better evidence of what is original and therefore must not be destroyed and what is recent addition and may reasonably be removed than the written confession of the restorer himself. What better place for a copy of the record than the restorer's workshop?

FASHIONS IN ETHICS

Without going so far as to say that each case must be judged on its own merits, the flexibility and reasonableness of a code of ethics can be assessed only by trying it out as cases arise in everyday work. Such guidelines can be interpreted rigidly or loosely, but they do put certain forms of conduct beyond the pale.

If the purpose of restoration is the conservation of a object so that it can be seen, or even used, in its original concept and original beauty with complete historical accuracy, then the adherence to such guidelines cannot be merely a matter of fashion.

Fashion suggests a fluctuation, something cyclic, the values of one age to be returned to after a period of very different attitudes. Conservation cannot be allowed to become subject to fashion. Any move away from the values of preserving the evidence of the original nature of historic objects must involve destroying that evidence. This is an irreversible process which allows no return to the previous state. Fashion in conservation can only result in destruction of information. If guidelines are adopted, there is less chance of regression to more subjective and destructive methods of alteration. If correctly worded, and sensibly interpreted, guidelines can be useful and thus very lasting.

This paper first appeared in The Conservator *6 (1982), pp. 1–5.*

2

Cleaning and meaning:
The Ravished Image *reviewed*

Gerry Hedley

This article is not simply a book review. Gerry Hedley, a conservator, examines and answers many of the criticisms raised by Sarah Walden in her book The Ravished Image. *It reveals the arguments of both sides in a debate which seems to attract media attention every few years – indeed, it was not new in 1985. There seem to be few defections from one camp to the other but the dialogue is not entirely fruitless as it allows museums to re-evaluate and justify the objectivity of what they do to objects.*

Towards the end of her book *The Ravished Image* Sarah Walden sensibly observes that 'Schools of restoration continue to contend fiercely amongst themselves. . . . But there ought to be more common ground between them' (p. 143). At first sight her text hardly seems calculated to forge mutual understanding. Sensationally subtitled *How to Ruin Masterpieces by Restoration*, it frequently adopts a strident and exaggerated tone. She imagines Leonardo seeing paintings in a modern conservation studio, lying 'prostrate like patients, surrounded by technicians and machinery and bleeding slowly to death under the scalpel and the corrosion of fierce chemicals' (p. 7). Some reviewers responding to this high-impact style have been most critical. Others, especially in the daily press of Britain, have tended to take at face value the self-projection of the author as a sensitive aesthete battling against hordes of white-coated technicians. Very little space has been given anywhere to discussing her arguments about conservation practice. Within the profession we should reverse this emphasis. For the time being let us put to one side questions of style and accuracy, and focus instead upon the themes of the book.

Sarah Walden's main concern is with the cleaning of paintings, and, to a lesser extent, with the manner in which they are retouched. She believes that we have been led, by the attitudes of the twentieth century, to present paintings in a way that distorts their essence. Paintings, she says, 'must be made as attractive as possible to the twentieth-century mass audience' (p. 13). When a painting is restored, it is therefore necessary to 'bring out its highlights, to clarify, to sharpen – in short to make it more "acceptable" and "photogenic" ' (p. 13). Her argument is that our own contemporary prejudices are those of advertising: impact, rawness and readability (p. 19). National institutions inadvertently pursue these values through a widespread policy of overcleaning, particularly in the United Kingdom and the United States. What is more, they do this heavily under the influence of science, and at the expense of aesthetics. The domination of science and technology, she believes, excludes consideration of the wholeness of a painting and focuses attention upon material details. Ambiguity will tend to be obscured so as to inch a Titian a few years nearer to our own ideals, which are symbolized by what she calls Mondrian's gaunt squares.

This is a well-rehearsed viewpoint, and we should surely accept that our times influence the way we see. But the hypothesis does call for more thorough examination. Even if it were accurate as to mass taste, museum curators and conservators are not average members of the public. Much of their lives is spent in intimate contact with, and study of, great art from all periods; must not this, too, shape their visual sensitivity? It is, for instance, less than convincing that they are driven by the need to attract a mass audience and manipulate the images they work with accordingly. In fact art, at least that in the museums of major centres, seems to be popular regardless of the restoration policy of particular institutions. It is not noticeable that museums which Sarah Walden admires, the Metropolitan and the Louvre, are any the less attractive to, as Gombrich puts it, 'the hurried tourists', than is London's National Gallery. However, we ought not to shut our minds to the central tenet, which is that there is a way of seeing in the late twentieth century to which, in some degree, our collections have been made to conform. Walden essentially thinks we make them flat, bright and sharp.

It would be ridiculous to deny that much of recent art does indeed utilize bright colours, have readability, flatness and sharp lines. But equally much does not. How do the diffuse and brooding works of Rothko fit the mould? Are Pollocks readable? What of the subtle nuances of colour in Frankenthaler? Certainly flatness, and concern with plane, could be claimed as a dominant visual theme which was explored through the twentieth century. Yet even flatness has been elucidated with much greater sensitivity by art than is exemplified by photography. Think perhaps of Cubism at the beginning of the century, and, say, Yves Klein from Minimalist practice. In any case, while painters were painting ever flatter, conservators were busy finding ways, when lining, of making old paintings ever less flat.

I am not denying the influences that Sarah Walden adduces, merely querying their selection in isolation. As soon as we so much as glance back across twentieth-century art, we find numerous examples which fog, to use a photographic metaphor, the simple schema she establishes. Probably an overriding visual influence has been, not advertising, but the acceptance of formal values as meaningful art. No doubt we do see a work of Titian differently because we have seen Barnet Newman or Clyfford Still. This, however, is rather more sophisticated and difficult to unravel than the notion that we see it as an advertisement or a photograph.

There is little point in extending this type of speculation. I should have thought that it is not really possible, by definition, to know exactly how our times condition us, let alone how particular individuals impose that conditioning on past cultures. Still, Walden presents a simplified formula with great confidence. Would it not be better to look more closely at paintings and the history of art to try to assess how they were intended to be seen? Conservators are better equipped to study these aspects than they are to be sociologists. It may be wiser to concentrate upon the actual paintings.

Still, Sarah Walden is right to emphasize that people will see things differently at different periods, or more simply that they will be affected by fashions. Conservation, therefore, always runs the risk of being peculiar to its time. Indeed, this is crucial to a basic concept of conservation: reversibility. In professional conservation this is the most widely accepted guideline that we have. Nothing ought to be done that cannot be undone. It is an impossible goal, but it is one for which we all strive and are surely closer to attaining than our forerunners. Why do we do it? It is not merely because something may go wrong with our beautiful restoration, and in the future it may have to be re-done. There is, of course, a more fundamental reason. Reversibility ensures that we can hand the work of art on, intact, to a future generation. They will then have the option to present it as they choose. Perhaps they will decide to apply thick yellow varnishes, maybe they will add thin greyish layers (in emulation of glair varnishes) to early Italian works. We could have no philosophical objection so long as they attempt to do it reversibly. In fact, a similar situation prevails today with regard to cleaning, galleries choosing to show their works with differing layers of aged varnish. Naturally, we will dispute amongst ourselves the aesthetics involved, and the relationships to the original works, but in principle, unless we break the code of reversibility, we do not cut off options for the future. However, it is exactly that which Walden believes is happening during total cleaning.

We should look then most closely at the attitude of the book to the crucial question of cleaning. Cleaning and retouching involve, inevitably, an aesthetic intervention by the restorer, although its limits are quite tightly defined. Sarah Walden correctly suggests that, in cleaning, the restorer 'faces multiple choices: he can retain the old varnish; he can thin it, keeping only a fine film; he can remove it entirely; or he can clean some areas more than others' (p. 132). This amounts to just four choices, only three of which actually involve cleaning. Each of these approaches, selective, partial or total cleaning, involves a particular emphasis on various contributors to the aesthetic experience, such as harmony, colour or the effects of age (Hedley 1985). Walden is right to point out that we cannot return the painting to the authentic. But this does not render the whole process of cleaning arbitrarily subjective. Whichever method is chosen will emphasize particular aesthetic aspects and will stand in a definable relationship to the original work. Though we cannot any longer have the artist's original intent, we can be aware of how the limited interpretative intervention implicit in different types of cleaning is conditioning the way that we see a painting.

This degree of relativity will continue to exist so long as we must deal with paintings which have undergone changes with time. Unlike Walden, I feel it is no bad thing that we are able to experience works, by the same artist, displayed in marginally but significantly different manners, in London, Paris and New York. Ideological and cultural concepts will, no doubt, cause us individually to prefer one mode of cleaning to another. But it is hardly going to be appropriate to attempt to impose a homogeneity on what is admittedly a field of relativities.

What I should have found immensely stimulating, from Sarah Walden, would have been a careful exposition of her approach to the aesthetics of cleaning, illustrated by actual examples of problems she or others have resolved. She has trained in Italy and worked at the Louvre and is therefore well placed to discuss this type of 'European' approach. Her stated goal is 'to hold together the fragile unity of the painting' (p. 96). There are only a limited number of ways to achieve this. Yet in response to the rhetorical question 'What should the restorer do?' she can only call forth the usual vague litany: no dogmatic rules; infinitely flexible techniques; constantly responsive to individual works of art. Scratch any conservator, including those who have paid too little attention to aesthetics, and they will all too readily gush these grandiose but hollow phrases. It is well meant; it just does not take us very far. I am sure it is possible to be more precise about what we do, but if not, then sticking to specific examples of what has been done will be a good deal more informative.

Still, the book was evidently not written to tell us what Walden does, but to criticize the work of others. She claims unambiguously that, in museums, 'the policy of over-cleaning has continued to be widespread, particularly in the United Kingdom and the United States' (p. 139). From the foregoing, and indeed the general tone of the book, it is apparent that she feels this to be not merely a debate about aesthetic appearance but

23

a warning that irreversible damage is being done. Unfortunately, Walden makes it less than clear what she means by over-cleaning, and since this is central to the book it does rather hinder discussion. Several possible interpretations do suggest themselves from the text. To facilitate discussion I shall take the liberty of a little speculation.

She may mean that literal physical over-cleaning is occurring. Original paint, probably glazes or scumbles, is being removed. Could this really be what she is claiming to be happening, not just as in occasional accident, but deliberately and as a matter of policy? It does not seem to be the view of Brealey at the Metropolitan (Stoner 1981: 26); though critical of the aesthetics behind some of total cleaning, he has indicated that trained conservators do not habitually remove glazes and scumbles. Surely today this is an accurate view. Most conservators are terrified of removing anything in the way of original paint. I suspect that some of those who have trained recently in America, working mostly on nineteenth-century paintings, though they will have been limited aesthetically, will be all too aware of the dangers of soluble layers. Removing original paint is surely the stuff of our nightmares not of our policy.

Another interpretation suggests itself. Maybe she is not claiming original matter is being lost but is referring to a point made by Gombrich in the 1960s. He wrote,

> Is it not possible, on the other hand, that the removal of all perceptible layers of veiling make a painting look flat? The illusion of space and form may well be lessened when the bare pigments on the canvas obtrude too forcefully on our attention.
>
> (1963: 92)

A sort of aesthetic over-cleaning. This is a serious point, the more so when presented with Gombrich's both scholarly and cunning use of the interrogative. For only the very rash or the very knowledgeable can deny that many things are, indeed, possible. When it comes to these intricacies of perception I doubt if any of us could safely claim to reside amongst the enlightened. However, this particular view ought to be verifiable by a relatively simple perceptual experiment. Even looking at differentially cleaned areas of paintings should make it apparent, for one can certainly see the emergence of space as varnish is removed. This would make a most interesting project. Naturally, the gravity of the charge of over-cleaning is greatly reduced once the removal of original paint is excluded.

My last suggestion as to the meaning of 'over-cleaning' lies in between the two so far discussed, and concerns the notion of patina. Patina is an element which runs strongly through the book. This time Walden offers a definition:

> Patina is the by product of time, and in the case of painting is an accumulation of a number of facets of the ageing process. The craquelure itself is one. The slow transformation of texture and transparency undergone by each pigment and medium is another; and the interaction with a deteriorating varnish is a third. The overall effect is as distinctive, evocative and intangible as the vintage of a wine.
>
> (p. 125)

In passing we might note how patina has changed with time. In 1949 Brandi wrote, 'what we call patina can more often than not be shown to consist either of glazes or of tinted varnishes' (1949: 183). In 1962 Kurz was writing that 'it is simply a layer of varnish which has become yellowish' (1962: 58). In 1985 Walden has reduced it, from the point of view of the surface layer, to merely the interaction with a deteriorating varnish. Patina is evidently fading all too fast; a tinted varnish, a yellowish varnish and now an interaction. At this rate we shall lose it more quickly from the written word than its adherents fear from paintings!

Looking more seriously at Walden's definition from the point of view of cleaning, it is only this last aspect, 'the interaction', which would be vulnerable to varnish removal. We know, too, that most varnishes are, in any event, nineteenth-century or later in their application, so any interaction would probably have little to do with the Old Masters. All the other facets of ageing to which she alludes would still be present. There is nothing inherently wrong with an adherence to the notion of patina. It represents in part the aesthetic view that effects of time enhance the beauty of paintings. They improve over their moment of creation. Sarah Walden seems to hold this view, and the book ends with the well-known passage by Addison describing Time the Painter, 'He also added such a beautiful brown to the shades and mellowness to the colours that he made every picture appear more perfect than when it came fresh from the master's pencil' (Joseph Addison 1711). Perhaps, then, it may be felt that something important to a particular aesthetic, though probably not original, is being irreversibly lost: the interaction. Future generations might not have the option of retaining Sarah Walden's patina in its entirety. If so, a calm and measured discussion of her idea of patina would have been much more helpful. What exactly are these interactions of paint and varnish? How do they appear? Are they removable during cleaning, can they be simulated when gone? Is it the aspect of age or of harmonizing which is most valued, or is it their particular interrelation?

I would not deny the possibility of interface effects between paint and varnish. Rees Jones cautiously stressed this aspect from the technical side in 1962: 'the boundary between paint and varnish may be anything but clear; it may be indeterminate geometrically and operationally' (Jones 1962: 61). Looking at cross-sections one can frequently perceive visual differences at the interface between paint and varnish; whether these actually have a visual effect when a picture is seen in the normal way is not known. This is one of the reasons why it is not usually appropriate for total cleaners to attempt the removal of every last trace of residual oil varnish left after cleaning resin varnishes from the surface.

Over-cleaning is an emotive word which needs careful expression. I suspect that Walden would define it as a possible combination of all three of the explanations I have offered: This would accord with a description she offers of the changes in perception of the third dimension at different stages of cleaning,

> An unrestored painting, still covered in discoloured varnish, has a flat look. . . . As this varnish is thinned, the third dimension suddenly reappears. . . . So satisfying is this change that the temptation to continue can be powerful. But should the restorer succumb – as he frequently does – the effect will be reversed and a new flatness will re-emerge as the patina and glazes begin to disintegrate under the swab.
>
> (p. 137)

Mainstream total cleaners would agree with much of this, they would affirm that they do not remove glazes, and we would thus be left with only the patina as the point of controversy. At its most subtle patina is seen as serving a dual role: its yellowness harmonizes changed relationships, while its presence gives a sense of the passage of time (Philipot 1966: 138). That this duality is hardly touched on by Walden is but another indication of the tendency to believe that because there are 'subjective' elements, or more properly judgements which are not absolute, in cleaning, the subject is not amenable to intellectual analysis. Down that road we shall find, not only the unperceived influence of fashion, but also a fixation upon individual personalities who just 'know' how a painting should look.

Perhaps a technical observation is also pertinent to the issue of over-cleaning as it is here, I think, presented. Partial cleaners usually attempt to thin varnish until there remains still a perceptible yellow layer, though much diminished. Something close to Kurz's definition of patina is left. Total cleaners like to proceed until all natural resin varnish has been removed. Now the aesthetic behind total cleaning would, of course, be satisfied equally if varnish could be thinned to an imperceptible layer. Any paint/varnish interactions would then also be retained. The technical problem, with both partial and total cleaning, might therefore be seen as the fact that there exists no method for reliably thinning varnish, as opposed to removing it. Candid partial cleaners are prepared to admit that frequently the 'partial' effect is achieved by reapplying a thin layer after the dirty varnish has, inadvertently, come off completely in the cleaning. Aesthetically this is fine if we use Kurz's definition for patina, but it does rather undermine some of the technical arguments about the safety of the technique, as well as the aesthetic argument as to patina, if Walden's definition is adopted.

If ever there was a case for more science in conservation this is surely it. Can methods be found to thin varnishes reliably? If we use reagents can we avoid damage to original paint? All schools would find value in such a study. At present the techniques of cleaning are not objectively scientific. It is largely an empirical craft, illumined by little more science than one PhD thesis, some work from the IRPA in Brussels and the chart of a gentleman called Teas. There is no such thing as scientific cleaning.

The author is, in fact, most unhappy with the relationship of science to conservation. She suggests that, 'In recent years the balance of power between technicians and theoreticians of art has shifted drastically towards the former, reflecting the supremacy of the scientific method that has pervaded the profession' (p. 120). She is moved to enquire, 'Why is it that there has been no counter-revolution [*sic*] in this area against the excesses of the scientific method?' (p. 16). Yet she is by no means completely anti-science. Walden urges the maximum knowledge, 'historical, art historical and scientific' (p. 21). She does not want science restricted but better directed: 'It is not necessarily in less, but in better, more self critical science that the answer lies, and in more restraint and refinement in its use' (p. 17). The conservator, she believes, 'should stand mid way between scientist, artist and art historian.' These last are unexceptional views on which there is probably a consensus in America and Britain.

As to the reputed present dominance of technology, that is worth considering. There is certainly some truth in Walden's view that aesthetic implications of cleaning and retouching have not received very much attention in the last twenty years. In part this has been due to the hegemony which the practice of total cleaning had acquired. This meant that those training, during that period, tended to take for granted their aesthetic interpretation of the painting through total cleaning. With agreement in this area, attention naturally focused on other questions. Principally these concerned the practice of lining and the feasibility of employing reversible synthetic polymers to varnish and retouch. Without doubt, the way that a painting looks at the end of treatment, its whole appearance, has in some quarters received less attention than it should. This was compounded by the fact that numbers of students were trained in environments where they did not have exposure, or even ready access to, great art. Grandma's portrait usually raises only limited aesthetic questions, but often very difficult technical problems.

In the United States, through the influence of Brealey, this area is rightly attracting fresh attention. In Britain, with its record of fierce controversy about cleaning, there has never been quite the same lack of cognizance of the relevant aesthetic issues.

Fortunately, there is so much to indicate that a sense of aesthetics is not dead that I see no cause for gloom. Consider those last twenty years: our main concern has been with lining. Was not that an issue which was eminently about the whole aesthetic appearance of the front of the painting? Insensitively Walden gets this wrong: 'It is an ironic fact that the most solid advances in the field of conservation have been to do with the back of the painting rather than the front' (p. 148). Conservators, rather than curators, were alerted to the awful texture changes that could be and had been imposed on paintings. From the 1930s they were able to apply a rather basic science and come up with new technological methods to line paintings that could preserve the delicate surface. What is more, such application of science has, in the long run, led to more and more caution in the use of treatments. Many of us are now minimalists. There is much to learn from that history. It is true that there was a period during the 1950s and early 1960s when a new tool, the vacuum hot table, was used too much. Today, though, we have matured as we have developed new methods and greater understanding. Contemporary techniques are, according to Walden, 'amongst the most successful developments of contemporary conservation, [and] can help preserve the finest most sensuous impasto remaining from the Venetian High Renaissance, or the swirls of modern action painters' (p. 149). A profession which can integrate technology and aesthetics in this way is evidently capable of doing so in other areas. There is need for direction rather than counter-revolution.

The book does focus upon an interesting aspect of the critical response to totally cleaned works. People sometimes feel that these appear too sharply defined. Contrasts seem exaggerated and outlines seem too clear and harsh. This perception is unlikely to be due to cleaning alone. It will probably be related to the retouching policy, as well as to the nature of the original painting. How little discussion of retouching takes place nowadays is quite surprising since it can be decisive to the final appearance of a work. The point can readily be made, even if we confine ourselves just to the illusionistic retouching of totally cleaned paintings. At one end of the scale might be the type of painting one frequently sees in smaller American museums: a worn or badly damaged painting, with an impressive, perhaps optimistic attribution. Often these types of paintings are cleaned, revealing extensive damage, and then retouched rather cursorily. Extensive retouching may not overlap the original paint, but its texture and transparency are often awry. The cleaned work will now hang as an obvious wreck made worse by the visible modern inpainting which does nothing to integrate a sense of the, admittedly lost, whole.

At the other end of the spectrum, we find retouching which is not only superbly illusionistic but produces a very high finish. This is usually applied to works less damaged than the former example, though galleries certainly have characteristic retouching. This type of approach can produce the clarity of line to which Walden refers. She believes this finish to be related to our twentieth-century way of seeing. There could, however, be other explanations.

Is it not possible that the relatively contrasting image revealed by total cleaning tends to lend itself more readily to a precise finish, while on the other hand the more suppressed image of a partially cleaned painting lends itself to a more diffuse finish? The logic may be more in the type of cleaning than in anything else. It is certainly true that the National Gallery in London, which is most consistent in applying total cleaning, has evolved gradually to producing more and more highly finished works through retouching. I doubt that this is an iron law. Many other galleries display totally cleaned works with more restrained retouching. Yet it does perhaps explain some of the critical response to the 'tidied up' images. Retouching is usually reversible, so we need have no qualms for the future, but there are definite problems in retouching so that the appearance of age is greatly diminished. This is especially so when total cleaning has revealed sets of relationships which have changed from the original intent. The whole area could benefit from more appraisal and Sarah Walden genuinely describes some of the dangers when she says it is, 'when the restorer is tempted by his own virtuosity into encroaching further and further into the original work – strengthening, tidying, or perfecting a hypothetical finish – that the strength of the painting is sapped' (p. 155).

Throughout the book Walden also makes much of the need for restraint, the avoidance of extremes, for caution and balance. She urges less conservation as a routine, and counsels considering doing nothing. Such axioms always bear repetition, and though she seems unaware of it they are views shared by many of her colleagues. Given the fondness of the book for medical analogy, it is surprising that the attention now directed towards preventative conservation such as environmental control was not appraised. She worries greatly about the work being done in museums, but in fact restoration is done far more rapidly and routinely by commercial restorers, working for dealers, than it is in institutions. Anyone who has gazed down a row of cleaners and retouchers, busy at their easels, in a typical London studio, or who has seen the huge looms on which multiple glue-paste linings are performed each week, is not likely to forget the experience. These places are veritable production lines for restoration and handle the vast bulk of present-day work in Britain. Largely craft-orientated, and pretty much free of science, they have escaped Walden's fire. Paradoxically, she feels that it is the art market, to which this productive little industry is tailored, which will 'within the next decade at the most' demand to be supplied with relatively untouched works. No wonder she does not address her book to professional conservators if the free market is so soon to sort the matter out! Bizarrely, she urges us to beware of the welfarism of state museums and praises the merits of private owners.

There are occasions when Sarah Walden writes with warmth and enthusiasm, especially when she is describing her working methods. She could probably have written a most interesting book describing her solutions to difficult problems of conservation. There is quite a lengthy section on technique which makes interesting reading. Though it has many inaccuracies, it does try to pursue the relationship between style and technique. This is never easy and Walden is to be commended for making an effort. She sets up a dichotomy between the notion of durability and the pursuit of artistic finesse, and explores it with a consistency not found elsewhere in the book. Ultimately it does not prove to be a very useful analytical dialectic since she encounters too many artists who could do both, or displayed either one without the other, and cannot establish it as an operational driving force in art history. Despite that, it is worth reading, though rather too loose and anecdotal. Material facts are more necessary in this type of analysis than amusing stories. A more profitable line of enquiry might be to explore the link between style and the development of the versatility of the oil medium. Technique would need to be seen as a means to an end, as well as a craft in which durability figures.

The Ravished Image is the first book on the cleaning of paintings to appear in Britain since 1968. Unfortunately, many in the profession, out of key with its method and style, will find it wildly polemical. Yet it does contain the seeds of serious arguments. Conservators ought, I believe, to give more time to comprehending the difficult and complex issues involved in diverse approaches to cleaning and retouching; they ought, as always, to be cautious. The book has raised these matters, but it has not developed them.

Many of the ideas within the book are not new. They were presented in former discussions by Brandi, Kurz and Gombrich, amongst others. Short though their contributions were, the book does not supplant them, primarily because it neglects scholarship and succumbs to sensationalism. As a conservator Walden had the opportunity to bring the experience of praxis to the more academic writings of her mentors; without that she adds little to what has gone before.

In writing a book for the 'mass inexpert audience' whose taste and sensitivity she decries she must have been aware that even the most carefully wrought arguments would lose something in the reading. Style matters. In opting for sensationalism Walden should not be surprised if the book develops misinformed and frenetic controversy. Others will simply be dismissive. Either way, this is a shame.

A generation ago Gombrich lambasted the National Gallery for the absence of the scholarly spirit from the cleaning debate. It was a fair point. I hope our generation is not about to make the same mistake, for as Gombrich concluded then, and as we should take to heart now, 'Such methods of controversy may be quite effective in the short run – but what is meanwhile to happen to the pictures?' (1963: 93).

This paper first appeared in The Conservator 10 (1986), pp. 2–6.

REFERENCES

Addison, J. (1711) *The Spectator*, 5 June.
Brandi, C. (1949) 'The cleaning of pictures in relation to patina, varnish, and glazes', *The Burlington Magazine* 91.
Gombrich, E. (1963) 'Controversial methods and methods of controversy', *The Burlington Magazine* 105.
Hedley, G. (1985) *On Humanism, Aesthetics and the Cleaning of Paintings*, Canadian Conservation Institute.
Jones, R. (1962) 'Science and the art of picture cleaning', *The Burlington Magazine* 104.
Kurz, O. (1962) 'Vanishes, tinted varnishes and patina', *The Burlington Magazine* 104.
Philipot, P. (1966) 'La notion de partine et le nettoyage de peintures', *Bulletin IRPA* 9.
Stones, J. H. (1981) 'John Brealey's trained and sympathetic eye', *Museum News* 59 (7).
Walden, S. (1985) *The Ravished Image*, London: Weidenfeld & Nicolson.

3

Solvent abuse
Michael Daley

Michael Daley not only reveals more of the history of the debate surrounding the cleaning of works of art but also exposes the passion and anger felt by those who appear powerless to affect decisions concerning this process. Decisions to interfere with the integrity of objects must have an underlying scientific rationale but objects also have other attributes which are less easy to measure or define and which the conservation/restoration process can alter or destroy. Both conservators and curators must have answers to the questions Daley raises; as custodians our duty is to the object and to the public which Daley partly represents.

Late one night in 1970, an elderly man mounted the steps of the portico at the National Gallery and painted 'MURDERERS' on the doors. The miscreant was the 'society' painter Pietro Annigoni, who fourteen years earlier had protested more conventionally in a letter to *The Times* (14 July 1956):

> A few days ago, at the National Gallery, I noticed once more the ever-increasing number of masterpieces . . . ruined by excessive cleaning. . . . I do not doubt the meticulous care employed by these renovators, nor their chemical skill, but I am terrified by the contemplation of these qualities in such hands as theirs. The atrocious results reveal an incredible absence of sensibility.

The tenacity of these practices was confirmed recently when a curator from New York's Metropolitan Museum of Art condemned the 'strident tones' produced by 'the exuberant cleaning of paint surfaces for which the National Gallery has, unfortunately, become famous'. It is not just artists and curators who are offended – so too are many restorers. Sarah Walden memorably savaged the philosophy in her polemical book *The Ravished Image*.

The object of the Gallery's notorious and dogmatic insistence on removing every last trace of varnish is to maximize the strength of a painting's colours. But this goal has been thought suspect and dangerous since antiquity. Pliny records the destruction of a painting by Aristides Tebano. The great seventeen-century connoisseur Baldinucci recalled how a magnificent painting, when washed, 'crumbled and fell to the ground in minute fragments'. The very desire to 'freshen up' colours, Baldinucci saw, is a function of vulgarity and ignorance and, when implemented, robs paintings of beauty and historical authenticity. Degas concurred: 'Time has to take its course with paintings as with everything else, that's the beauty of it.' Goya had warned, 'The more one retouches paintings on the pretext of preserving them, the more they are destroyed.' The original artist, if alive today, could not match, he said, 'the aged tone given the colours by time who is also a painter'.

The National Gallery falsifies the art it seeks to preserve. Stripping paintings down to an alleged 'original' surface does not reveal the painting as it once was but merely exposes the combined injuries suffered and decayings undergone. The original colours and the relationships between them no longer exist. Each colour ages differently: some darken, some fade, others remain constant. The removal of all layers of varnish amplifies the chemically induced discordancy. Such cleaning, therefore, reveals not the 'original' painting but its spruced-up corpse. This tasteless deception is compounded by a meticulous filling-in of all the numerous losses and abrasions with fresh, perfectly matching paint. A seamless surface of clean, bright colours emerges whose glossy, synthetically varnished 'perfection' creates a plausible but deceiving impression of miraculous recovery.

This approach, Annigoni explained, needlessly exposes the painting to assault by solvent and scalpel, jeopardising thereby the very surface as the master left it, 'aged, alas! as all things age, but with the magic of glazes preserved and with those final accents which confer unity, balance, atmosphere, expression – in fact all the most important and moving qualities in the work of art'.

Artists and connoisseurs have, for a century and a half, alleged precisely such violations and destruction of glazes. The Gallery has sometimes changed its defences, but never its philosophy. It denied during the nineteenth century that Old Masters had employed glazes at all – yet Titian is known to have employed as many as forty layers and Leonardo, it has recently been discovered, over thirty. By the end of the nineteenth century restorers were widely reviled as well-connected, failed artists – 'ignorant daubers' – who, being paid piece-rate, contrived to 'undo and redo' every painting. To facilitate their own 'repaints', they rubbed paint surfaces down almost to the canvas or panel, obliging scholars to address only qualities of design and composition. Henry Layard recalled how even churches provided no sanctuary: 'The celebrated altarpiece by Titian in the Church of the Frari . . . has been "restored" seven times. . . . The once splendid altarpiece by Giorgione in the Church of his native town Castelfranco retains little but the composition.'

The National Gallery's contribution to this mania began in the 1840s with hasty cleanings of magnificent paintings by Rubens, Titian, Velazquez, Veronese, Poussin and Canaletto. Disbelieving onlookers held the pictures to have been 'flayed', 'scoured', 'scrubbed', 'laid bare' and 'smudged'. The outcry forced the Keeper to resign and the Government to set up a parliamentary committee of inquiry at which the Gallery's restorer refused to identify his solvents. The Keeper's and the restorer's evidence so conflicted that, it was remarked, 'an impression of want of candour' was created.

This century, cleanings greatly subsided, with scarcely more than one picture a year being treated. But with the evacuation of the pictures and two restorers during the last war to a secret cave in Wales, the process, unwatched, took off once more. Over sixty paintings were cleaned, provoking, when they were exhibited in 1946, a renewed outrage which filled the correspondence columns of both *The Times* and the *Daily Telegraph* for over a year. This time the Director, Sir Philip Hendy, was prepared. Swiftly and pre-emptively, he set up his own 'official' inquiry. Two 'outside' restorers served under a 'lay' academic, J. R. Weaver (who lent his name to the enterprise). This committee, professing to disregard all questions of taste and judgement and seek only ascertainable facts, held 'industrial tests' to have scientifically proved that the Gallery's solvents could not possibly harm paintings. This reassurance, relayed to the nation in an article written by Weaver himself, has not worn well.

The opposite is the case with J. Morris Moore, the first of many critics and the founder of the National Gallery Reform Association, who said in 1852 of Canaletto's *Stonemason's Yard*:

31

That picture has been literally flayed, the transparent colour on the shadowed side of the beams . . . has been nearly rubbed off . . . the effacement of half-tints and shadow has [produced] unmeaning and reliefless surfaces . . . the linear perspective is forced into direct antagonism with the aerial . . . *the chalky, veiled appearance . . . is owing to the solvent having disturbed some portion of the body pigment.* The sky has a smudged appearance [as a] result of an improper action of strong solvent.

When the painting was next cleaned by the Gallery in 1955, it was conceded that Moore's observations were 'not wholly unjust': the shadows were indeed rubbed and the sky was damaged. The claim, however, that solvent had left oil paint with a 'chalky, veiled appearance', remained unacknowledged. But during the last great cleaning controversy, that of the early 1960s, an eminent conservation scientist, S. Rees Jones, Head of the Department of Technology at the Courtauld Institute of Art, confirmed that solvents, whatever Weaver contended, could indeed impart 'a matt, chalky quality' to oil paint. This they achieve by leaching organic material from it, thereby leaving the paint more brittle and fragile and, in effect, prematurely aged.

Director Sir Philip attacked scientist Jones under cover of the Gallery Report (which carries no correspondence), but even so was forced to concede that leaching occurs. Putting a figure of 4 per cent to the amount of soluble material present in old oil paints, he held that the phenomenon was inconsequential and that any resulting 'surface mattness' was easily disguisable with varnish. Nonetheless, 'experimental data on this subject are needed . . . there is still much to be learnt'. In 1954, six years after the Weaver Report, he had more frankly admitted that, 'What actually takes place when a solvent comes into contact with a varnish or a medium [oil] or a pigment is still fundamentally a mystery'.

Sir Philip Hendy's response was in turn challenged in the scholarly press by Rees Jones and a second Courtauld scientist, P. L. Jones, who charged the National Gallery's scientists with misleading the public and failing to understand the nature of oil paint. He repudiated their reported contention that oil paints were as impermeable to solvents as synthetic materials like Formica and alleged the claimed upper figure of 4 per cent for leachable material to be inaccurate. The research from which it had been taken had made clear, he said, that that figure referred to the proportion of loss in the entire paint film, including its pigments. With the pigment discounted, the potential loss of organic material in the oil paint amounted to 25 per cent, and with common solvents like acetone to as much as 47 per cent. P. L. Jones's own research at the Courtauld Institute had shown leaching to be capable of consuming as much as 70 per cent (by weight) of an artificially aged oil film.

The Gallery Director was in some difficulty. The scientific expertise used so effectively in previous controversies to counter aesthetic criticisms was now itself suspect. The artistic consequences of the cleaning techniques underwritten by the Gallery's scientific department were under great attack from the country's most distinguished artists, critics and scholars: Francis Bacon and Frank Auerbach; David Sylvester and Laurence Gowing; Professor Anthony Blunt, then Director of the Courtauld Institute; Professor Ernst Gombrich, then Director of the Warburg Institute; Dr Otto Kurz, the Warburg's chief librarian; John White, Manchester University's Professor of Art History. Once again, Sir Philip responded under cover of the Gallery Report, dismissing the charges as meriting attention only in so far as their authors held prestigious positions. With some triumph he gave his account of events: first, he invited the Gallery's scientific adviser to prepare a statement of the claims made by the Gallery's many critics; then he set up inside the Gallery a special committee which included himself, his Keeper and his scientific adviser; and finally he invited the scientific adviser to submit his statement to the committee (on which he sat) so that it could, in secret session, 'evaluate' the Gallery's own form-ulation of its critics' contentions. They then found 'no valid scientific criticisms of the present National Gallery cleaning policy'. The present state of scientific understanding as revealed in the technical literature shows the earlier conclusion to have been both complacent and obtuse. Papers delivered at a 1990 Conservation Congress reported variously that:

> Cleaning science barely exists. . . . Swelling and leaching of moderately aged paints are substantial. . . . Pigment sensitivity to solvents has been neglected by researchers. . . . Methods of removing this disfigured [varnish] film are a continuous source of controversy or even polemic . . . we may never fully characterise or understand the surface of an aged, varnished, grime-laden paint film. . . . The effect of solvents on paint films is not completely understood. . . . It is also known that solvents cause oil films to swell. Does the oil film eventually return to its original state or is it permanently changed?

I recently asked the present Director, Neil MacGregor, whether the Gallery is confident that its restorers fully understand the precise nature and extent of the impact their solvents have on paint films being cleaned and whether the Gallery is confident that no leaching of organic material (with consequent embrittlement) has occurred during the last thirty years. I also asked whether any research has been carried out on these matters by Gallery staff since the cleaning controversy of the 1960s. Mr MacGregor instructed Dr Nicholas Penny, the Clore Curator of Renaissance Art, to reply on his behalf. He has not responded to these questions.

As it happens, evidence of the scale of solvent-inflicted injury exists in the restoration dossiers which the Gallery keeps on every painting. Each dossier is said to contain a record of all tests and treatments, scientific analyses, materials deployed (for example, solvents, varnishes, glues), as well as a comprehensive photographic record of treatments. I have asked to see five dossiers and been allowed to see two, *The Entombment of Christ*, attributed to Michelangelo, and *The Adoration of the Kings* by Bramantino, neither of which contained any technical record of treatments. The absence of record of tests on material removed by cleaning swabs – the only certain method of detecting unwitting removal of pigment – is particularly regrettable. Five requests to see this material have proved unsuccessful.

In the case of the Michelangelo *Entombment*, it has been said that no material now exists other than that published in the 1970 Report. But that account contained no analysis of material removed from the painting on cleaning swabs and no information on any prior testings of solvent strengths and mixes. It discloses only that 'the discoloured varnish was easily removed with the neutral organic solvents customarily used for cleaning (in this case a mixture of acetone and white spirit)'. Acetone is the strongest of the commonly used solvents and is stronger than neat alcohol. It is known to swell old dry oil paint as well as varnish. The combination of acetone and white spirit swells oil paint more than either substance can in isolation. The more powerful the swelling of paint induced by a solvent, the greater is the quantity of material leached. Leaching is known to erode the surface of a paint film and to cause embrittlement of its substance. Embrittled glazes are more easily detached from sounder, more elastic underlying paints.

The question of whether pigments or glazes are removed along with varnish is central to all disputes. The Gallery's claim to be able to distinguish between, for example, a brown toning glaze and a superimposed, browned varnish is not convincing. Restorers recently testing a new cleaning agent were obliged to apply it to the flesh tones and not to the brown background because, even with the aid of a microscope, polarized light and ultra-violet light, 'no visual distinctions were possible, it was difficult to observe the degree of partial cleaning in these dark areas'.

The photographs in both of the two dossiers I have examined indicate solvent-inflicted injuries. One in the *Entombment* dossier shows the effect of a test patch of solvent on one of the painting's figures. A pencilled note from the restorer, Helmut Ruhemann, observes that 'the cleaned strip here looks more unfinished than the uncleaned parts' – which is true: the cleaned section has a reduced tonal and colour range, not an enhanced one as would be expected with dirt removal. Ruhemann's note continues, 'This effect no longer shows after complete cleaning of the face.' This too was true – after cleaning, the values of the entire face were reduced to those of the initial test strip. The awkward comparison simply ceased to exist as the 'cleaning' progressed.

Permission to publish that photograph here was refused. The Gallery intends to include the photograph in a future exhibition. Nor could any other photograph from the dossier be made available: the Gallery, it was said, permits publication only of those photographs previously published by itself. The photographs in the Bramantino dossier record, among many changes, a clear loss of shading on a pink stone container in the foreground. When this loss was drawn to the attention of the restorer, she replied: 'I agree that the absence of any modelling on the lower side of the convex curve is odd. It is possible that a red lake glaze has faded.'

The now missing glaze had in fact survived for five centuries prior to the present cleaning during which it disappeared. Photographs taken before and after the cleaning have been published by the Gallery in the current National Gallery Technical Bulletin. Permission to publish them here was offered on two conditions: that *The Spectator* be able to assure the Gallery of a sufficiently high standard of photographic reproduction; and that the author of the accompanying article be prepared to submit it to the Gallery for prior approval in order to ensure that, as a press officer put it, 'the photographs are used or interpreted in a way they [the curators] would find acceptable'. When asked whether such a precondition was usual, the officer replied, 'Yes, it's the standard thing with particularly delicate matters like cleanings.'

The Bramantino cleaning is described in the National Gallery Technical Bulletin (no. 14). The function of these Bulletins is unclear. In them, the Gallery's restorers describe their own actions and decisions in language which suggests a disinterested reporting of uncontroversial and verifiable 'facts'. And yet often the content of these accounts is less than complete. The Bramantino report, for example, gives no indication of solvents used and offers no explanation for the altered state of the stone container. A delicate matter indeed.

This paper first appeared in The Spectator 30 (Jan. 1993), pp. 55–8.

4

Working exhibits and the destruction of evidence in the Science Museum

Peter R. Mann

Science underpins conservation; it is ironic then that scientific collections in museums have been among the last to receive specialist conservation support. History of science and natural science collections are now beginning to attract the attention of the conservation profession. Here Peter Mann discusses those aspects of science and industry museum practice which appear to contradict their very purpose. It will be interesting to see how the objectives of conservation can be incorporated into the dynamic methods of object interpretation and exploitation practised by these museums.

The purpose of this article is to try to explain why it is that so many curators of technical artefacts, particularly transport artefacts, subscribe to the ethic of the museum profession that their duty is to preserve evidence, yet devote much of their professional lives to the destruction of that evidence. Why is it that a thoughtful and dedicated curator such as John Hallam, in his paper in the Museum Association's *Manual of Curatorship*, should accept that a museum is a 'collection of artefacts assembled for preservation as evidence of man's material culture and environment' and then devote 8,000 words to exploring various ways in which artefacts may be restored, modified, worn out through operation and otherwise compromised, so that little uncorrupted evidence remains to be placed before the public? And all without a trace of irony. The paper is in fact excellent, and one with which few technical curators would take exception.

Are such curators dishonest, thoughtless and uncaring? Are they schizophrenic? Or is it that the dominant ethic of the profession is in fact inappropriate to technical artefacts and that they are intuitively acting out a more appropriate, though unexpressed, ethic which has yet to be defined?

The question of whether museum objects should be demonstrated is one which is a constant source of debate both inside and outside the museum profession. There are those who take a conservative view: since the purpose of a museum is the preservation of material evidence it must be wrong to compromise that evidence by wearing out artefacts through operation. At the other end of the spectrum are a few curators of car collections who insist that the best way to preserve a car is to maintain it in good working order and run it regularly. In the middle are the generality of technical museums, all of which demonstrate artefacts to a greater or lesser extent. Such divergent views cannot be reconciled. An analysis of the arguments shows that the reason the debate is invariably fruitless is because the protagonists fail to recognize that they start from different assumptions and work towards different objectives. A historical survey of the policy and practice of sectioning and operating artefacts in the Science Museum, London, serves to clarify these issues. It shows how the sectioning and operating of artefacts can be justified, but only by rejecting the dominant ethic of the museum profession.

THE CONSERVATIVE VIEW

The underlying ethic of the museum profession is that the primary objective of a museum is the preservation of material evidence, which may then be exploited in a variety of ways for the public benefit. Since such preservation of evidence is the primary objective, it follows that any exploitation of the artefact should not compromise that evidence.

Clearly, sectioning an artefact, or wearing it out through operation, must compromise the evidence and hence cannot be allowed. It is a concise, logical argument. However, it rests on the belief that the primary objective is indeed the preservation of material evidence and on the assumption that the only evidence in the artefact is of a material nature. If either primary objective or assumption were changed, then it would be necessary to modify the conservative ethic which results.

THE WORKING VIEW

It may seem implausible at first that some curators should believe that operating cars preserves them, so let us see how this comes about. It is a fact that museums have often allowed their cars to deteriorate on exhibition or in store through simple lack of care and attention. Private individuals who run their own old cars point out that theirs are in better condition than those in museums and conclude that running cars helps to preserve them. This conclusion is false. What in fact is going on is that the decision to run a car necessitates the application of sufficient resources to keep the car in good enough condition for it to be run. If equivalent resources were put into conserving a car in static condition it would in fact preserve the originality and evidential value of the car far longer than would be the case for the running car with all the attendant maintenance, repair and substitution of parts. Running a car concentrates the mind on keeping the car running but not on conserving the car. What the protagonist of running cars is really saying is that if your objective is to run a car then the best way to keep the car in running order is to maintain it in running order. The running of the car has become of more importance than the preservation of its originality and its value as material evidence. It would seem, therefore, that the primary objective has changed, though in a way which is as yet unclear. Equally, it would seem that there has been some change in the underlying assumption of the object as material evidence. By the end of this article I hope to make plain these changes in assumption and objective.

Few curators hold such a strong working view, but those who operate objects all share it to some degree. And since they also tend to believe in the importance of the preservation of evidence it is not surprising that there is confusion in their minds, that they are unable to explain their position even to themselves, and that those holding the conservative view fail to understand them. This leads technical curators into the most improbable justifications for their behaviour.

The view that the best way to preserve a car is to maintain it in good working order and to run it regularly is incorrect. Let us be quite clear that working any machine causes wear and tear which requires maintenance, repair and substitution of new parts to keep it running. It may happen imperceptibly, it may happen rapidly and cata-strophically. Either way, the originality and evidential value of the artefact are com-promised, and no amount of justification and rationalization can alter that.

JUSTIFICATIONS

Technical curators, particularly transport curators, become defensive when taxed with the problem of the destruction of evidence. They know instinctively that what they are doing is in some way wrong, but equally they feel that there is something instructive, inspirational or, at the very least, just plain fun in people being able to see old machinery working. They adopt a variety of defensive strategies to paper over the cracks and say: the wear, degradation and other risks are actually very small; we always replace with original parts or with parts made to the original pattern and the right type of materials; we keep records of everything we do and keep all the original parts when they are removed; operating objects in museums is only a natural extension of their original working life and hence causes no ethical problems; operating objects is the best way of preserving them. These answers are all unsatisfactory as they make no attempt to address the basic problem of the destruction of evidence. In reality what they are is a series of rationalizations to help technical curators cope with the guilt of the destruction of evidence. Since they fail to address the problem itself, they fail to satisfy the logic of the conservative view and leave even those holding the working view feeling uneasy.

Those who take the conservative view sometimes suggest that the answer for newly acquired objects is to acquire two specimens, one to lay down as an archival specimen and one to operate; for old objects the answer is to make a reproduction to operate. Such sug-gestions are usually rejected by technical curators on the grounds of the cost and space of duplicating objects, and a feeling that a reproduction is no substitute for the 'real thing'; but also because they have an instinctive feeling which they cannot or dare not express, that operating objects is in some way more important than preserving them.

I have lumped sectioning and working together as if they were equal in the destruction of evidence. In fact their effects are slightly different. Sectioning is usually a unique event. There is therefore time to work out in advance what part of the artefact is to be removed so as to control the amount of destruction involved. In the case of working a machine, a series of *ad hoc* decisions must be made throughout the period of operation as to whether to carry on modifying the machine in order to keep it running. The process is cumulative and inexorable. Whilst nominally under the curator's control it is all too easy to end up with a completely reproduction machine and a large box of worn-out 'original' parts.

SCIENCE MUSEUM POLICY ON WORKING EXHIBITS

Let us now look at the policy and practice of the Science Museum in addressing these prob-lems to see what light it can throw on the assumptions and objectives of technical museums.

The Departmental Committee on the Science Museum (better known as the Bell Com-mittee after its Chairman Sir Hugh Bell) reported in 1911 and 1912. The recommen-dations of this committee, actively pursued by successive directors, were the mainspring of policy in the Science Museum between the wars, and the general outline of those policies is still with us today. The Science Museum had working exhibits before the Bell Report, but the approval of the Report enshrined the technique as a necessary part of the interpretive process:

> In the Machinery Division of the Museum many of the objects have been arranged so that the visitor may examine internal details of construction and study moving parts in successive positions. . . . Such methods of exhibition are most efficacious, and when well devised they greatly increase the educational value of the objects. . . . They ought to be applied so far as possible throughout the collections.

This was immediately echoed in the 1913 Annual Report (perhaps not surprisingly as Sir Hugh Bell became the first Chairman of the Advisory Council), and succeeding Annual Reports give ample evidence that the museum was eager to extend the policy of sectioning and working objects. Nor were the science collections immune to this desire to make things work. In 1934:

> The second feature of the modern plan which has a direct bearing on Division IV [Astronomy, Mathematics, Chemistry, Optics, etc.] is an attempt to make the exhibits dynamic rather than static, to employ all the resources of power and art to make exhibits attractive, self-active or operable at will.
>
> (Advisory Council Report 1934: 27)

When the advisory Council was reconstituted in 1951 it began a major review of policy in the Science Museum. As part of this process a paragraph-by-paragraph analysis was carried out of the Bell Report forty years after its publication. Commenting on the paragraph about working exhibits quoted at the beginning of this section it reported that: 'This principle has been generally applied as far as possible and nothing is placed in the collections without consideration of the possibility of increasing the instructiveness by making it work.' This review of policy appeared as an appendix to the Advisory Council Report for 1952 entitled *Report on the Policy of the Science Museum* and recommended an extension of the practice of working demonstrations:

> (iv) Active and static displays. The essential characteristic of the laboratory, workshop or factory is change . . . Museums on the other hand are traditionally static . . . but it ought to be considered whether more opportunities should not be afforded for visitors to see the real thing being done. The active display is very much more attractive to visitors of what ever type than the static . . .
>
> (Advisory Council Report 1952: 38)

The Report went on to survey the methods by which this could be achieved. Subsequent Annual Reports continued to record new exhibits which were sectioned or working. Presumably it was axiomatic that the technique was followed and no specific justification was thought necessary even when the museum started entering cars in the Brighton Run in 1954 and steaming locomotives in 1975.

What the Annual Reports show is that the Science Museum has had a consistent and repeatedly expressed policy of wanting to section and operate objects. The purpose of this policy was to make the objects in the museum more understandable to the visitors.

SCIENCE MUSEUM PRACTICE IN WORKING EXHIBITS

It is not known when the Science Museum first sectioned an artefact or operated a working exhibit, but certainly the practice was started before the Bell Report enshrined it as an act of policy. Dickinson regarded the appointment of W. I. Last in 1890 to the post of Keeper of the Machinery and Inventions Division as:

the dawn of the third period in museum technique that I have mentioned, that of making a museum a living institution by such arrangements that the whole public can be made to understand what they see and derive educational advantage from a visit, arrangements contemptuously stigmatised by superior persons as 'making the wheels go round'.

(Dickinson 1933/4: 9)

In conducting the following survey of working exhibits in the Science Museum I have tried to use as examples artefacts which are clearly 'real full-sized' objects rather than models or reproductions. I do not intend to engage in a discussion of whether a contemporary model is a 'real' object which must be preserved at all cost, or whether it can be regarded merely as an ephemeral piece of display material. It is irrelevant to this discussion except in determining the number of objects being operated. If a model is not a 'real' object it does not matter; if it is a 'real' object it can be treated as part of the discussion of 'real' objects.

The 1914 Annual Report stated that in the Machinery and Inventions Division there were 184 working objects, in the Naval Division 91, whereas in the Scientific Apparatus Division there were only 49. An indication of the nature of the 250 or more working objects in the engineering collections can be obtained from the catalogues of these collections where the entries identify most, but not all, of the working exhibits. Thus the 3,091 catalogue numbers contained 1,086 'real full-sized' objects, of which 33 were working and 65 were sectioned, and 182 working models. In other words, 10 per cent of the 'real, full-sized objects' were working or sectioned, and nearly 7 per cent of all objects were working. Unfortunately, the science catalogues do not systematically record which objects were working so that it is not possible to identify from these catalogues the 49 working objects noted in the 1914 Annual Report.

Most of the working objects were engines and pumps, for example an 1862 Maudslay vertical engine (still working in the East Hall) and an 1860 Lenoir gas engine (no longer working), but they also included an 1863 Glover dry gas meter (still on exhibition but not working), and an 1864 Holtzapfel ornamental turning lathe. The sectioned objects included a 1906 Dursley-Pedersen cycle gear, an 1858 Giffard locomotive injector, a c.1894 Miller's apparatus for purifying gold, and an 1897 Singer lock-stitch sewing-machine.

As the years passed, the sectioning and working of objects broadened out into new areas of the collections. Radio demonstrations were proving very popular in 1927; cine projectors, stroboscopes, zootropes were working in 1929; an 1810 handloom for weaving silk was being demonstrated in 1931; in 1932 five ophthalmic instruments were arranged so as to be seen in operation and a polarizing microscope and strain-viewer in 1935; the same year an early postal franking machine in the mathematics collection went into operation; twenty working exhibits were to go into the new Illumination Gallery in 1938; a sectioned and working combine-harvester was the centrepiece of the new Agriculture Gallery in 1951; the same year saw the operation of a Geiger counter and a Dines anemometer.

Many of these objects would have been operating under light loads and perhaps would be more accurately described as moving rather than working. However, vehicles are invariably highly stressed when working and it was not long before they too were being operated. In 1936 the 1888 Benz car was put into working order and demonstrated in the museum grounds and at the start of the Brighton Run (it did not take part in the run itself). In 1939 nine horse-drawn carriages went to the Jubilee Show of the Royal Agricultural Society in Windsor Great Park of which four paraded. The 1902 Ivel tractor led the procession of tractors around the Grand Ring at the Royal Show at Cambridge in 1951. The 1903 Wolseley became in 1954 the first car entered in the Brighton Run by the Science Museum.

For the 65 years in which Reports were issued, in the period 1912 to 1983, there were an average of 4.42 mentions per year of sectioned or working exhibits (excluding those objects which were definitely not 'real full-sized' objects).

It had been my original hope to estimate the number of objects which are currently sectioned or operating in the Science Museum but it became clear that this was unrealistic. Such a survey must await the future completion of the computerized catalogue. However, it would be true to say that every gallery contains sectioned or working exhibits, and the Public Services Division is only too aware that each new exhibition brings with it new demands from curators for yet more sectioned and operating objects. There is certainly sufficient evidence to say that the museum's stated policy of sectioning and operating objects has been put into effect. Only the shortage of resources has prevented its even wider use.

THE PRICE TO BE PAID

If it is necessary to section and operate artefacts to explain how things work then the Science Museum has shown that it is prepared to pay the price of the destruction of evidence which inevitably results. But are there any bounds to the price it is prepared to pay? Is the museum prepared to sacrifice prime objects, or only those of lesser significance? Is is prepared to destroy an artefact completely or allow only a limited degradation? Is there an unacceptable level of risk (for example the crashing of an aircraft may be a rare event but the consequences are catastrophic, whereas crashing a car may be more likely but the consequences less serious)? Is it prepared to section and operate old objects, or only those newly manufactured or newly acquired? These questions are explored by looking further at the practice of the museum.

PRIME OBJECTS

If the Science Museum were concerned about the destruction of evidence it might be expected to exclude those it regarded as prime objects. However, it is not obvious that this has been the case. The prime objects which have been sectioned or operated include the 1797 Boulton and Watt engine, the Parsons turbines, all four Harrison chronometers and the 1888 Benz car.

In 1924, erection of the engines in the new East Hall began, 'one at least of which will shortly be arranged so that it can be seen in motion' (Advisory Council Report 1924: 4). By 1927 the 1797 Boulton and Watt engine had been motorized, and in 1936 the museum was proud to record that it had been operated during the Watt bicentenary exhibition and that its operating sound had been radioed across the Atlantic to the Franklin Institute in Philadelphia, who reported that it could be heard quite clearly. The periodic demonstration of this engine has remained a feature of the East Hall ever since.

The Parsons steam turbines involved sectioning rather than operation. In 1927 the museum acquired the radial flow steam turbine originally fitted in 1894 to Turbinia. Although replaced by an axial flow turbine in 1896, it was nevertheless the first steam turbine to power a ship.

From 1924 the Science Museum made repeated efforts to acquire on loan from the Lords Commissioners of the Admiralty the four chronometers designed and constructed by John Harrison between the years 1728 and 1759, which he made to win the £20,000 prize offered by the government for a timekeeper of sufficient accuracy to determine longitude at sea. The chronometers had not been working for over 100 years when Lt Cdr R. T. Gould began in 1920 to clean and overhaul them. The Science Museum acquired them all on loan – No. 2 in 1925, No. 3 in 1932, Nos. 1 and 4 in 1935 – and all four were exhibited in operation until they were sent to the recently opened National Maritime Museum at Greenwich in June 1936. Three of the four were again in the Science Museum in 1952 for the special exhibition 'The British Clockmakers' Heritage', and two were kept in operation throughout the exhibition.

The 1888 Benz car is the oldest car in this country and the only survivor of the first production batch of cars. It was acquired in 1913 in a rusty and dilapidated condition, although E. A. Forward seems to have carried out a trial run at that time. In 1936 the car was driven to Hyde Park for the start of the Brighton Run, although it did not take part in the run itself. Forward also gave a few demonstration runs in Exhibition Road but was clearly of the opinion that it should not attempt extended runs. However, in 1957 the car was restored and entered in the Brighton Run. In the event, the car ran out of control and crashed into an MG saloon at some traffic lights at Purley, breaking the front fork of the Benz. With the brakes fully applied the car was still travelling at 10 m.p.h. on a wet, downhill road. The car was repaired and had an additional band brake fitted to the transmission for the 1958 run. This time the car completed the run, but even so was involved in a slight accident when manoeuvring at 2 m.p.h. between two lines of traffic at Crawley. For safety reasons the car had to be manhandled down the steeper slopes.

ACCEPTABLE LEVELS OF RISK AND DESTRUCTION

The purpose of the preceding section was simply to establish that the Science Museum does section and operate prime objects, rather than to record any loss of evidence which may result from so doing. But what levels of degradation do occur and how likely is it to occur?

Significant cumulative degradation is quite common, but catastrophic destruction comparatively rare. Cumulative degradation occurs as a result of wear or as a result of modification, and both usually take place over a long period of time. The wear itself may amount to significant degradation even if all the component parts are still original to the artefact. And, in an attempt to reduce further wear, the artefact may be modified and parts replaced. Cumulative degradation through modification may occur even without wear in order to improve the reliability of repeatability of a demonstration by an artefact whose operation is only marginally satisfactory.

A good example of such modification is that of the horizontal pendulum seismograph built by J. J. Shaw and installed in Gallery 45 in 1935. With the exception of some of the clocks, this may well be the object with the longest record of operation in the museum. In order for the seismograph record to include a timing signal it had to be supplied with timing signals from another working exhibit in the Time Measurement Gallery, the Shortt free pendulum clock which was acquired in the same year and which controlled the public clocks in the East Block. Although comprehensive records are not available, it would seem that the seismograph was modified on at least five occasions in order to improve its accuracy, reliability and sensitivity. The then curator Dr

McConnell, in recommending a new pen and ink recording system in 1983 wrote, 'the original Shaw seismograph has already been so considerably modified over the years that little of the original remains. Its value lies rather in its demonstration function' (Technical File 1938–348). After being out of action for several years the seismograph has been modified again and is now back in operation. The importance which the museum attaches to this working exhibit is indicated by the frequent references in the Annual Reports to the public and media interest in its recording of major earthquakes.

Degradation through straightforward wear (though accelerated by poor design) is shown by the motorized, sectioned Coventry-Climax portable fire-pump which has been operating continuously in the Firefighting Gallery since 1966. By 1982, in the absence of any lubrication, the cam lobes had been severely scored and the faces of the cam-followers gouged out to a depth of 3 mm. This was no doubt aggravated by the chromium plating (applied by the manufacturer in preparing the engine for exhibition) breaking up and acting as a grinding paste. In order to keep the engine and pump running, a new camshaft and new followers were substituted and the engine modified so that it could be continuously lubricated.

The catastrophic destruction of an artefact through operation is comparatively rare. However, the Science Museum has been associated with one case, the Bristol Bulldog aircraft, which is something of a *cause célèbre* in the transport museum world. In 1939 the Bristol Aeroplane Co. Ltd presented the Science Museum with a 1931 Bristol Bull-dog aircraft, then one of the standard single-seat fighters of the RAF. After being displayed for a short time, it went into store for the duration of the war but remained there after the war was over. In 1956 Bristol wrote saying that they would like to include the aircraft, which appeared to be the only one surviving, in a historical display they were planning for Bristol's 50th anniversary in 1960. In return for its loan they offered to put the aeroplane into a fully airworthy condition, and the museum agreed. Progress on restoring the aircraft was rather slow but on 21 April 1961 the museum gave permission for it to be flown. The following month the museum decided to submit it to a Board of Survey for returning to the donor because 'The Bulldog is not required . . . for exhibition in the foreseeable future, and is not of such historical or technical significance that it should remain in the Museum store' (Guttery 1963: 3, 22) and in June Bristol were duly advised that the aircraft was again their property. After passing its test flight satisfactorily Bristol presented the aircraft to the Shuttleworth Trust. On Sunday 13 September 1964 it crashed at the Farnborough air show when its engine failed to pick up after a loop, and struck some fencing, the aircraft turning over. The pilot was later reported to be comfortable in hospital but the Bulldog suffered irreparable damage. The aircraft has never been rebuilt and the pieces are reputed to be housed by Shuttleworth and the RAF Museum. The fact that it was not still a Science Museum object at the time of the crash is simply a matter of timing.

OLD OBJECTS

It is often the case that people take a different view of the sectioning or operation of a newly made object as opposed to an 'old, historical' object. If I were to section a new Rolls-Royce car for display it would be regarded as a first-class way of obtaining an interesting and informative technical exhibit. But if I were to section our 1904 Rolls-Royce which has been in the museum since 1935, there would be howls of rage at this wanton destruction. It might be expected, therefore, that the museum would not section or operate an object which was already regarded as old. It may well be the case that the museum is reluctant to section objects which have been in its possession for some time. Unfortunately, it is difficult to test this as it is actually quite difficult to find out when many of our objects were sectioned. Certainly the museum has no compunction about sectioning and operating objects which are old at the time of acquisition. Nor does it have any compunction about starting to operate old objects which have already been in its possession for some time without previously being operated.

As an example of an old object being put back into service on arrival at the museum, nothing could be better than the Wells Cathedral clock. It is certainly the object with the longest period of operation, both in the outside world before coming to the museum and also since arriving there. It is:

> the second oldest surviving clock in England and was probably already in use by 1392. It continued in use until 1835, when it was replaced by a modern one, and the old movement was removed to the crypt of the Cathedral. In 1871 it was lent to the Patent Office Museum . . . [transferred to the Science Museum with the Patent Office Museum in 1884] . . . and the clock has since been on public exhibition in working order.
>
> (Ward 1955: 18)

The present curator Dr Vaughan says that about 1984 one of the pinions was replaced and another is now so worn that the clock keeps stopping. A decision will shortly need to be taken as to whether to carry on replacing worn pinions or finally to retire the clock.

Other old objects in the science collections have also been put back into operation. The museum has a number of fine dividing engines, at least three of which have been operated since being acquired. Two came from A. J. Bennett, one believed to have been made by John Troughton in 1778 by copying Ramsden's engine of 1777 and put on exhibition in Gallery 42 in working order (though probably operated only by special request) in 1935, and another Ramsden-type engine which contributed to the war effort when it was lent to its donor in 1942 who used it to produce upwards of 2,000 sextants for the Admiralty. The third to be operated was a *c.*1895 Cooke circular dividing engine acquired from its makers, put into operation in 1954, and still under push-button operation in the Mathematics and Computing Gallery.

Another of the museum's scientific instruments to go back into service was the 1885 Isaac Roberts twin equatorial telescope. This had been purchased in 1936 and then stored in a number of packing-cases without being exhibited. When it was realized that the new observatory domes at Herstmonceux would be ready before the telescopes, the Royal Greenwich Observatory asked to borrow our telescope. In recommending the loan H. R. Calvert wrote, 'It will have the advantage that the telescope will be overhauled and put into working order so that it will be ready for use in our own observatory if we can get nothing better.' The telescope was collected on 24 September 1956, installed by August 1957, arrived back at the museum on 4 July 1961, and was assembled in our observatory by 30 November 1961. It was used in the museum for the first time in May 1963.

Some of the oldest objects to be operated were textile machines. None seems to have been used before the First World War, and immediately after the war the collection was in store, although a catalogue was produced in 1921. In 1928 the collection came out of store for exhibition in Gallery 24 of the new East Block, and the first to be demonstrated may have been an 1810 handloom for weaving silk in 1931. The gallery was reopened to the public after the Second World War in early 1947 and, by 1957, twenty-seven of the machines could be demonstrated. Among the oldest to be demonstrated were an eighteenth-century manual stocking-frame and a 1796 hand rib-knitting machine, first demonstrated in 1958 and 1961 respectively. This paper could have been written almost entirely around the many proud references to the working of textile machinery contained in the Annual Reports.

THE SCIENCE MUSEUM TODAY

The Science Museum has probably been operating objects longer than any other museum in the world. What this survey shows is that, broadly speaking, the sectioning and working of artefacts has always been part of the Science Museum, that this was a deliberate act of policy of which the museum was proud and sought to extend, that although most prevalent in the engineering collections it involved all parts of the museum. Every gallery in the Science Museum now has sectioned or working exhibits of one kind or another. This has been done with the specific intention of making the objects more understandable to the public. In other words, it is an interpretive technique to improve the exploitation of the artefacts for the public benefit. Whilst the museum could suddenly decide it is no longer going to section or operate artefacts, in reality it is almost inconceivable that the museum could now turn its back on this method of display.

As the Science Museum has so much experience of running objects it might be reasonable to suppose that it would have come to terms with the problems which this undoubtedly causes. But this turns out not to be the case. The museum runs an apparently random assortment of new, old and prime objects. It allows cumulative damage to occur until any sense of originality or evidential value is negated. That this is comparatively rare is only because of the shortage of the resources to do it more often, and because for many objects it takes many decades of operation to achieve significant degradation. That there have been so few cases of catastrophic destruction may simply be due to the lack of resources to demonstrate the type of object potentially susceptible to such catastrophes.

There are two reasons for the apparently random way in which objects are used and for the absence of any guidelines governing their use. First, the Science Museum's curators have very individual responsibilities and act largely independently of each other. Whilst they do talk to each other, overall policies are very difficult to obtain. When the question comes to be asked, if it ever does, as to whether a particular object should be kept running or pensioned off, it is always faced by an individual curator who may never have faced the problem before, and who may be trying to account for the first time for the actions of several generations of curators. Second, nobody has ever identified, or faced up to, the central paradox of the technical museum: the need to preserve evidence and the need to demonstrate objects. The result is a basic uncertainty as to what is the correct, or even what is the most reasonable, course of action to follow. So let us look again at this central paradox.

TOWARDS A NEW ETHIC FOR TECHNICAL MUSEUMS

As far as I am aware, the Science Museum has never stated as policy that it subscribes to the dominant ethic of the museum profession that the primary objective of the museum is the preservation of material evidence. However, in talking to Science

Museum curators whose experience goes back thirty-five years it is clear that individual curators do subscribe to that ethic. I have no reason to doubt that pre-war curators also subscribed to that view. It is after all self-evident that we are in the preservation business; we acquire and keep artefacts which are undeniably material evidence of the cultures that produce them.

Why then has the Science Museum devoted so much of its resources to the destruction of evidence through the sectioning and working of artefacts? The answer is that, whilst paying lip-service to the dominant museum ethic, the Science Museum is in fact acting out a more appropriate, though unexpressed, ethic for technical museums. That more appropriate ethic is that the primary objective of a technical museum is the exploitation of the artefact for the public benefit rather than the simple preservation of material evidence. This change in the primary objective of the technical museum is in turn based on a fundamental change in the underlying assumption of artefacts as material evidence to one of objects as also including functional evidence. What the museum is doing is to accept the destruction of one form of evidence so that another 'more important' form of evidence can be revealed to the public by the sectioning and operation of artefacts. As Kenneth Hudson has said, the Science Museum is at its best when acting as the 'National Museum of How Things Work'. If it is necessary to section and operate artefacts to explain how things work and to interest and excite people, then the museum has shown that it is prepared to pay the price of the destruction of material evidence which inevitably results.

To that extent the technical museum in general, and the Science Museum in particular, is different from the other broad categories of museums of archaeology, natural history, fine and applied arts. Because the Science Museum has seen its primary objective as explaining how things work rather than maintaining an encyclopaedic archive of arte-facts, it has adopted a different strategy for the treatment of objects. In other types of museum, even when objects have a functional nature, such as a teapot or a violin, they will generally have been collected for their aesthetic qualities or their historical associations. It is not that such museums have adopted a certain ethical position on the operation of objects, it is that it just did not occur to them to operate objects for they had no need to do so. For the technical museum it is not a matter of principle as to whether or not to operate objects; some objects will inevitably be operated. The 'principle' has become the more pragmatic (though no less difficult) decision as to which objects to operate, and the balance to be struck between the medium-term needs of exposition and the long-term needs of preservation.

I asked at the beginning of this paper whether technical curators were dishonest, thoughtless and uncaring, or whether they were schizophrenic. The answer is now clear. Because they have been labouring under an inappropriate ethic derived from other types of museum, they have been living in a schizophrenic state in which their actions contradict their beliefs. They are not dishonest, thoughtless and uncaring, but merely confused.

What is needed is that technical curators should come out of the closet and admit that they are in the business of destroying evidence. They should recognize that this is a necessary by-product of fulfilling their primary objective of exploiting their objects for the public benefit. They should cease their agonizing over the ethics of sectioning and operating objects, for no ethics are involved. Instead curators should concentrate on working out the circumstances in which it is appropriate to section or operate objects in order to meet the objectives of their museum, and the balance which they think appropriate between the medium-term needs of exposition and the long-term needs of preservation. Only then will they be able to function as 'whole' curators and carry out both exposition and preservation without suffering the confusing effects of the tension between the two.

The practical problem of balancing the conflict between exposition and preservation in the field where it is at its most severe, namely motor vehicles, will be dealt with in another paper.

This paper first appeared in Museum Management and Curatorship *Vol.8 (1989), pp. 369–87.*

NOTE

Peter Mann was formerly Curator of Road Transport, Science Museum, London, 1978–1993, and now works as a freelance Museum Consultant.

REFERENCES

Dickinson, H. W. (1933/4) 'Museums and their relation to the history of engineering and technology', *Transactions of the Newcomen Society* 14: 1–12.
Hallam, J. (1984) 'Conservation and storage: technology', in J. M. A. Thompson (ed.) *Manual of Curatorship*, London: Butterworth, 323–32.
Report of the Departmental Committee on the Science Museum and the Geological Museum Part I (1911), Part II (1912), London: HMSO.
Ward, F. A. B. (1955) *Handbook of the [Science Museum] Collection Illustrating Time Measurement – Part II Descriptive Catalogue* (3rd edn), London: HMSO.

5

The role of the scholar-curator in conservation

Peter Cannon-Brookes

The role of the specialist – the archaeologist, geologist, historian, etc. – is becoming undervalued in museums. Increasingly we are seeing the employment of more generalized conservators, collections managers, interpretation officers and others. Peter Cannon-Brookes's comments on the role of the specialist art historian in conservation apply equally to other disciplines.

One of the more discouraging aspects of the assault on curatorial professionalism during the last decades has been the lack of progress made with regard to consolidating the role of the scholar-curator in the processes of conservation. In the *Tate Gallery Report* for 1970–2, Sir Norman Reid drew attention to the crucial role of the scholar-curator in conservation and stated:

> The contact between restorer and curator requires to be continual and very close. Many of the problems in conservation, which arise from day to day, and sometimes from hour to hour, involve historical and critical issues; they can hardly be solved except in consultation with an experienced curatorial staff of the kind which is only found in the largest galleries.

Considerable weight was given to this problem in the booklet, *After Gulbenkian*, published in 1976, but after twelve years it is much to be regretted that, notwithstanding a number of reports and much debate, so little thought is devoted to the role of the scholar-curator, and that to a considerable extent this continues to reflect contemporary attitudes of both curators and conservators.

Sir Norman Reid's statement not only presupposed the existence of expert curatorial staff in close proximity to the studio with adequate time at their disposal but also a clear understanding by all parties of the nature and obligations of the partnership. Succeeding reports have rightly drawn attention to the necessity of providing high-quality technical training for the conservator, but with few exceptions they have tended to avoid drawing attention to the limitations of the competence of the conservator after receiving that training. The International Institute of Conservation (UK) Report, published in 1974, draws close attention to the unacceptably high proportion of conservation work in United Kingdom museums and art galleries then being carried out by curatorial and technical staff who had received no specific training to undertake it, while the corollary was ignored. Indeed the likelihood that conservators are, consciously or unconsciously, by desire or through necessity taking decisions for which they do not possess either the scholarly knowledge or the relevant curatorial experience still tends to be forgotten. The conservator usurping the role of the curator is almost as dangerous for museum and art gallery collections as the more familiar problem of untrained curators and technicians dabbling in conservation.

Little has changed since the mid-1970s, and at the basic level few curators, or for that matter conservators, currently receive appropriate training designed to enable them to communicate meaningfully with colleagues specializing in the other disciplines, and the management of conservation services ignores this factor only at great peril. This process of communication begins with the technical examination of the object, and the curator may read the evidence provided by the physical condition of the object with very different eyes from those of the conservator. The physical condition in which the object has come down to us enshrines much of its history, but that evidence is best read by the scholar-curator whose task it is to accumulate a much deeper, specific knowledge of related material than the technological familiarity based on representative examples which forms part of the training of the conservator. Thus, although the art curator is primarily concerned with the historical and aesthetic aspects of the work of art in his care, and the art conservator is concerned with the technical aspects of their fabrication and physical well-being, the overlaps of responsibility are obvious and generally accepted. In response to the every-increasing pressures experienced in the museum environment, it is only too easy to forget the fundamental division between those specializing in the different disciplines: the curator and the conservator jointly undertake the technical examination of the object; and only then, the curator, in consulation with the conservator, agrees what shall be done to an object; and the conservator, in consultation with the curator, will decide how that operation will be carried out, and then undertakes it personally or supervises the agreed treatment.

The presumption that the art conservator has been trained to an adequate level of technical competence, so as to be able to select an appropriate course of action and carry it out, is generally accepted, though his obligation to agree courses of action with his curatorial partner tends to receive less emphasis, for practical as well as historical reasons. Precisely the same principles apply to the scientific disciplines and, for example, the conservator of fossils must work in close liaison with an experienced palaeontologist or taxonomist if physical evidence at variance with the norm is not to go unrecognized and be destroyed inadvertently. There is a tendency to accept these principles in theory and then to add hastily that, of course, it is not practicable to apply them to routine conservation treatments. Such arguments might be politically realistic but they reveal a deep lack of understanding of the whole nature of museum collections and the uniqueness of each specimen or work of art. The batch relining of oil-paintings is now mercifully something of the past, and even shards are rarely treated in this manner today. Each object presents it own individual problems, often unsuspected before the joint technical examination and the commencement of its conservation, and it can be argued that there is no such thing as routine conservation treatment.

Unfortunately, all too many curators continue to stand condemned by the condition of their collections, although the blame may well lie with their senior management or employers, and the decades of neglect which has been publicized since the 1960s has tended to undermine disproportionately the standing of the traditional scholar-curator *vis-à-vis* the professionally trained conservator, but without in any way diminishing the functional importance of his role in the conservation dialogue. In the United Kingdom at least, his situation has been greatly aggravated by the inexorable decline in the quantity and quality of the scholarly output of the museums, and the intellectual impoverishment of those institutions thereby implied. Nevertheless, before any curator can enter into the conservation dialogue, he must have established an intimate relationship with works of art, and in particular with those in the collection for which he is responsible.

Education and display are increasingly undertaken by specialist in-house staff, but while administrative functions of curatorial departments grow ever more onerous, the actual physical contact between curators and their collections grows less every month. Furthermore, academic art history, as taught in most university departments for the last twenty years, provides only a starting-point for developing the deep relationship with works of art, that of aesthetic sensibility combined with deep historical knowledge which is the foundation for the contribution to be made by the art curator in the conservation dialogue. The curator of the art collection must possess a more highly developed aesthetic sensibility than those colleagues who are responsible for archaeological, scientific or technological collections, whilst other specialist skills are required of them, but the demand for knowledge in depth is the requirement shared by all scholar-curators.

In these days of instant communication and popularization of museum collections it is easy to lose sight of the fact that all museum activities must be based on secure foundations of sound scholarship and that the integrity of the museum objects must be jealously guarded. If not, museums and art galleries can become so easily just congenial settings for trivial mass entertainments, their very collections suspect. Such complaints have often been voiced before, and many view the decline of the scholar-curator with considerable disquiet, but the implications for the conservation of collections have been insufficiently publicized. Clearly the traditional priorities of the scholar-curator have little in common with the philosophy of the local authority amenities and leisure services complexes, or indeed the new commercial orientation of the British national museums. For them the multifarious talents of 'show-biz' and high-profile marketing are more immediately in demand when high aesthetic and scholarly standards are not in themselves conducive to the high attendance figures and increased earnings which remain the only yardsticks of success intelligible to the local authorities and HM Government alike.

It is self-evident that the interpretation of a museum object presupposes a specialist knowledge of not only that particular object but also its intellectual context, and thus adequate provision for the scholar-curator is a prerequisite for the institution carrying out collections-based interpretative and educational functions. Less familiar is the requirement for trained scholar-curators, present in adequate numbers, as a prerequisite for the conservation of the museum's collections, and the maintenance of their individual expertise by regular access to high-quality collections and library resources. The demands to be made of experienced scholar-curators are of crucial importance in the operating of existing conservation units as well as the strategic planning of future conservation services, since by their nature highly trained and experienced scholar-curators, actually or potentially able to fulfil their role in conservation, will tend in the foreseeable future to be concentrated in relatively few national and provincial museums and art galleries. However, these scholar-curators will neither appear by magic nor survive prolonged intellectual starvation, and any assessment of conservation requirements must take due cognizance of the demands to be placed on other museum disciplines in order that an increasing amount of conservation work is carried out to the required standards. The principal weakness of the IIC (UK) Report in 1974 was its failure to recognize the integrated nature of the problem, and thus to appreciate the necessity of training scholar-curators as well as conservators for the operation of conservation services. Since then the situation has further deteriorated and there remains an urgent need to assign adequate resources to the training and servicing of scholar-curators as an integral component of the conservation of museum collections.

This paper first appeared in Museum Management and Curatorship *Vol. 7 (1988), pp. 323–5.*

REFERENCES

Cannon-Brookes, P. (1976) *After Gulbenkian: A Study Paper towards the Training of Conservators and Curators of Works of Art*, Birmingham.
The Tate Gallery (1972) *The Tate Gallery 1970–72*, London.

6

Do objects have a finite lifetime?
Susan M. Bradley

In this article Susan Bradley gives a succinct introduction to those factors which can lead to the deterioration of objects in museums. Such information is vital if sensible and cost-effective decisions are to be made concerning preventative conservation.

A very small percentage of all the objects ever made are now in museums, galleries, institutions or private collections. Most objects were lost when they were damaged in use and thrown away, reused in another form, destroyed during attacks on settlements and war or have deteriorated during burial or when forgotten in buildings. Once an object has been excavated or rediscovered, modern society expects it to last for ever. It is as if the very act of putting an object into a museum will preserve it. Despite what we read about the conditions in museums, it is true that many objects have only survived because they were in museums. However, having become part of a collection, not all objects are equally able to survive. This is because some objects are made of very durable materials whereas others are made of materials which are subject to rapid deterioration.

There are several factors which influence the survival of objects in museums. Although the material the object is made from is important, the history of the object before it entered a museum collection will affect its chances of survival since this may have altered its stability. The role of conservation and the potential for deterioration in the museum must also be considered.

Once an object is in a collection every effort should be made to ensure its survival. If the preservation of an object proves to be beyond the present state of conservation theory and practice then a complete record including illustrations or photographs must be made.

WHY OBJECTS WERE MADE AND WHAT HAPPENS TO THEM

The purpose for which an object was made, what it was made from, how it is used and whether it was buried will determine whether it has survived long enough to be part of a collection in the twentieth century. For instance, objects made for domestic use would have been heavily used and are likely to have been broken or worn out and thrown away. In addition, unless they were to be used in a grand household, the items were generally of poor quality. Thus only relatively few of the artefacts made for domestic use have survived. Objects which have been passed on in households are more likely to have survived than objects which have been buried. Some objects are also likely to be excavated in an unstable condition.

Broken and sometimes salty ceramics, salty stone, corroded metals, bones and water-logged textiles, leather and wooden objects are excavated from settlement sites. Buried porous ceramics and stone may have been permeated with ground-water containing soluble salts which cause continuing deterioration once the objects are lifted. Stone which has not been buried is also affected by ground-water permeation and many other weathering processes which cause the stone to lose at least some of its carved surface. Metal objects may have already started to corrode prior to burial. During burial total mineralization of some objects occurs. Even if the metal is totally mineralized, iron objects particularly can undergo post-excavation alteration of corrosion products which causes lamination of the objects. Waterlogged materials present special problems since they are dimensionally unstable and will shrink if allowed to start drying out. The conservation of waterlogged materials is still not a routinely successful process.

Ceremonial and decorative objects made from gold, enamels and gemstones have survived for generations because they are symbols of power. Objects of this type, found in burials, have often survived in good condition, because of the durable nature of the materials. During the excavation of the Sutton Hoo ship burial a gold and garnet belt buckle and a purse were discovered in near perfect condition. Other artefacts in the burial mound had suffered considerable corrosion and only a few fragments of the organic material from the boat, body and textiles survived.

Ethnographic collections contain many objects made from low-durability materials such as grasses, feathers, poorly tanned skins, paper, textiles and foodstuffs. Ethnographers also collect objects made specially for them during collecting trips. On arrival at their destination these objects can be found to have insect infestations and therefore need to be fumigated. The insects can have caused serious damage to the objects, which will need to be repaired. Some of the objects collected will have been made for the celebration of an annual festival and were therefore expected to have a short life. Their construction is often crude and they may be easily broken. They can present particularly difficult preservation problems.

Objects which were made for decorative and artistic purposes probably have the greatest chance of surviving intact and of being in museum collections now. This is because they were always valued, were handled infrequently and with extra care and have never been buried. Oil-paintings and prints and drawings have survived for these reasons even though *prima facie* it seems that they are made of at least some non-durable components.

Artefacts which were used for transport and are in museums now include cars, trains and aeroplanes. These later means of transport have suffered differential wear of components and contain components such as rubber tyres which suffer from considerable wear, having a short working lifetime, and will need to be replaced. Rubber itself is difficult to conserve. Corrosion of the metal body and moving components has often occurred during use and the subsequent period of neglect. The replacement or conservation of worn parts is the subject of a debate amongst conservators and engineers, who are usually responsible for the restoration and maintenance of this type of object.

The survival of many objects prior to entering a museum is random and fortuitous. Those objects made by great artists and artisans are most likely to have survived because they were protected by patrons and subsequent owners. In general, objects which have not been buried are in a better condition than buried objects and cause fewer problems in the museum. The continuing deterioration of archaeological objects can cause serious problems for conservators, but some modern materials such as early plastics are equally difficult to deal with.

Once the object is in a museum it becomes part of a collection in which it will be used and demands apart from those of conservation are made upon it.

THE PURPOSE OF MUSEUMS

The purpose of a museum with regard to the objects in its care is protection by means of security and conservation. The purpose with regard to the public is curation, which includes study of the collection by visiting academics and students; exhibition, which includes the loan of objects for exhibition in other institutions and countries; and education, which may involve handling of objects in the collection by students, school parties and occasionally by other members of the public.[1]

The effect of security is to limit access to the objects in the collection. This is of definite assistance to their survival since only those qualified to handle the collection and interested in the academic value rather than the financial value of the objects are allowed to come into contact with them. The effect of conservation should be to stabilize and secure the object and to ensure its survival.

The purpose of studying an object is to learn what it is, what it was used for, what it was made from and how it was made and how it relates to other similar objects. As a part of this study the objects may be analysed, and this can involve the permanent removal of a small sample. Objects are therefore valued for what can be learned from them in terms of technology as a result of scientific examination as well as for aesthetic reasons.

During the study of the objects they must be handled by both museum staff and bona fide students. The most common cause of damage to museum objects is handling. When objects are moved and examined, it is possible for damage to occur to even the most stable of materials. It is therefore important that all museum staff are trained in correct handling procedures and that guidelines for handling of objects by students are drawn up and enforced by supervising museum staff. Common problems which can occur are picking objects up by handes which are not secure and tearing of paper when pages are turned.

When objects are loaned to other institutions they are subjected to handling during packing and unpacking, vibration and changes in environmental conditions during the journey. This may cause damage to the objects especially if they are fragile. One of the jobs of the museum conservators will be to advise on the suitability of objects for loan. However, other considerations may be involved in the selection of objects to go on loan and the conservator's views may be ignored. The object will then have to be conserved to make it safe to travel.

The education department will want to use the collection actively in its work. In 1983 the British Museum Education Department organized an exhibition entitled 'Please Touch', in which the public were encouraged to handle objects. The period of the exhibition was limited to five weeks at the request of the conservators, who felt that even the twenty hard stone objects chosen could suffer damage from being constantly handled. As a consequence of the success of this exhibition and its follow-up, 'Human Touch' held in 1985, a series of Roman sculptures in the Wolfson Gallery has been made available for touching to the partially sighted. Making part of the collection available to the partially sighted is a legitimate part of the museum's activities, but it contravenes one of the conservation principles of restricting handling to trained staff and a limited number of others.

Whatever approach is taken towards the purpose of having objects in a museum, the job of conservation is to ensure their continued preservation.

THE ROLE OF THE CONSERVATOR

At first glance it often seems that the conservation department in a museum is working towards an aim which is not shared by other departments. This is not true, since everyone is concerned with the survival of the objects. Although permanent preservation is very much easier to achieve if the objects are never handled and kept in dark rooms at constant relative humidity and temperature, the role of the conservator should not be to separate the objects from the staff of the museum and the public but to ensure that the objects can be safely used for the proper purposes of the museum. To do this the conservator may use active or passive methods of conservation. Active methods involve intervention on the object, for instance stabilizing a bronze which is affected by bronze disease by using benzotriazole. Passive methods include surveying the collection, advising on how an object may be used, whether it can be exhibited or loaned, and recommending safe environmental conditions. The purpose of environmental control is to slow down or prevent deterioration. There may be objects which are inherently unstable and for which special provisions for use and exhibition must be made.

In order to identify objects in need of conservation a regular programme of collection surveys should be undertaken by conservators in conjunction with curatorial staff. In addition, the curatorial staff may find objects during the course of their work which they think are in need of conservation. The conservation work programme needs to be sufficiently flexible to accommodate the emergencies which these activities may produce.

Because of the numbers of objects in museum collections it is not always possible for the conservator to carry out a full conservation treatment of every object. The collection surveys highlight those objects in need of urgent conservation and it is possible to carry out this essential work without undertaking the cosmetic work which is often required for objects which are to be exhibited. For instance, a ceramic vessel may be made secure by breaking down old insecure joins and remaking them. Cleaning the shards and touching in areas of repair to tone in with the ceramic are both-time consuming and cosmetic and are not necessary if the object is not being exhibited or photographed for a catalogue. The main purpose of the conservation process is to stabilize the objects.

DETERIORATION OF OBJECTS IN THE MUSEUMS

Some objects in museum collections are actively deteriorating. This is not because the environment in the museum is bad compared with other places but because the objects themselves are unstable. It is not uncommon to hear people say that an object has lasted hundreds or even thousands of years and is now actively deteriorating in a collection. In fact objects have been deteriorating ever since they were made. The rate of deterioration may have been slow until a critical point was reached when an equilibrium was disturbed and the reaction gathered momentum.

Reactions involved in the corrosion of metals and deterioration of natural organic polymers are well documented. They can be slowed down by controlling environmental conditions to reduce the amount of water in the air and to stabilize the temperature. Both moisture and heat affect the rate at which reactions proceed. Corrosive gases can be removed from the atmosphere by the use of filters and scavengers and the careful selection of materials used in the storage and display of the collection since these materials can give off appreciable quantities of corrosive gases.[2]

There are no categories of materials from which objects are made which can be specifically identified as stable. For instance, flint is a stable stone, but soft limestones, such as some Egyptian limestones which were used for sculpture in antiquity, are prone to deterioration because of their clay and salt content.[3] Ceramics may normally be considered stable but low-fired ceramics which have been buried can contain salts which cause exfoliation of the surface through migration and crystallization. Gold is a stable metal, but other metals, such as bronzes from the soil of Western Asia, are particularly unstable and often suffer from bronze disease. Iron objects, especially those from archaeological digs, suffer from active corrosion and lamination following excavation. Lead corrodes and silver tarnishes in museums due to the presence of corrosive gases in the atmosphere, which are largely derived from man-made pollution.

If objects were new and unused when acquired by museums they would be easier to preserve. Environmental conditions play an important role in controlling the deterioration mechanisms to which materials are susceptible. To prevent migration of salts, stone and ceramics should be kept at 35–40 per cent RH, but corrosion of lead and tarnishing of silver can be prevented only by removal of the gases which initiate the reactions from the atmosphere.[4]

Organic materials, which include paper, textiles, feathers, leather, bone, ivory and wood, are affected by fluctuations in relative humidity and temperature which cause them to expand and contract, putting strain on objects and causing warping, cracking, flaking and structural deterioration. They also suffer structural deterioration from ultraviolet (UV) and visible light. Some pigments used in the decoration of objects fade on exposure to light and in some cases undergo chemical change. Organic pigments such as gamboge are very susceptible to fading. Earth pigments tend to be unaffected by light but vermilion (cinnabrite, HgS) becomes black on exposure to light, forming metacinnabrite which also has the formula HgS^3. All these reactions can be controlled by limiting the exposure of the objects concerned to light.

Some objects are unstable because of the mixture of materials used in their manufacture. Renaissance enamels and some types of glass are examples of this. Glass which has a high lead content does not suffer from weeping and crizzling and it has been suggested that lead acts as a stabilizer in glass because it increases water resistance.[6] Window glass and glass for enamels made in the fourteenth and fifteenth centuries had a low lead content. As a consequence this type of glass is often unstable, exhibiting weeping and crizzling. Both conditions are caused by moisture attacking the glass. Weeping glass is characterized by the formation of water droplets or a film of water on the surface of the glass. Crizzling is characterized by the presence of surface crazing or an increase in opacity accompanied by leaching out of water-soluble alkali. In an analysis of Limoges enamels which exhibited signs of deterioration it was found that the opaque flesh and white colours which were not deteriorating had a high lead content whereas the blue, mulberry, green and purple enamels which were deteriorating had a low lead content.[7] The researchers who carried out this work suggested that the enamels should be stored and displayed at 42–48 per cent RH. In a study of the deterioration of ethnographic beads, an RH of 35–40 per cent was suggested[8] and, in a study of weeping glass, Bimson and Organ suggested an RH of below 42 per cent. They also recommended that unstable glass objects should be stored in showcases so that they could be readily viewed without handling.[9] The different recommendations on environmental conditions are confusing and the only way to judge which is correct is to compare the reasoning behind the recommendations and establish how successful their use has been.

Another example of composition making an object inherently unstable is that of the sugar skulls made in Columbia for the 'Day of the Dead'. Within a year of being purchased, the skulls started to turn brown. An investigation attributed this to a reaction between amino acids from protein in the icing-sugar decoration and reducing sugars from the breakdown of sucrose. This is a well-known chemical reaction, the Maillard reaction.[10] There is no proven way in which the reaction can be prevented but a recommendation of low relative humidity and low temperature storage was made, as this should result in a slowing down of the rate of the reaction.

Even stable objects can be damaged accidentally during handling or by workmen who are working on adjacent areas of the building. Members of the public can also inflict deliberate damage. At the least this can be in the form of chewing-gum stuck on to free-standing objects, and at the worst, paint sprayed on objects or the firing of a gun at a painting. Damage of this type may be avoided by putting all objects into secure showcases, but this often prevents a full appreciation of the collection. Barriers which stop people from touching an object are normally adequate to prevent opportunist vandals from causing any damage. The vandal who travels with serious intent is always more difficult to deal with.

THE PREVENTION OF DETERIORATION

There are several questions which should be asked about collections:

> Are the objects in good condition?
> If objects are not in good condition, are they stable or actively deteriorating?
> At what point can an object be considered a write-off?
> Have any objects been known to deteriorate to this point?

Many objects have already started to deteriorate before they enter a museum collection and have therefore probably never been in good condition at any time during their life in the museum. New or recently made objects should have entered the collection in good condition but since some materials, such as early plastics, rubber and acidic paper, deteriorate rapidly they may soon show signs of deterioration. Only by careful regular observation is it possible to tell whether an object is stable or actively corroding. If the latter is true, the circumstances should be investigated and any proven methods for preventing deterioration implemented.

Potentially 'active' bronzes in the collections of the Department of Western Asiatic Antiquities in the British Museum have shown no sign of deterioration since they were put on exhibition in showcases dehumidified to below 40 per cent RH. Similarly effective methods of controlling the deterioration of modern plastics and rubber have not yet been identified, but work is in progress on this problem. For instance, recent work on sealing rubber objects into airtight bags with an oxygen scavenger has shown promising results.[11] However, this means that the objects are not readily available for study and display purposes. An object is probably a write-off at the point when it ceases to have a recognizable form. Bronze disease has been observed to cause complete break-down of an object to a powder, at which point the object has totally lost its form and is a write-off. Lead point drawings can become invisible when the lead is corroded to basic lead carbonate, but the image is still visible under ultraviolet light and the object is therefore not a write-off. Although the deleterious effects of light on prints and draw-ings are well known, fading of the image to a point where it is not visible is a very rare occurence. Prints may, however, become seriously discoloured.

In the British Museum the Prints and Drawings Collection is exhibited only in a series of temporary exhibitions which each lasts up to six months. Light levels during these exhibitions were formerly maintained at 50 lux and less than 75µ watts per lumen of UV. The light level has recently been increased to 80 lux because of the difficulty of viewing detailed images at 50 lux and the short period of exposure to light which the prints and drawings experience. After exhibition they are returned to solander boxes and folders where they remain in the dark until they are required for study purposes or for re-exhibition. With a collection of 1–2 million objects the exhibition of individual prints and drawings is limited. The period of exhibition of Japanese painted material is being restricted to a maximum period of two months at 80 lux, as happens in Japan. For painted material the concern is not that the image will cease to exist, but that the colours will fade or change and the work cease to be as the artist had intended. The approach of limiting the period of exhibition can be taken to all light-sensitive objects if an exhibition record is kept so that the accumulated period of exposure is available when decisions on the future exhibition of the collection are made.[12] Because of the com-posite nature of most objects, including prints and drawings, only an arbitary limit on the total lux exposure can be set. For the storage and display of all organic materials, the effect of light which can cause structural deterioration, fluctuations in relative humidity which affect dimensional stability and cause cockling of paper, fluctuations in temperature which can cause expansion and contraction, and the presence of pollutant gases which can increase acidity, are all important factors. The literature is specific about what is an acceptable relative humidity and temperature, and 55±5 per cent RH and 19 or 20±2 °C are normally quoted.[13] However, there is increasing evidence that drier conditions are in fact more suitable for ethnographic collections and for libraries.[14,15] The risk of biological attack and hydrolytic breakdown is decreased at a low RH but unfortunately materials such as leather show a reduction in flexibility. If objects are handled carefully this need not be a cause for concern. An advantage of opting for a lower RH level is that many other materials in the collection, such as metals, stone and some ceramics, will be stabilized because some of the mechanisms involved in their deterioration will be arrested. Unless a full air-conditioning system is installed, full control of relative humidity and temperature cannot be achieved. The effects of fluctuations in humidity are more damaging than the effects of fluctua-tions in temperature as long as the temperature is not excessively high. The main requirement is for the relative humidity to be stable whatever level is chosen, but it is easier to maintain a stable level close to the median relative humidity of the building. It is also easier to maintain a totally stable environment in a small volume than in large storerooms and exhibition galleries. Sensitive objects may require an inert environment as well as controlled environmental conditions. This could include the use of evacuated airtight bags, oxygen scavengers and inert gases such as nitrogen.

Objects made of materials with serious deterioration problems can be difficult to stabilize and more radical approaches may need to be taken to ensure their survival.

These include making a replica of the object, which can include a hologram, or buying two objects. The object can then be kept in a totally stable environment whilst a replica or duplicate object is used for study and exhibition.[16] However, the cost of making a replica is high and the cost of purchasing a duplicate object can be prohibitive and a major rethink of how we use objects may be necessary. If airtight bags and oxygen scavengers are used for the storage of some objects, those objects will not be readily available for study and display because they will have to be taken out of the bags and rebagged at the end of the study period. This will involve extra staff time and costs. Objects may be displayed by using a specially sealed box in which the required environment has been created inside a showcase. This has been used successfully for several objects in the British Museum when conditioned silica gel was used to create a constant relative humidity in airtight perspex boxes inside showcases.[17] A system could be developed for the creation of inert atmospheres inside similar boxes.

CONCLUSION

Many objects have survived to the present day only as a result of being in a museum. However, museums are not just places where objects are kept, they are also places of research, education and exhibition. The combination of these activities with conservation has resulted in the survival of collections, and should continue to do so. However, there is much that is unknown about the deterioration of many types of objects. There is some understanding about the effects of light and how light levels relate to the deterioration of materials. In the 1950s an investigation of the rate at which light caused structural deterioration of fibres such as silk and jute was carried out and a study of the effects of light on cellulose resulted in the calculation of damage functions.[18,19] However, no similar work has been carried out to study the rate of deterioration caused by humidity and temperature. Work on the effects of pollutant gases has not resulted in a clear understanding of rates of deterioration which could be applicable to antiquities. The definitive work on environmental conditions for the prevention of deterioration has yet to be carried out. There is also considerable scope for an improvement in interventive methods of conservation. Even so, the prognosis for the survival of many objects in museums is good. For instance, as long as the tarnishing of silver can be prevented there is no reason why silver objects should not last indefinitely. However, sugar skulls are unlikely to survive indefinitely no matter how much effort is put into researching the mechanism of deterioration and devising innovative storage conditions. The actual survival time of objects cannot be predicted, but will be closely linked to the ability of human beings to maintain a friendly and stable environment, and this applies not just in museums, but also to all man-made objects and buildings which are part of our daily lives.

This paper first appeared in S. Keene (ed.) (1990) Managing Conservation *(United Kingdom Institute for Conservation of Historic and Artistic Works of Art), pp. 24–7.*

NOTES AND REFERENCES

1 Wilson, D. M. (1989) *The British Museum Purpose and Politics*, London: British Museum Publications.
2 Blackshaw, S. M. and Daniels, V. D. (1979) 'The testing of materials of use in storage and display in museums', *The Conservator* 3: 16–19.

3 Bradley, S. M. and Middleton, A. P. (1988), 'A study of the deterioration of Egyptian limestone sculpture', *JAIC* 27: 64–86.

4 Bradley, S. (1989) 'Hydrogen sulphide scavengers for the prevention of silver tarnishing', in *Environmental Monitoring and Control*, Edinburgh: SSCR, 65–7.

5 Daniels, V. D. (1988) 'The blackening of vermilion by light', in J. Black (ed.) *Recent Advances in the Conservation and Analysis of Artefacts*, London: Summer Schools Press.

6 Morey, G. M. and Bowen, N. L. (1927) 'The decomposition of glass by water at high temperatures and pressures', *Journal of the Society of Glass Technology* 11: 97–106.

7 Smith, R., Carlson, J. H. and Newman, R. M. (1987) 'An investigation into the deterioration of painted Limoges enamel plaques, c 1470–1530', *Studies in Conservation* 32: 102–13.

8 Lougheeds, S. (1986) 'The deterioration of glass beads on ethnographic objects', presented at the IIC Canadian Group Annual Meeting. Winnipeg, 18 May 1986.

9 Organ, R. M. (1957) 'The safe storage of unstable glass'. *The Museums Journal* 5 (11): 265–72.

10 Lohenis, G. (1986) 'An investigation into the deterioration of sugar skulls', London: British Museum Department of Conservation Internal Report, VI 3.

11 Gratton, D. (1990) 'Ageless oxygen absorber project status', a letter circulated to everyone who expressed interest in the project, 6 April 1990.

12 Bradley, S. M. (forthcoming) 'The effect of light on ethnographic material', in *Proceedings of the Ethnographic Colloquium* held in the British Museum, November 1989.

13 Thomson, G. (1986) *The Museum Environment* (2nd edn), London: Butterworths.

14 Levinson, J., personal communication regarding the storage of ethnographic collections in the American Museum of Natural History.

15 Burgess, H. D., personal communication on storage at the National Archives of Canada and the the National Gallery of Canada; Lawson, P., personal communication on experience of conditions in library stores.

16 Oddy, W. A. (1975) 'Comparison of different methods of treating waterlogged wood as revealed by stereoscan examination and thoughts on the future of the conservation of waterlogged wood', in W. A. Oddy (ed.) *Problems of the Conservation of Waterlogged Wood*, Maritime Monographs and Reports no. 16: 45–50

17 Johnson, C., Rae, A., Wills, B., Ward, C. and Lee, J. (forthcoming) 'Organic materials', in S. M. Bradley (ed.) *A Guide to the Storage, Exhibition and Handling of Antiquities, Ethnographic and Pictorial Art*, London: British Museum Occasional Paper no. 66, British Museum Publications.

18 Stromberg, E. (1950) 'Dyes and light', *ICOM News* 3.

19 Harrison, L. S. (1953) 'Report on the deteriorating effects of modern light sources', US National Bureau of Standards report no. 2254, The Metropolitan Museum of Art, New York.

7

Audits of care: a framework for collections condition surveys

Suzanne Keene

A rational and cost-effective policy for both preventative and remedial conservation relies upon accurate information about the condition of existing collections. Suzanne Keene's article describes how statistical sampling might be used to provide this information.

Collections condition surveys are surveys undertaken in order to assess, or audit, the condition of collections as a whole, rather than to identify individual objects requiring action.

This paper introduces a general methodology for assessing the condition of museum collections. It includes definitions of the data which need to be collected, and a method of surveying, based on examining a statistically designed random sample of objects in the collection or collections, thus making the most effective use of scarce conservation expertise. Then, the analysis of the data is described, and a checklist for the resulting report is presented.

BACKGROUND

In 1988, the National Audit Office published a report, *Management of the Collections of the English National Museums and Galleries.*[1] In it the Auditor General remarked that 'this represents a major breakdown over many years in the proper stewardship of national assets', i.e. the collections of the national museums. The report was swiftly followed by a sitting of the Commons Public Accounts Committee, to which the Directors of the Victoria and Albert and British Museums gave evidence.[2] This evidence elicited much press comment.

This initial interest in the state of publicly owned collections is being pursued further by the National Audit Office, which is extending its interest to local authority museums, in its recent report, *The Road to Wigan Pier.*[3]

Clearly then, the condition of museum collections generally is now a matter of public concern, as it has been for many years to conservators and others in museums. The question is, can the general condition of collections be measured? Can a simple, practical measure of performance in this vital museum function be devised?

Condition surveys of objects in collections are not uncommon. But they are often very time-consuming, since they generally aim to examine every single object. A variety of methods of recording the results is in use. If we are to be able to determine the state of collections on a large scale, and compare the results from one collection to another, or from one institution to another, a more practical and general methodology will have to be developed. A framework for this is presented here, for debate and further work.

INTEREST IN COLLECTIONS CONDITION SURVEYS

The Office of Arts and Libraries is currently encouraging and developing the use of performance indicators for museums. The condition of collections is one such important indicator. Collections condition is also a central factor in the 'Cost of Collecting' formula, developed by the OAL.[4] The Museums and Galleries Commission has also assisted the project; it is interested in a standard surveying methodology for use in connection with its work on curatorial standards. The Conservation Unit's forward plan includes work on assessing collections condition.

Several other bodies have expressed great interest in, or adopted, the methodology, such as the Public Record Office, the Oxford Joint Libraries Board, and national museums.

Work abroad, in the USA and in Europe, is discussed below.

THE RESEARCH PROJECT

As a result of the reports described above, the Museum of London decided in 1989 that the general condition of its collections should be assessed. As a social history museum, these are extremely large and varied, and include almost every sort of material except natural history. The museum's interest coincided with that of the Office of Arts and Libraries. A research project was therefore part funded by them, to develop a generalized approach to collections condition assessment, using the MoL surveys as a test bed.

THE WORKING PARTY

The general framework for these surveys was thus first developed in the museum. Following this, a working party was assembled in 1990, made up of those known to have undertaken surveys, or with useful expertise, or whose institutions had a particular interest in surveys.

Working party members

Suzanne Keene:	(Chair) Museum of London
Louise Bacon:	Horniman Museum and Gardens
Lawrence Birney and Chris Gregson:	National Maritime Museum
May Cassar:	Museums and Galleries Commission
Mike Corfield:	National Museum of Wales
Velson Horie:	Manchester Museum
Nick Umney:	Victoria and Albert Museum

EXISTING WORK ON SURVEYS

The working party members between them found information for the UK on well over twenty surveys past or present, in six museums, two libraries, some museum 'umbrella' bodies, and the National Trust. Most surveys have been object-by-object. Very large amounts of data are being collected, but most of these projects have placed more importance on surveying itself – collecting data – than on analysing, reporting, and making use of the results. One objective of the proposed framework is to correct this imbalance.

There is some other work on general surveys, for example, museums in Scotland.[5] These, however, do not include detailed surveys based on objects in collections. Other published references are to work on surveys of particular collections, rather than on how surveys can in general be undertaken. Some useful information has been assembled on data collection and terminology.[6]

At the same time, work on terminology is proceeding at the Getty Institute, and in the ICOM Conservation Committee Working Group for Documentation. There is a great deal of work on conservation matters, including information and data in Europe, under the EUREKA umbrella and by the International Standards Organisation.

DIFFERENT TYPES OF SURVEY

In fact, at least three types of survey are needed to provide a truly comprehensive view of collections preservation:

Conservation assessments

Assessments of the preservation environment, in the broadest sense, covering institutional policies, procedures, available staff and skills, the history of the collections and space and physical resources for their preservation. Work on these has been completed in America. The Getty Conservation Institute together with the National Institute for the Preservation of Cultural Property have developed a standard Conservation Assessment, to be used for 'planning, implementing and fundraising'.[7]

Collections condition surveys

Data on the condition of objects and collections themselves – the subject of this report. These are the exact complement to Conservation Assessments.

Curatorial assessments

Curatorial assessments of the importance of the object as part of the collection. This sort of assessment is clearly essential for prioritizing action to be taken as a result of condition surveys, and for allocating resources.

As well as these general surveys, object-by-object surveys will still of course be required for other purposes. For example, a collection condition survey may show which collections are the highest priority; to plan work, one will need to know which objects are the highest priority, and for this an object-by-object survey is essential.

At a more detailed level still, instrumental or microscopic examination and recording of individual objects or parts of objects is required to investigate exact mechanisms of deterioration, and this may in time influence the form of surveys (see, for example, Pretzel).[8]

The concepts, definitions and framework for surveying which has been developed by the working party is presented below.

THE NEXT STEPS

Using the methodology

The benefits of using a general method of assessing collections condition could be substantial, and are set out above. The Office of Arts and Libraries and the Museums and Galleries Commission are both interested in developing such a method, as the OAL has done with the 'Cost of Collecting' formula.

Field testing

The survey methodology needs to be thoroughly tested. Three aspects need to be examined:

Surveyor bias

Different surveyors need to survey the same collections (probably even the same objects) to see whether the definitions of damage factors and condition rating enable them to arrive at comparable results.

Differences between collections

The same surveyors need to inspect similar collections in different institutions, to see how much genuine variation there is.

Blind testing

A few institutions which have not been involved in the development should be persuaded to try out the method.

Survey software

Although simple software has been adapted for part of the task (see below), it is probably desirable for a standard package to be developed, which would be available for any museum to use in collecting data and analysing the results.

Writing or developing software which will design sampling procedures is a separate project.

Communicating and debating the results

Collections condition is a very sensitive topic. Both curators and conservators can easily perceive survey results as criticisms of their stewardship. Recommendations could radically affect how resources are distributed in museums. It is very important that the project is fully debated by the museum community, and it is envisaged that one or more special seminars should be devoted to this.

Any method of recording collections condition which is developed in the UK should also be promoted for use by the international and overseas organizations mentioned above.

Recommendations

The working party recommended that work proceeds to complete this project, in co-operation with the Conservation Unit, the Museums and Galleries Commission, and the Office of Arts and Libraries, as appropriate. As described above, the NEXT STEPS are:

- communicate results through a special seminar or seminars;
- adopt the framework as the potential standard to be used in museums;
- undertake field tests;
- complete the work on sampling design – probably involving software development;
- prepare guidelines and instruction manual.

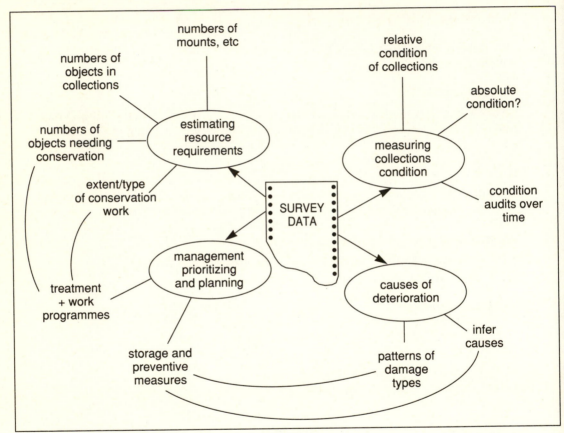

Fig 7.1   The uses of collections condition surveys

THE SURVEY FRAMEWORK

Objectives of surveys

The uses of collections condition surveys are summarised in Fig. 7.1. As a result of a collections condition survey, the institution should be able to:

- give a quantified assessment of the condition of the objects in the collection, and

compare results for one collection to those for another (audit condition);
- produce concrete evidence as to the major causes of deterioration;
- assess whether the collection is generally stable, or if its condition is deteriorating (diagnose trend);
- state what steps are needed to slow or halt deterioration (identify means of affecting trend);
- assess resources needed;
- assess the benefits to be gained from different actions;
- recommend priorities.

Data to collect

Table 7.1 sets out the objectives of surveying, and relevant factors to be investigated. On this depends what information or data are needed. Survey data quickly amount to large quantities, which are difficult to handle and to understand. It is recommended that only essential data are collected. There are six main aspects of collections which can provide data:

Administrative data

These are the main groupings used in the analysis of the data and reporting on it: collection, subcollection, object identification, store, location.

Description of object

The amount of data here is optional, and may vary according to individual institutions' or collections' needs. It may include: simple name, materials, type, manufacturing processes (e.g. photographic process). Data which might relate to condition are included here: fragility (the object may be fragile but in perfectly good condition); completeness; working or not (these do not necessarily reflect deterioration).

Damage

The working party agreed that eight general terms were sufficient to describe damage to objects. For a particular collection, it is useful to list all the terms which could describe damage to it under these headings, for reference during surveying (Table 7.2).

Major structural damage	Chemical deterioration
Minor structural damage	Biological attack
Surface damage	Bad old repairs
Disfigurement	Accretions

Condition

The following definitions of condition grades have been agreed:

C1 GOOD
  Object in the context of its collection is in good conservation condition, or is stable.

C2 FAIR
  Fair condition, disfigured or damaged but stable, needs no immediate action.

C3 POOR
  Poor condition, and/or restricted use, and/or probably unstable, action desirable.

Table 7.1 The objectives of surveys, and the data needed

Survey objective	Relevant factors	Type of data needed
Audit condition	Condition of individual objects Statistics on collections condition	Condition survey Damage types and severity
Identity causes of deterioration	Environment: space, enclosures, supports/mounts, growth of collection, humidity, temperature, light, contaminants, pests, provenance Use: display, handling, repairs/ conservation, examination, running/operation of objects	Observations Environmental records Environment now Damage types/severity
Diagnose trend	Condition: past vs. present, likelihood and rate of future change i.e. vulnerability and stability Factors which have caused/ likely to cause change	Condition past (? inferred) Condition present Condition predicted future (= stability) Present and likely future environment Present and likely future use
Affect trend	Change environment (see above) Modify use (see above) – display conditions, handling/use procedures, conservation procedures, running or working Modify object – treat or restore	Most potent causes of deterioration
Assess resources needed	Space, buildings, plant (HVAC, etc.) Equipment (racks, cupboards, etc.) Material (for mounts, etc.) Time, skills Costs	Size of task (e.g. number of objects, volume, storage area, etc.) Nature of task (e.g. mounting, treatment, redo store, new store) amount/cost of resource (e.g. conservator-years, sq. ft of storage)
Assess benefits	Present use, potential use, information potential, relevance to institution's purpose, monetary value, uniqueness, quality of workmanship, physical quality (e.g. wholeness), aesthetic quality	Present use (e.g. objects displayable, books readable, drawings accessible) Curatorial assessments [value] Number of objects being success- fully preserved (= in condition defined acceptable)
Recommend priorities	Institutional objectives Resources vs. benefits Consequences of 'do nothing'	Conservation/preservation policies Cost/benefit calculations using above data Vulnerability of objects/collections Judgement re deterioration or not

C4 UNACCEPTABLE

Completely unacceptable condition, and/or severely weakened, and/or highly unstable and actively deteriorating, and/or affecting other objects: immediate action should be taken.

'Action' means something done to the object itself, rather than to its surroundings or environment. Data on damage will give information on why the object has been assigned its rating.

Discussion of condition grades

A summary grading of each object's condition was agreed by all to be essential, as the main means of assessing and quantifying preservation. However, there are a number of different aspects to 'condition', and all of these have been used in different (or even in the same) surveys (Buck in 1971;[9] Walker and Bacon in 1987;[10] the author in 1990[11]). There was considerable debate among the working party over these definitions.

The aspects of condition that were identified were:

Insecurity (Buck 1971, and V. & A.): mechanical stresses, stability or vulnerability
Disfigurement (Buck 1971, and V. & A.): appearance of object
Conservation priority (Horniman, Museum of London and others): how urgently is conservation needed?
Condition rating (National Maritime, Public Records Office): usually good, fair, poor

It was eventually concluded that the condition of an object needed to be defined in the context of its particular collection. For example, a pot which is in separate sherds may be in GOOD condition as part of an archaeological archive, while the definition for an applied arts ceramic collection may place it in the UNACCEPTABLE category.

There was also doubt about the number of grades: between three and five. Four grades have been used in many institutions (British Museum, Horniman, Museum of London, National Museum of Wales). Allowing a fifth grade means that the majority of objects are assigned the middle, indeterminate grade, which does not give very useful information. Three grades are too few.

Data on work required

General categories of work are, in ascending order of elaboration:

- None
- Clean
- Mount, box or support
- Remount
- Treat/conserve

Further categories tailored to individual collections could certainly be defined: rebinding books for libraries, for example.

The survey method

The work so far has only pulled together and made more systematic what is already common to most surveys: data collection, more familiar as the survey form. A new departure for most people is the use of sampling, in which only a proportion of objects in the collection is examined, rather than every object.

Table 7.2 Broad damage types, and the sorts of damage which the broad headings include

Each general term includes all the more specific types of damage shown below.

| | Structural damage | | | | | | | |
	Major structural	Minor structural	Surface damage	Disfigurement	Chemical/internal	Biological	Accretions	Bad old repair
General	Separate Pieces/part; loose crack; large tear likely to spread; large holes; major splits; parts missing; mechanical disorder	Crack; small tear; puncture; small holes; small splits; obviously weak; loose attachment; bent; warped; creased; distorted elements e.g. feathers	Flaking/lifted paint, etc; peeling; paint/surface losses; bruised; cupped; delaminated; crazed; dented	Scratched; stained; abraded; discoloured; faded; tarnished; colours bled	Crumbling; friable; desiccated; exudations; grease; salts	Insect attack; moth; woodworm; foxed; rodent damage; mould; mildew	Dirty; encrusted; surface salts; deposits; greasy	Adhesive; misalignment; staples; Sellotape; greasy patches
Furniture	Very loose joint; separated attachment		Lifted veneer					

Material					
Paper	Very badly crumpled with split; very badly crease with split; very badly distorted/ rolled	Cockled; crumpled; folded	Skinned	Acid; yellowed; chemically changed edges; matt burn; redox sports; metal impurity	Tape; Sellotape
Books	Separated or nearly separated spine cover			Acid paper; red rot	
Textiles, fibre	Split seam; badly creased with split; seriously crumpled; crushed	Shrunken; detached fibres		Deteriorated silk; acid dyes	Clumsy stitching; alterations
Pictures			Cupped paint; losses; flaking paint; lifted paint	Blanched; deteriorated canvas	
Ceramics/ glass		Chipped; small crack		Salt damage; crizzled	Encrustations
Metals				Corroded; rusted	Solder

The basis for this is a statistical method, by which we can learn what we want to know about the population (the whole collection) from statistics gathered about a sample.[12,13] If the sample is correctly chosen, i.e. selected randomly from the population, then it is possible to know how *accurate* the estimate about the population is, and how much *confidence* we can place on the results.

There are several advantages in using a sampling method. Surveys take less time, which is important, because, as we well know, conservators are in short supply, and surveying itself does nothing directly to improve the condition of the collection. Fewer objects, examined more carefully, will give more reliable results than many objects examined only cursorily. If huge quantities of data are collected, it is very difficult to make sense of them, whether they are analysed by hand or by computer. Finally, we can admit that surveying is rather boring, and so if reliable results can come from looking at fewer objects, this is cause for celebration!

The sampling method has been developed in collaboration with Clive Orton, of the Institute of Archaeology, to whom grateful thanks are due.[14] It is based on a technique known as cluster sampling. This is an alternative to true random sampling, in which items are selected from a list, and those chosen found and examined. In most museums this would be impossible – often, there is no list; and if there were, it would take far too long to find the objects. Cluster sampling is based on sampling geographical locations of objects i.e. their store locations.

Sampling units

The basis for condition survey sampling is the store location. For survey purposes, a store location is the smallest physical grouping of objects – a tray, a shelf, a box of objects on a shelf, or a group of objects on the floor. If a shelf has some freestanding objects, and others contained in a box, then each group counts as a separate store location, and so on. The actual sampling method has been initially reported,[14] but is still being developed. It is based on selecting every nth store location, and within that every xth object – as one might select every nth house, and within houses, every xth person to interview.

Sample size

Sample size depends on several factors. These are well explained for the non-expert.[12] GCSE texts on statistics are also very helpful.

Time for surveying

It is actually helpful to set a limit on the time to be spent on the survey, as this is then one known quantity. We spent six person-months on surveying part of the Museum of London collections; two months each on costume, paper (art on paper, printed ephemera, business archives), and social history objects. Time included all survey stages, including analysis and reporting, and proved adequate.

Statistical confidence limits

How sure do we want to be that the results from the survey can be extrapolated to the whole collection? This has to be simplified into statistically meaningful terms. What most conservators are most interested in is, 'How many objects are in condition C4, needing urgent conservation?' or perhaps in C4 and C3 combined. Most of us would agree that given the slender resources we have to actually do anything about this, to be 95 per cent sure that the proportion given by the sample applies to the collection as a whole would be good enough. We could settle for 68 per cent, or 99 per cent, which are the other two commonly used confidence limits, but the higher the confidence limit, the wider the range of figures we will end up applying. In statistical terms then, what we want to know is:

> What proportion of objects is in condition C4 (or C3 + C4), to 95 per cent confidence limits?

Statistical accuracy

When survey result are multiplied to give an estimate for the whole collection, the result will be expressed as a range. Say 1,000 objects were surveyed, and 80 objects were in condition C4. If there are 10,000 objects in the whole collection, then we could not truthfully say that 800 objects altogether were likely to be in condition C4: the real result would probably be more like 'between 740 and 860', or 800 ± 60.

There is a payoff between confidence limits and range; the wider the range settled for, the more confident we can be in the result, and vice versa.

Collections size

It seems paradoxical, but it needs to be appreciated that it is not the size of the collection that determines the size of the sample needed, but its variability. So a sample of, say, 1,000 objects out of a collection of 5,000 will be only very marginally more reliable than a sample of 500 objects from the same collection. This may seem to fly in the face of common sense, but it is so. But what is meant by 'variability' in survey terms? For survey purposes, this is simplified to mean numbers of objects per location, and the proportion of objects in the different grades of condition.

Statistical sample design

Before a survey can be designed, therefore, information has to be obtained on all these factors. This is done by means of a pilot survey (see below). The data from this are used to calculate the sample size required. The next step is to design the best possible way of selecting the objects to be sampled.

For the most effective survey, and the most reliable results, a statistician should use the results of the pilot survey to calculate a sampling design. An example might be: every 8th object from every 4th store location. Work on this is not yet complete, but results to date are summarized in Keene and Orton (forthcoming)[14] and can be used by statisticians.

However, if no statistician is available, rule-of-thumb will have to be applied. There is no magic percentage sample which will always give accurate results. The minimum useful sample size in surveys generally is around a thousand objects, so for reasonable sized collections this should be used; for small collections, apply common sense. One in four objects (25 per cent) should be sufficient.

Using an informal method like this has the advantage that it is very simple to extrapolate the results from the sample to the collection as a whole. Statistical techniques can still be used, if wished, to calculate the range and the confidence limit for the whole collection. The disadvantages are that too few objects may have been surveyed to give reliable results, or the optimum selection procedure may not have been used; or more objects may have been surveyed than necessary, meaning that scarce specialist time may not have been put to the best use; and that unnecessary quantities of data may have to be analysed.

There is also the likelihood that the selection may not be properly random. This is extremely important, because only if it is will statistics about the sample be valid for the collection. To guard against this, in an informal sample (say every 10th object) the first object must be selected randomly by drawing a ticket, etc., and subsequent objects must be chosen according to a predetermined systematic procedure.

Monitoring condition over time

How to detect change over time was discussed in some detail. If a new random sample of the collection was to be taken for each resurveying exercise, there would be few if any objects common to both surveys. Any real change in the overall state of the collection might be masked by the variability introduced by the sampling procedure. The best way around this may be for subsequent surveys to include a subset of the original sample in the new sample, perhaps around a third of the original. More detailed logging of data on the subset may be required in order to spot differences more easily. The subset would provide a bench-mark against which the other parts of the survey can be measured. The subset itself would have to be randomly selected.

There is some work based on this and on using particular types of object as tell tales of condition.[15,16]

Survey procedures and sampling

There are six distinct stages in a survey, and sufficient time needs to be allotted to each of them:

Agree statement of survey purpose

- Describe collection(s) and define terms
- Quantify task and test data collection (pilot survey)
- Analyse pilot survey results and design sampling procedure, whether formal or informal
- Collect data (surveying itself)
- Analyse data and write report

Record the purpose of the survey

It is very useful to set out in writing beforehand what the survey is expected to achieve. This needs to be agreed by collections care staff (conservators or other), by curators and by management.

Describe the collections and define terms

The collection must be concisely described, and the main types of objects identified, for use later in analysing the data. What is included under the different damage headings should be set out, and the condition grades defined in the context of the collection. (See above, 'Data to collect'.)

Undertake pilot survey

A pilot survey is essential, to quantify the task approximately, find out how many objects can be surveyed in the time available, to test the method of collecting data and to refine the data definitions. About 20 per cent of the total survey time should be allocated to the pilot survey, and to analysing and using the results. This is an important stage.

To undertake a pilot survey, allocate a certain number of person-days for it. Allow at least half a person-day for analysis and writing up. Use the rest of the time to assemble the information set out in Table 7.3. The store locations and objects surveyed should be evenly distributed in the collection. The rules can be adjusted at this stage to ensure this. Time taken must be the overall time: i.e. including meal breaks, getting to the store, etc. This is why it is best to allocate a certain time, and see how many objects are examined during it.

Table 7.3 Information to be derived from pilot surveys

Quantification

1 Time spent on pilot survey (pre-determined): _____

2 Number of storage locations surveyed in the time: _____

3 Number of objects surveyed in the time: _____

4 Total number of storage locations (counted in pilot survey): _____

5 Mean number of objects per location (total of number of objects divided by number of locations surveyed): _____

6 Approximate total number of objects in collection (mean number per location × total number of locations): _____

7 Number of objects that could be surveyed in the time allocated for the survey. Allow at least 3 person-days for analysis and report writing (number surveyed per person/day × person/days for survey) _____

Variability

For each of the locations surveyed:

Location identity	Total number of objects	Number surveyed	Number and per cent in each condition rating			
			C1	C2	C3	C4

Analyse pilot survey results and sampling procedure

Pilot survey data is recorded on survey forms. Its analysis is set out in Table 7.2. Design the sampling procedure, that is, how to select which objects to examine in the real survey.

It is hoped in due course that a computer package will be developed, which will take pilot survey results and design a sampling procedure. At present it is necessary for a statistician to design this. The basis of the method is set out in detail elsewhere.[14]

If no statistician is available, then rule-of-thumb has to be applied as described above (see **'Statistical sample design'**).

Collect data: the survey itself

Data can be collected either on paper or on computer. An example of a form used for surveying a historic photographs collection is shown in Fig. 7.2.

COLLECTIONS CONDITION SURVEY	Conservation Section:				Survey Code:					Initials:	Date:	

Damage categories:
MAJOR structural damage
MINOR structural damage – cracked, distorted, loose joints
SURFACE damage – flaking, crazing, lifting, abraded
DISFIGUREMENT – stained, scratched
CHEMICAL deterioration – acid paper, corrosion, rubber
     and plastic breakdown
BIOlogical infestation – mould, insect, rodent
OLD sub-standard repairs
ACCRETIONS dirt, oil, deposits

Condition grades:
1 GOOD Good conservation condition, stable
2 FAIR Disfigured or damaged, no immediate action
3 POOR Probably unstable, needs remedial work
4 UNACCEPTABLE Actively deteriorating

Collection: _____
Store: _____
Sub-collection: _____
Run/group/location: _____
Storage type: _____

Totals for cond. grades:
1 ___ 2 ___ 3 ___ 4 ___

Totals for work: Treat _____ Rem _____ Mount _____ Clean _____

Total in location: _____
Total surveyed: _____

IDENT. NO.	SIMP NAME	MATERIALS	MAJ	MIN	BIO	CHEM	SURF	DISF	OLD	ACCR	Work TRMC	Cond. grade	REMARKS
Totals:													

USE NEW SHEET FOR EACH LOCATION

Fig. 7.2 An example of a survey form

Alternatively, a computer can be used. Few surveys have been conducted using computers to date. An adaptation of the widely available program 'Microsoft Works' has been set up and tested.

This provides a form for entering survey records. The records can be listed and counted, and simple analysis such as percentages performed, using pre-designed forms. The results can then be printed out.

Collecting data on paper has some advantages, in that it is easier to understand the results if the forms themselves are used for analysis. But it is impossible in practice to do some kinds of analysis – for instance, cross-tabulate condition by type of damage – by hand, and extra volumes of paper are really the last thing museums need.

Analyse and present data

Detailed research has been conducted into the analysis of the Museum of London survey data.[17]

Descriptive information

Different collections, subcollections, object types; analysis of other descriptive information collected (fragility, broken, etc.)

Analysis: Simple lists.

Output: Lists of objects types, stores, collections, etc. Because a sample only is collected, 'object type' has to be fairly broad; for instance, if 'object name' was analysed many kinds of object would not have been included in the sample. Even so, this is a very quick way of producing an accurate description of a collection.

Quantitative information

Total numbers of:

Objects in collections, subcollections, object types

Objects in different stores

Objects in different condition grades (therefore needing or not needing conservation)

Objects which have suffered different types of damage

Objects needing mounting, etc.

Analysis: Counts of cases (object records) by different groups; statistics – standard deviation, maximum number, minimum number; cross-tabulations; percentages.

Output: Lists, tables, diagrams such as pie diagrams, histograms, bar graphs.

Condition of collections

The main measure is the proportion of objects in different condition grades and types of damage suffered; correlation between type of damage and condition grade.

Analysis: Cross-tabulations of object type (or other grouping: e.g. store) by priority, with percentages. Log-linear or contingency analysis to compare the condition of different object groupings. Percentages of objects with different types of damage. Correlation of damage and priority.

Output: Tables and figures, as above. Percentage and other bar graphs.

Amount of work, and other resources required

Conservator or other person-years (months, etc.) needed to undertake necessary work; resources required

Analysis: Calculations of quantitative information as above together with data on resources: price, number of objects conserved per year, etc.

Output: Again – tables, bar graphs and figures.

Conclusions on survey data analysis

All this is very simple information, invaluable for collections care and management, and planning conservation. However, it is characteristic of collections survey data and information that it can be analysed in the same way at many different hierarchical levels (Fig. 7.3). This means that many separate, though similar, analyses need to be performed. These in turn result in numerous tables, diagrams, etc. It takes very considerable work and thought to make full use of the information, to draw conclusions, and to quantify and plan work. It is also quite a task to extract a general view.

The complexity of actually making use of the information from surveys is the main reason for urging that only essential data be collected.

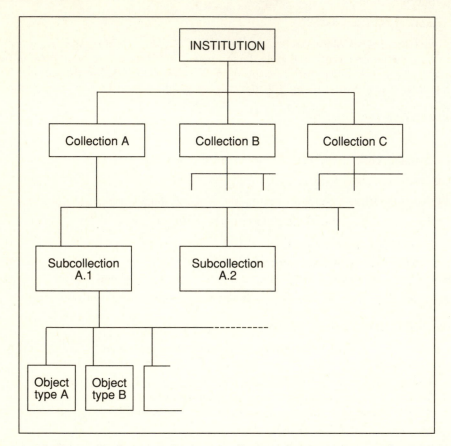

Fig. 7.3 The hierarchical nature of museum collections data. Large or complex institutions will have more organizational tiers in their collections than this.

SURVEYS REPORTS

The form of survey reports

Different collections often need separate mini-reports of their own. If the collections of a whole institution are being surveyed, then these individual reports have to be digested and summarized so that the whole picture can be appreciated. This is a considerable job.

Table 7.4 Checklist of topics for survey reports

Collections condition report	Conservation assessment
The context of the collection	
Provenance	
Age and growth	
Past conservation provision	
Environment	*Environment*
	Space
	Equipment: racks, etc.
Summary	Supports, mounts, protection Humidity +
	temperature control
	Light
	Contaminants
	Pests and biological agents
Use and procedures	*Uses and procedures*
	Display
	Handling
Summary as relevant	Working or demonstration
	Public access or study
	Archive function
Descriptive information	
Collections descriptions	
Types of object	Summary
Main materials	
Damage	
Nature of damage	
Analysis of data	
Condition	
Analysis of data	
Comparisons and discussion	
Inferences	
Causes of deterioration	
Quantification	
Numbers of objects	
Resources required	
Possible action	**Possible action**
Collections management	*Collections management*
	Improve store or building
	Improve environment
Summary	Eliminate pests
	Rack or mount or protect
	Control or alter use

77

This has been illustrated in the Museum of London survey reports, where the objective was to survey the collections of the institution as a whole. Here, there are no less than fifteen separate reports on subcollections; these are drawn together into a report discussing the results under four main object types, reflecting the conservation specialities in the museum. Finally, a brief summary dealing with the collections as a whole was presented to the Board of Governors.

It will be helpful for surveyors to have some suggestions for the main headings that reports ought to cover. Naturally, people can adapt these to their own particular circumstances. The objectives of surveys were discussed above. Reports on surveys ought to address these issues.

Checklist of survey report topics

Table 7.4 gives a checklist of the areas that a report might cover. This is potentially a lot of information, but much of it can be brief. Report headings should therefore include those below. Areas which would be gathered in depth through a complementary conservation assessments survey are shown under that heading, although they would need to be touched on in a collections condition survey report.

CONCLUSIONS ON THE SURVEY FRAMEWORK

The suggested framework has been agreed by all the working party members. It can be used by anyone wishing to make use of it, or of elements in it. We hope that it will eventually be refined and generally adopted by museums in the UK.

This paper first appeared in M. Norman and V. Todd (1991) Storage *(preprints for the UKIC conference, 'Restoration '91').*

NOTES AND REFERENCES

1 Comptroller and Auditor General (1988) *Management of the Collections of the English National Museums and Galleries*, London: National Audit Office Report, HMSO.
2 Committee of Public Accounts (1988) *Management of the Collections of the English National Museums and Galleries*, first report, London: House of Commons.
3 The Audit Commission (1991) *The Road to Wigan Pier*, London: HMSO.
4 Lord, B., Dexter Lord, G. and Nicks, J. (1989) *The Cost of Collecting*, London: HMSO.
5 Paine, Crispin (1990) 'Survey of collections surveys', MDA Information.
6 Craft, Meg and Jones, Sian (1981) Written documentation, 9th Annual Meeting, Philadelphia, AIC. A booklet which simply publishes a number of condition report forms used in America, without comment.
7 Anon (1991) *The Conservation Assessment. A Tool for Planning, Implementing, and Fundraising*, Washington D.C.: Getty Conservation Institute and National Institute for the Conservation of Cultural Property. (Obtainable from the NIC, 3299 K Street, NW, Suite 403, Washington D.C. 20007; enclose US dollar cheque or draft for $25.)
8 Pretzel, Boris (1990) 'Colour changes occurring in photographs by Lady Hawarden', *Victoria & Albert Museum Conservation Department Science Section Internal Report* no. 71/90/BCP.
9 Buck, Richard D. (1971) 'What is condition in a work of art?' *Bulletin of the American Group-IIC*, 12 (1). Sets out Buck's scheme for four terms descriptive of condition.
10 Walker, Kirsten and Bacon, Louise (1987) 'A condition survey of specimens in the Horniman Museum: a progress report', in J. Black (ed.) *Recent Advances in the Conservation and Analysis of Artifacts*, London: University of London. The first report of full-scale collections condition surveys.
11 Keene, Suzanne (1990) 'Assessing collections condition', Conservation Department Research Report, Museum of London internal report, unpublished. Report on the first part of the OAL-funded project.

12 Rowntree, D. (1981) *Statistics without Tears*, Harmondsworth: Penguin Books.
13 Cochran, G.W.G. (1963) *Sampling Techniques*, (2nd end), London: Wiley.
14 Keene, S. and Orton, C. (forthcoming) 'Measuring the condition of museum collections', *Proceedings of the 1990 Conference on Computing in Archaeology*.
15 SPNHCC-CC Assessment Sub-Committee (1990) 'Defining standard procedures for assessing the condition of a fluid-preserved collection', in *Preprints of the 9th Triennial Meeting*, Paris: ICOM Committee for Conservation, 437–40. First steps towards assessing and recording the condition of natural history collections. Some discussion of whether a random selection of objects should be surveyed, or the same designated objects each time.
16 Robert Waller, Canadian Museum of Nature, personal communication.
17 Keene, Suzanne (1991) 'Analysis of survey data', Conservation Department Research Report, Museum of London internal report, unpublished. A detailed report on the exploratory analysis of the MoL data.

APPENDIX

Details of printout of survey data analysis.

Historic photographs survey

Location	Count	Sample	Pri 1	Pri 2	Pri 3	Pri 4	Mean pri
9–6–6	212	10	5	2	3	0	1.8
Business Archiv	212	10	5	2	3	0	1.8
Percent:			50%	20%	30%	0%	
8–7–1	15	4	0	2	2	0	2.5
Henry Grant	15	4	0	2	2	0	2.5
Percent:			0%	50%	50%	0%	
10–6–3	1130	11	5	6	0	0	1.5
Jean Straker	1130	11	5	6	0	0	1.5
Percent:			45%	55%	0%	0%	
6–2–8	147	10	0	5	5	0	2.5
Mixed cupbs 6	147	10	0	5	5	0	2.5
Percent:			0%	50%	50%	0%	
7–4–7	276	10	1	3	6	0	2.5
Mixed cupbs 7	276	10	1	3	6	0	2.5
Percent:			10%	30%	60%	0%	
11–6–8	1230	10	0	10	0	0	2.0
Pat. Smith	1230	10	0	10	0	0	2.0
Percent:			0%	100%	0%	0%	

Statistics for this collection:

		Pri 1	Pri 2	Pri 3	Pri 4	Mean p
	Totals:	11	28	16	0	2.1
	Percent:	20%	51%	29%	0%	

Sample of　55　objects from 3010 in sampled location
Max. objs/location:　1230　Min. objs/location 15
SD:　487

Historic photographs survey

Run/gp/loc		Image no.	Prior.	Ma	Mi	Bi	Ch	Su	Di	Ol	Ac	Work
Business Arc	9–6–6	nn.	1	1			1		1			TMC
Business Arc	9–6–6	nn.	1		1		1		1			TMC
Business Arc	9–6–6	nn.	1		1		1	1	1			TMC
Business Arc	9–6–6	nn.	1		1		1	1	1			TMC
Business Arc	9–6–6	nn.	1	1			1	1	1			TMC
Objects in this priority:			5									
Business Arc	9–6–6	nn.	2		1		1					TMC
Business Arc	9–6–6	nn.	2		1		1		1			TMC
Objects in this priority:			2									
Business Arc	9–6–6	nn.	3		1		1		1			TMC
Business Arc	9–6–6	nn.	3		1			1				TMC
Business Arc	9–6–6	nn.	3		1		1	1				TMC
Objects in this priority:			3									
Objects in this location:		10										
Objects with damage:				2	8	0	9	5	7	0	0	
Henry Grant	8–7–1	1528/54	2		1			1			1	TMC
Henry Grant	8–7–1	1528	2	1				1				TMC
Objects in this priority:			2									
Henry Grant	8–7–1	1528/25A	3		1			1				MC
Henry Grant	8–7–1	1528/25B	3		1			1				MC
Objects in this priority:			2									
Objects in this location:		4										
Objects with damage:				1	3	0	0	4	0	0	1	
Mixed cupbs	7–4–7	nn.	1		1		1	1			1	TM
Objects in this priority:			1									
Mixed cupbs	7–4–7	nn.	2				1	1			1	TM
Mixed cupbs	7–4–7	nn.	2				1	1	1		1	TM
Mixed cupbs	7–4–7	nn.	2				1	1	1		1	TM
Objects in this priority:			3									
Mixed cupbs	7–4–7	nn.	3				1		1			M
Mixed cupbs	7–4–7	nn.	3				1				1	M
Mixed cupbs	7–4–7	nn.	3				1	1	1		1	TM
Mixed cupbs	7–4–7	nn.	3				1	1				M
Mixed cupbs	7–4–7	nn.	3					1			1	TM
Mixed cupbs	7–4–7	nn.	3					1			1	TM
Objects in this priority:			6									
Objects in this location:		10										
Objects with damage:				0	1	0	8	8	4	0	8	
Mixed Cupbs	6–2–8	nn.	2				1	1	1			TR
Mixed Cupbs	6–2–8	nn.	2				1	1	1			TR
Mixed Cupbs	6–2–8	nn.	2				1	1	1			TR
Mixed Cupbs	6–2–8	nn.	2				1	1	1			TR
Mixed Cupbs	6–2–8	nn.	2				1	1	1			TR
Objects in this priority:			5									
Mixed Cupbs	6–2–8	nn.	3				1	1	1		1	TR
Mixed Cupbs	6–2–8	nn.	3				1		1			TR
Mixed Cupbs	6–2–8	nn.	3				1	1	1			TR
Mixed Cupbs	6–2–8	nn.	3					1	1			TR

Name	Loc	Obj										Code
Mixed Cupbs	6–2–8	nn.	3					1		1		TR
Objects in this priority:		5										
Objects in this location:			10									
Objects with damage:				0	0	0	9	8	10	0	1	
Pat. Smith	11–6–8	501/67/22	2		1		1	1				TMC
Pat. Smith	11–6–8	/30	2		1		1	1				TMC
Pat. Smith	11–6–8	/11	2		1		1	1				TMC
Pat. Smith	11–6–8	/14	2		1		1	1				TMC
Pat. Smith	11–6–8	/22A	2		1		1	1				TMC
Pat. Smith	11–6–8	/27A	2		1		1	1				TMC
Pat. Smith	11–6–8	/33A	2		1		1	1				TMC
Pat. Smith	11–6–8	/0A	2		1		1	1				TMC
Pat. Smith	11–6–8	/6A	2		1		1	1				TMC
Pat. Smith	11–6–8	/11	2		1		1	1				TMC
Objects in this priority:		10										
Objects in this location			10									
Objects with damage:				0	10	0	10	10	0	0	0	
Jean Straker	10–6–3	R5106	1	1			1	1	1			TMC
Jean Straker	10–6–3	R5109	1	1			1	1	1			TMC
Jean Straker	10–6–3	R5111	1	1			1	1	1			TMC
Jean Straker	10–6–3	R5113	1	1			1	1	1			TMC
Jean Straker	10–6–3	R5115	1	1			1	1	1			TMC
Objects in this priority:		5										
Jean Straker	10–6–3	R5117	2		1		1	1	1			TMC
Jean Straker	10–6–3	R5119	2		1		1	1	1			TMC
Jean Straker	10–6–3	R5121	2		1		1	1	1			TMC
Jean Straker	10–6–3	R5122	2		1		1	1	1			TMC
Jean Straker	10–6–3	R5124	2		1		1	1	1			TMC
Jean Straker	10–6–3	R5126	2		1		1	1	1			TMC
Objects in this priority:		6										
Objects in this location:			11									
Objects with damage:				5	6	0	11	11	11	0	0	

Statistics on this data file

Total sample	55	objects from	3010	
Max.objs/loc	1230	Min. objs/loc-		15
Variance:	237123	SD:	487.0	

Historic photographs collection: pilot survey data summary

Runs		Storage groups		Locations		Objects		Priorities			
Run	Sub-col	T-grps	Samp.gp	T-locs	Smp.loc	T-objs	T-samp	Pr1	Pr2	Pr3	Pr4
R.01	HenryG	8	G.4	2900	L.2	65	12	2	1	6	3
								17%	8%	50%	25%
R.02	Mounted co	8	G.3	179	L.2	170	34	0	36	0	0
								0%	106%	0%	0%
R.03	Postcds	4	G.4	365	L.2	3	1	0	0	0	1
								0%	0%	0%	100%
R.03	Postcds		G.4		L.7	17	4	1	1	1	1
								25%	25%	25%	25%
R.03	Postcds		G.3		L.12	20	3	0	2	1	0
								0%	67%	33%	0%
R.04	HenryG	15	G.3	2100	L.1	25	6	0	1	2	4
								0%	17%	33%	67%
R.05	Mixed5	24	G.3	324	L.3	52	10	0	0	2	8
								0%	0%	20%	80%
R.05	Mixed5		G.3		L.8	87	4	1	1	0	2
								25%	25%	0%	50%
R.05	Mixed5		G.3		L.13	406	14	7	4	3	0
								50%	29%	21%	0%
R.05	Mixed5		G.3		L.18	20	4	0	2	2	0
								0%	50%	50%	0%
R.05	Mixed5		G.3		L.23	142	27	4	11	8	4
								15%	41%	30%	15%
R.06	Mixed6	28	G.2	255	L.8	147	10	0	5	5	0
								0%	50%	50%	0%
R.07	Mixed7	16	G.4	560	L.7	276	10	1	3	6	0
								10%	30%	60%	0%
R.08	HenryG	31	G.7	295	L.1	15	4	0	2	2	0
								0%	50%	50%	0%
R.09	BussArch	21	G.6	910	L.3	12	2	1	0	0	1
								50%	0%	0%	50%
R.09	BussArch		G.6		L.6	212	10	5	2	3	0
								50%	20%	30%	0%
R.10	JeanStr	9	G.6	36	L.3	1130	11	5	6	0	0
								45%	55%	0%	0%
R.11	PatSmith	8	G.6	78	L.8	1230	10	10	0	0	0
								100%	0%	0%	0%
R.12	Slides	33		33	L.1	739	26	0	3	7	16
								0%	12%	27%	62%

Totals:		Groups:		Locations:		Objects:			Priority totals:		
		205		8035		4768		Pr1	Pr2	Pr3	Pr4
	Max:	33		2900		1230		37	80	48	40
	Min:	4		33		3		18%	40%	24%	20%
	SD:	9.65624		866.62		363.653					

Samples:	Groups:	Locations:	Objects:
(counts)	18	19	202

Samples of objects:
	Total:	202
	Max:	34
	Min:	1
	SD:	8.85087

Run: i.d. of run   T-locs: Number of locations in sampled group
Sub-col: Name of sub-collection   Smp.loc: i.d. of sampled location
T-grps: Number of groups in run   T-objs: Number of objects in sampled location
Samp.gp: i.d. of sampled group   T-samp: Number of objects surveyed

8

Preventive conservation

Getty Conservation Institute

The Getty Conservation Institute is a major contributor to both new research and training in preventive conservation. This article describes the basic approach and current areas of interest.

In 1826, King Ludwig I of Bavaria began work on a new building to house his extensive collection of European paintings. The Alte Pinakothek was constructed on a site that was then well outside the city of Munich, a controversial decision at the time. One reason for the choice of location was simple: it was believed that the clean air would better preserve the paintings. The decision was, in a sense, an act of preventive conservation. Until recently, conservation as a profession devoted itself almost solely to the care of individual objects. Mending or restoring an object – whether a Roman bronze, a painting by Rembrandt, or a Chinese textile – was the primary function of the conservator. Today the demands for conservation can no longer be met satisfactorily by this approach. As both the number of museums and the number of objects within museums proliferate, concentrating exclusively on individual objects severely limits conservation care for the bulk of a collection. Even the most generously endowed institutions lack the financial and personnel resources to provide individual attention to every object in need. For those institutions with fewer funds, sustaining any conservation programme remains a secondary or tertiary consideration. If a major portion of our heritage is to survive, it must be cared for collectively rather than individually. For the conservator this means focusing on ways of preventing or slowing the deterioration of objects through control of the collections environment. It means, in short, preventive conservation.

ADVANTAGES AND OBSTACLES

Preventive conservation can be defined as any measure that prevents damage or reduces the potential for it. It focuses on collections rather than individual objects, non-treatment rather than treatment. In practical terms, the handling, storage and management of collections (including emergency planning) are critical elements in a preventive conservation methodology.

In the long term, it is the most efficient form of conservation, not only for museums, but particularly for libraries and collections of ethnographic, natural history and geologic materials. With comprehensive preventive conservation, the need for individual treatments can, over time, be reduced to more manageable levels, putting personnel and financial resources to more effective use.

Despite its advantages, preventive conservation even where understood is more accepted in theory than in practice. The rate of deterioration in a group of objects can be slow and not fully appreciated except over long periods. Because the deterioration rate is difficult to quantify, the results of preventive conservation are not easily measured, nor are the results visually dramatic since preventive conservation does not involve improving the appearance of objects. In comparison, attending to the immediate conservation needs of an important or frequently exhited piece can seem far more significant – and urgent.

There are other institutional issues as well: the focus, in this age of limited resources, is often on survival. While preserving collections is obviously essential, for many museums and other collecting institutions conservations is not the primary concern.

'Museums are trained to survive', observes Marta de la Torre, Director of the GCI Training Program.

> In order to survive, you have to justify your existence. Organizing large exhibitions is much easier to justify than conserving objects – because, in fact, conservation is not an end in and of itself. It's something that you do so that you can use those objects for another purpose.

By seeking to control a museum's environment, preventive conservation, in the short term, can require a substantial outlay of funds. It means putting money into things that may have no visual impact, and therefore lack appeal to the public upon whose support the institution depends.

'The easiest thing in the world is to create a museum', says Paul Perrot, the director of the Santa Barbara Museum of Art. 'The next easiest thing is to add galleries to it. But when it comes to the operation of these galleries – whether it's the guards, the curators, or the conservators – the funds are not there because there's no glamour to it.'

These issues, while serious, are not likely completely to obstruct the movement towards preventive conservation. In part because few alternatives exist. Already there is a growing body of scientific research that is leading to practical applications. Nevertheless, for preventive conservation to be effective for a particular collection, technical knowledge has to be matched with an administrative commitment to integrate preventive conservation into the operation of an institution.

ACQUIRING TECHNICAL KNOWLEDGE

The scientific research framework for preventive conservation involves four progressive stages: (1) identifying threats to collections, (2) substantiating the risk, (3) identifying cost-efficient means to measure the risk, and (4) developing methods to reduce or eliminate the risk.

The basic problem for collections is object deterioration. 'Objects deteriorate from either internal forces or external influences', explains Jim Druzik of the GCI Scientific Program. 'Of those two, the external influences on an object are vastly larger than the internal instabilities. Things that have existed for half a millennium have very little residual internal instability – so when they begin to deteriorate, it's purely an environmental effect.'

The first step, then, is analysis of the museum environment. It is precisely in this area that the GCI Scientific Program has concentrated much of its efforts. Following a 1984 study, with the California Institute of Technology, on the relationship between outdoor and indoor concentrations of ozone, the Institute examined a number of outdoor pollutants and their penetration into the museum environment, research also conducted collaboratively. These investigations led to a series of studies on indoor-generated pollutants. 'More and more, indoor-generated air pollution is becoming an issue that the conservation field wants to have resolved', says Druzik.

> It seems every time one turns around one sees a bronze or other susceptible material corroding in museum storage in what is supposed to be a stable environment. Corrodants such as formaldehyde, and formic and acetic acids are being liberated by wood products and attacking a wide range of diverse materials.

With outdoor- and indoor-generated pollutants, a number of threats have been identified and the risks substantiated. The next stage – finding inexpensive means to measure the risks – has also been completed.

'We've identified, and called to the attention of the conservation field, low-cost, highly sensitive monitors', Druzik reports.

> The next step is developing efficient, clever control techniques that can be applied in historic houses, older buildings, storage rooms, and display cases where the curator or conservator simply does not have the advantage of a full blown air conditioning system with particle and chemical filters built into it.

Microenvironments have been the subject of several GCI projects, including the development of a prototype display case for the Royal Mummies at the Cairo Museum and a study of the optimum storage conditions for the Dead Sea Scrolls at the Israel Museum in Jerusalem. The knowledge acquired in both projects has wider applicability for the preservation of organic materials.

In another area of preventive conservation research, the GCI conducted a joint study on pest control with the University of California, Riverside. The study quantified and confirmed the effectiveness of pure nitrogen as an 'extremely promising' alternative to toxic chemical pesticides in microenvironments.

A major environmental factor for any collection is the design of the building housing it. Many of the world's museums and other collections are located in humid environments where North American and European design solutions to environmental control are too costly and architecturally inappropriate. Recognizing that much indigenous architecture is designed in a way to maximize human comfort with minimal mechanical systems (or none at all), the Institute has begun a study of passive and semipassive systems in tropical countries. Its findings could help lead to the development of cost-efficient environmental controls.

A BASIC APPROACH

Preventive conservation does not always require expensive or complex care strategies. In many institutions, much can be done by applying common sense.

For objects in storage, reducing the potential for physical damage can be achieved through such modest procedures as restricting access, exercising care in handling, and whenever possible placing objects in individual boxes or containers.

When it has been determined that some material within the museum environment is producing corrodants, the obvious course is to remove the offending material. If this is not easily done, either sealing off the material or placing some barrier around it can reduce the potential for harm. Alternatively, creating a protective barrier around the objects can help minimize long-term damage.

Routine building maintenance can serve the cause of preventive conservation. Ensuring that windows and roofs are in good repair can prevent moisture damage and help moderate temperature fluctuations that place stress on objects. Keeping both exhibition and storage space clean and free from dust (as well as from insects and rodents) is essential. Improving ventilation and air circulation through the use of low-tech fan and filters will also benefit a collection.

THE MANAGERIAL COMPONENT

Because preventive conservation relies greatly on controlling the museum environment, it involves decisions beyond the conservator's traditional authority. 'If you're going to control your environment you have to focus on your building and the different envelopes of protection', says de la Torre.

> It might be a question of reviewing the heating and air conditioning systems (if those exist), or creating new storage, or changing the exhibition cases, or controlling the visitor pattern. You have all these things that are really not within the realm of the conservator. It's an administrative decision.

Since 1987, the GCI has offered an annual course in preventive conservation to mid- and senior-level conservators. The approach is macro to micro, beginning with an assessment of the building envelope and working down to the creation of micro-environments. While technical information constitutes a major portion of the course material, the importance of conservators being skilful advocates of preventive conservation is also emphasized.

Kathleen Dardes, a conservator by training, co-ordinates the course. She believes that for preventive conservation to be incorporated into museum operations, conservators must not only develop collection care policies, but convince others of their necessity.

> You can be as clever as possible when it comes to dealing with technical matters, but if you can't speak about these things to the director in language he or she can clearly understand – which means understanding the financial implications as well – and if you can't communicate to curators and exhibition designers, and if you're not prepared to work with museum colleagues, then nothing's going to happen. It makes no difference how much you know.

De la Torre concurs. 'We need to start selling preventive conservation as a feasible and viable alternative to the management of collections', she says.

> We need to start talking very convincingly to curators and museum directors, saying, if you're going to be putting new demands on the collections, you must make sure you're protecting them as well – and here are new methods of protecting them that are less expensive and more efficient.

At the same time, institutions need to foster a general appreciation of collections care. Lawrence Reger, director of the National Institute of Conservation in Washington, D.C., thinks the public has a genuine interest in the more 'hidden' aspects of a museum's operation, and that institutions can do a better job of sharing the conservation process with the public. Reger believes museum patrons are now more receptive to supporting a museum's operational needs. 'People want recognition', he explains. 'I think they're willing to take on the redoing of a storeroom, as long as they get some kind of recognition. I think our goal has to be to promote this and help institutions bring this to the fore.'

TO PRESERVE AND PASS ON

Like nature conservation, preventive conservation of cultural heritage requires a change in attitudes and habits. The first level of awareness is simply understanding what preventive conservation means; the second is accepting it as a legitimate collections care strategy. The final and most important stage is when preventive conservation becomes an integral part of an institution's consciousness and is put into practice routinely.

Within the last decade the number of US organizations promoting preventive conservation awareness has grown. Their ranks include the American Institute of Conservation, the Institute of Museum Services, the National Gallery of Art, and the National Institute of Conservation (NIC). In 1990, the NIC and the GCI concluded a two-year project to develop a methodology for museum professionals to amass and evaluate information on the condition of their collections. The project report, *The Conservation Assessment: A Tool for Planning, Implementing, and Fundraising*, is now being used by museums and federal funding agencies in the USA as a basic guideline for undertaking conservation assessments. But preventive conservation holds perhaps the greatest potential for institutions located in less affluent regions of the world, where the funds and personnel for individual treatments are in short supply. As Reger observes: 'In countries with very limited resources, this is, frankly, the best approach to take.'

There is, however, no collecting institution that would not profit from a preventive conservation programme. 'After all,' says Paul Perrot, 'preserving cultural objects for the future is a fundamental part of a museum's mission. Our historic charge is to make sure that these resources are not only collected and studied, but preserved and passed on.' For that reason, says Perrot, preventive conservation

> is good business, as well as effecting an ethical concern for objects that are within our care ... We will certainly not arrest the march of time, but we can slow it down sufficiently so that these objects can be more true to themselves in years to come.

This paper first appeared in Conservation, the GCI Newsletter 7 (1) (1992), pp. 4–7.

9

Paintings: the (show) case for passive climate control

Emil Bosshard

Microenvironments are currently in vogue with conservators and curators. More reliable and flexible than most mechanical air-conditioning systems they are now widely used in temporary and travelling exhibitions, and in protecting particularly vulnerable objects. Emil Bosshard's example of a silica gel-based enclosure demonstrates their potential.

Climatic conditions kept as uniform and as constant as possible: these are the prerequisites demanded by restorers and museum technicians when works of art are to be handed out on loan, transported or permanently exhibited. If a work of art is to be placed in an exhibition hall with dubious, unstable or merely unpredictable climatic conditions, a climate-controlled showcase is needed for the more sensitive exhibits. Usually the air-conditioning of such showcases is limited to maintaining a certain relative air humidity. The methods for reaching this objective are manifold, and have already been published in detail elsewhere,[1] so that we can refrain from listing them again here. A basic distinction has, however, to be drawn between active and passive climate control.

In the case of an active, motor-operated system, electrical and physical assemblies are used for cooling, warming, humidifying, dehumidifying, demineralizing and circulating. Such apparatus, with complete automatic control by means of thermostats and hygrostats, are certainly most impressive from the technical point of view. They have disadvantages, however, which must not be underestimated: they function only as long as there is electricity available, they are very expensive, they need maintenance and are very susceptible to damage. Experience has shown that their reliability is limited in duration. It must in fact be stressed that a climate-controlled showcase that functions imperfectly and erratically is much more harmful for the object displayed in it than if no climate control at all is used.

Considerably safer in this regard are passive climate-control systems, which avoid the need for energy supply and have no moving parts. For about thirty years now hygroscopic materials, maintaining the climatic conditions at original loading time, have been inserted into closed showcases. These are materials which emit or absorb humidity, and which are thus able to stabilize the relative humidity in the showcase. As is well known, silica gel had proved to be particularly efficient in this respect: in the form of silica gel granulate, it is now being used in museums throughout the western world. The fundamentals of this system and experience with it have been documented in numerous reports.[2] Particularly informative were the results of its practical application obtained by F. Schweizer and A. Rinuy in the 1980s.[3] It was shown, in fact, that by using efficient buffer material and relatively air-tight showcases, it is possible to stabilize the climatic conditions for long periods of time.

WHAT ABOUT CASES IN USE TODAY?

In the traditional climate-controlled showcases, the painting (or several together) is mounted with its frame in a case made of glass or acrylic glass where the silica gel, usually placed behind or under the painting, is commonly concealed by means of a textile covering.[4] This system offers the advantage that the showcase does not have to be tailor-made to suit the measurements of the painting, so that, if necessary, it can also be reused for another exhibit. It has also certain disadvantages, such as:

The painting is placed into a rather unsightly and (especially when acrylic glass is used) highly light-reflecting case, which spoils the aesthetic pleasure of viewing the work of art.

The second defect is technical: the efficiency of such showcases is directly dependent on their intrinsic airtightness and on the ratio of buffer material used to the internal air volume. Now, this type of showcase has a considerably larger air space around the painting than is actually necessary. The bigger the showcase, the less airtight it is likely to be.

A further disadvantage becomes evident when exhibits are sent out on loan: the work of art is removed from its normal surroundings, it goes on a short (or long) trip, during which it is exposed – as is well known – to hardly controllable climatic conditions, and finally arrives at the pre-conditioned display case prepared for it. Although the climate conditions for that display case may have been agreed upon in advance, the lending conservator has practically no possibility of checking them, let alone changing them, when he or she arrives with the exhibit. Thus, even with optimal precautions, the exhibit passes through three different climatic environments: (a) at the home museum; (b) in a case during transit (quite apart from packing and unpacking); and (c) in the host display case. After the exhibition, the same condition changes occur again in the reverse sequence.

It is possible to eliminate these short comings by making the modifications described below:

The showcase is reduced in size, until the painting itself (without frame) is separated on either side by only 5–10 mm from the inside surface of the case. In this way, the air volume to be conditioned will be so reduced that small quantities of silica gel will suffice. The showcase thus becomes so compact and flat that it can be fitted into the picture frame. With a front of non-reflecting glass, which is practically invisible, it will now be not more disturbing than a painting under glass. The advantages with respect to loan and travel are considerable. The painting can now be encapsulated in its usual climatic environment and can be packed into the transport box on its own showcase. In this way, it proceeds to the host museum and back well protected against variations of relative humidity and against physical contact of any kind.

DESIGN

Such a type of showcase was developed by Ben Johnson and George Wight in California in the early 1980s. In co-operation with the Thyssen-Bornemisza Collection, the system has been further improved and brought to near perfection, so that now a standard climate-controlled showcase is currently available.[2] It consists of a plexiglas box with a normal width (depending on the painting's thickness) of 3.5 to 8 cm and with a front of non-reflecting glass. The whole inner rear side is fitted with a wooden lattice 1 cm thick, whose openings hold 'Art-Sorb' silica gel[6] contained in small fabric bags. The fabric bags in turn are held in place by a fine metal mesh.

The painting, usually on a wooden panel, is put into the cover, with some felt buffers in between (see schematic drawing, Fig. 9.1). The latter keep the panel at a distance of about 5 mm from the front and sides of the made-to-measure showcase, and thus permit the air to circulate freely between the front side and the rear side of the panel. The panel, from the direction of the rear (i.e. the wooden lattice), is softly pressed towards the front into the cover by means of several foam-rubber or felt buffers. As a result, the inside of the showcase is used approximately as follows: one-third of its volume is occupied by the painting, one-third by the bagged silica gel with its wooden lattice, and one-third remains as free air space.

The conditioning of the silica gel is carried out by exposing it, for three to four weeks, to the desired relative humidity (RH), or even better to a RH which is about 3 per cent higher than desired, since the RH diminishes slightly after the showcase is closed. Then the showcase is closed without the use of screws, by putting the rear side over the front side with the painting, and sealed by covering the joints in the side walls with an air-tight adhesive tape. Also enclosed, but visible from behind, is a paper hygrometer, which permits the approximate degree of relative humidity to be read without having to open the showcase.

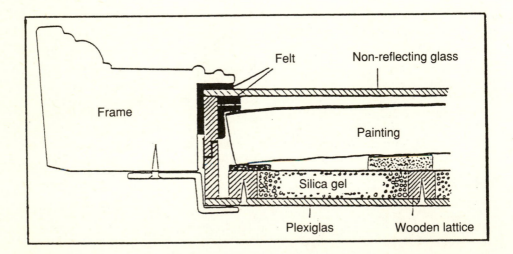

Fig. 9.1 Schematic cross-section of a climate-controlled case as used by the Thyssen-Bornemisza Collection (Emil Bosshard)

TEST RESULTS AND EXPERIENCES

At the present time, the Thyssen-Bornemisza Collection in Lugano has fifty-eight paintings in showcases with stabilized air-conditioning as described above. Originally, these cases were intended as a protection for sensitive wooden panels during temporary exhibitions and badly air-conditioned museums. Since the method proved to be so reliable, it was decided to leave the paintings in their showcases after the exhibitions. Many of them have, at the time of writing been in their cases for six years without interruption and without any maintenance. The paintings are on thin German and Dutch wooden panels, as well as Italian ones on thick panels.

Basically, the time during which the closed showcase can maintain its relative humidity depends on the following factors:

- the airtightness of the case: the more hermetic it is, the longer the climatic conditions remain constant;

- the quantity and the moisture-retentive capacity of the buffer materials;

- the relative degree of humidity of the air surrounding the case: the greater the difference between internal and external relative humidity conditions, the faster the change that will occur inside the showcase.

It must be assumed that a showcase designed in this way is never completely airtight. On the one hand, plexiglas itself is to a limited degree permeable to air. On the other hand, any change in air pressure and temperature, as occurs for instance during transport by air, will doubtless cause a certain movement of air into or out of the case.

Now, how does the relative humidity inside the showcase behave? In order to determine this, two test programmes were carried out. One was empirical, measuring and recording once a week the behaviour of such a showcase in an unclimatized room over a period of two years. While the RH in the room fluctuated by 30 per cent, that in the showcase varied by only 2 per cent (Fig. 9.2).

Parallel to this, another test programme was carried out in 1988/9, under accelerated laboratory conditions, by Mervin Richard of the National Gallery of Art in Washington, D.C. He had calculated a half-life of two years for these cases, and postulated that if the showcase with an RH of 50 per cent inside was continually exposed to an environment with only 30 per cent RH, the RH inside the case would decrease to 40 per cent within about two years. Inside the display cases described here, the volume of silica gel constitutes approximately one-quarter of the air volume. The result is an intended over-capacity, a clear overkill. It ensures a rapid levelling out of RH fluctuation, even in case of a sudden change in temperature. In his tests with a climatic chamber, Mervin Richard noted that a temperature change of 10°C causes the relative humidity inside the case to change only by about 2 per cent.[7]

SUDDEN SHARP CHANGES ELIMINATED

The results obtained show by these tests that this type of display case can ensure controlled and stable climatic conditions (with respect to humidity only, not to temperature) over many years without any maintenance. Although the relative humidity inside will doubtless alter towards the value of the humidity of the room, this will occur very slowly. It is especially the case that, if the painting hangs in a room which in winter has too low and in summer too high an air humidity, this buffered showcase will provide

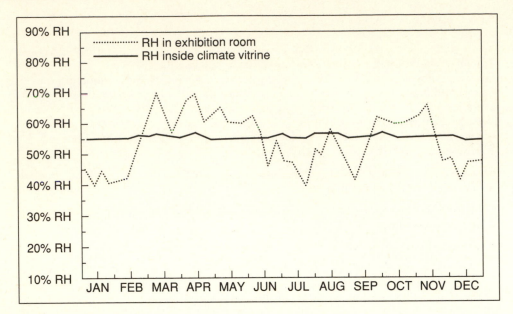

Fig. 9.2 Empirical RH test in Lugano 1989 (Emil Bosshard)

effective protection by balancing out its own average value to correspond with the average relative humidity of the room. Detrimental sudden and sharp changes of relative humidity inside the case are thus almost completely eliminated.

This paper first appeared in Museum *173 (1992), pp. 46–50.*

NOTES

1   G. Thomson (1986) *The Museum Environment*, London: Butterworths.
2   T. Padfield (1966) 'The control of humidity and air pollution in show cases and picture frames', *Studies in Conservation* 2: 8–30; N. Stolow (1966) *Controlled environments for works of art in transit*, London: Butterworths; G. Thomson (1977) 'Stabilisation of RH in exhibition cases: hygrometric half-life', *Studies in Conservation* 22: 85–102.
3   F. Schweizer and A. Rinuy (1980) 'Zur Mikroklimatisierung zweier Vitrinen mit Ikonen fur eine temporare Ausstellung', *Maltechnik-Restauro* 4: 239–43; F. Schweizer (1984) 'Stabilisation of RH in exhibition cases: an experimental approach', ICOM Copenhagen Conference, 17, 50–3, 84.
4   A. Rother and B. Metro, 'Climate controlled show cases for paintings', *Museum* 37(2)(146).
5   Manufacturer's address on request.
6   Produced by Fuji-Davison Chemical Ltd.
7   These test results vary according to size of vitrine and temperature range. All tests were made with empty vitrines. The results can be expected to be even better with vitrines filled with panel paintings.

10

Silica gel and related RH buffering materials, conditioning and regeneration techniques

Nathan Stolow

Silica gel is the most popular buffer for maintaining microenvironments, yet exactly how it should be used is given relatively brief coverage in the literature. Nathan Stolow is well known for his pioneering work on the transport of objects. Typical of Stolow's writing, this paper is a mine of practical information.

1 DESCRIPTION

Silica gel is an artificially prepared inert crystalline colourless chemical substance composed of silicon and oxygen. Its most important physical property is its high absorptive capacity for water vapour. It has extensive industrial use as a drying agent, and also has found use in a limited way as an absorbent for airborne pollutants. The use of silica gel for humidity-buffering purposes, as in museum applications, is of recent origin (dating from the 1950s). Only a small part of silica gel production is devoted to such use. The method of preparation of silica gel for humidity-buffering purposes is detailed below. Essentially the dry gel is exposed to a humid atmosphere for a fixed period of time until the crystals have absorbed a known amount of moisture. The moisture content is determined by removing samples, weighing, heating to dryness, re-weighing and then calculating the moisture content (dry basis). By consulting the isotherm curves which relate the moisture content of the silica gel (actually the equilibrium moisture content – EMC) to given ambient RH conditions, one can arrive at the degree of exposure to produce the required conditioned gel. Silica gel prepared in this manner can then be stored in polyethylene bags, or other humidity-tight containers for further use.

The 'indicating' type of silica gel is one in which the particles are coated in the manufacturing process with small quantities of cobalt salts. When dry, the gel crystals are deep blue, and as the EMC increases the colour shifts to progressive shades of mauve and pink. Whatever the form of the gel, complete drying out can be achieved by heating to 250°C under well-ventilated conditions for a period of about one hour.

Silica gel can be regenerated and reconditioned many times and still retain its absorption capacity. Of particular interest are the sorbents 'Art Sorb' silica gel, Kaken Gel (Nikka Pellets), and Montmorillonite and the standard silica gels whose isotherms are reproduced here in Fig. 10.1.

It is seen that Art Sorb silica gel has a higher absorptive capacity than the standard Davison gel, and likewise the sorbent Kaken Gel (or clay-like material) is also more absorbent. For ordinary buffering applications up to control levels of 40–50 per cent the standard gel is quite satisfactory and is cheaper and more commonly available. In

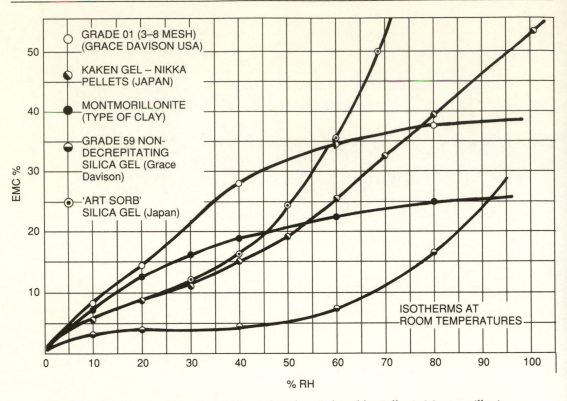

Fig. 10.1 Isotherms of 'Art Sorb' silica gel, Kaken Gel (Nikka Pellets), Montmorillonite and standard silica gel

situations where high levels of RH maintenance are required, e.g. above 60 per cent, RH the more absorptive gels and buffers are recommended. Also included in the figure is the type of silica gel which is non-decrepitating. This is a gel that does not readily disintegrate on direct wetting with water – but, as noted, has a low absorption capacity. Kaken Gel completely disintegrates to a 'mud' if directly wetted, while the other grades of silica gel will break down into small crystals. These reactions are worth taking into account in establishing conditioning techniques.

For a given sorbent the equilibration to a particular EMC depends on its initial moisture content, the ambient RH, particle size, depth of crystals in the exposed 'bed', degree of air movement – assuming that the temperature remains constant throughout the process.

The time taken for say the EMC to go from 0 to 30 per cent, for which the 01 gel will produce a buffering level of 45 per cent RH, may take weeks if the conditioning environment is 45 per cent RH. By spreading the gel crystals thinly over a large surface area and boosting the ambient RH to 80 per cent the absorption process will be speeded up. However, in this case the EMC increase must be monitored to avoid overconditioning. Whatever the conditioning procedure, it is important to have at hand the isotherm curve which governs the property of the particular grade of sorbent.

If one started with 100 g of dry 01 type silica gel and the final equilibrium weight in a 50 per cent RH ambient environment was 130 g, the

$$\text{EMC} = \frac{132 - 100}{100} \times 100 = 32\%$$

Suppose now that the equilibrated gel was transferred to an environment of 70 per cent RH. The gel would progressively pick up moisture and eventually the weight of the gel would stabilize at 136 g, and the

$$\text{EMC} = \frac{136 - 100}{100} \times 100 = 36\%$$

Suppose the conditioned gel is now exposed to a drier environment, moisture will be lost until a lower EMC value will be reached. The desorption process, however, takes place more slowly than absorption and moreover the phenomenon of hysteresis applies. If the gel is heated in an oven to dryness (0 per cent EMC) the normal sorption characteristics are regained upon re-exposure.

The gel with an EMC of 30 per cent, if placed in a sealed glass jar, will generate an RH level of at least 45 per cent RH. If other absorbent materials are present the resultant RH after a period of conditioning (equilibrating) will depend on the nature of these materials, their initial moisture contents, their isotherm characteristics, their masses and the air volume. The period of effective buffering action of conditioned silica gel in a display case or vitrine will be governed by the airtightness of the case. It will be necessary therefore to test the gel over intervals of time to determine its EMC and establish the need for replenishment or regeneration.

The industrial suppliers of silica gel and other sorbents specify sizes of the crystals, or beads, in screen or mesh sizes. Some of the typical particle size designations are:

- 3–8 mesh (USA) 6 mm to 2.4 mm screen opening
- 6–16 mesh (USA) 3.4 mm to 1.2 mm screen opening
- 8 mesh (USA) 2.4 mm screen opening

2 NORMAL CONDITIONING TECHNIQUES

If it is desired to prepare silica gel for creating or buffering an enclosed environment to say 50 per cent, it is first necessary to provide the constant environment of 50 per cent RH (or more) for conditioning the dry gel. Consulting Fig. 10.1 it is seen that the EMC must be raised from 0 to 32 per cent. If a gallery or other open space is already stable at 50 per cent RH (or more) it is a simple matter to spread a quantity of gel in large areas, as in cafeteria or photographic trays, or even on large sheets of polyethylene film or paper on tables or other surfaces. It is advisable to put canopies over these surfaces as there may be dust or dirt accumulation over the period of time required. The time required for equilibration depends on layer thickness, and screen mesh-size – as well as frequency of 'stirring' to expose fresh quantities of gel.

On the basis of the bulk density of silica gel as 700 kg/m^3, a tray of dimensions 60 × 90 cm could be loaded with 5 kg dry gel, which gives a layer thickness of about 1 cm. It may be useful to play a fan over the surfaces to speed up the absorption equilibration as shown in Fig. 10.2. It should take about 2–3 weeks to reach the required EMC of 32 per cent, somewhat less time if the ambient RH is at higher level, say 60 per cent. The EMC is determined at intervals by removing 10 to 20 g samples for moisture content testing as described in Section 4.

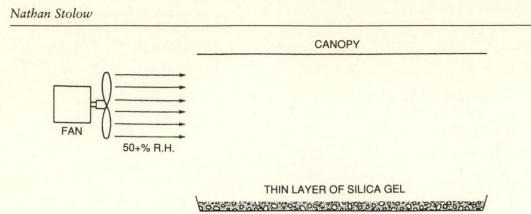

CANOPY

FAN

50+% R.H.

THIN LAYER OF SILICA GEL

TRAY

Fig. 10.2 Conditioning technique using a fan over a tray of silica gel to speed up the process

If an environment chamber is available, it can conveniently be set for 60 per cent or even higher and the gel can be conditioned in probably less than two weeks. Another method for conditioning involves the use of a domestic-type humidifier of the evaporative type (revolving drum) with hygrostat control and tent-like enclosure. This is schematically shown in Fig. 10.3. The hygrostat controls tend to be coarse, with the desired level overshooting before the unit is cycled to the off position.

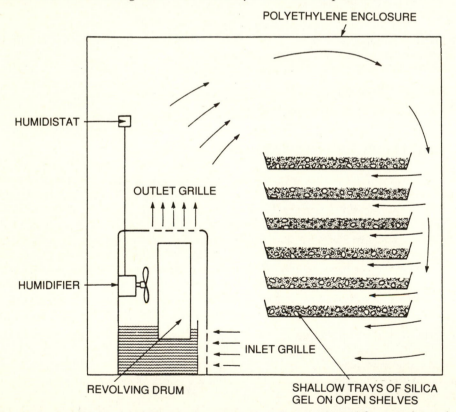

POLYETHYLENE ENCLOSURE

HUMIDISTAT

OUTLET GRILLE

HUMIDIFIER

INLET GRILLE

REVOLVING DRUM

SHALLOW TRAYS OF SILICA GEL ON OPEN SHELVES

Fig. 10.3 Conditioning technique using an evaporative-type humidifier (revolving drum) with hygrostat control with a tent-like enclosure

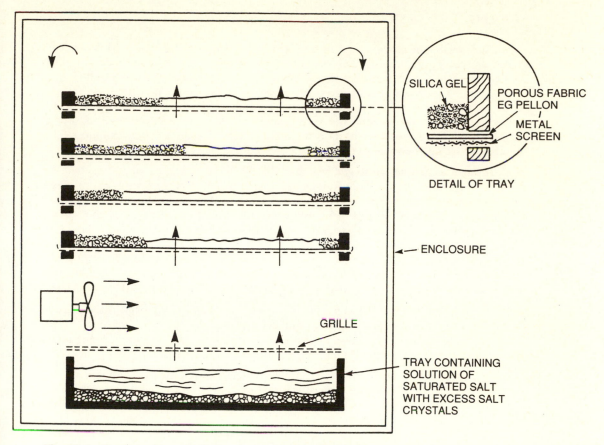

Fig. 10.4 Conditioning technique using saturated salt solutions

Still another method employs saturated solutions of certain salts which create a constant RH environment for the conditioning procedure. Some of the salt solutions and resulting RH levels at room temperatures are as follows:

Saturated solution of*	RH
lithium chloride	12
magnesium chloride	34
magnesium nitrate	55
sodium bromide	59
sodium chloride	75

* It is important that the saturated solution of the salt be in contact with a large bulk of undissolved crystals.

A typical arrangement for this is in Fig. 10.4. It is important to prevent spillage of the control solution. A fan helps to speed up the RH distribution and attainment of equilibrium. The salt solutions and undissolved crystals should be stirred up every few days.

3 RAPID CONDITIONING TECHNIQUES

The silica gel, again in trays, can be exposed to 95 per cent RH which with care can speed up the required moisture absorption to 2–3 days or less. One method is to place the gel in an insulated moisture-impervious enclosure together with a humidifier running at full capacity, that is at 95–100 per cent RH. One must be careful to prevent condensation at the walls from dropping on the gel. Again the EMC should be determined at various stages along the way. There may be a tendency to overshoot the required EMC as the gel absorbs moisture quite readily in a saturated environment. The equipment set-up is similar to that in Fig. 10.3.

Still another technique, although less desirable, is direct spraying of the gel with a known weight of water. This technique is rather difficult to carry out with any precision as there is a tendency to overwet the more accessible layers of gel and underspray the concealed portions. Also the gel crystals tend to break down, a phenomenon known as 'decrepitation'. Clay-like materials like Kaken Gel will form into a mud. Where it is important to retain the mesh size, the spray technique is not to be used. There tends to be less decrepitation by spraying if the gel is already partly conditioned. Thus, if the silica gel is conditioned to an EMC of 25 per cent (35 per cent RH), the amount of sprayed water to be added can be calculated to bring the EMC to 32 per cent (50 per cent RH).

The spraying can be carried out in a large polyethylene bag and the bag then sealed for a few days to allow for distribution of moisture throughout the silica gel mass. Occasional shaking of the bag speeds up the process. As usual in these techniques the EMC should be determined on small samples of gel removed at intervals.

However prepared or conditioned, the sorbent material should be stored in sealed bags or containers labelled as to the type of gel, mesh size, EMC, description of conditioning process, temperature, and to include information on subsequent regeneration procedures.

4 MEASUREMENT OF EMC

The equipment and technique for EMC measurement of silica gel and related sorbents need not be complicated. There are expensive instruments available which give direct readings (moisture testers). The method described here is simple using commonly available apparatus:

Apparatus

- adjustable hot plate – 600 W
- surface thermometer to measure up to 350°C
- small aluminium pans (kitchen-type) (weight approx. 0.4 g)
- weighing scale (beam balance) sensitive to 0.02 g
- tongs or long forceps for handling the pans
- small, heavy-gauge polyethylene bags with closures for storing samples of gel to be measured

Procedure

(a) Put hot plate into operation until its temperature as indicated by the surface thermometer reads more or less steadily at 250°C (about 30 minutes of operation);

(b) Weigh an empty aluminium pan, weight in grams (W_p);
(c) Before removing silica gel sample, e.g. Art Sorb, stir or shake tray so that the sample will be representative. Remove about 20–30 grams of 'conditioned gel' to a small polyethylene bag – and temporarily seal;
(d) Record time of removal of silica gel sample and describe details of the conditioning technique used;
(e) Transfer about 10 grams of the bagged sample to the weighed empty pan. Then weigh pan plus sample (W_i);
(f) Transfer a second sample of the gel to another empty pre-weighed pan. This will be a duplicate test so that there will be two results to average. Make sure that each of the pans has an identifying mark; e.g., I and II;
(g) Place the pans plus samples on the hot plate. After 5 minutes shake gently to shift around the crystals and permit more even drying. The particles may be cautiously stirred with the forcep tips. Make sure that no particles of crystals are shaken out of the pans. Wire gauze discs may serve as protective covers during the heating interval;
(h) After 10 minutes take pan off hot plate with forceps and tongs and quickly weigh on balance (time to weigh about 10 s). Record time of heating and weight (pan + sample);
(i) repeat every 10 minutes until two repeat weights are constant. The final dry weight pan + sample is W_f grams. The same series of weighings is carried out on the duplicate sample II.

Note: If the gel is of the indicating type the appearance when completely dry is deep blue throughout the crystal sample.

Calculation of EMC:

$$EMC = \frac{W_i - W_f}{W_f - W_p} \times 100 \ (\%)$$

Example

weight of pan empty = 0.4 g (W_p)
weight of conditioned gel + pan = 12.6 g (W_i)
weight of heated gel + pan = 9.7 g (W_f)

$$\text{thus EMC} = \frac{12.6 - 9.7}{9.7 - 0.4} \times 100 = \frac{2.9}{9.3} \times 100 = 31.2\%$$

If the first sample produces this result, 31.2 per cent EMC, and the second (duplicate) sample is measured as 31.8 per cent EMC, the average of the two is therefore 31.5 per cent EMC.

The EMC determinations should always be done on duplicate samples to give more confidence in the result. Now by consulting the established relationship of the curve in Fig. 10.1, it is seen that 31.5 per cent EMC corresponds to a potential RH control level of close to 55 per cent RH for the Art Sorb grade of silica gel.

If the EMC level desired is not yet reached, the conditioning procedure as outlined above is repeated or continued. The spent silica gel samples after the moisture determinations are accumulated in a separate container as dry gel for further use.

5 WHEN DOES THE SILICA GEL NEED RECONDITIONING OR REGENERATION?

The first indication is when the measured RH in the display case or other enclosed environment reads less (or more) than that required. It is important to establish that the recording devices, e.g. thermohygrographs, are reading accurately (quite often they need calibration). If, for example, the silica gel is drying out (also shown by increasing blue colour if indicating silica gel is employed) then it is time to check on the EMC of the silica gel by the hot plate technique described in the previous section. If the results then prove that the EMC has fallen to an unacceptable level it is necessary to institute a reconditioning procedure – or to exchange the 'spent' gel with a fresh stock of standby gel conditioned to the proper EMC level.

If the gel needs very frequent replacement or regeneration, e.g. every 6 months, then the construction of the display case and the disposition and quantity of gel should be re-examined. For long-term stability and low maintenance the case should be fairly air-tight, opened rarely, and the gel exposed over broad surfaces in the approximate proportion of 20 kg per cubic metre.

This paper first appeared in N. Stolow (1987) Conservation and Exhibitions *(London: Butterworth-Heinemann), pp. 241–6.*

11

Conservation in the computer age
Richard Hall

Museums are turning from mechanical to electronic monitors for measuring the museum environment. Richard Hall's paper demonstrates some of the advantages of a technology which is enabling major advances in the understanding of the effects of the environment on objects.

INTRODUCTION

Parks Canada Atlantic Region, at its headquarters in Dartmouth near Halifax, has just installed a microprocessor-based environmental monitoring system to keep a distant eye on a number of its far-flung acquisitions. The system is not only capable of monitoring a number of important variables at distances of up to 1,000 miles in one area, correcting variations in the atmospheric conditions surrounding valuable artefacts, but also of notifying professional conservators when there is trouble.

The first phase of the Parks Canada programme will see installation of sensors in five locations, ultimately in twenty-one. For example, the famous house Green Gables, in Cavendish, Prince Edward Island, will have monitors and furnace controls to permit staff at Parks Canada headquarters in Dartmouth to regulate temperature and relative humidity (RH) during the winter, a particularly crucial time. During the summer, control is extremely difficult, according to Eddy Patterson, Chief of Conservation for the region, because the house is in constant use, with doors and windows having to be opened for the public. Green Gables is approximately 300 miles from headquarters.

Almost 1,000 miles from Dartmouth lies the site of the first Viking settlement in North America, on the far northern tip of Newfoundland. It was here at Leif Eriksson's tiny colony, L'Anse aux Meadows, that fragile remains were discovered by the Norwegian explorer, Helge Ingstad, and his team in 1960. Most valuable is a bronze cloak-pin left by one of the Vikings. Patterson emphasizes that 'Metals are normally stable, especially bronze, but in this case the artifact is highly mineralized and fragile. This requires keeping it in a special container even within an environmentally controlled showcase with other iron and small organic objects.' Similarly, the historic site of Fort Anne in Annapolis Royal is destined to house the charter of Nova Scotia after a special provincial ceremony in 1987, and this will require a special showcase to house it since parchment requires a steady 50 per cent RH with less than 5 per cent variation. At the Alexander Graham Bell National Historic Park in Baddeck, Nova Scotia, sensors are to be installed in the storage area containing a wide range of scientific artefacts. The last site being considered is Signal Hill where Marconi's kites are housed – these were used for the first transatlantic wireless telegraph transmission in 1901.

THE PROBLEM

Engineers and curators faced with inherently inaccurate manual monitoring systems turned for help to two professional sources of advice: John Perkins, Project Coordinator at the Getty Conservation Institute in California; and Canadian Applied Technology (CAT) of Concord, Ontario, which specializes in the design, manufacture and installation of data acquisition systems for environmental and industrial monitoring applications. John Perkins has designed the conservation requirements and CAT have provided an off-the-shelf system with customized software, a system unique in North America because of its comprehensiveness.

The reliability and validity of readings are everything when the fate of valuable artefacts is at stake, and to be aware of the dynamics of an environmental system, and thus to be able to take appropriate remedial action ahead of time, is true preventative conservation. Manual systems very rarely permit this, since a typical example of such a system is a series of thermohygrographs in various locations taking continous measurements. The paper charts are collected on a supposedly regular basis to be transcribed, analysed then filed. This information is supplemented by periodic measurements of light levels (lux – usually only within the visible spectrum range), with other variables measured usually on an 'as needed' basis. Rarely is there any comprehensive, ongoing and reliable data collection system established and maintained. Not surprisingly it is also rare for any in-depth follow-up to be undertaken using manually collected data. Indeed, John Perkins has ventured to speculate that:

> most of the data collected by this type of system would prove to be woefully inadequate if it were ever required, and while it is not possible to solve all the problems plaguing monitoring systems, I do believe that microprocessor-based technology can offer substantial assistance.

With more conservation facilities now acquiring computers to assist with laboratory operations, it makes sense to use them to facilitate part of the conservator's job – environmental monitoring and preventive conservation – which otherwise is not possible because of the massive labour involved. According to Perkins:

> In all fairness, there are good reasons why the manual systems outlined above represent the status quo. First is the cost in time and money of a comprehensive system, and, secondly, it can become discouraging to be collecting information which cannot be acted on. People who start out with the intention of having a comprehensive system gradually let them lapse.

A truly comprehensive system would naturally incorporate alarm and safely features, too, but in terms of conservation, what conservators need to know retrospectively for optimum management of artefacts are the longer-term trends and characteristics. This 'picture' of the situation is the information needed to make decisions about the suitability of the environment which objects are to be kept in. The picture is made up of summary statistics – maximum and minimum values, daily and weekly averages, and standard deviations; and for this, analysis and manipulation of data need to be performed.

John Perkins has summarized the problem in that to achieve the two requirements of analysis and manipulation, data must have both reliability and validity. In the broad sense, 'reliable' must mean that the data gathered actually represent what they are supposed to, whilst validity refers to the strength of confidence in their correctness. For example, if readings are taken every day on a single thermohygrograph, to measure the temperature and RH levels in a five-room exhibit over a period of one week, this can be seen as reliable, but are the data valid? What about the accuracy of the recorder, or variations in values in different parts of the laboratory? Perkins points out that monitoring the 5 per cent modal band of a 50–60 per cent RH range requires an accuracy of 2 per cent or better. If one merely needs to know whether the ambient environmental conditions are between 40 and 70 per cent, much more total error is acceptable.

The total error is the sum of all individual components' error, and one of the disadvantages of manual systems is that they have a great capacity to introduce unquantifiable error, most of it human. Every time a recorder runs down, a chart goes round twice or a week's data are lost because the operator was sick, the system error increases. A similar potential for error is inherent in computer-based systems, but it is much easier to control and this yields greater validity.

HARDWARE AND SOFTWARE

The Parks Canada Atlantic Region system is designed to monitor constantly temperature, RH and incident light levels at up to nine different artefact storage and display areas. Its secondary functions are to control the conditioning of environments and to act as a security system when required. There are three components: sensors, data loggers and a system controller, all man–ufactured by CAT. The sensors combine temperature and RH functions with a range of 0–100 per cent with an accuracy of ±2 per cent for 0–80 per cent and ±3 per cent for 80–100 per cent. Between −14 and 115 degrees Celsius, accuracy is ±0.3 per cent. These sensors are film capacitors and should be calibrated once a year by having the data logger send a reference voltage and monitoring the response. The light-level sensor is a braodband silicon cell with a bandwidth of 300 to 1100 nM giving a linearized output of mV/watt/m^2 and can have filters applied to it to tailor it to any spectrum range from ultraviolet through visible to infra-red.

Conventional light meters, or lux meters, just measure illumination – not total radiant energy – and only within visible wavelengths, thus ignoring the more damaging ultraviolet and infra-red, though it is these forms of radiant energy which cause particularly rapid deterioration.

The data logger, a CAT 2200+, plays the role of ever-present observer and is an intelligent system with 32K of RAM for data storage, 32K EPROM for program storage, special RS232 channels for communication, and an operating software package. The system offers 23 analog input channels and 16 digital input/16 digital output channels. It is calibrated to take average readings every few seconds, determined by the user, and if these are exceeded, a warning is directed to a specified location. This can take a variety of forms depending on the extent of the excess – a message to the controller, automatic telephone calls to the fire station – in fact up to twelve telephone numbers can be dialled. Since it is possible to monitor such a variety of events, it is possible to tailor the system at each location from simple environmental monitoring to sophisticated preventive conservation packages, including security, fire, smoke, water, intrusion, visitor-use evaluation and maintenance timing.

Again, to quote John Perkins:

All of these activities are controllable from any computer or terminal that has

ASCII protocol, over ordinary telephone lines, or if necessary, by radio link, offering great flexibility.

The system controller software package is in many ways incidental to the rudimentary functioning of the system since the bulk of the operational capacity is in the data-logger component. But the PC used need not only be truly dedicated since data can be programmed for transmission during the night leaving the computer free for analysis during the day when it is a simple matter to design the generation of a summary report that can be automatically produced at regular intervals and sent online to anybody with a terminal or a Datapac connection.

Initially, sensors will be installed in appropriate showcases at these sites; later, small air-conditioning units will be added, also regulated by the monitoring network. The kind of accuracy possible with the new microprocessor-based system is of the following high order:

(a) Records of RH and temperature are individually identifiable with an accuracy of ± 2 per cent from up to 10 separate locations, and incident light levels from at least two locations.

(b) Discrete areas of a single site can be monitored for occurrences of intrusion, fire flood, smoke, and visitor frequency, and these data can be gathered on a continuous basis for 24 hours a day, at locations physically removed from the lab – by up to 1,000 miles, if necessary – without the use of a dedicated microprocessor at the site.

(c) Data can be stored for up to 36 hours, be instantly accessible, and log maximum and minimum values for each record together with calculated standard deviation values. At least two average monitoring values can be changed for each record, that is, the range of monitoring.

(d) Other advantages would be: power failure proofing; to be able to assign high and low alarm values to various artefacts; and to be informed automatically if limits are exceeded.

(e) Finally, the system is operable with a minimum of supervision, on preferably less than one person-day a week.

This paper first appeared in International Journal of Museum Management and Curatorship 6 *(1987), pp. 291–4.*

12

Museums tune in to radio
Graham Martin and David Ford

Martin and Ford, of the Victoria and Albert Museum, describe a wireless system for environmental monitoring. A wide range of different types of continuous electronic monitoring devices is now available, each useful in slightly different applications.

The restrictions of hard-wired environmental monitoring equipment and the high labour costs of battery – operated systems have led to the interest in the use of radio transmission as a means of obtaining data from within display cases and the like.

Only recently, with the relaxation of the statutes regarding low power radio transmitters at particular frequencies and developments in technology, has radio transmission become possible. This contribution describes a system purchased to satisfy data collection from an area in the museum which is subject to continuing changes of display.

Recently, the museum acquired the Meaco Museum Monitor, which is the first radio telemetry system for relative humidity and temperature data collection. It is distributed and marketed by Meaco Sales and Marketing. The system's main usage within the museum will be in the North and South Court temporary exhibition spaces currently occupied (until February 1993) by the *Sporting Glory* exhibition.

At present the system comprises twelve combined relative humidity/temperature monitors. The number of monitors is dependent on the application. Each monitor has its own liquid crystal display of temperature and humidity, in addition to a small onboard transmitter. All power for the monitor is supplied by dry cell batteries which will last for one year or longer depending on the application.

SYSTEM FLEXIBILITY

Communication to a PC receiving station is the basis of the system. The PC's printer and disk drive give hardcopy, flexibility and data security. The interval between readings is selectable and we have chosen 30 minutes. Since the system is highly flexible it may be used in a variety of other configurations. By employing suitable relay stations or hard wiring, the base station can be sited anywhere, provided the receiver unit is within approximately 200 metres of each of the monitors.

Radiotelemetry enables live on-line data alarm conditions to be set to activate light-emitting diodes, to warn curators that the conditions are out of specification. Readings may also be observed on each individual monitor's LCD.

Advantages of such a system are the collection of live data from numerous maintenance-free source points and logging the data at a central work station which can also provide hard copy on paper. The major economic advantage is the absence of wires that require channelling in walls or suitable conduits, thereby saving considerable disruption to the fabric of the building and allowing a 'movable' system.

EASY TO MOVE

Since the telemetry system's inherent feature is wireless data transfer, the monitors, measuring a mere $101 \times 76 \times 40$ mm, can be moved to different locations without cumbersome wiring or fixtures; this is a highly desirable feature in equipment for a temporary exhibition.

A radio frequency survey and transmission test may need to be carried out by the manufacturers to ensure as far as possible that there is no interference from other radio waves of a similar nature.

Each monitor, based on the Meaco HK 100, is accurate to $\pm$ 3 per cent relative humidity and $\pm$ 1°C with no distortion of data resolution through transmission. Data logging is achieved by custom-written software for the system as supplied by Meaco Sales and Marketing. A suitable sized hard disk is supplied to contain a year's data for the relevant number of loggers; the current maximum is 250 monitors. Full printout facilities giving various options are supplied with the system.

The telemetry system saves many person/hours in the collection, analysis and presentation of data. In the future more applications, such as UV content and lux monitors, will be available. With the advance of information technology and research these data will become invaluable in the day-to-day running of museums. The software package allows standard statistics and graphical analysis to be performed and output to spreadsheet packages will be available.

A similar system has also been developed by Exeter-based Hanwell Monitors. A radio-linked system is being installed at Bath's Roman Baths, and a monitoring system, linking a number of outstations by phone, has been developed for Lancashire Museums Service. This is also able to monitor light and ultraviolet levels.

This paper first appeared in Museum Development *(November 1992), pp. 15–16.*

13

Fresh-air climate conditioning at the Arthur M. Sackler Museum

Michael Williams

Air-conditioning systems tend to be the province of specialist designers and engineers. As the requirements of museums are often more rigorous than those of other organizations, it is useful to have a basic understanding of how these systems work before one is commissioned. Michael Williams gives a readable account of the main considerations in the design of HVAC systems.

INTRODUCTION

Museum climate-control efforts began with a closed dry space. Then central heating was added, followed in turn by humidification, mechanical cooling, dehumidification, particulate filtration, noxious gas absorption and, currently, accurate digital control. Museum standards always have stretched contemporary technology to provide an appropriate environment for sensitive objects. It is now considered critical to maintain both a stable temperature and relative humidity, and to provide clean, totally filtered air.

The standard which was applied to the design of the Arthur M. Sackler Museum at Harvard University called for temperature variations of only ± 2.5°F (~1.5°C) and relative humidity control to ± 5 per cent. Particulate and basic gas filtration (activated carbon) were also to be programmed. During design development and construction, growing concern over inappropriate elements in the museum environment tightened these specifications further to eliminate the injection of corrosion inhibitors through standard steam humidification, add provisions for formaldehyde filtration, and increase the accuracy of the control system. While this constant improvement, resulting from a growing ability to control a total environment, is the correct response for the preservation of our collections, it does present a wide array of challenges to all museums. How soon should we upgrade? How can we retro-fit an older structure? How can we afford to operate this system? These and other similar questions face all museum managers. The process of design, construction, modification and operation of the climate-control systems at the Arthur M. Sackler Museum dealt with many of these concerns and presents some solutions.

DEFINITIONS

To understand environmental control, we need to understand the ingredients. Temperature (dry-bulb) is a measurement of the heat present, and only the temperature of most interior spaces is controlled by normal domestic and commercial central-heating and air-conditioning equipment. Many museum objects, however, are adversely affected not only by abrupt temperature variation but also by changing moisture content. Changes in moisture levels can create expansion or shrinkage, and at very high or low levels can cause permanent damage. Moisture content should not be confused with relative humidity. Relative humidity (RH) is a measurement, expressed as a percentage, of the moisture content relative to the amount of water which that body of air could hold if saturated at the same temperature and pressure. For example, in a 22°C room at 50 per cent RH, there is vastly more moisture in the environment and, therefore, in an object than at 16°C at 50 per cent RH. Unlike air and other gases, most objects are more sensitive to changes in RH than to changes in environmental moisture content. Museum managers should specify stable levels of both temperature and RH to ensure the safety of their collections.[1]

Humidification is the process of adding moisture to the air in a conditioned area. It is usually accomplished by injecting steam or water into a moving air path. The moisture evaporates into the air which is then delivered to the space. Dehumidification is the reverse. Moisture is removed from the environment by passing moving air over a cold surface. The excess moisture condenses (dew) as the temperature of the air drops. The cooled air is then reheated and delivered to the space.

Particle filters are screens or bags constructed of a permeable mesh placed across the air stream to remove almost all airborne dirt. Gaseous filters (activated carbon, potassium permanganate) are chemicals placed in trays in the air path to remove inappropriate gases from the air. Both are essential to meet current museum climate-control standards.

To maintain optimum environmental conditions, climate-control designers rely on mechanical systems. Heating, ventilating and air-conditioning (HVAC) systems include fans with heating and cooling elements (coils), usually mounted in boxes called air handlers. These air handlers also contain the filters. They are connected to the spaces (display galleries, stores) by sheet-metal ducts or plenums (sealed architectural spaces designed to move air). Automatic sensors measure temperature and relative humidity in ducts and open areas. They control motors driven by air pressure which open and close heating and cooling valves and air dampers. Pneumatic controls send signals between sensors and motors by changing the air pressure in the connecting pipes. Digital controls send electronic signals on thin connecting wires. Digital systems also can convert pneumatic signals to digital, and vice versa. Digital control systems using computer logic and memory are capable of sophisticated control sequences: if x then y actions. They can also monitor conditions and send alarms. Because of these and other capabilities, direct digital control (DDC) is appropriate for many museums.

DESIGN

Precise control, economical operation, simplicity, reliability and low capital cost were the basic principles outlined in the climate-control programme for the Arthur M. Sackler Museum. In addition, the building programme required that the facility should perform a number of functions unrelated to the display and storage of the art collections. The offices, shops, darkrooms, library, lecture hall, etc., required different types of environmental control. Faced with a complex building and strict requirements, the mechanical designers elected to approach each function separately. They recognized that they could obtain the most accurate control of the art galleries and storage areas by controlling both humidity and temperature throughout the entire building. To do so, however, would have eliminated the economy of operation required by the owners. By approaching each function independently, the design could provide the most efficient solution for each requirement.

Offices have openable windows for ventilation, as required by the programme, and individual heating/cooling recirculating fans for independent temperature control. The work and meeting areas needed independent air handlers designed to provide temperature control with a combination of heating and cooling coils, plus the ability to use outside air for free cooling or heating if appropriate. Lobbies and corridors required only simple heating (no cooling) and ventilation systems to provide partial temperature control. Exhaust fans were specified for all spaces requiring positive ventilation (kitchens, rest rooms, fume hoods, copy machine rooms, equipment rooms, etc.). Finally, the art galleries and storage areas utilized central air handlers to provide both temperature and humidity control. These units incorporated the larger cooling coils required for dehumidification during the summer, provisions for steam humidification, and extra space for all the filters required. The result of these different approaches was the creation of a number of microclimates within the envelope of the new museum. This environmental configuration is common today in new and renovated museums.

Conventional contemporary humidification/dehumidification practices are the basis of the design for the total climate control of the art galleries and storerooms. In order to maintain stable conditions, the system needed to perform four interrelated functions: heat, cool, humidify and dehumidify. In New England, the climate may require any combination of these functions during any of the seasons. There are times in summer when the spaces will need heat and/or humidification, and periods in winter which require cooling and/or dehumidification. A good museum climate-control system should always be able to cope with that unusual weather condition which occurs once every few years. In addition, the design should eliminate any steam or water piping in or over the conditioned spaces to prevent collection damage from the inevitable leaking pipe.

In standard heating/cooling design, a thermostat in the conditioned space sends a signal to the air handler telling it to heat or cool the air to a set point, which will correct the temperature in that space and maintain a stable level. Complexity in the design of these systems arises, however, when one large air handler serves many unrelated spaces. A gallery, for example, filled with people and tungsten lights, might require cooling while the adjacent collection storage area, served by the same air handler, with no lights or people, may simultaneously require heating. The solution can take one of two forms. In some cases adjacent spaces with similar use patterns and heat loss/gain characteristics are grouped together to form a zone. A single thermostat in the zone controls an air handler for this group of spaces. Many buildings, because the spaces cannot be divided into zones easily, or because multiple air handlers cannot be located properly, or because more specific stability is required, use a design with remote heating coils. In such a configuration, a large air handler sends cool air to all the spaces it serves. This cool air will remove any unwanted heat. If the thermostat in any space calls for heat instead of cooling, a heating coil mounted in the supply duct serving just that space heats the air destined for the area. The room air is then returned to the main unit. Some air is exhausted to make room for the fresh outside air required for ventilation. The fresh air is mixed with the remaining returning room air, then heated or cooled to re-establish the cool discharge temperature. The remote heating coils then reheat the air when required to maintain space temperatures. In such a reheat system, the designers sacrifice operational efficiency for more precise control of the temperature in each room.

Recently, the efficiency of the reheat system has been improved by programming a computer to take the input from all the room thermostats and determine the optimum discharge temperature of the main air handler. If all the spaces require heats, for example, it is far more efficient to heat all the air just a few degrees than it is to cool it to an arbitrary temperature, then reheat it all again. Likewise, it is better only to cool the air to the level required by the warmest space, rather than cool to a level set for the worst possible condition and reheat most of the air most of the time. Engineers also use variable air volume devices (VAV) to reduce energy use. These devices reduce the flow of air to the space is too cool. With the reduced air flow, smaller reheat coils provide the heat required for the room. If most of these boxes go into this heating mode, the main fans reduce the volume of air discharged to reflect this reduced need for cooling, thereby saving energy. Fig. 13.1 illustrates a typical reheat/VAV system operating spaces with different heating/cooling requirements. This approach was selected for Harvard's new museum. Smaller museums will often utilize either the single-unit system or the multi-zone configuration.

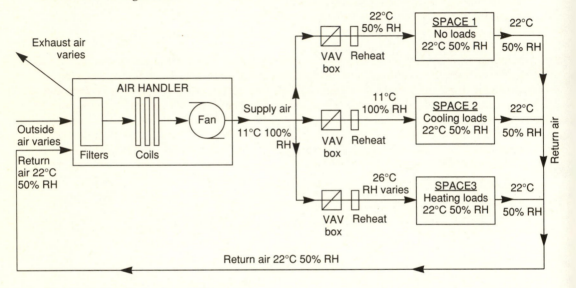

Fig. 13.1 Standard reheat VAV system

Humidity is much more difficult than temperature to control. Although there are many aspects of this problem, the primary difficulties converge around moisture migration, condensation and humidity measurement. Airborne moisture, like heat, will move to equalize distribution throughout the environment. If it is dry outside, interior moisture will move to exterior areas, and vice versa. The effect of this movement of moisture within museums, particularly where humidity-controlled areas abut uncontrolled spaces, is often difficult to control or overcome. The curatorial desire for open doors from galleries to uncontrolled public areas can cause severe migration of moisture in or out of controlled spaces. If the climate-control equipment is not large enough or if the migration is too great, then loss of humidity control will result. Sealed areas or building envelopes, plus vapour barriers which slow moisture migration just as insulation retards heat equalization, are essential. This can be very difficult to establish in older buildings without undertaking major renovations.

Condensation occurs when moist air cools and reaches its dewpoint (100 per cent RH). Particularly in climates with cold winters and in buildings without vapour barriers or insulation, condensation can be very serious. Major damage is often caused by condensing moisture freezing in the exterior walls of a porous structure. Bricks and stone spall (break apart), mortar fails, wooden structural members rot, plaster stains and decays, and so on. Even in new museum structures, condensation can be a serious problem. Any surface which is cold (metal window-frames, for instance) will collect condensation which can damage the building or its contents. The problem is not limited to cold weather either. During warm, humid weather, cold pipes or ducts will create the same situation with equally problematic results. In many older facilities, the damage caused by efforts to control humidity can be greater than the benefits derived. This is particularly true for historic buildings where it is often impossible to modify the significant interior surfaces for the installation of insulation and vapour barriers. Very few museums in northern climates have avoided this problem totally.

Humidity is difficult to measure accurately without the use of equipment which requires significant maintenance, calibration and operation. Because most standard humidity sensors are inaccurate and unpredictable, many mechanical engineers hesitate to rely on them for control. To maintain 50 per cent ± 5 per cent relative humidity, as programmed for the Arthur M. Sackler Museum, the sensors needed to be accurate to ± 2.5 per cent. Available sensors which maintain this accuracy require frequent and unrealistic maintenance and calibration. A few new digital sensors and some high-quality industrial pneumatic sensors seem better and appear to be able to maintain ± 5 per cent. With a 10 per cent inaccuracy built in by the best sensors, a climate-control system which relies on humidity sensors has no room for error in other aspects of its operation. Most designers of museum systems, therefore, now specify at least partial reliance on dewpoint control.

Dewpoint control is based on the well-defined and accurate relationship between dewpoint, wet- and dry-bulb temperatures and relative humidity as defined by the psychometric chart. It also relies on the demonstrated reliability of temperature sensors. In practice this means that, if air is cooled to 11°C and then reheated to 22°C, the RH will be 50 per cent or less in a space kept at 22°C. When the air is cooled to 11°C, excess moisture condenses and the air is dehumidified. If at 11°C the air is saturated (100 per cent RH), when it is heated to 22°C the moisture content remains the same but the relative humidity drops to 50 per cent. The reheat/VAV heating and cooling system adapted by the designers for the new museum is often used in connection with the dewpoint dehumidification system for accurate control. Fig. 13.1 shows a 11°C discharge from the main air unit. This guarantees that the spaces will not exceed 50 per cent RH at 22°C as long as no moisture migrates into the spaces or ducts from the unconditioned areas.

Humidification is required when the air is less than 100 per cent RH at 11°C. The designers in this case did rely in part on a humidity sensor in the return air duct which measured the moisture at 22°C. If it fell below 50 per cent, steam was injected into the 11°C air path until the return air humidity sensor read 50 per cent again. Because the 11°C air could absorb only up to 100 per cent RH before the excess water condensed, it was impossible to over-humidify the space. By injecting steam into cool rather than reheated air, the engineers avoided the major danger of gross over-humidification and eliminated some of the impact of the relative humidity sensors' known inaccuracy.

CONSTRUCTION

Construction problems and last-minute refinements are to be expected with any complex building, and the Arthur M. Sackler Museum was no exception. One issue which arose during the project involves the use of plenums constructed of gypsum drywall to deliver air to and return air from the galleries. The use of plenums reduced capital costs by avoiding costly sheet-metal ducts. To operate effectively, however, plenums must be airtight. Unconditioned air from other interior and exterior sources entering the circulation path makes humidity and often even temperature control impossible. We decided to remove the plenums and install metal ducts for the return air system. Based on our experience, it is our opinion that plenums in a museum climate-control system probably should be avoided if at all possible.

During construction, new museum environmental issues developed. We were fortunate to be able to incorporate these improvements into our new building. These changes included the substitution of clean stand-alone steam humidifiers for standard steam humidifiers which would have injected steam from the central steam system where corrosion inhibitors are added to protect the piping and boilers. This airborne contaminant adversely affects not only the art but also the inhabitants.[2] In addition, we are currently adding potassium permanganate filtration to remove formaldehyde, a probable threat to people and art. Formaldehyde is present in many products, including carpet, fabric and many building materials. As the gas escapes from these materials and enters the environment, it can react with a wide variety of museum objects creating, at fairly low concentrations, significant damage. It is also considered a health threat.[3]

Design and construction of museum climate-control systems is a complex undertaking. Based on our experience, it is our view that an independent review of the design concept by a firm skilled at troubleshooting and energy conservation is critical prior to final acceptance of any design. It is also our opinion that these systems require the highest-quality design skills, construction expertise and mechanical components.

MODIFICATION

At the end of the lengthy construction and start-up process, we were able to establish proper conditions in the galleries and art-storage areas. But there were still serious concerns. Control problems resulted in major fluctuations in space conditions. The stand-alone steam humidifiers failed to operate properly and consistently. The future operation of the original system would have required large maintenance and monitoring expenditures in order to avoid damage to the collections caused by suddenly shifting conditions. In addition, the initial energy consumption information indicated that the system would strain resources for years to come.

The museum management elected to modify the system. With the construction capital expended, it was clear that the cost of these changes would have to be recovered from energy savings. A consulting engineer[4] agreed to produce a simple, reliable modification that would pay for itself in three years. The design principles that the consultant adopted were logic and simplicity. They sought to eliminate extra parts and features which, in their opinion, often only exacerbated the problem. Given their inaccuracy, humidity sensors would not control any operations. Complicated steam humidifiers would be replaced with proven spray coil units. Where accurate control and measurement were required, only the best components would be used. To reduce operational costs, however, they had to redesign the standard solution to humidity control, i.e. the cool/reheat cycle. Their solution, which they call 'fresh air climate conditioning', represents an innovative possibility for both improved control and reduced operational cost. This efficient approach may have applications in many museums.

Gallery and art-storage spaces are subjected to a variety of environmental loads. Solar and lighting loads add heat, while people will add both heat and moisture. If the spaces are adjacent to either exterior areas or different interior conditions, the walls of the room will conduct heat or moisture. If the gallery or storeroom is well insulated and the walls are sealed with vapour barriers, the effect of the surrounding environment on the conditioned areas will be minimal. The consulting engineer indicated that the amount of heat and moisture added by people to typical museum spaces is insignificant when compared to the three major variable loads: solar gain, lights, and the outside air pumped in for ventilation.

Solar loads are related not only to the museum's architecture but also to the season. As the angle of the sun decreases in winter, solar loads increase as more sunlight pours in through vertical glazing. Solar heat at the Arthur M. Sackler Museum was insignificant in all controlled areas except one. On the upper floor of galleries (fourth floor) a large south-facing window was installed temporarily until a bridge could be constructed between the Fogg and Sackler Museums. The bridge has not yet been built and the window remains as a large solar source. The engineers indicated that solar film and shielding were required to reduce the gain and maintain temperature control.

Lighting loads for the galleries are substantial. In most cases, our small galleries carry at least 1,000 to 2,000 watts of display lighting; the larger ones more. This source of heat is constant during open hours, but when the museum is closed, the spaces are dark. The storage areas have much lower light loads and are usually dark except during infrequent use by appropriate staff. This pattern is typical of all museums and presents a challenge to the climate-control system. Both solar and lighting loads are variable, changing with the season, weather, time of day, and type of space. The climate-control system must be able to remove this extra heat from specific areas without adversely affecting other areas not subject to the same heat source.

Outside air is the most difficult variable to control. In New England there are very few days when outside conditions are 22°C and 50 per cent RH. On most days both the temperature and the humidity require conditioning. Solar, lighting and outside air loads all affect the temperature of the space, but only outside air affects the moisture level. By separating the loads, the engineers were able to pinpoint those which required specific control. They also pointed out two ways for unconditioned outside air to enter the spaces. First, it is intentionally added to the space by the air handlers for ventilation as discussed above. Second, air will also leak into the spaces around doors, ducts, etc.

To control humidity, it seemed logical to control the only major humidity variable, outside air. The consulting engineer's design, illustrated in Fig. 13.2, conditions the outside air as it is added to the system: fresh-air climate conditioning. The fresh air is always injected into supply air for the spaces at 11°C and 100 per cent RH. This conditioning is accomplished by separate air handlers with heating and cooling coils, and spray coil humidifiers. The incoming outside air is heated above 11°C. The air is then fully saturated with moisture (100 per cent RH) by passing through the cooling coil, which is constantly sprayed by a fine mist of cool water. This mist is produced by a pump which sends pressurized water out through nozzles arranged in an appropriate pattern. 'Washing' also cleans the air of large particles and some water-soluble gases, and hot air is cooled by the spray and the resulting evaporation. Steam humidification adds heat, but water washing removes heat and becomes a form of low-cost cooling. As the air passes

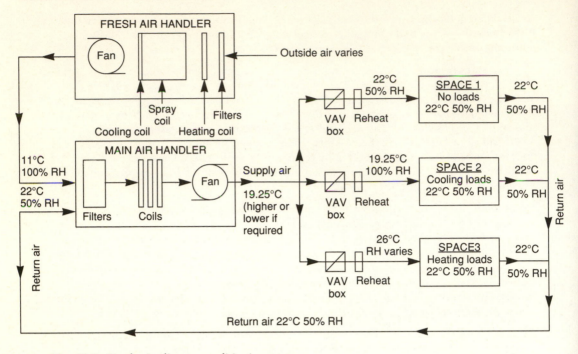

Fig. 13.2 Fresh-air climate conditioning system

through the wet cooling coil, it is also cooled to exactly 11°C. The cooling/heating functions are controlled by a highly accurate duct thermostat which ensures that the conditioned fresh air is always 11°C. The spray unit runs constantly, to maintain 100 per cent RH.

The engineer's design sets out to eliminate the penetration of outside air by pressurizing the spaces. By eliminating the exhaust function of the original air handler (compare Fig. 13.1 to Fig. 13.2), the main air unit supplies more air to the space than it returns. The amount of this difference is equal to the amount of conditioned outside air injected into the supply flow. The pressure will then increase in the spaces, and as this increases, the air will seek the leakage points and escape outward to the surrounding, unpressurized areas. The resulting exhaust of the spaces through leakage controls the flow of outside air into the spaces by eliminating that flow. It also allows excess heat or moisture to escape. The escaping air is constantly being replaced by the extra air supplied by the air handler. Our field experience indicates that, to control humidity with any system, positive pressurization of spaces is essential.

In the original sequence of operation, most of the returning air and all the new outside air was first cooled to 11°C, then reheated to 22°C. Now only the outside air is cooled to 11°C. The return air is left untouched. When the two are mixed together the resulting air temperature is 19.25°C (based on 75 per cent return air mixing with 25 per cent conditioned fresh air). The 19.25°C air is sent to the spaces and the reheats have only 2.75°C to heat, not 11°C. The energy savings are major. The new design, however, still did not address the lighting and solar loads. The cool, 11°C air of the original system could always be used by any space requiring cooling to offset these loads. The warmer 19.25°C discharge was not cold enough for this purpose. The consultant reasoned that the air should be only as cool as required by the space with the highest solar, lighting or other load. Sensors were placed in these areas to indicate when the spaces get too hot (or cold). This information is used to cool (or heat) all the air to just the right temperature for this worst case. Other areas less affected by these loads can adjust the specific room temperature with their reheats. This adjustment of the main-supply air temperature does use more energy, but provides precise response to varying load patterns. It also provides more specific control in each gallery.

Finally, we elected to install a new direct digital control system to control the operation of the climate-control air handlers. Our direct digital system is simply a number of stand-alone control units networked together. If one fails, the others will still operate. Central computers not only lack this feature but are also more difficult to connect to many remote points. With microcomputers talking to each other, it was easier to use multiple units positioned for easy conversion from the old pneumatic system. This system is also infinitely expandable as our needs grow. There are additional major advantages in these systems for museums since they are highly accurate and reliable, and they can send alarms based upon accurate information to any point. Old computer monitoring systems usually used separate sensors from those used to operate the air-handling equipment. This often resulted in false or confusing alarms when the sensors read differently. DDC uses the same information both for alarms and for control, and DDC systems can collect and save data on any condition. This is very useful in troubleshooting. They also permit central operation of the equipment, which often means prompt action to correct a serious problem.

OPERATION

Start-up and initial debugging of the modified system occurred just as we opened the new museum to the public. After the busy opening, the consulting engineer and museum staff spent six months running the new system, repairing and modifying as we went. In general the design worked well but it was plagued by two problems. First, the spray-wash humidifiers could not saturate the air to 100 per cent RH. After a variety of experiments, the problem was solved by using a finer nozzle and adding additional nozzles to the standard pattern. The other problem was more difficult to correct.

The original design specified a variety of fans and systems for the whole building. This was economical from an operational standpoint, but meant that the climate-controlled areas would have to function in an unpredictable surrounding environment, and the areas around these controlled areas would often be closer to outside conditions than to the controlled environment. The engineer and Harvard had assumed that the pressurization of the spaces would prevent unconditioned air from affecting the spaces. We found, to the contrary, that some building dynamics were making pressurization impossible. Particularly in winter, more air was leaving the building than was entering. In one area the extra air provided by the new system was not enough. Pressurization could not be maintained, and inappropriate air was leaking into the controlled spaces. To restore pressurization, the building is being tightened to restrict excessive exhaust of heated air.

In a similar way, we discovered that duct leakage can be very serious. Unconditioned air was being sucked through leaks in ducts on the roof and in other unconditioned areas. The application of sealer to these leaks and a waterproof membrane onto the roof ducts eliminated this problem. Our experience with rooftop units and ducts does indicate, however, that for any sort of museum application they should be avoided.

Economically, the system has met our objectives. The most recent review of our energy consumption compared to a projected spending with the original system indicates that our utility costs are about $2.25 per square foot per year versus $4.00. This saving is entirely attributable to the modifications to the climate-control systems.

CONCLUSIONS

Fresh-air climate conditioning is a simple, logical approach to museum climate control. Our experience at the Arthur M. Sackler Museum indicates that it is an economical alternative to the standard cool/reheat design. It is, on the other hand, not necessarily more reliable or accurate than the standard approach. Fresh-air climate conditioning requires tight ducts and well-insulated sealed spaces, since it is not tolerant of outside air penetration into the controlled areas, which the standard design with its high energy use can often overcome. But in a well-sealed building, with balanced total-building air intake and exhaust, this different approach has real advantages, and the cost savings are major. The design is easily incorporated into standard air-handling equipment, and the capital costs are moderate, with very few control dampers and moving parts. This alternative has proved to be precise, simple, reliable and efficient.

This paper first appeared in International Journal of Museum Management and Curatorship *5 (4) (1986), pp. 329–36.*

NOTES

1   G. Thomson (1978) *The Museum Environment*, London; Butterworths, 213–14.
2   P. Volent and N. S. Baer (1985) 'Volatile amines used as corrosion inhibitors in museum humidification systems', *The International Journal of Museum Management and Curatorship*, 4: 359–64.
3   P. B. Hatchfield and J. Carpenter (1986) 'The problem of formaldehyde in museum collections', *The International Journal of Museum Management and Curatorship* 5: 183–8.
4   Exergen Corporation, 307 West Central Street, Natick, Mass. 01760, USA.

14

Light and environmental measurement and control in National Trust houses

Sarah Staniforth

Sarah Staniforth describes the regime for monitoring and controlling the environment in National Trust houses where care of the contents has to be balanced with care of the building.

INTRODUCTION

Although the theme of the conference is the conservation and analysis of archaeological artefacts, and a relatively small proportion of the National Trust collections are of this category, the principles of preventive conservation apply as much to artefacts as they do to the decorative and fine art collections which make up the main part of the contents of the National Trust houses. There are now some two hundred historic houses and castles in the care of the National Trust in England, Wales and Northern Ireland.

The Conservation Service of the National Trust, which employed its first member of staff in 1975, now has twenty-five conservation advisers and conservators on the staff. It also takes advice from museum conservators. Much of the remedial conservation treatment is carried out by freelance conservators.

Great emphasis is placed on the preservation of the contents of the houses, and the key to this is to have a good practice of preventive conservation. There are two advisers in the Conservation Department, who, in collaboration with the Housekeeper and the twelve regional conservators, are responsible for the implementation of environmental measurement and control in the houses. The 'Bible' of the housestaff is *The National Trust Manual of Housekeeping* which explains the need for the right levels of light, heat and relative humidity, as well as giving instruction in methods of cleaning, handling, moving and storing the various objects found in National Trust collections (Sandwith and Stainton 1984). The first chapter, 'The right environment', will be familiar ground for *aficionados* of *The Museum Environment*; Garry Thomson has helped the National Trust considerably in its efforts to come to terms with these matters (Thomson 1986).

LIGHT

The recommended maximum levels for light are the same as those for museums, that is, up to 50 lux for the more sensitive materials such as textiles and works of art on paper, and 200 lux for oil-paintings. The specification for ultraviolet radiation is no more than 75 microwatts per lumen.

1 Measurement of visible and ultraviolet radiation

Each of the sixteen National Trust regions has an ultraviolet monitor, and this is used to test ultraviolet filters on installation, and every six months from then on. Every house has a light meter which is used to determine the levels to which blinds are raised when the houses are open to the public. We have found it unrealistic to ask that light meters be used on a daily basis to adjust the blinds according to the weather; the housestaff are too few to be able to cope with such an extra demand on their time. However, there are a few houses in which the enthusiasm of the housestaff does encourage them to tend the blinds assiduously, with the help of their light meters.

The majority of the houses take a series of readings in every room at the beginning of the season. They are asked to take readings in two locations in the room (usually one near a window and one away from it) and to set the blinds at different levels to ascertain how this affects the readings. They then repeat the readings in different weather conditions, which should give them a feel for the correct setting of the blinds. They may discover that it is impossible to reduce the light levels sufficiently, and a set of dark blinds may be recommended in addition to holland blinds (see section 3).

2 Protection against ultraviolet radiation

This is the first line of defence against photochemical damage and is uncontroversial; the filters are transparent and colourless, and therefore do not affect the quality of light in the rooms; most people are unaware of their existence unless they examine the windows very closely. The majority of rooms rely on daylight for their illumination, and therefore all sources of daylight are filtered to eliminate the ultraviolet content.

A campaign to install ultraviolet filtering has been carried out during the last ten years or so, and now almost all houses have been protected. However, the operation has not been without its problems. The first of these has been with the use of UV-absorbing varnish, which was the first method of protection used. The varnish is applied to the inside of window panes, and dries to a transparent colourless film when new. Unfortunately, in a number of houses this varnish has crazed and begun to peel off at any stage between two and five years from the date of its application. This has almost certainly been caused either by thermal expansion and contraction of thin old glass, which has occurred at a different rate to that of the varnish, or by condensation, and results in extremely disfiguring islands of varnish forming, not unlike the appearance of a bituminous varnish on a painting, although luckily not so dark!

Where the varnish has deteriorated in this way on a window it has been replaced with UV-absorbing films. These are transparent and colourless polyester (Melinex) sheets which are coated on one side with a layer of water-activated and pressure-sensitive adhesive. There have been some unfortunate instances in which we have found that the films are not absorbing enough of the UV wavelengths, and the level is found to be greater than 75 microwatts per lumen after the windows have been treated. When this has occurred it has been necessary to have the film removed and replaced with a filter with better UV-absorbing properties.

These problems have arisen when the UV-absorbing material is incorporated in the adhesive, as is the case for films supplied by many manufacturers. There seem to be great problems with quality control; sometimes not enough absorber is added to the adhesive formulation or the adhesive is not thick enough when applied to the polyester. Filters in which the UV-absorber is dyed into the polyester, as well as being added to the adhesive, are generally superior in all respects. Their UV-absorbing properties are good, and they are long-lasting; the filter protects the film itself from photochemical deterioration. They are generally guaranteed for five years, but the suppliers suggest that the films will probably last for ten years or more. We cannot comment on this as no film has been in place for that long.

To avoid the installation of faulty filters, we now test samples of film before application. It is important to test a piece of every roll used, to ensure that the quality is consistent between batches. The absolute characteristics of the filters may be determined by recording a spectrophotometric transmission curve. A transmission spectrophotometer is a standard piece of analytical equipment in chemistry laboratories. Although it is unlikely that museums will have their own instrument, analytical services of local universities will almost certainly be able to help.

Garry Thomson suggests the following specification for the transmission curve of a UV-filter. Transmission at 400nm should be less than half the transmission at 550nm. Transmission at 320 and 380nm should be less than 1 per cent of the transmission at 550nm (Thomson 1986: 17).

3 Reduction of visible light levels

In many ways, the National Trust has an easier task in controlling visible light levels than museums. The main reason for this is the relatively limited opening hours. Most of the houses are open from 2 p.m. to 6 p.m. no more than six days a week (24 hours per week). All the houses (with the exception of the few that are managed by local authorities) are closed from the end of October to the beginning of April. That makes the total number of opening hours per year 720 hours compared with four times that for the majority of museums. When houses are closed, shutters are drawn, which eliminates daylight and provides additional security. Dark blinds are used in rooms without shutters. In this way, the contents of a room are only illuminated when the house is open to the public and when the room is being cleaned.

Daylight usually enters rooms through side windows rather than through roof lights. Systems of electronically controlled louvred blinds are unacceptable because of interfering with the architecture of the building. The expense and maintenance costs also discount their use. However, there are two houses in which they have been used to reduce the light levels entering through roof lights. The basic method of reducing visible light levels is by using roller blinds fitted to the inside of the windows. Traditionally these would have been made from window holland, a glazed linen, but this is now unobtainable and a synthetically treated cotton is used. In appearance this is virtually indistinguishable from holland. One set of blinds is cream-coloured, and if it is necessary to reduce levels still futher, a second darker-coloured (dark green, navy or black) blind is fitted. The levels are set as described in section 1. In some houses sun curtains are used instead of blinds, as their appearance is more in keeping with the character of the house. The most important function of sun blinds and curtains is to eliminate sunlight, by far the most damaging radiation to enter a room. Obviously the range of visible light levels falling on the objects in a room will cover a wider range than those obtained when a photocell-controlled system is used.

The need to protect the contents from damaging light levels is explained in many of the guidebooks for the houses. Typical wording can be found in the guidebook for Attingham Park: 'Visitors will find that the windows are fitted with holland blinds, which reduce the harmful effects of daylight upon furniture, paintings, textiles and other vulnerable materials.'

TEMPERATURE AND RELATIVE HUMIDITY

Regular readings of temperature and relative humidity were started in 1982, as described in the following sections. As with light levels, we cannot hope to have the close control possible with museum-type air-conditioning installations; these can seldom be accommodated within the structure of a historic house. However, we aim to keep the relative humidity (RH) within the range 50–65 per cent. Temperature (T) control is less critical, particularly as the houses are closed to the public during the winter months. During this time it is only necessary to heat the houses to keep the relative humidity as constant as possible and to prevent water freezing in pipes.

1 Measurement of relative humidity

The housestaff are asked to keep a weekly record of temperature and relative humidity. These spot readings are generally taken on one day each week, in at least four rooms (if possible facing the four points of the compass) and outside. They are recorded between 0800 and 0900 in the morning and between 1500 and 1600 in the afternoon. These readings are then plotted on a graph. The houses are equipped with whirling hygrometers or electronic instruments. The weather conditions and whether the heating is on or off are also indicated on the graphs. Where the room is well buffered against changes in temperature and RH, the spot readings give a good indication of the conditions in the room. However, we have found that in some locations the RH fluctuates greatly, falling to minimum in the middle of the day when there is solar gain increasing the temperature, and rising to high levels during the night. The extremes are often missed by the spot readings. Where 24-hour records are needed thermohygrographs or solid-state memory temperature and relative humidity recorders have been installed.

The use of electronic recording devices has made an enormous difference to our capacity for controlling the environment in the houses. Obviously the fundamental requirement for control is to have reliable records, and the housestaff have only limited time for helping the Conservation Department with this work. The advantage of electronic equipment is that it requires infrequent attention. We extract data quarterly. Since autumn 1985, one hundred recorders have been installed in the houses.

2 Control of temperature and relative humidity

The fundamental method of controlling RH is through temperature control. If the RH is high, it can be reduced by raising the temperature. In the early 1980s the Government Department of Energy operated an Energy Efficiency Survey Scheme. They agreed that surveys to review environmental control for conservation in historic houses which open to the public and which recommend energy-efficient improvements to plant, controls, instrumentation, etc. qualified for grant assistance. With this help, the National Trust commissioned thirty short surveys and six extended surveys from Bob Hayes, a consultant civil engineer.

By looking at meteorological records and the outside readings recorded by the house-staff, we established that an increment of 5°C between outside and inside temperature will keep the RH within a house between 50 and 65 per cent for all but exceptional weather conditions (Staniforth and Hayes 1987). This can be achieved by using weather-compensating controllers on central heating systems. An obvious prerequisite for this method of control to work is that the heating systems for the showrooms are not connected to those for the domestically occupied parts of the house! Unfortunately, this has often been the case, and as the flats are invariably on the end of the heating circuit, unnecessarily high temperatures, and therefore dangerously low relative humidity, have occurred in showrooms. This low level of heating can also be supplied by using electric heaters controlled with humidistats (Staniforth, Hayes and Bullock 1994).

Where there is no requirement for heating during the winter, it is useful to consider the possibility of direct RH control through dehumidification. The average external RH in the UK during the winter months is between 80 per cent and 90 per cent. Unheated houses will therefore tend to be damp during the winter. A study carried out at Monk's House near Lewes in 1985 showed that dehumidifiers can achieve the same measure of RH reduction as heating, using as little as one-fifth of the energy input, provided that the space can be made relatively draught-proof (say one air change per hour) (Hayes 1985). In the several areas that are now being controlled in this way, we have found that the most crucial factor is to ensure good draught-proofing. In a room this will involve ensuring that there are no gaps around the windows and doors, and that the chimney is blocked. The draught-proofing is generally a case of trial and error, until the RH recordings show that the dehumidifier is in control of the atmosphere.

In stores, a sealed area can be simply and cheaply constructed by making a polythene tent. This approach has been used at Calke Abbey. The building underwent a complete restoration between 1985 and 1989. The contents of the house were removed during this time and were stored in an indoor riding school. A tent was constructed by fixing polythene over a scaffolding and timber batten frame, to enclose a volume $6 \times 10.5 \times 5$ metres. Two refrigerative dehumidifiers with a condensing capacity of 3 litres a day at 10°C and 80 per cent RH were installed. The RH was reduced to 60 per cent over a six-week period while the RH outside the tent in the riding school had an average of 80 per cent. As refrigerative dehumidifiers tend to ice up in cold weather (the defrost cycle does not clear the condensing coil), two 50W greenhouse heaters were fitted next to the cold coils. These were plugged into a froststat set at 5°C. This prevented the dehumidifiers icing up, even during the excessively cold spell during February 1986. In subsequent projects, when low temperatures are likely to occur, dessicant dehumidifiers which are effective at all temperatures, are used rather than refrigerative.

This method of controlling RH has many applications throughout the National Trust. It would be equally applicable in areas of museums that do not require heating. But for its successful operation it is essential that the area to be controlled is well sealed.

CONCLUSION AND FUTURE PLANS

This is a very brief account of light and environmental control in National Trust houses. Our aim for the future is to complete the installation of ultraviolet-absorbing filters, to check and replace filters as their UV-absorbing properties decrease (if this happens), to complete the installation of sunblinds and sun curtains, and to provide a method of blackout during closed hours in all properties. We will continue surveys of the environments in the houses, which will enable us to improve the control of relative humidity using the heating systems in the houses. We hope to improve storage conditions throughout the National Trust properties by building polythene tents and using dehumidifiers to control the RH in unheated areas.

It is a great challenge to adapt museum methods of environmental control to the very different circumstances of historic houses, but one which all the members of the Conservation Department and their advisers are tackling with great relish!

This paper first appeared in J. Black (ed.) (1987) Recent Advances in the Conservation and Analysis of Artifacts (London: University College London Press). It has been updated for this volume.

REFERENCES

Hayes, R. (1985) *'Monk's House, Rodmell – a case study in atmospheric humidity control using a dehumidifier – extended energy survey report'*, internal National Trust document.

Sandwith, H. and Stainton, S. (1984) *The National Trust Manual of Housekeeping*, London: Allen Lane.

Staniforth, S. and Hayes, R. (1987) 'Temperature and relative humidity measurement and control in National Trust houses', to be published in *Preprints of 8th Triennial Meeting of ICOM Committee for Conservation*.

Staniforth, S., Hayes, R. and Bullock, L. (1994) 'Appropriate technologies for relative humidity control for museum collections housed in historic buildings', to be published in *Preprints of the IIC Conference on Preventive Conservation*, Ottawa.

Thomson, G. (1986) *The Museum Environment* (2nd edn), London: Butterworths.

15

The Clore Gallery for the Turner collection at the Tate Gallery: lighting strategy and practice

Peter Wilson

In recent years there has been increasing interest in the use of natural light in museums – its special qualities can enliven an otherwise uninspiring space. The rigorous enforcement of 50 lux and 200 lux standards makes the effective use of natural light almost impossible. Peter Wilson describes how an understanding of long-term exposure can be used to design a lighting system that meets conservation standards and yet preserves the desirable qualities of daylight.

THE LESSONS OF THE RECENT PAST

Designed by the architects Llewelyn-Davies, Weeks, Forestier-Walker and Bor, the last major extension to the Tate Gallery was opened in 1979.[1] It was supposed to represent the ideal compromise between the requirements of display and the preservation of paintings. Yet when it opened there was immediately considerable critical disquiet about its extravagant superstructure of lighting control hardware.[2] Soon, there was equally vigorous criticism not only of the hardware itself but also of its efforts to deal with rapidly changing conditions of weather.[3] One point which seemed largely to have escaped notice, even in the technical press, was that, in most circumstances, the building delivered superbly well those display conditions which the brief required of it. The brief had been drawn up in the climate of the received wisdom of the early 1970s (for the most part emanating from the conservation lobby – a group to which the present author then unashamedly owed primary allegiance). It had attempted to mitigate the worst effects of the National Gallery solution where daylight merged inextricably with artificial light behind a translucent diffusing ceiling. The 1979 building had skylights of clear glass so that in theory the weather could be experienced and the sunscreening was programmed to ignore small variations of natural light. But, nonetheless, the brief had decreed that the lighting should be uniform, constant (i.e. varying only between narrowly defined limits) and should maximize the use of daylight whilst excluding all trace of direct sunlight from the building envelope. All this was satisfactory achieved and yet the result was, in terms of display, a failure. Why?

TOWARDS A NEW POLICY

When the chance came to reassess our lighting brief, and to think afresh for the Clore Gallery, it was necessary to take a critical look at our existing lighting-control philosophy. This was as important for the conservator as for the curator because the rigid standards which had previously been applied were in danger of being abandoned since they produced a visually unsatisfactory result in a daylit gallery. At the time, David Loe of the Bartlett School of Architecture and Planning at University College London (who had worked on the lighting design for the 1979 building) was doing some very relevant work which suggested that the illuminance (light level) chosen in the existing standard needed to be adjusted upwards.[4,5] Were there other factors which needed reconsideration? First of all the reasons for providing daylight at all were re-examined. Sir Norman Reid, the Tate Gallery's director throughout the period of the design and construction of the previous building, had, we later discovered, expressed the need succinctly in an interview given to the press:

> we had a strong liking for the variation which natural light produces. If the environment is dead level you do get a sensation, after a bit, almost of boredom, because nothing ever changes. Whereas, in this country, natural light has extraordinary variations, which can change in ten minutes.[6]

There were, however, obvious advantages in excluding natural light altogether, since without a glazed or partially glazed roof the building would be both better insulated and subject to much lower solar gains. As a result the air-conditioning plant could be smaller, as could its ducts. Even with a sophisticated and variable artificial lighting system to replace daylight, the building would be less costly, and more display space could be bought for the money available. However, neither the curators nor the trustees were prepared to consider this possibility seriously: they were instinctively against it. Yet they were, in general, equally unable to articulate clearly just what it was in daylight, as opposed to artificial light, that was required for the good viewing of art.

This needed investigation. We took as our starting point the last brief, because clearly we had removed whatever quality it was that was needed for a successful daylit gallery. Did the light need to be brighter? Conservation considerations apart, this could be achieved with artificial light, so higher illuminance alone could not be the essential quality. Did the light need to be less uniform? This also could be achieved with artificial light. So did it need to vary with time? Yes it *did*: at last we were beginning to establish a quality of daylight that we must include. Could we not vary the artificial lighting with time? No, everyone agreed that the quality of natural light most prized was its unpredictability and unevenness! This realization seems in retrospect rather obvious, but it was very hard to formalize at the time, in spite of Sir Norman Reid's clear statement. There remained one puzzling question: daylight is not always varying in an obvious way and yet it was generally perceived to be superior in all weathers, times and seasons. It seemed that there was an element of 'psychological set' in the visitors – when looking at paintings under natural lighting, however modified, they seemed to remember the exterior conditions far longer than any period of adaptation of the perceptual system of eye and brain would explain. It was a question of expectation; in midsummer on a brilliantly sunny afternoon the light in the gallery *ought* to be brighter than on a rainy November afternoon.

An informal analysis of written comments received at the information desk supported this view. Most criticism of the 1979 building's lighting came on sunny summer days when the light levels in the galleries were actually very similar to those achieved in the winter. In summer the louvre system in the 1979 building has to close partially to exclude direct sunlight, but it is actually often possible for this louvre configuration to require concurrently artificial lighting as back-up because on clear days relatively little light comes from the north sky. The subjective effect is of louvres unnecessarily closed and artificial light needlessly applied. In fact, it was the very changeability of English daylight which had beaten the designers of the 1979 building – the narrow range of illuminances permissible *inside* the building could only be achieved with rapid, sometimes noisy and always noticeable, response from the external louvres. The desired variation of daylight *was*, despite the Tate Gallery's aspirations, being suppressed.

FROM ILLUMINANCE CONTROL TO ANNUAL EXPOSURE QUOTAS

Clearly the Clore Gallery brief had to encourage the design of a building which would allow the full range of variation of natural lighting to be reflected in the galleries. The light on the gallery walls would have to be constantly changing its colour, intensity and distribution in response to the exterior conditions, though this was not difficult in itself, since a greenhouse does precisely that! However, we had to meet the requirements not only of display but also of conservation. The problem for the conservation scientist was to reconcile science with conservation. It was obvious that the recognized illuminance standards were arbitrary, whilst Loe's work had demonstrated that they were inadequate, and since those standards were founded on display criteria and not conservation considerations, we could justify an increase based on his work. Nevertheless, the system now proposed would seemingly lead to even higher illuminances and we had to be sure that we would not be needlessly exposing works of art to excessive light. The natural variation of daylight is large, but how could we preserve its character without a tremendous increase in annual exposure? One fact is obvious and also crucial: every hour spent at, say, 100 lux above the target average illuminance needs to be compensated by an hour spent at 100 lux below that average illuminance. This whole strategy could be achieved only if, apart from the exclusion of daylight at all times when the galleries were closed, the periods spent at below-average illuminances were acceptable to the public, and so the building had to look brightly lit at the lowest possible illuminance. The times when below-average (and this does not mean inadequate!) illuminance would be psychologically most acceptable would be when there is little or no daylight at all: i.e. at the latter end of days in the winter months. Under these circumstances the galleries would rely wholly on artificial lighting. It was crucial to ensure that this would be effective even at relatively low levels of illuminance.

We had to be able to set a criterion for acceptability (in conservation terms) for a lighting solution which had the potential of continuous variation. Spot readings of illuminance would tell us nothing as the value might, for example, have been half as great two minutes beforehand and double a minute later. The present author had, in 1979, tried to lay the ground rules for such a new approach by 'entering a plea for the replacement of an adherence to arbitrary [light] levels with an approach based on a consideration of total exposure'[7] in a review of Garry Thomson's *The Museum Environment* [8] which had appeared the previous year.

Thomson, whilst championing his long-established illuminance standards, knew only too well that alternative strategies based on total exposure *were* possible and recommended them to those who could not afford a stricter regime of automatic control. He also acknowledged the shortcomings of the then current generation of control systems:

> sometimes a work of art may be caught in a light that reveals unexpected or rare beauty. This is the nearest we may be able to get to identifying the peculiar quality of daylight – its infinite variability . . . out of doors everyone has felt exhilaration when the sun, emerging from cloud, exerts its pervasive influence . . . such opportunities are lost . . . under heavily controlled daylight.[9]

In retrospect, it is possible to affirm that our insight into our problem owed much to Thomson's book. Our much-needed criterion was also provided by him: 'Instead of aiming to achieve a steady illuminance . . . we can work out the total annual dose of illumination, or exposure, equivalent to this'.[10] We judged that our criterion for exposure should be that the potential damage by light would be no greater than it would be in a gallery operating at a constant 200 lux over an 8-hour day, $6\frac{1}{2}$ days aweek, every week of the year. Such a control regime would allow an exposure of:

$$200 \times 8 \times 6.5 \times 52 = 540,800 \text{ lux hours per annum}$$

So we had a little over 0.5 million lux hours as an annual target.

We could be confident that exposure control was practicable only if we could have a method of recording or logging the total exposure on each display wall. This requirement could be met: again we were indebted to Thomson, whose pioneering experiences with data logging were available to us,[11] and the Clore Gallery would certainly need an extensive data-logging system. The brief was being worked up at a time of rapid and significant development in the field of electronics and microcomputing. Equipment was becoming vastly more sophisticated and costs were falling all the time. It appeared that we would be able to have a photocell monitoring the illuminance on each major display surface in the building and be able to integrate the results of frequent spot readings to provide a running exposure total for each wall. About this time it became obvious that an exciting possibility had emerged: if we extended the logging specification to include position monitoring of the sunscreening and control of the motors driving it, the lighting control strategies applicable to the building would then be limited only by the size of the computerized logger and the sophistication of its software. Such a computer could control the artificial lighting as well. Furthermore, we could proceed with as innovative a strategy as we liked, and not only could we monitor its performance and modify its control system in the light of experience, but also mimic earlier strategies, or adopt entirely new ones, as yet undefined. All this was a far cry from the hard-wired logic circuitry of the control system of the building we had only just completed, in which a simple modification to a time delay in the lighting switching programme had necessitated the removal and replacement of no fewer than forty-two small electrical components!

THE DESIGN PHASE: PRACTICAL REFINEMENTS

Our initial briefing for the design team, though not formalized into a document, was roughly as follows: the galleries would be naturally lit, and they would have external sunscreening, probably using wide louvres of the type used on the 1979 building. There would be no need for total uniformity, whatever the external conditions; rather the interiors should echo the variability of daylight. The louvres would need to close tightly to exclude daylight during non-public hours. It also made sense to specify that louvres could be partially opened to reduce overall exposure on any wall which was tending to receive excessive illumination over a significant period (a month, say). Artificial lighting needed to be even, but not dull. The architect rejected the notion of imitating daylight and instead offered the solution of 'uplighters' to counter the problem of the oppressive darkness of the ceiling above the lighting. This was a problem experienced not only in the 1979 building but also in recent relighting schemes in the older galleries of the Tate Gallery.

The design team came up with a system of vertically glazed roof sheds which reflected the light down onto the 'picture zone' of the gallery wall through a slot via a suitably angled central baffle. The design process moved rapidly to an intensive period of model testing. It was of great benefit to the Tate Gallery to be treated as a 'technical' client by the consultants and thus to be able to contribute directly to the model-testing phase. Many valuable ideas were formulated during the course of these discussions.

The model was tested under a standardized artificial sky which mimics an overcast day. Under these special conditions we needed a uniform internal illumination so that we could be sure that the design did not light one wall excessively rather than another. If this were the case, there would be scant chance of achieving similar annual exposures on all walls. Our aim was that variations of intensity round the walls would result from the directional variations of daylight and not be an artefact caused by the building itself. The testing process revealed that, under overcast conditions, there were optimum louvre positions which maximized the ratio of internal/external illumination (the so-called 'daylight' factor). These optimum positions involved angling the louvres above the horizontal so that their upper surfaces were reflecting additional light onto the baffle. This effect was dubbed 'scooping'.

The daylight factor associated with any particular louvre position could be calculated. Moreover, in combination with available statistical data,[12] it could be used to calculate those louvre positions which would achieve our target exposures. The optimum position could be reduced for times when the target would be likely to be exceeded. The louvres on any aspect could, in addition, be closed or partially closed to exclude direct sunlight from the picture zone. It should be emphasized that it has always been intended that such positions would be preprogrammed. There was no question of having a system which responded to changes as they occurred: this was positively undesirable as it would damp out precisely those unpredictable changes of natural light that we had been at such pains to preserve.

REALIZATION: 'IN-SERVICE' REFINEMENTS

At the time of writing (December 1986), the commissioning of the logging system lies before us, and the performance specification for sunscreening control and data logging finally produced by the Tate Gallery in March 1982 has undergone substantial revision. We are to have a computerized system[13] which allows on-line monitoring (current data being available to the system operator in coloured mimic diagrams on screen). This is designed to calculate and store hourly, weekly, monthly and annual exposures for each display surface, to monitor temperature and relative humidity in each gallery, and to control each louvre bank from its own 'look-up table' of positions, as well as to monitor and record those positions so that the causes of apparent anomalies in the recorded exposure data can be resolved. This mass of data will be put to good use: real 'daylight factors' will be available to replace those of the model. Long-term 'high spots' and 'low spots' can be identified and corrected. It also allows the construction of complex, user-definable, artificial lighting control algorithms which remove the possibility of the on–off flashing Christmas-tree light syndrome to which the 1979 building is prone. The system is furnished with a 'fourth generation' control language[14] which allows a technically aware user to generate new control routines and modify old ones without being a computer programmer. The system has the capacity to take over control of the 1979 building, using the new strategies, and the Tate Gallery is well advanced with its plans to provide similar louvre and lighting systems for the older display galleries.

FUTURE DEVELOPMENTS

The Tate Gallery changes its displays frequently (although in fact the Turner oil-paintings in the Clore Gallery will not be moved very often) and the system described above offers the potential of an object-by-object rather than a wall-by-wall quota. This is a longer-term aim which is not yet realizable, but the integration of data from the Tate Gallery's projected mainframe-based collections management system[15] with logged environmental data, using a spreadsheet software, is under active consideration.

All this affordable high technology has been applied to give visitors a seemingly low-technology space in which to view the works of art. Indeed, they should not be conscious of the intervention of technology. It is perhaps appropriate to temper euphoria with a note of caution. We have relaxed an arbitrary lighting rule which had been imposed to preserve our collection. Our reasons for doing so are empirical but the justification is at best informed supposition. Conservators and conservation scientists are increasingly called to account for and justify their strictures – should we not also ask curators and the viewing public to demonstrate the genuineness of their affirmed desire for naturally lit galleries? Many questions remain to be asked: maybe views out are more important than natural light from above? The Clore Gallery has such a view, too, onto the front gardens and the riverbank. The control and monitoring systems we will have in the new building will give us a perfect experimental tool to vary subtly the lighting conditions, or to exclude daylight altogether, and to keep records of exactly what are the conditions experienced. The opportunity to test public response by questionnaire will enable us to separate fact from myth: the conservator may yet strike back!

This paper first appeared in Museum Management and Curatorship, *Vol. 6, No. 1 (March 1987), pp. 37–42.*

NOTES

1 D. E. Church (1979) 'Picture gallery lighting', *DOE Construction* 16.
2 Kenneth Robinson, 'Tate ah Tate', *The Listener*, 31 May 1979, p. 746.
3 William Feaver, 'The endurance test', *The Observer*, 27 May 1979, p. 14.
4 David Lawrence Loe (1981) 'Appropriate lighting conditions for viewing works of graphic art,' MPhil thesis, University College London.
5 D. L. Loe, E. Rowlands and N. F. Watson (1982) 'Preferred lighting conditions for the display of oil and watercolour paintings', *Lighting Research and Technology* 14(4): 173–92.
6 Dennis Barker on Monday column, 'Tate officials had to consult lists to remember who painted what abstract', *The Guardian*, 12 March 1979.
7 P. Wilson (1979) 'Review of: "The Museum Environment" by G. Thomson', *The Conservator*, pp. 46–7.
8 Garry Thomson (1978) *The Museum Environment*, London: Butterworths.
9 Ibid., 31–2.
10 Ibid., 30.
11 An account was later published: Garry Thomson (1981) 'Control of the environment for good or ill? Monotoring', *National Gallery Technical Bulletin* 5: 3–13.
12 D. R. G. Hunt (1979) Availability of Daylight, Watford: Building Research Establishment, Department of the Environment.
13 MICROFAST 2 from Lee Micromatics Ltd.
14 FLO-GEN from Lee Micromatics Ltd.
15 Provided by STIPPLE Database Services Ltd.

16

Construction materials for storage and exhibition

Ann Brooke Craddock

Conservators and curators have long been aware of the effects of gases emitted by storage and display materials on objects. The selection of materials is extremely complex as many which have been popular in the past and have excellent properties, such as wood, are now seen as potentially hazardous to certain types of object. At the same time curators are faced with a bewildering choice of new materials. Ann Brooke Craddock's article describes these concerns in detail.

Storage furniture and exhibition cases have traditionally been made of wood and wood products, with adhesives, papers, fabrics and metals used to join, line and decorate them. As is often the case, the tried and true methods are not necessarily the best. For the past two decades studies and direct observation have suggested that traditional materials used for storage furniture are contributing to the degradation of objects rather than to their protection. This essay attempts to present sufficient data to allow an informed choice among the construction materials that are within the reach of a given budget. While some of the information may appear very technical, it will be of use in discussing a collection's storage needs with architects, engineers and manufacturers.

Recent studies and actual damage in museum storage have demonstrated the dangers posed by wood, wood composites, adhesives and some of the traditional surface coatings. The off-gassing of volatile components, primarily acids from wood and formaldehyde from adhesives, has been shown to cause significant corrosion of metal objects. Studies have also identified more subtle, slower changes in photographs, paper, textiles and pigments. Nevertheless, until alternative materials can be developed to match the low cost of wood, its availability and the ease with which it can be used for construction, it is likely that wood will continue to be used to make storage furniture. It must be understood, however, that the use of wood-based construction materials will not result in the best possible protection of collections in storage and on display. Even the less volatile, less acid and more stable wood products only reduce the risk of damage to sensitive artefacts, but do not eliminate it. Wood-based building materials can be grouped in categories of greater or lesser 'harmfulness,' and the following pages will focus on the safer choices.

Solid wood is rarely used to construct cases, shelves and cabinets because it is expensive and has a low span-to-weight ratio. The material most commonly used for the purpose is plywood, which is made up of several thin sheets of wood laminated together by an adhesive. Also used are particleboard and fibreboard; both are mixtures of woody particles or fibres with adhesives. Sometimes Melamine or Formica is applied to the surfaces of these boards. Solid wood and composite boards may emit acids; in addition the composites will off-gas the degradation products of their adhesives. Evaluation of the relative merits of wood materials shows solid mahogany to be the safest, followed by exterior plywood. Before funds are committed to wood construction, alternatives should be considered.

Anodized aluminium and coated steel, if correctly manufactured, are the safest materials known.

WOOD

Over time wood releases primarily acetic acid, formic acid at one hundred times lesser concentration, and small amounts of propionic acid, isobutyric acid, alcohols and formaldehyde. The evolution and off-gassing of these organics increases dramatically at higher temperatures and at relative humidity above 80 per cent. Even after long periods of time wood may continue to evolve organic acids, and even 'aged' wooden storage cabinets may still be unsafe. If wood is used, no object, except other wood, ceramic, glass, or stone, should ever be in direct contact with its surface. Shelves and drawers should be lined with Mylar or glass. To lessen the danger of acid emission for wood-based storage units containing metal artefacts, it is extremely important to maintain low relative humidity and temperature and to avoid rapid fluctuations of these two factors (metals should not be exposed to levels of relative humidity above 45 per cent).

The potential acidity of wood depends on so many factors that only gross rankings of species can be made. Mahogany, walnut, spruce and some tropical woods such as iroko, ramin and obeche appear to be among the least acid and therefore reasonably safe woods, unless they have been treated with insecticides that may have undesirable residual effects. True mahogany, American (Swietenia group) and African (Khaya group), have also been tested and found to be safe. False, or Philippine mahogany (Schorea group), has not been tested, and therefore is not recommended. White pine is very acidic, yellow pine is not, but both give off many other organic gases that could harm materials other than metals. Oak, chestnut and steamed beech are the most dangerous woods and should never be used.

ADHESIVES

Most commonly used adhesives off-gas a considerable amount of formaldehyde. Under certain conditions formaldehyde crosslinks proteins and cellulose, and changes the colour of some pigments; under ambient museum conditions, it readily causes formate corrosion on metals and causes formate crystals to grow on unstable, weeping glass. Formate crystals on lead or alloys of lead are toxic if inhaled, and are also very difficult to remove.

Wood composition boards are predominantly fabricated with three adhesives or adhesive combinations – urea-formaldehyde, melamine-formaldehyde, or phenol-formaldehyde. The latter is significantly more stable than the urea or melamine-based adhesives; therefore, only composition wood products made with a phenol-formaldehyde adhesive are presently recommended for use in storage areas. Research on the effects of composition boards and their adhesives on museum collections has just begun. The following recommendations are drawn from these preliminary findings and from studies done by the plywood and particleboard industries. They are based on the most current information available, but recommendations may change as more research is published.

INTERIOR PLYWOOD, PARTICLEBOARD, AND MEDIUM-DENSITY FIBREBOARD

Most interior plywood, particleboard and medium-density fibreboard are fabricated with a urea-formaldehyde resin adhesive that is inexpensive and does not discolour the wood veneer. This adhesive gives off significant amounts of formaldehyde after manufacture because excess formaldehyde is used to react the resin. In addition, the formaldehyde is only loosely bound to the wood moisture and the resin after manufacture. For this reason newly made storage cases are especially likely to have high levels of formaldehyde. Even after airing and ageing, the cases are not safe because the urea-formaldehyde adhesive is never stable. Moisture or an increase in relative humidity or temperature can easily trigger a release of formaldehyde in significant amounts.

Interior plywood and particleboard manufactured earlier than nine years ago are especially suspect because they were made without any industry or government standards. More recently, in response to health concerns, the industries have begun to formulate the adhesives with lower formaldehyde-urea ratios and to incorporate formaldehyde scavengers to react with the excess chemicals. The Department of Housing and Urban Development's standard for manufactured homes requires that interior plywood have a formaldehyde emission of less than 0.2 parts per million (ppm) and that interior particleboard have an emision of less than 0.3 ppm. Emission certificates for each lot of board are available upon request. Yet, even at these levels, formaldehyde has rapidly corroded objects in newly constructed storage units, an indication that the standards are not low enough to prevent deterioration of certain metals and other materials.

If an institution has no option but to use a wood product with urea-formaldehyde adhesive, plywood that is laminated on all sides and edges appears to be the safest. Solid lamination has been shown to reduce formaldehyde emission to a level below that of unlaminated particleboard. In choosing a plywood one must not use a surface veneer grade below B, since the lower grade veneers have splits and knots that will allow more formaldehyde to escape.

Because its hardwood veneer provides an easily painted surface, architects and cabinet-makers prefer to use interior plywood. Exterior plywood is made exclusively of softwoods and does not have the fine surface finish of an interior plywood. However, exterior plywoods are manufactured with phenol-fromaldehyde adhesive, and therefore contain less formaldehyde than interior plywood and particleboard. The stamped initials of the American Plywood Association certify that a plywood was made with phenol-formaldehyde resins.

It is possible to find hardwood veneer with a phenol-formaldehyde adhesive by contacting a large lumberyard or the Hardwood Plywood Manufacturers Association. Manufacturers of interior plywood are also producing a board bonded with a more expensive isocyanamate adhesive. It does not have a significant formaldehyde emission problem but has not been tested on museum objects for the effects of its other volatile components. The interior plywood and particleboard industries are striving to improve their products and may, in the next few years, produce boards that will be acceptable for museum storage areas.

MELAMINE-COATED PARTICLEBOARD

Melamine-formaldehyde resin is about four times more stable than urea-formaldehyde, but not nearly so stable as phenol-formaldehyde resin. It is not waterproof and can be used only for interior products. Since it is considerably more expensive than urea-formaldehyde, it has been little used to date. Melamine-coated particleboard is heat-set; in the process most or all of the unreacted formaldehyde may be eliminated. Melamine-coated particleboard tested extremely well in one instance and is recommended by some conservators. Because of the demonstrated instability of melamine-formaldehyde resin, caution in its use is urged until more test results have been published.

EXTERIOR PLYWOOD, STRUCTURAL PARTICLEBOARD, ORIENTED STRAND-BOARD, WAFERBOARD

Exterior wood products are predominantly bonded with phenol-formaldehyde adhesive; it is more expensive than urea or melamine-formaldehyde resins, but is stable and impervious to moisture. The phenol-formaldehyde is reacted without excess formaldehyde, and it cross-links to form a stable resin that does not emit formaldehyde as it ages or is exposed to adverse conditions. Directly after manufacture some formaldehyde remains bonded to the moisture of the wood. If the boards are aired in dry conditions, this residue evaporates over a period of three months. At that point the formaldehyde levels drop to an amount about equal to the formaldehyde levels of an urban area and after six months to nearly undetectable amounts. The formaldehyde emission levels of phenol-formaldehyde resins are so low that they have been little studied in the industry and not at all by conservators.

Despite low formaldehyde levels, exterior wood products are not completely safe, and slight corrosion on test metals has been detected in museum studies. The corrosion has not yet been analysed, and the cause is not known. It could be the effect of the woods' emissions or other chemicals that are added to promote the cross-linking reaction of the adhesive.

HARDBOARD

Hardboard such as Masonite is composed of digested or pressure-exploded wood fibres, small amounts of wax-like petroleum materials, and sometimes small amounts of phenol-formaldehyde resins. There is little reported testing on the effects of hardboard on metals, except one test in which hardboard had no more negative effect than exterior plywood, a result to be expected since they have similar components. Tempered hardboard should be avoided because it is baked with oil, which gives off acids.

HIGH-PRESSURE PLASTIC LAMINATES

No published tests on high-pressure plastic laminates such as Formica are available. These laminates are a combination of melamine- and phenol-formaldehyde resins and kraft papers, fused with high pressure and heat. The industry claims that the products are completely inert and would prevent the migration of harmful volatile materials from the laminating adhesive or wood product beneath (usually particleboard). No tests have been published, but conservators have reported that they have observed considerable corrosion on test metals and significant formaldehyde levels in newly constructed cases made from high-pressure plastic laminates. No one has determined whether the corrosion is from the laminate or the adhesive. Until further information becomes available, high-pressure plastic laminates should be used with caution.

FIRE RETARDANTS

Products treated with fire retardants should be avoided whenever possible. If fire codes require them, one should use only wood treated with 'second generation', non-hygroscopic fire retardants that are resistant to high relative humidity. Even so, wood treated in this manner should not be stored uncovered and exposed to outdoor conditions. No museum object should ever be in direct contact with products treated with fire retardant.

SURFACE COATINGS

No surface coating can completely seal off the emission of acids from wood, or formaldehyde from resins and adhesives. Many surface coatings are themselves dangerous; they evolve harmful by-products immediately after application or as they age. Any oil-modified coatings, such as one-component polyurethanes, oil-based paints or alkyd paints, should not be used in storage because they evolve acids. Some acrylic (latex) paints have been found to have an adverse effect, others have not. Acrylics, because they are hygroscopic, can actually increase the rate of formaldehyde release. If an acrylic-based paint is chosen, it should be a vinyl-acrylic, *not* a polyvinyl acetate-acrylic. The two surface coatings that appear to be somewhat effective reducing emissions by approximately 85 per cent, and that evidently have not corroded metals, are two-part epoxies and moisture-cured polyurethanes with aliphatic hydrocarbons or xylenes as solvents. Both coatings are expensive, difficult to apply, have somewhat toxic solvents, and require extremely careful mixing and airing according to the instructions. They continue to off-gas solvents for well over a year, which could be detrimental to certain plastics and other finishes, including paint and varnish.

ALTERNATIVE CONSTRUCTION MATERIALS

Alternative case and storage construction materials include metals, paints and plastics carefully chosen for their inherent stability. Until recently aluminium and steel coated with a baked enamel paint have been recommended as safe construction materials because they do not corrode. It is now recognized that aluminium must be anodized to create an inert surface because it will otherwise emit peroxides as it oxidizes. For this reason aluminium runners should not be used for drawers containing sensitive materials.

A baked enamel coating on steel must be properly cured and fully cross-linked; if such a coating has not been sufficiently baked, it can off-gas formaldehyde that will quickly damage collections. The latest development for metal shelving for art storage is the use of powder coatings; particulate dry powder is given a static charge as it is sprayed onto a grounded substrate. This system is very promising and is used by at least one manufacturer of metal storage furniture. An alternative coating for steel is chromium plating. It is important to note that any metal product used must be of high quality with a continuous coating so that rusting in areas of flaking paint or scratches does not occur.

133

Metal storage units and various wire rack systems can be bought ready-made at laboratory furniture suppliers, architectural supply stores, hardware stores and even some large department stores. Metal shelves manufactured for libraries can often be adapted for other storage needs. Units can be custom built to precise design and manufacturing specifications by some companies. Any unit bought or built must be strong enough for its intended use. It must be of sufficient thickness or gauge and construction quality so that it will not warp or bend when loaded, or sway from side to side when moved. Care must be taken that metal units do not have sharp edges or protruding bolts or screws that could damage an object as it is moved in and out of a unit. These danger points must be padded with blotters, cotton muslin or carpeting. It would be best to use cotton or synthetic carpeting that has been heat-bonded rather than backed with adhesive. Many objects require some padding for protection and support, and shelves or storage trays are often lined with heavy acid-free, buffered paper; unbleached muslin; blotters; or acid-free, buffered corrugated board. These are hygroscopic materials and have the advantage of providing a moisture buffer during short periods of unexpected fluctuations in relative humidity. Water-absorbing materials should not be used for the storage of objects that are adversely affected by moisture, such as metals from burial sites, any metals with active corrosion, or 'weeping' glass. Any secondary padding material used in the storage of water-sensitive metal or organic materials should be inert; bubble wrap, polyethylene and other such materials of unknown property and manufacture must not be used.

The newest material on the market for custom-built storage units is a laminated honeycomb, fully expanded polystyrene. It has the advantages of inertness, great sheer strength combined with light weight, large sheet sizes, and no need for surface coatings beyond the polystyrene laminate. It can be laminated by the manufacturer or by in-house staff. No consensus has been reached on a suitable adhesive for this product.

Wooden units that are already installed and cannot be replaced by more suitable materials can be lined with barriers such as aluminium sheets, aluminium/polyester/polyethylene sheeting, aluminium honeycomb panels, or heavy aluminium foil if it is protected from puncture; even glass can be used. Other materials, less expensive, but not as effective, are buffered barrier papers of various kinds, sheets of ragboard, and polyester. Barriers made of these materials must be applied over *all* wood, including the undersides of shelves or drawers, and the fronts and backs of cabinets.

Lining with an impermeable barrier is most effective if the storage units have doors and a minimum of air circulation to exclude pollutants from outside sources. If aluminium sheeting is applied, an inert sealant must be used for the seams; it appears that certain of the sealants/adhesives used in computer systems are adequate.

The addition of a formaldehyde scavenger to existing storage and exhibition systems may also help reduce the danger to objects. A commercial product, Purafil, composed of activated alumina, potassium permanganate and other unidentified chemicals, is a complete formaldehyde scavenger. It reacts with formaldehyde and has no later off-gassing when exhausted. The Purafil system has a colour indicator that shows when it should be replaced. So far, it has been tested only with good ventilation, and its effectiveness without forced-air circulation has not been investigated. Activated charcoal filters and sheets also are effective formaldehyde scavengers, but they must be replaced periodically because the molecule is only adsorbed and not permanently reacted with the charcoal, nor are indicators available to signal saturation.

This paper first appeared in K. Bachmann (ed.) (1992) Conservation Concerns: A Guide for Collectors and Curators *(Washington D.C.: Smithsonian Institution Press).*

17

Indoor air pollution: effects on cultural and historical materials

Norbert S. Baer and Paul N. Banks

Norbert Baer and Paul Banks's review paper brings together information scattered throughtout the literature on the effect of air pollution on museum objects. Conservators are at last giving atmospheric pollution in museums the attention it deserves.

Traditionally, one has associated the development of awareness of air-pollution damage to cultural artefacts with the observations by Michael Faraday in London in the 1850s. He attributed the rotting of leather bindings and armchairs in the Athenaeum Club to SO_2 emissions from gas illumination, and the soiling of pictures in the National Gallery to particulate matter from smoke.[1,2] However, Brimblecombe[3,4,5] has demonstrated that such concerns were noted as early as 1284 when a Royal Commission was appointed to investigate air pollution from coal used as a fuel for kilns in London and Southwark. By the seventeenth century many references were made to the soiling of household materials. In 1658, Digby wrote: 'this coal hath in it a great quantity of volatil salt very sharp, which being carried on by the smoke doth dissipate it self, and fill the air . . . it spoils beds, Tapistries and all other household stuff'.[5] Similarly, Evelyn in his *Fumifugium* of 1661 wrote:

> the weary Traveller, at many Miles distance, sooner smells, than sees the City to which he repairs. This is that pernicious Smoake which sullyes all her Glory, superinducing a sooty Crust or Furr upon all its lights, spoyling the moveables, tarnishing the Plate, Gildings and Furniture, and corroding the very Iron-bars and hardest Stones with those piercing acromonious Spirits which accompany its Sulphure; and executing more in one year, than exposed to the pure Aer of the Country it could effect in some hundreds. . . . Finally it spreads a Yellowness upon our choycest Pictures and Hangings. . . .[5]

Despite these observations of material damage and warnings of serious health consequences, pollution levels continued to climb in industrializing England. Brimblecombe,[3] using a simple single-box model for the annual mean SO_2 and particulate levels in London air, estimates that SO_2 rose to mean annual levels of about 150 µg m^{-3} as early as the end of the seventeenth century and began to drop only at the end of the nineteenth century. Particulate levels followed in parallel with a peak mean annual value of 125 µg m^{-3} about 1880.

It was only some fifty years ago with the development of central air-conditioning systems that attention began to be paid to effective control of the museum environment. In 1933, the National Bureau of Standards undertook a study of alkaline-wash systems for the removal of SO_2 in library atmospheres.[6] The Folger Shakespeare Library,

Washington, D.C., installed such a system in the 1930s, but abandoned it due to maintenance problems. Since 1941, the National Gallery of Art, Washington, D.C., has had an alkaline scrubbing system. However, until recently, interest in air purification remained limited. A comprehensive survey in 1973 of 429 museums and galleries in the United Kingdom[7] revealed that only some 9 per cent of exhibition areas and 2 per cent of showcases have relative humidity control with similar estimates for air filtration. Only 10 per cent of those institutions with a conservation staff monitor atmospheric pollutants that cause chemical and physical damage to exhibitions. More recently, the Library of Congress (Madison Building), the Newberry Library (Chicago), the Prado (Madrid), and the National Library (Caracas) installed activated alumina systems while the National Gallery (East Building) again installed an alkaline-wash system for the removal of SO_x. It is now being recognized that, in addition to acidic gases, oxidizing pollutants can cause significant damage to cultural property.[8] Other concerns include emissions from building materials, the introduction of anti-corrosive chemicals from humidification systems, and the recirculations of vapours from chemicals used in conservation process.

INDOOR POLLUTANTS

Indoor pollutants in libraries, museums and historic houses originate for the most part from outgassing of structural or decorative materials, heating plants, activities of visitors and staff, and by the intrusion of outdoor pollutants. In special cases the artefacts themselves may emit significant and even dangerous amounts of polluting gases. The types of damage observed, principal air pollutants implicated, and methods of quantifying damage for different materials are given in Table 17.1.[9] The discussion which follows is classified by the source of pollutant emissions since control strategies and mitigative measures to be taken will, in general, be determined by the source.

Pollutants emitted from building materials

In a series of papers Toishi and Kenjo[10,11,12] reported that the air in new concrete buildings is usually alkaline due to the presence of minute aerosol particles. These particles are in the ultrafine particulate range (*c.* 0.01 μm). Among the damaging effects attributed to such alkaline aerosols were darkening of oil-paint films, loss of tensile strength for silk, discoloration of dyes and pigments, and the loss of precision for hair hygrometers. In general, indoor formaldehyde concentrations exceed outdoor concentrations. Urea-formaldehyde foam used as thermal insulation is the dominant source of formaldehyde. Another source is the various formaldehyde resins used in plywood, particleboard and other building materials. Where these materials are heavily used for partition walls and furnishings, formaldehyde concentrations can reach 1 ppm or more, enough to cause eye and upper respiratory irritation.[13]

Pollutants introduced by HVAC systems

Much of the SO_x, NO_x, O_3 and particulate matter detected in the library or museum environment is introduced by way of the HVAC system. Even in buildings with HVAC systems lacking pollutant gas removal capability, the ratio of indoor to outdoor concentrations is typically less than one due to reaction of the gases with building surfaces or with objects in the collections. The introduction of a well-maintained, effective, pollutant filtration system permits the removal of substantially all of the SO_x, O_3 and

Table 17.1 Indoor air pollution damage to materials

Material	Type of impact	Principal air pollutants	Other environmental factors	Methods of measurement
Metals	Corrosion, tarnishing	Sulphur oxides, hydrogen sulphide and other acidic gases	Moisture, air, salt, particulate matter, ozone	Weight loss after removal of corrosion products, change in surface characteristics
Paintings and organic coatings	Discoloration, soiling	Sulphur oxides, hydrogen sulphide, alkaline aerosol	Moisture, sunlight, ozone, particulate matter, micro-organisms	Surface reflectivity loss, chemical analysis
Paper	Embrittlement, discoloration	Sulphur oxides	Moisture, physical wear, acidic materials introduced in manufacture	Decreased folding endurance, pH change, molecular weight measurement, tensile strength
Photographic materials	Microblemishes, 'suphiding'	Sulphur oxides, hydrogen sulphide	Particulate matter, moisture	Visual and microscopic examination
Textiles	Reduced tensile strength, soiling	Sulphur and nitrogen oxides	Particulate matter, moisture, light, physical wear, washing	Reduced tensile strength, chemical analysis (e.g. molecular weight), surface reflectivity
Textile dyes	Fading, colour change	Ozone, nitrogen oxides	Light, high temperature	Reflectance and colour value measurements
Leather	Weakening, powdered surface	Sulphur oxides	Physical wear, residual acids introduced in manufacture	Loss in tensile strength, chemical analysis, shrinkage
Rubber	Cracking	Ozone	Sunlight, physical wear	Loss in elasticity and strength, measurement of crack frequency and depth

Source: Adapted from Yocom and Baer.[9]

particulate matter from the make-up air (see Table 17.2). Some question obtains as to the effectiveness of NO_x removal. Many conservation procedures involve the use of such toxic solvents as acetone, benzene, N, N-dimethylformamide, toluene, trichloroethylene and xylene.[14] In siting intakes for make-up air in HVAC systems, particular care must be exercised to avoid entertainment of vapours emitted from solvent exhaust systems. In 1982, the Herbert F. Johnson Museum of Cornell University discovered extensive coatings of diethylaminoethanol (DEAE) on artefacts in its art collection. It was determined that the source was DEAE routinely added to steam lines to prevent corrosion. The steam lines had been tapped to provide humidity for the museum climate control system. In August 1983, the museum was closed for a clean-up after a majority of the museum staff reported eye and respiratory irritations, skin rashes and other health problems.[15] Ethylene oxide (EtO) has been a routine fumigant in some archives and ethnographic collections. Growing concern about the health effects of EtO exposure and observation that many fumigation chambers have been inadequately maintained, operated and vented have reduced its use in conservation practice.[16]

Pollutants emitted by artefacts and exhibition cases

NO_x from cellulose nitrates

Cellulose nitrate, made by reacting purified cellulose from cotton linters or purified wood pulp with nitric acid in the presence of sulfuric acid, is a well-known source of NO_x emissions in libraries, archives and museums. It was discovered in the nineteenth century, and a few products are still made from it. Cellulose nitrate preparations were among the first plastics invented, and as such found a tremendous range of use until more satisfactory materials replaced them. Widely used products based on cellulose nitrate include photographic films,[17,18] 'acetate' recording discs,[19] imitation silk, lacquers, adhesives and pyroxylin-coated or impregnated fabrics including pre-vinyl 'imitation leather'.[20] Cellulose nitrate continuously emits NO_x as it ages. The largest and potentially most devastating source of NO_x emissions in collections of cultural property is photographic materials. The NFPA *Fire Protection Handbook* notes that, 'When a large quantity of nitrate film decomposes in a small room or vault not provided with adequate vents, the gas pressure may be enough to force out masonry walls.'[20,21] Cellulose nitrate was the first flexible film base, supplanting glass plates, and all early motion pictures and many still negatives were on nitrate film base. The manufacture of nitrate-based photographic film continued until 1951. The most serious problem occurs with nitrate motion-picture film because of the large, compact masses of film, often in closed containers, which prevent the escape of NO_x, creating an autocatalytic reaction, whose endpoint can in extreme cases be spontaneous ignition.[22] Many disastrous fires have been caused by the ignition of nitrate motion-picture films, and elaborate precautions, including reduced temperature, frequent inspection for advanced deterioration, and extensive provision for venting of evolved gases, are required for the safe storage of this material.[23] In addition, NO_x emitted by nitrate film bases is a recognized hazard for other film materials in their vicinity.[24,25]

The emissions of NO_x from cellulose nitrate plastics in other industrial applications is recognized in a fire protection standard specifying extensive venting.[26] Pyroxylin-coated or impregnated cloth has been in almost universal use in library rebinding and to a lesser extent in publishers' bindings since its introduction in 1922.[27] It has been speculated that the higher levels of NO_x found in testing the air in the stacks of the Library of Congress might be caused by emissions from the large amount of this cloth.[28]

Table 17.2 Measured indoor–outdoor pollution levels for archives, libraries and museums

Institution	Pollutant	Dates measured	Exterior concentration	Interior concentration	Filtration system	Note nos.
NARS (Archives Building)	SO_2	Nov. 1977	32–40 ppb	<3 ppb (10x reduction)	Particulate	(68)
NARS (Archives Building)	SO_2	Dec. 1982– Jan. 1983	7–34 ppb[a] daily average	2–25 ppb	Particulate	(68)
National Gallery (East Building)	SO_2	Feb. 1983	7–34 ppb[a] daily average	≤1 ppb	Alkaline wash	(68)
Library of Congress (Madison Building)	SO_2	Jan. 1983	7–34 ppb[a] daily average	≤0.5 ppb	Purafil	(68)
Tate Gallery (London)	SO_2	1980–3	12–80 ppb	0–4 ppb	Activated carbon	(69)
Victoria & Albert (London)	SO_2	Jan–Feb. 1983	22–60 ppb	3–42 ppb	None	(69)
NARS (Archives Building)	NO_x	Sept. 1977	41 ppb average	20–80 ppb	Particulate	(68)
NARS (Archives Building)	NO_x	Dec. 1982– Jan. 1983	10–527 ppb[a]	10–252 ppb	Particulate	(68)
National Gallery (East Building)	NO_x	Feb. 1983	40–92 ppb[a]	7–50 ppb	Alkaline wash	(68)
Library of Congress (Madison Building)	NO_x	Jan. 1983– Feb. 1983	46–318 ppb[a]	4–154 ppb	Purafil	(68)
NARS (Archives Building)	O_3	Sept. 1977	97 ppb	0–42 ppb	Particulate	(68)
NARS (Archives Building)	O_3	Dec. 1982– Jan. 1983	1–21 ppb[a]	≤0	Particulate	(68)
National Gallery (East Building)	O_3	Feb. 1983	1–21 ppb[a]	≤0	Alkaline wash	(68)
Library of Congress (Madison Building)	O_3	Jan. 1983	1–21 ppb[a]	≤0	Purafil	(68)
LA County Museum (Los Angeles)	O_3	July 1982	200 ppb average	<10 ppb	Activated carbon	(66)
Sainsbury Centre (Norwich, UK)	O_3	Sept. 1981	56 ppb maximum	40 ppb maximum	Particulate	(65)

[a] Measured at 24th and L Streets NW by the District of Columbia.

Volatile acids from storage materials

Oak and Douglas fir are among the wood species giving off acetic, formic and tannic acids. These have caused significant damage to lead objects, which in some cases have been converted entirely to amorphous masses of lead carbonate after long storage in oak cupboards.[29] Adhesives such as polyvinyl acetate emulsions can lead to similar effects. Lead formate was observed growing on bullets on display in the National Air and Space Museum in a case with a painted plywood back.[30] Other effects associated with acid emissions from wood are corrosion of zinc and vitreous enamel to create formates.[31] Nockert and Wadsten[32] identified sodium formate on the glass lids of sealed boxes used to store archaeological textile fragments. They determined the source to be cardboard in the boxes. Padfield[30] found calcium acetate and calcium formate in a 1 mm thick corrosion crust on an aragonite cowrie shell stored in a Douglas fir box with a glass lid.

Silver tarnishing has been associated with sulphides emitted by certain rubbers, paints, degraded casein through the action of *Thiobacillus*, and finished textiles used in mounting displays.[29,33] Black spots of copper sulphide corrosion have been observed on bronze archaeological artefacts in museums in Scandinavia, the United Kingdom, Germany, France and Italy.[34,35,36] Though it is assumed that the spots are the result of reaction between H_2S and the copper of the alloy, the source of the H_2S remains unidentified, with the possibilities including intrusive air pollution, microbiological decomposition of organic materials, outgassing of showcase materials, or carbonyl sulphide.[36] In a series of papers, Graedel noted the importance of carbonyl sulphide in the sulphidation of copper and other metals. He also proposed that such reactions are initiated by ozone.[37,38,39] A most interesting example of this phenomenon occurred when black spots of copper sulphide were observed on a polished metallographic specimen left for less than a week on a clean bench in a flow of filtered air at 100 feet per minute.[40] Microscopically small coloured spots or blemishes have been observed on silver-gelatin microfilms after storage of from two to twenty years. The spots are attributed to local oxidation of the image silver, resulting in the formation of coloured colloidal silver. Possible atmospheric pollutants responsible for this damage are peroxides, ozone, sulphur dioxide, hydrogen sulphide and nitrogen oxides. Storage in cool, dry air free from oxidizing gases or vapours is recommended for preventing the development of microblemishes.[41,42,43]

A number of simple tests for tarnishing or corrosive action by materials for proposed used in display cases or conservation procedures have been described.[29,44,45] Such tests should be interpreted with caution since it is seldom the case that a single simple process takes place during the test. It is probable that local pH, local potential and catalytic activity of the surface affect the kinetics of tarnishing.[46] In a recent study, Dawson demonstrated that many pesticides in routine use in museums cause irreversible damage to a broad range of artefacts.[45]

Intrusive air pollutants

The criteria pollutants, SO_x, NO_x, O_3 and total suspended particulates, represent a significant form of indoor pollution. All institutions with climate-control systems undertake at least some filtration to remove particulate matter. Some have installed systems to remove SO_x and, in impacted areas, ozone. NO_x is currently removed only as a by-product of filtration for the other criteria pollutants. A growing body of evidence indicates that these pollutants are appropriately the concern of archivists, conservators, curators and librarians. However, the literature reveals few if any quantitative relationships (damage functions, dose-response relationships, etc.) between pollutant concentrations and damage.

Sulphur oxides (SO_x)

The role of sulphur dioxide in the deterioration of paper has been accepted since the 1930s. Early experiments[48,49] relied on unrealistically high SO_2 concentrations of 5000 ppm interacting with damp paper. Working with concentrations of 10 ppm, Grant[50] showed that SO_2 deposition increased with increasing aluminium sulphate/rosin sizing of the paper. A comparative study of identical copies of twenty-five seventeenth- and eighteenth-century books in two English libraries, one in a normally unpolluted atmosphere of rural Chatsworth, the other in the badly polluted urban atmosphere of Manchester, revealed a significantly higher level of paper acidity in the Manchester library copies.[51] This acidity was greatest at the page edges and decreased greatly towards the centre of the page, which might be considered the initial sheet acidity. Wallpapers form an important part of the indoor surface area available for SO_2 sorption. Spedding and Rowlands[52] measured the sorption characteristics of polyvinyl chloride (PVC) and conventional wallpapers on exposure to maximum initial SO_2 concentrations of 150 µg m^{-3}. Sorption depended largely on surface finish and design pattern, with greater sorption by conventional wallpapers. The researchers suggested that SO_2 sorption accelerated the deterioration of wallpaper.

It has been observed that leather initially free of sulphuric acid will accumulate up to 1 per cent acid by weight per year if exposed to an atmosphere containing SO_2. The mechanism is thought to involve the metal ion catalyzed conversion to sulphuric acid of the SO_2 absorbed by the collagen of the leather. Using sulphur-35 labelled SO_2, Spedding *et al.*[53] showed that it is sorbed evenly over the leather surface, with the limiting factor in uptake being gas-phase diffusion to the surface. Sulphur oxides are capable of causing deterioration to natural and synthetic fibres. Cotton, like paper, a cellulosic fibre, is weakened by sulphur dioxide. Under circumstances where sulphuric acid comes in contact with a cellulosic surface, the product of reaction is water-soluble with little tensile strength.[54] In field tests in St Louis, cotton duck, exposed to varying SO_x levels, showed a direct relationship between loss in tensile strength and increasing SO_x concentration.[55] Zeronian[56] exposed cotton and rayon fabrics under accelerated ageing conditions of light and water spray with and without 0.1 ppm SO_2. Loss in strength was 13 per cent in the absence of SO_2 and 22 per cent in the presence of SO_2. In a study of nylon fabrics exposed to 0.2 ppm SO_2 under similar conditions, he found that nylon fabrics lost 40 per cent of their strength under the SO_2-free conditions, and 80 per cent of their strength in the presence of SO_2.[57] The degradation of nylon 66 by exposure to light and air is increased by the addition of 0.2 ppm of SO_2 to the air. Chemical properties and yarn tensile properties both reflect this damage.[58] Results demonstrated that the mode of degradation is not changed, although SO_2 accelerates the rate of reaction. Among proteinaceous textiles, silk is most vulnerable to the effects of light, acidity and sulphur dioxide, demonstrating much greater loss in strength than wool.[59]

Under normal conditions of temperature and relative humidity, paper, acetate film and other photographic materials are oxidized at a very slow rate. One of the most serious factors in the preservation of photographic materials is the presence of large quantities of oxidizing gases: hydrogen sulphide, sulphur dioxide and, to a lesser extent, NO_x peroxides and ozone.[25] The effect of these pollutants is usually yellowing and fading of the silver of the image. The paper base may also be degraded and stained. Acidic gases will degrade gelatin, paper and the film base of negatives.[25]

Nitrogen oxides (NO_x)

Damage to textiles has been attributed to NO_x.[60] Such damage appears both as a loss of fibre strength and fading of textile dyes. Significant reduction in breaking strength and increase in cellulose fluidity were observed for combed cotton yarns exposed in Berkeley, California, to unfiltered air when compared to exposure to activated-carbon-filtered air.[61] Both sets of samples were unshaded and exposed at a 45-degree angle facing south. Though the authors did not isolate the effects of individual pollutants, they implied that compounds associated with photochemical smog, especially NO_x, were the probable cause of increased damage. In an Environmental Protection Agency (EPA) chamber study of the effects of individual pollutants on twenty dyed fabrics, it was demonstrated that NO_2 at 0.1 to 1.0 ppm produced appreciable dye fading, and SO_2 at 0.1 to 1.0 ppm caused visible fading on wool fabrics.[62] It was also concluded that higher temperatures and relative humidities increase dye fading, and that the rate of fading as a function of exposure time appeared to be non-linear.

Ozone (O_3)

Only recently have conservators expressed concern over growing ozone concentrations, especially in areas subject to photochemical smog. Measurements in the National Gallery (London) showed concentrations of 0.5 µg m^{-3} in the exhibition rooms when ambient concentrations reached 80 µg m^{-3}.[8] In a recent study,[63] no significant concentrations of ozone were found in the National Archives, National Gallery (East Building) or Library of Congress (Madison Building). This study was conducted in winter 1981–1983 when the maximum ozone concentration reported in Washington D.C. was 21 ppb, substantially less than one would expect in summer or fall. In photochemically smoggy areas, e.g. Los Angeles, indoor ozone concentrations for typical buildings were found to lag in time and somewhat in value, though at times exceeding 200 ppb, about 70 per cent of ambient values, in a typical office building and laboratory.[64] A similar ratio was reported for the Sainsbury Centre for Visual Arts, opened in 1978, in rural eastern England, where the indoor ozone concentrations were typically 70 ± 10 per cent of ambient concentrations during the summer measurements period, with a peak indoor concentration of 40 ppb. During a photochemical episode the level in the gallery could exceed 70 ppb for many hours.[65]

Effective ozone filtration by activated carbon was observed for the Huntington Library Gallery, San Marino, and the Los Angeles County Museum of Art, where ozone concentrations remained below 10 ppb.[66] In laboratory experiments rubber, fabrics and plastics appeared to react with ozone.[64] Cass and co-workers, studying the effect on watercolour pigments, concluded that ozone at the concentrations found in photochemical smog can fade or alter the colour of pigments, in particular alizarin-based lakes and yellow pigments used in Japanese woodblock prints and in watercolours, and that ozone could pose a threat to the preservation of works of art.[66,67]

Particulate matter

Particles and aerosols constitute a broad class of pollutants damaging to cultural property. Dust, soot, residues of tobacco smoke, alkaline aerosols from setting concrete, and textile fibres are all encountered in the soiling of works of art. The only effective protection for collections as a whole is full, ducted air-conditioning with filtration to remove particulate matter and pressurization to reduce infiltration.[8] However, the effectiveness of such systems will be greatly reduced if the system is not properly maintained, or if measures to control pollutants introduced by visitors are not taken. An obviously avoidable problem is smoking in libraries or in museums where exhibition rooms are made available for receptions. Paintings in club rooms often demonstrate a tarry, water-soluble brown stain associated with smoking.[8] Among the 2,000+ compounds given off

Table 17.3 Air quality criteria for archives, libraries and museums

Authority installation	SO_x	NO_x	O_3	Particulates	Note nos.
ANSI-PH	Suitable washers or absorbers			Preferably HEPA	(70)
ASHRAE	Canister-type filters or spray washers of chemical pollutants in outdoor air			85% DSM	(63)
BML	0	0	0	0	(63)
CCI	Should not exceed 10 ppb. Consider central air purification in high ambient areas			95% $\geq$ 1 µm 50% 0.5–1 µm	(71, 72)
LC	Purafil system in use			95%	(63)
NBS	1 µg m^{-3} (0.4 ppb)	5 µg m^{-3} (2.5 ppb NO_2)	25 µg m^{-3} (13 ppb)	75 µg m^{-3} TSP (HiVol)	(63)
N–PNB	$\leq$ 10 µg m^{-3}	$\leq$ 10 µg m^{-3}	$\leq$ 2 µg m^{-3}	High-rating DSM	(73)
ROM-C	Charcoal or equivalent filtration to remove SO_x, NO_x, O_3			99% $\geq$ 10 µm 95% $\geq$ 1 µm	(63)
T	$\leq$ 10 µg m^{-3},	$\leq$10 µg m^{-3}	0–2 µg m^{-3}	60–80% MBT	(8)

Key: ANSI-PH = American National Standards Institute – Photographic Standards; ASHRAE = American Society of Heating, Refrigeration, and Air Conditioning Engineers; BML = British Museum Libraries; CCI = Canadian Conservation Institute; LC = Library of Congress (Madison Building); NBS = National Bureau of Standards; N–PNB = Newberry Library – PN Banks Planning Study; ROM-C = Royal Ontario Museum Conference; T = G. Thomson; DSM = Dust Spot Method; MBT = Methylene Blue Test.

in tobacco smoke are carbon monoxide, acetone and hydrogen cyanide, while tar and nicotine dominate the particulate matter.[13] There is very little information available on the chemical composition of indoor particulate matter. Lead concentrations are generally low, though concentrations as high as 2 µg m^{-3} have been measured in rooms painted with lead-pigmented paints or near major roads.[13]

INDOOR AIR QUALITY CRITERIA

Most attention to indoor air quality standards for cultural property has been directed to the intrusive pollutants: SO_x, NO_x and particulates. The essential questions are:

- What are the relationships between indoor concentrations and ambient outdoor levels?
- What air filtration strategy is appropriate and cost-effective?
- What are the appropriate environmental criteria?

Fundamental to answering these questions are measurements of indoor air quality and the development of quantitative relationships between pollutant concentration levels and damage. At present, many of the available data are qualitative or even anecdotal. Typical results of measurements of intrusive air pollution concentrations in museums, libraries and archives are given in Table 17.2.

The National Bureau of Standards (NBS), under a contract with the National Archives and Records Service, convened an experts workshop which suggested air quality criteria for storage of paper-based archival records.[63] These criteria are compared in Table 17.3 to other standards and specifications for libraries and museums. Subcommittee R of ANSI Z39, National Information Standards Organization, is drafting the standard, 'Environmental conditions for storage of paper-based library and archival holdings', which is based in part on the NBS study.

CONCLUSIONS

There is substantial evidence that indoor air pollution causes significant damage to cultural property. Certain sensitive materials, e.g. photographs, silver objects, paper, leather and dyes, demonstrate effects of immediate consequence. In the absence of quantitative dose-response relationships, the trend has been towards best available technologies criteria for SO_x, NO_x, ozone and particulates. Other pollutants are considered on a case-by-case basis.

This paper first appeared in International Journal of Museum Management and Curatorship *4 (1985), pp. 9–20.*

ACKNOWLEDGEMENTS

This work was supported in part by a grant from the National Endowment for the Arts, and the article is based on a paper presented at the 77th Annual Meeting of the Air Pollution Control Association in San Francisco, California, 24–29 June 1984.

NOTES AND REFERENCES

1 C. T. Eastlake, M. Faraday and W. Russell (1850) 'Report on the protection by glass of the pictures in the National gallery', House of Commons, 24 May.
2 A. Parker (1955) 'The destructive effects of air pollution on materials', London: National Smoke Abatement Society.
3 P. Brimblecombe (1977) 'London air pollution, 1500–1900' *Atmospheric Environment*, 11: 1157–62.
4 P. Brimblecombe (1978) 'Air pollution in industrializing England', *JAPCA* 28: 115–18.
5 P. Brimblecombe (1978) 'Interest in air pollution among early Fellows of the Royal Society', *Notes and Records of the Royal Society of London* 32: 123–9.
6 A. E. Kimberly and A. L. Emley (1933) *Study of the Removal of Sulfur Dioxide from Library Air*, Washington, D.C.: US Department of Commerce, Standards Bureau, Miscellaneous Publication 142.
7 International Institute for Conservation, United Kingdom Group (1978) *Conservation in Museums and Galleries: A Survey of Facilities in the United Kingdom*, London: IIC-UK.
8 G. Thomson (1978) *The Museum Environment*, London: Butterworths.
9 J. E. Yocom and N. S. Baer (1983) 'Materials', *The Acidic Deposition Phenomenon and Its Effects: Critical Assessment Review Papers* (North Carolina State University), chapter E-7.
10 K. Toishi and T. Kenjo (1967) 'Alkaline material liberated into atmosphere from new concrete', *Journal of Paint Technology* 39: 152–5.
11 K. Toishi and T. Kenjo (1968) 'A simple method of measuring the alkalinity of air in new concrete buildings', *Studies in Conservation* 13: 213–14.
12 K. Toishi and T. Kenjo (1975) 'Some aspects of the conservation of works of art in buildings of new concrete', *Studies in Conservation* 20: 118–22.
13 National Research Council (1981) *Indoor Pollutants*, Washington, D.C.: National Academy Press.
14 N. S. Baer (1984) 'Risk assessment as applied to the setting of solvent toxicity limits', *Adhesives and Consolidants*, London: Preprints of the Tenth International IIC Congress 1984, Paris.

15 W. Biddle (1983) 'Fear of contamination still impedes museum', *New York Times*, 18 September.

16 M. Ballard and N. S. Baer (1984) 'Ethylene oxide fumigation: results and risk assessment', preprint, Annual Meeting of the Society of American Archivists.

17 R. A. Weinstein and L. Booth (1977) *Collection, Use, and Care of Historical Photographs*, Nashville: American Association for State and Local History.

18 R. N. Sargent (1974) *Preserving the Moving Image*, Washington, D.C.: Corporation for Public Broadcasting and National Endowment for the Arts.

19 A. G. Pickett and M. M. Lemcoe (1959) *Preservation and Storage of Sound Recordings*, Washington, D.C.: Library of Congress.

20 M. Johnson (1976) 'Nitrocellulose as a conservation hazard', preprints of papers presented at the Fourth Annual Meeting, AIC, Washington, 66–75.

21 F. D. Miles (1955) *Cellulose Nitrate*, London: Oliver & Boyd.

22 J. W. Cummings, A. C. Hutton and H. Silfin (1950) 'Spontaneous ignition of decomposing cellulose nitrate film', *Journal of the Society of Motion Picture and Television Engineers* 54: 268–74.

23 National Fire Protection Association (1974) *Standard for the Storage and Handling of Cellulose Nitrate Motion Picture Film*, Boston: NFPA no. 40–1974.

24 J. F. Carroll and J. M. Calhoun (1955) 'Effect of nitrogen oxide gases on processed acetate film', *Journal of the Society of Motion Picture and Television Engineers* 64; 501–7.

25 Eastman Kodak (1979) *Preservation of Photographs*, Rochester: Eastman Kodak, Kodak Publication no. F–30.

26 National Fire Protection Association (1980) *Code for the Storage of Pyroxylin Plastic*, Boston: NFPA no. 40E–1980.

27 M. F. Tauber (1972) *Library Binding Manual*, Library Binding Institute.

28 J. C. Williams, personal communication.

29 H. J. Plenderleith and A. E. A. Werner (1971) *The Conservation of Antiquities and Works of Art* (2nd edn), London: Oxford University Press.

30 T. Padfield, D. Erhardt and W. Hopwood (1982) 'Trouble in store', *Science and Technology in the Service of Conservation*, London: Preprints of the Ninth International IIC Congress 1982, Washington, DC, 24–7.

31 E. W. Fitzhugh and R. J. Gettens (1971) 'Calclacite and other efflorescent salts on objects stored in wooden museum cases', *Science and Archaeology*, Cambridge, Mass.: MIT Press, 91–102.

32 M. Nockert and T. Wadsten (1978) 'Storage of archaeological textile finds in sealed boxes', *Studies in Conservation* 23: 38–41.

33 A. E. Werner (1972) 'Conservation and display: environmental control', *Museums Journal* 72: 58–60.

34 H. Brinch Madsen and N. Hjelm-Hansen (1982) 'A note on black spots on bronzes', *Science and Technology in the Service of Conservation*, London: Preprints of the Ninth International IIC Congress, Washington, D.C. 125.

35 W. A. Oddy and N. D. Meeks (1982) 'Unusual phenomena in the corrosion of ancient bronzes', *Science and Technology in the Service of Conservation*, London: Preprints of the Ninth International IIC Congress 1982, Washington, D.C., 119–24.

36 N. Hjelm-Hansen (1984) 'Cleaning and stabilization of sulphide-corroded bronzes', *Studies in Conservation* 29: 17–20.

37 T. E. Graedel, G. W. Kammlott and J. P. Franey (1981) 'Carbonyl sulfide: potential agent of atmospheric sulfur corrosion', *Science* 212: 663–5.

38 T. E. Graedel, J. P. Franey and G. W. Kammlott (1983) 'The corrosion of copper by atmospheric sulphurous gases', *Corrosion Science* 23: 1141–52.

39 T. E. Graedel, J. P. Franey and G. W. Kammlott (1984) 'Ozone- and photo-enhanced atmospheric sulfidation of copper', *Science* 224: 599–601.

40 M. Goodway, personal communication.

41 R. W. Henn and D. G. Wiest (1963) 'Microscopic spots in processed microfilm: their nature and prevention', *Photographic Science and Engineering* 7: 253–61.

42 R. W. Henn, D. G. Wiest and B. D. Mack (1965) 'Microscopic spots in processed microfilm: the effect of iodide', *Photographic Science and Engineering* 9: 167–73.

43 Eastman Kodak (1981) *Storage and Preservation of Microfilms*, Rochester: Eastman Kodak, Kodak Pamphlet D-31.

44 T. J. Collings and F. J. Young (1976) 'Improvements in some tests and techniques in photograph conservation', *Studies in Conservation* 21: 79–84.

45 W. A. Oddy (1973) 'An unsuspected danger in display', *Museums Journal* 73: 27–8.

46 A. T. Kuhn and G. H. Kelsall (1983) 'Methods for the testing of tarnish', *British Corrosion Journal* 18: 168–73.

47 J. E. Dawson (1984) 'Effects of pesticides on museum materials', Sixth International Biodeterioration Symposium, Washington, D.C.

48 W. H. Langwell (1952) 'The permanence of papers, Part II', *Technical Bulletin* 29: 21.
49 W. H. Langwell (1953) 'The permanence of papers, Part III', *Technical Bulletin* 30: 2.
50 R. L. Grant (1963) 'Some factors affecting the attack on paper by atmospheric sulfur dioxide', PhD thesis, University of Manchester.
51 F. L. Hudson (1967) 'Acidity of 17th and 18th century books in two libraries', *Paper Technology* 8: 189–90.
52 D. J. Spedding and R. P. Rowlands (1970) 'Sorption of sulphur dioxide by indoor surfaces. I: Wall-paper', *Journal of Applied Chemistry* 20: 143–6.
53 D. J. Spedding, R. P. Rowlands and J. E. Taylor (1971) 'Sorption of sulphur dioxide by indoor surfaces. III: Leather', *Journal of Applied Chemistry and Biotechnology* 21: 68–70.
54 T. C. Petrie (1948) *Smokeless Air*, no. 67, p. 62.
55 R. J. Brysson, B. J. Trask, J. B. Upham and S. G. Borras (1967) 'Effects of air pollution on exposed cotton fabrics', *JAPCA* 17: 294.
56 S. H. Zeronian (1970) 'Reaction of cellulosic fabrics to air contaminated with sulphur dioxide', *Textile Research Journal* 40: 695–8.
57 S. H. Zeronian, K. W. Alger and S. T. Omaye (1971) 'Reaction of fabrics made from synthetic fibers to air contaminated with nitrogen dioxide, ozone, or sulphur dioxide', *Proceedings of the Second International Clean Air Congress*, New York: Academic Press, 468–76.
58 S. H. Zeronian, K. W. Alger and S. T. Omaye (1973) 'Effect of sulfur dioxide on the chemical and physical properties of nylon 66', *Textile Research Journal* 43: 228–7.
59 J. E. Leene, L. Demeny, R. J. Elema, A. J. de Graaf and J. J. Surtel (1975) 'Artificial aging of yarns in presence as well as in absence of light and under different atmospheric conditions: condensed final report', ICOM Committee on Conservation, 4th Triennial Meeting, preprints 75/10/2, 1–11.
60 D. Harrison (1975) *Who Pays for Clean Air: The Cost and Benefit Distribution of Federal Auto-mobile Emission Controls*, Cambridge, Mass.: Ballinger Publishing.
61 M. A. Morris, M. A. Young and T. A.-W. Molvig (1964) 'The effect of air pollutants on cotton', *Textile Research Journal* 34: 563–4.
62 N. J. Beloin (1973) 'Fading of dyed fabrics exposed to air pollutants', *Textile Chemist and Colorist* 5: 128–33.
63 National Bureau of Standards (1983) *Air Quality Criteria for Storage of Paper-Based Archival Records*, Washington, D.C.: National Bureau of Standards, NBSIR 83–2795.
64 R. H. Sabersky, D. A. Sinema and F. H. Shair (1978) 'Concentrations, decay rates, and removal of ozone and their relation to establishing clean indoor air', *Environmental Science and Technology* 7: 347–53.
65 T. D. Davies, B. Ramer, G. Kaspyzok and A. C. Delany (1984) 'Indoor outdoor ozone concentrations at a contemporary art gallery', *JAPCA* 31; 135–7.
66 C. L. Shaver, G. R. Cass and J. R. Druzik (1983) 'Ozone and the deterioration of works of art', *Environmental Science and Technology* 17: 748–52.
67 K. Drisco, G. R. Cass and J. R. Druzik (1984) 'Fading of artists' pigments due to atmospheric ozone', Preprint no. 84–83.6, APCA, 77th Annual Meeting.
68 E. E. Hughes and R. Meyers (1983) *Measurement of the Concentration of Sulphur Dioxide, Nitrogen Oxides and Ozone in the National Archives Building*, Washington, D.C.: National Bureau of Standards, NBSIR 83–2767.
69 S. Hackney, (1984) 'The distribution of gaseous air pollution within museums', *Studies in Conservation* 29: 105–16.
70 American National Standards Institute (1981) *American National Standard Practice for Storage of Processed Safety Photographic Film*, New York: American National Standards Institute, ANSI PH 1.43–1981. Related Standards are PH 1.45 (plates) and PH 1.48 (prints).
71 R. H. Lafontaine (1978) 'Recommended environmental monitors for museums, archives and art galleries', *Technical Bulletin* (CCI) 3: 1–22.
72 R. H. Lafontaine (1979) 'Environmental norms for Canadian museums, art galleries and archives', *Technical Bulletin (CCI)* 5: 1–4.
73 P. N. Banks (1980) 'Addendum to Planning Report 7: preliminary statement on environmental standards for storage of books and manuscripts', Chicago: The Newberry Library.

18

Managing museum space
U. Vincent Wilcox

Space is the most limited resource in museums. Vincent Wilcox's article suggests that an audit of the spaces operated by a museum is essential if a rational approach to their deployment is to be developed. The basic principles have wide applications – not simply in museums of the size of the Smithsonian.

SPACE AS A RESOURCE

Of all the resources critical to museum operations, space is perhaps the least understood. Consequently, it tends to be poorly managed. Poor management causes considerable trauma to staff, damage to collections, and significant waste of other such critical resources as finances and staff time. Space is money. It should be controlled accurately and cost-effectively with the rigorous attention that is demanded by modern accounting principles. Space is also power. It represents personal position, prestige and job security. It is reflective of an organization's personnel structure. Personal work space and parking space are perhaps a staff member's most precious possessions, next to salary ranking.

The trauma of poor space management is also experienced by our museum collections. Staff will be very vocal in their complaints when their own space is changed, but the sufferings of the collections may not be recognized for years, until the accumulated effects of deterioration begin to impact upon research and exhibition. There never seems to be enough space for collections, and we often find them relegated to the halls, attics and basements of our facilities, where conditions are marginal for preservation.

Space management is an integral part of collections management. In service of our mission to preserve collections for future generations, it is absolutely essential to provide a stable, secure and rigidly controlled space in which to house and protect them. All our specialized knowledge, techniques and procedures for collections care and conservation are rendered insignificant without the appropriate space and facilities/services required to support them.

Modern techniques for resource management can be applied to space. Recognizing this, many organizations in the commercial sector have developed a number of new tools and technologies to assist in managing it more effectively. Among these are specifically designed computer programs variously referred to as CAD (Computer-Aided Design) and CAFM (Computer-Aided Facility Management). Such programs permit the space manager to track, inventory, define and adapt physical space, and to provide projections for future space needs based on predicted growth and changes within the organization. CAD systems provide graphic displays of the physical configuration of any given space, while CAFM systems produce spreadsheets, calculations and projections of future requirements, and provide a method for tracking and documenting usage. They can also set schedules for facility maintenance and inventory property contained within the spaces.

Museums have been slow in using modern resource management techniques. One of the reasons is ignorance. Another is simply the lack of time and resources to set aside for planning and implementation, and for investigating the new technologies. Museums seem to operate in a constant state of crisis-management. Planning takes time, and is difficult to accomplish when there are always so many problems to solve. Good space management does require time and planning, and it involves staff from all museum operations.

Unfortunately, space problems cannot be simply resolved through the purchase of CAD and CAFM computer systems. The computer cannot be considered the medicine that will magically heal all the ills of bad management. As registrars and collections managers have learned, through often bitter experience with automated collections information systems, the computer does not solve problems, it only automates them. Before a computer system can be used appropriately, the problems must be understood, and the functional requirements and expectations of the system clearly described.

Parallels can be drawn between space management and collections management. Not only are the two processes closely interlinked in practice, but both involve resources that may be characterized as commodities. Commodities have physical characteristics that can be described, and special values that can be applied to them. Space, like a collections object, can be defined by size, shape and material composition. Its special values are such characteristics as environmental conditions, and levels of maintenance and security. Space also has a market value, a price tag that can be applied to it according to established formulas. To manage collections, we select critical bits of information about our objects and put them in an information system, providing greater capability for tracking and inventory control. To manage space, we select critical bits of information about space and the facilities contained in it. Through the use of space inventory data we can achieve more control over the use of space, and provide for better maintenance of the facility as a whole.

Before we attempt to inventory space, it is necessary to define the critical bits of information that are important in the process of making decisions concerning space use, allocation and maintenace. Space must be named and classified, and a standard terminology, or dictionary, developed. This is similar to the process we use for naming and classifying collections objects. Even more importantly, we must define an 'information architecture' that illustrates the functional relationships of these various bits of information within the context of general museum operations. The information architecture defines what information is important, and how it is used. Without an information architecture, we face the risk of developing beautifully structured and logically conceived systems and programmes that are functionally useless. A number of museums have, unfortunately, created functionally deficient collections information systems because of their failure to understand their real needs, needs that would have become evident had an information architecture been created.

The failure of museums to develop standardized methodologies for space management is probably symptomatic of a more serious problem. Museums tend to suffer from the lack of a common understanding of what staff do, and how they go about specifically accomplishing their duties. We take many of our tasks for granted without full comprehension of the complex implications they have upon space and facilities. To manage space, we must have accurate information regarding what goes on within it. Failure to understand the functional relationships of the various programmes and activities within museums have resulted in the inefficient use and maintenance of existing facilities. It has also manifested itself in the construction of new structures whose very design, though beautiful to behold, renders the spaces contained within them unsuitable for use. Collections will deteriorate just as rapidly in new, beautiful space as they will in old, ugly space, if the space itself is not properly designed for the purpose of collections preservation.

DEVELOPING A SPACE PLAN FOR THE SMITHSONIAN INSTITUTION

As an enormous complex of many different museums, offices and programmes, and with growing collections now estimated in excess of 136 million objects and specimens, the Smithsonian Institution is confronted by major space management issues. With literally millions of square feet of space, both owned and rented, in many different facilities within the Washington area, and, in fact, around the world, it simply has no exact idea of the amount of space it controls, or its specific characteristics. With the constant addition of new programmes, new staff and new collections, there is a tremendous amount of 'chum' or turnover of space as programmes, people and collections are moved from place to place and old facilities are remodelled for new functions.

The buildings themselves range from only a few years to over a hundred years old, and most of the spaces were never designed to accommodate the new technologies and activities which they now contain. Environmental systems are often inadequate, not just for collections, but for people as well. The work performed by conservators and scientists requires special safety and ventilation systems. Electrical and other power systems are often inadequate to support computers, ultra-cold freezers, and sophisticated analytical instruments, for which even the most minor interruption of power can cause serious problems. The very construction of our older buildings renders the introduction of modern climate control systems difficult if not impossible. The maintenance of 50 per cent humidity, for example, inside older structures during the cold Washington winters can cause condensation, which aggravates building deterioration and destabilizes the interior environmental controls. The introduction of water sprinkler systems as the most effective means of fire protection causes great concern among conservators, to whom water is almost as great a threat to collections as fire. Many programmes, although fundamental to the operation of the museums, are basically incompatible with one another and compromise the spaces that contain them. Animal preparation and study laboratories are, for example, high-risk areas for pest infestation. For convenience they may be located near the collections storage areas, where pest infestation represents a serious problem. For similar convenience, staff have used these same areas for food consumption, which is neither safe nor particularly appetizing.

These problems are certainly not unique to the Smithsonian, but represent situations that are generic to museums everywhere. It can be considered an axiom in facility and space management that the resolution of one problem often results in the creation of a new one. Again, the parallel can be drawn with collections management. There is no one right way to manage space or collections, merely a series of compromises that must be made, based on knowledge and available information.

The Smithsonian is about to embark upon a major effort to inventory its space. As part of this inventory it will investigate the various CAD and CAFM technologies available for the purpose of automating the space inventory data. For several years, a few of the organizations within the Smithsonian have been experimenting with these technologies. The basic building plans for the Museum Support Center are in CAD, for example. CAFM is used to monitor some preventive maintenance activities for engineering systems. However, no Institution-wide application of these technologies has previously been attempted.

As part of the preparations for the acquisition of appropriate CAD/CAFM technology within the Smithsonian Institution, considerable time and effort has been devoted to the process of defining an information architecture for facility management. Simply described, this is a model, in diagram and text, of the basic functions involved in facility management, and the information used in support of these functions. This project is part of a larger programme to develop an information architecture for all the operations within the Smithsonian, particularly in collections management. Although the Smithsonian automated its collections information many years ago, each museum has its own database. As yet, the Institution has not systematically integrated or connected its various databases within a single communication network. The information architecture programme is an attempt to remedy this situation by developing a full understanding of how information is used and how it flows between the various functions and organizations within the Institution.

Although still far from completion, this project has drafted two major classification products, one being the functional classification of museum space, the other being a functional classification of basic facility services. More important, perhaps, is the profound effect of the process upon staff. The staff involved in the project, coming as they have from many different functional operations, have developed a greater understanding of their own activities, those of their colleagues, and the effects of these activities upon one another. It has also resulted in a more complete understanding of the process of management.

FACILITY TERMINOLOGY DEFINITIONS

Within the Smithsonian Institution, as in most large museums, a variety of terms is used to identify and designate space. Few of them are exclusive or well defined. What is one person's laboratory is another person's office. The same functions may be carried out in both. Facility services can vary enormously in support of the same activities. No standards for space terminology existed, nor is there any consistency in the definition of facility services required.

The facility terminology definitions, currently still in draft form, are designed to remedy the problem of inconsistent nomenclature. They attempt to define, in a simplified format, museum space according to function. They divide museum space broadly into six categories:

Administrative facilities

In this category are included administrative and programme spaces devoted to a wide range of functions, including photography and visual imaging; publications; offices and administrative activities; computer operations; training, conference and assembly areas; and basic human services, which encompass lounges, food services, medical and even residential facilities.

Building services space

This category incorporates all general facility services from loading docks to equipment storage, circulation corridors, workshops for craft services, energy plants and waste removal.

Collections facilities

The various types of collections storage facilities are defined in this category, including those for alcohol collections, oversized objects, and the specialized storage systems requiring cold temperatures or the use of movable equipment. Also included are study storage and 'open' storage arrangements, and collections processing and examination areas.

Exhibits facilities

Exhibit space is defined according to such characteristics as permanent/temporary, two/three dimensional, oversize, and compatibility for public performances. Also included are exhibit design and productions spaces, which are specifically differentiated from the various craft services, such as sheet-metal working and carpentry, included under building services.

Library and archive facilities

Although similar in many respects to collections facilities, the various functions associated with the use and management of libraries and archives are differentiated, as the patterns for using these resources differ significantly from those associated with object and specimen collections.

Scientific research, conservation, examination and treatment facilities

In this final category are placed the various sophisticated laboratories for research and conservation. Although collections are often used and examined in these spaces, the special safety, ventilation, and utility requirements are distinctive.

Each of these categories is broken down into subunits based on functional activities and the facility services necessary to support them.

During the process of defining these terms, it was discovered that a number of very different functions or programmes had similar facility requirements. For example, spaces for hazardous waste management were similar to those used for storing and processing collections materials preserved in alcohol. Similarly, closely related programme functions might have very different facility requirements. The same space used for processing fluid-preserved collections of fish is not particularly suitable for processing African ethnology. Some effort was made to combine functions possessing similar requirements in order to simplify the classification, even though in actuality the functions would be allotted separate spaces. The characteristics for collections supply storage and maintenance supply storage, for instance, are similar, although the spaces should be kept separate.

A simple definition is provided for each function, along with a list of synonymous terms. Exclusions are also noted. A brief description of the minimal facility requirements is given, assuming current building and safety standards and codes are applied as required. A cross-reference index is also being developed.

Applying this classification scheme to existing museum space is not, however, a simple task. The scheme is based on the assumption that we can, and will, differentiate our spaces according to function. Rarely do we find this to be the situation in current practice. Our circulation spaces (corridors and hallways) may also be used as collections storage spaces and collections work spaces. Our exhibit areas may also be used as exhibit preparation areas and temporary collections storage areas. Seldom do any of the spaces meet the minimum requirements defined in the terminology as necessary to support the operations carried out within them. The terminology is based on an ideal, not reality. This may be considered a significant deficiency. If properly taken into consideration during an inventory, however, it can also be considered a strength. A checklist of the minimal facility requirements defined for each function or operation can be developed. As the spaces are inventoried, the deficiencies within each space can be noted and documented.

FACILITY SERVICES DEFINITIONS

Concurrent with the space classification effort has been the task of defining the various services involved in facility management. A draft definition of these services has been a direct product of the information architecture programme. Broadly described, these services are identified below.

Managing planning and policy

Basic to all organizations is a planning function that seeks to integrate all the operations within a coherent long-range plan, and to develop policies for daily operations.

Managing cleaning

One of the most important services is the process of maintaining a clean facility. Not only is this important for cosmetic purposes, it is fundamental to the health and safety of both people and collections. Specialized cleaning techniques are employed depending on the characteristics of each space.

Managing safety

The workplace is now governed by numerous regulations for the maintenance of a healthy and safe environment. Safety services include a variety of activities from routine inspections to the inclusion of fire protection and suppression systems within the structural components of the individual spaces.

Managing security

Security is a significant concern to museums with objects and equipment of high intrinsic value. As a service, it includes not only inspections and guard supervision, but sophisticated looks and alarm devices to be installed in designated areas.

Managing utilities

A very broad and inclusive service, utilities represent all the basic power, light and communications systems necessary to daily operations within any space. It also includes climate control.

Managing facility structure

All space is defined by the physical characteristics of the structure that contains it. The walls and ceilings must be painted or finished, the exterior of the structure maintained and secured against leaks, and the physical dimensions modified as needed as the activities within them grow and change.

Managing pest control

Pest control in museums has advanced significantly from a routine process of fumigation to a complex methodology including environmental monitoring and modification. The application of Integrated Pest Management methodology to museums has necessitated its identification as a separate facility service.

The process of identifying the different facility services illustrates rather dramatically the difficulties associated with space allocation. Just as the various functions and operations conflict with one another, so do the various services conflict, with each other and with the very functions they serve. A very secure space, with limited access and locked doors, may fail to meet safety standards, and may inhibit staff who need to gain entrance in performance of their duties. The inclusion of water sprinkler systems as a safety requirement has already been noted as perhaps endangering collection materials. The inclusion of sophisticated climate control and other utility systems in storage areas to promote collections preservation may compromise security, as regular access is needed by building engineers and contractors to service the equipment. There can be no easy formula for making the necessary compromises. However, the use of these space and facility service definitions assists the space manager to collaborate with staff in making informed decisions, with the complex interaction of space and the activities contained within it properly understood.

USES OF A SPACE MANAGEMENT SYSTEM

Once an inventory of space has been completed, using the facility terminology and facility service definitions as standards, and the data incorporated in an automated system based on an integrated information architecture, the Institution will have a functional space management system. This system can be used to achieve three goals: more efficient and cost-effective use of its existing space; better maintenance of its facilities; and more effective planning for new space and facilities. From the perspective of the conservator and collections manager, each of these also serves the goal of better collections care.

The inventory of existing space, using the facility terminology, will define what and how much space is being used for which functions. It will also show how these spaces may be deficient for the functions contained within them. For example, what proportion of all space currently used for collections storage meets the defined minimum requirements, in terms of security, climate control and accessibility, that we consider essential to the proper care and use of these materials? What other space exists, currently used for other functions, that might be more appropriate? What modifications can be made to existing space to eliminate the deficiencies? Where can we find temporary space for special conservation or processing projects? While it is true that staff may well know the problems and deficiencies from their own experience, the space inventory will provide full and proper documentation that can be used for setting priorities for space use, and for making informed decisions and compromises over space allocation.

The various facility service requirements can also be applied specifically to each space to improve facility maintenance. The system will enable maintenance staff to define the levels of care needed for each space and more effectively monitor these conditions. What cleaning techniques should be used in a collections storage area? How often should cleaning be done? Who needs to be involved in co-ordinating custodial service? All these factors may be noted, and the system can distribute schedules for services. Keeping staff informed of procedures and schedules is an important use of a CAFM system. The schedules generated by the system also permit better use of personnel resources, and can enable staff to document and track all activities that may affect the use of any given space. It should enable conservators, for example, to have ready access to information regarding all maintenance activities that are performed in and around collections. With this information they can more effectively co-ordinate with maintenance staff to assure that facility maintenance and collections maintenance are accomplished to the mutual benefit of both the facility and the collections.

Finally, the system permits more accurate projection of future space needs, and provides the kind of documentation necessary for architects and space planners to programme new facilities. The system can track the changes in space use over time, and predict space needs years in advance. Collections growth, when translated into specific square feet of storage space, with well-defined environmental and other facility service conditions properly noted, can be documented in the system and used in programming new space that will meet the stringent requirements for collections care. A space management system, using well-defined and classified space inventory data, is the primary vehicle for communicating facility and space needs to architects and planners, who, more often than not, have no idea of the specialized space needs of museums. The system will provide space programmers with the basic information and understanding necessary to develop facilities that not only look good, but do provide proper space for collections care and use.

In another sense, the physical process of developing and using a space management system is perhaps even more important than the actual data itself. Space is the single, common denominator affecting all staff and activities. The process of space planning requires the staff to work together in developing a common understanding of precisely what goes on in a museum, and the complex interaction of all the functions and activities. Staff will recognize the extent to which they must consider the impact their duties and activities may have upon colleagues, the facility, the collections and the organization as a whole, resulting in a more closely united staff and better management.

Finally, perhaps it is not unreasonable to expect in the future a complete integration of the space management and the collections management systems in the computer. If this is accomplished, then each object in the collection can be directly associated with the spatial and facility requirements necessary to support and preserve it. This is a goal which is both practical and feasible, and certainly would facilitate our efforts to provide optimum care and preservation for the collections.

This paper first appeared in S. Keene (ed.) (1990) Managing Conservation *(United Kingdom Institute for Conservation of Historic and Artistic Works of Art), pp.7–10.*

19

Museum collections storage
John D. Hilberry and Susan K. Weinberg

John Hilberry and Susan Weinberg give a wide-ranging introduction to the basic principles of storage. Whilst a few of the materials mentioned have now been superseded, it provides a useful overview of the main elements requiring consideration in the design of a store.

Storage facilities for museum collections should not only be safe and secure for the objects, but convenient and accessible to the staff. These goals can be achieved through thoughtful planning, good design and careful monitoring of the construction process.

The size, design, location and relationships of storage areas must be considered in the initial plan and design for a new or renovated museum building. The architect or planner should never assign collections storage to leftover space. He must recognize from the outset that museums require a variety of storage areas, not only for collections but also for maintenance supplies, food, trash, exhibition materials and office supplies. Although all these facilities are often away from public view and house materials not currently in use, they are not interchangeable, and one or two large areas should not be designed for 'miscellaneous storage'. Storage for museum supplies other than the collections may actually present a hazard to safe and secure storage of museum objects. For instance, paint storage constitutes a substantial fire hazard, while the storage of food, garbage and trash invites vermin which may greatly harm the objects in the collections.

This article will address many aspects of the planning, design and implementation of safe and secure storage for museum collections. Although many of the facilities discussed may be too elaborate for a small museum, it is hoped that the basic facts and suggestions will aid both the museum professional who is planning a new multimillion-dollar facility and the one who is planning storage renovations in a small historic building.

THE MASTER PLAN

Before storage facilities can be designed, a long-range comprehensive plan should be developed. A well-thought-out master plan is essential for effective phased development in a new or renovated building. Each storage room must not only be properly designed and equipped, but it must relate correctly to all other facilities in both size and location.

The first questions to consider are: What kinds of storage will be required? How much of each kind of storage is required, both now and in the future? Where should each be located?

One should develop general architectural plans for much more storage than can initially be completed. Raw space can be built and finished later, or facilities can be designed so that they may be expanded. Without a master plan, however, future expansions are almost certain to be expensive and to disturb some important established relationships.

Planning for an unpredictable future may be difficult, but one should keep in mind that plans do not have to be perfect to be useful. The biggest errors are probably made when planners fail to confront the overall patterns of growth, which can be predicted with some effort and objectivity. It is far better to develop a workable plan that can be modified than not to plan at all and run the risk of costly modifications or an unworkable facility in the future.

HOW MUCH STORAGE IS REQUIRED?

Determining the amount of storage space that will be required is one of the planner's most difficult and important tasks. If the galleries are also being expanded, he will be tempted to think that storage requirements will be reduced, because many objects will be removed from storage for exhibition. Since objects in storage are much denser than are gallery installations, the reduction in required storage space will generally be small and short-lived. The only way to predict storage requirements is to imagine the kind of organization that may exist twenty years in the future. Growth is often an accelerating process, so that one might get an idea of future growth by looking back thirty or forty years and asking whether past rates of growth will continue. One can also learn by visiting other museums similar in size and type to the facility under consideration.

Having talked with other museum professionals, we believe there is no substitute for systematically listing the storerooms that will be needed in the future and attempting to imagine the type and quantity of material that might be kept in each area. In the case of large collections, it probably will not be possible or reasonable to make a projected volumetric survey of the entire collection, although ideally this would be an appropriate basis for planning. At the very least, one should consider each storage area and estimate its appropriate size by comparison to familiar spaces. This way the total anticipated storage area is made up of correctly identified parts, even though the anticipated size of the parts has been determined intuitively. The most serious mistake is not to over- or underestimate the size of a particular storeroom, but to forget about it or ignore the necessity for it all together.

WHERE SHOULD OBJECTS STORAGE BE LOCATED?

The location of stored objects is an essential part of good planning. Storage is not an area that can be tucked away indiscriminately at the convenience of the planners. While fewer people will walk to a given permanent storeroom than to the exhibition galleries or the director's office, the relationship between these rooms and other parts of the museum is critically important.

In a new or renovated facility, it is often considered cost-effective to locate storerooms at the basement level, but this may increase the possibility of water damage by flooding. An investigation should be made of local soil conditions, land contours near the building, the adequacy of the storm sewer system and the likelihood of heavy rains. Particular attention should focus on below-grade entrances such as the delivery truck ramp and the basement entrances to ensure that in the case of a flash flood or extraordinary rain, the water will not enter the building and flood the collections storage area. All basement-level exterior walls should be waterproofed with an appropriate sealant to help prevent seepage.

Another possible location is the top floor of the building. This, too, is a sensible, cost-effective use of space, allowing the ground floors to be dedicated to public use. If collections are stored immediately below the roof, however, extra precautions should be taken to prevent water leaks from damaging them. Regardless of what floor is used for storage, the storeroom should not have windows. Exterior windows are not only a possible entry route for leaking water, but a security and conservation risk as well.

The different types of object storerooms should not necessarily be grouped together in one location. They may have different functional relationships. For example, the holding rooms should be close to the shipping and receiving area and should be controlled by the registrar or collections manager. On the other hand, storage for the permanent collection would not have this requirement, but might better be located close to the curatorial office.

Storerooms can vary greatly in size. There may be some small rooms or vaults for objects like jewellery or coins, which are especially vulnerable to theft. Much larger rooms would be required for painting storage racks or industrial shelving holding large objects. In general, rooms should range from 2.5m to 3.5m. Ceiling heights may vary from 6m × 6m to 10m × 20m or higher.

Museum storerooms must also be designed to accommodate the variety of equipment that is used to house objects properly. Several types of racks, shelves and cabinets can be used in a single storeroom as long as the administrative responsibility and the climate control requirements are the same. The size and shape of each room should be determined, however, with a view to the kinds of equipment that may be installed.

For permanent storage it is best to separate different categories of museum objects. The entire collection should not be kept in one large space unless it is homogeneous, nor is it appropriate to provide one large storage space with wire mesh screen subdividers or partitions of lightweight construction. It is essential to have a carefully considered series of rooms, each thought of as an individual medium-security vault, separated not only from the rest of the building, but from other storerooms. Partitions should be of masonry, fireproof, light- and airtight, and difficult for a burglar to penetrate. Different kinds of objects require special climate control, lighting, equipment and various levels of security. In an art museum, for example, large contemporary paintings should not be stored in the same room with gold jewellery, medieval tapestries, old master drawings or ancient bronze vessels. Likewise, in a natural history museum, animal skins and fossilized bones must not be stored together because their humidity requirements vary.

Objects storage must also be separated by curatorial responsibility. A number of curatorial departments should not have direct access to a single storeroom. If an object is discovered to be damaged or missing, it is essential to know who is responsible for a particular area.

The main permanent museum object storerooms will take up a relatively large space and should be a major planning consideration. Although access to these rooms may be infrequent, the routes and arrangements are critical for maintaining good access control. In an active museum, the storerooms may in fact be the scene of continuous curatorial activity and may be used as a study centre.

It may be desirable to arrange the storerooms close to responsible curatorial offices. On the other hand, many museums may find it more advantageous to locate the object storerooms together in a more remote part of the building. Some may even find it necessary to house the collections off-site with the related curatorial staff. In any case, the spatial relationships are extremely important. If there is a freight elevator and a passenger elevator used by staff, they should both stop in a space immediately outside of the museum object storeroom area, but never open directly into a secured space. The storerooms should be grouped off a common corridor with controlled access to that corridor. It should never be possible for anyone, staff or public, to loiter outside the storage areas unobserved.

Objects may be frequently moved between the storerooms and the registrar's office, conservation laboratory, photography studio, shipping and receiving area and the galleries. Visiting scholars will be taken to examine objects. These relationships and movement routes must be studied carefully. Ideally these routes must all be off-limits to the public and must also be directly and easily negotiated. Objects are most liable to damage when they are moved. Therefore, awkward corridor configurations, bottle-necks, ramps and other arrangements that require special care on the part of the object handler or technician should be avoided. Other considerations, such as prevention of water damage, maintenance of proper climate conditions and security will also affect the selection of locations for the permanent object storerooms. The most important thing to remember is that location is critical and must be carefully considered in the planning process.

DESIGN OF STORAGE SPACE

The architect and the museum staff must both be involved in the design process. Only if the problems and goals of the project are clearly identified during the planning phase can the architect effectively begin the design process.

Ceiling heights, sizes of doors and widths of corridors must be decided upon first. Ceiling height affects both floor-to-floor heights and the total volume of the building. It is important to realize that functional vertical space is not the distance between the floor and the underside of the structure above, but rather is the workable space between the floor and whatever pipes, ducts, lighting fixtures or other equipment may be overhead. 'Ceiling height' does not necessarily mean that there is an actual ceiling installed, for most storage rooms will probably not require a ceiling. While it is important to have adequate usable height, one should remember that it is costly to increase the height of the structure unnecessarily.

All storage areas may not require the same ceiling height. Certainly coins, decorative arts or insect specimens can be adequately housed in rooms with a normal 2.5m ceiling. On the other hand, contemporary paintings, dinosaur bones or architectural elements may require at least 3m to 3.5m. However, if stacking shelf units are used, a high ceiling height will be useful even for small objects. The effective ceiling height can be increased in selected areas by rerouting ducts and pipes and avoiding suspended lighting fixtures.

Once the ceiling height of the storage areas has been decided, that figure must be co-ordinated with the sizes of entry doors, corridors and freight elevators that link storage areas with the shipping and receiving area and the galleries. Bottlenecks must be carefully avoided. Unhappy surprises can be prevented when the location and sizes of ducts, pipes and other overhead obstructions are anticipated and controlled. In designing the width and configuration of corridors, one should try to avoid difficult corners or ramps and assure that museum objects and handling carts can be safely and easily manoeuvred.

Careful consideration should next be given to the storeroom doors. Each doorway should be as large as the adjacent corridor system – generally between 2m and 3m high and between 1.5m and 2.5m wide. A double-door system with one fixed leaf and one operating leaf is best. The operating leaf allows easy access for people and small objects, while the release of the fixed leaf will accommodate larger objects. A transom above the double doors will provide extra height.

Planning and common sense should be used in the determination of door sizes. Large doors provide greater flexibility, but are more costly. Specific areas may require larger doorways than the standard 1.5m and 2m openings used in other areas.

Doors can be made to swing in or out of the storeroom. Ordinarily doors swing into rooms; however, consideration should be given to allowing storeroom doors to swing out. Such doors do not consume valuable interior space, and security is somewhat improved, as one cannot kick in a door if it swings out. If doors do swing out into the corridor, however, they must be made to swing completely around so that they lie flat against the wall, otherwise they will inhibit movement in the corridor.

Both the door and frame will probably be constructed of painted steel. A small reinforced window is recommended so that security officers can examine the room superficially for flooding, smoke or intruders without opening the door. In most cases this small window will not cause a significant compromise of security or conservation standards.

CHOOSING SECURITY HARDWARE

The selection of security hardware for storeroom doors is a complex problem. The help of an experienced registered hardware consultant is mandatory. The museum administrator must decide what kind of system is appropriate and can be afforded and maintained. The most basic decision is whether anyone can enter a storeroom by his actions alone. For instance, can the curator of the collection housed in a given store-room simply take out his key, put it in the lock and enter the room? Or must he obtain the co-operation of another person to do so, and if so, who is that person, where is his office and to whom is he responsible? A commonly accepted procedure is to require that a staff person telephone the security office and identify himself by name or code number, he may also be observed by closed circuit television. A simpler procedure would require that the staff member ask a security guard to accompany him to open a two-key lock on the storeroom similar to the lock on a safety deposit box.

Another way to ensure security is to operate the door latch electrically by a circuit that can only be activated if two separate switches are closed simultaneously. One of these switches is in the security office, the other is at the store room door and must be oper-ated by a key. Systems are now being developed that use a personnel identification card, similar to those used for 24-hour banking services, rather than a key. These cards trans-mit identification information into the electronic monitoring system as well as permit operation of the door lock. In either case, two people are required to take specific action before gaining entry, and no one person has free acess to storage. The mechanics of this operation are the job of the hardware consultant and electronic security specialist. Staff members involved in the design process must, however, understand the basic function of the hardware and monitoring systems and feel comfortable with the trade-off between protection and convenience.

Each time a storeroom door is opened, the security staff should be notified. In a small museum this may mean only that if intrusion occurs during closed hours, the alarm system will notify either the alarm company or the police department. In a larger, more complex system, computers may record not only entry, but the date and time, who entered and how long they stayed. The design and administration of a staff and police response procedure is as important as the design and construction of the physical facilities and electronic hardware.

There are other hardware considerations besides the locking system. The hardware consultant will have to select hinges, closers, holders, flush bolts and kick plates for each door. The more precisely the staff member can describe what the door should do, the more likely the result will meet expectations and needs. This requires close co-operation with the architect, electronic security specialist and hardware consultant.

BASIC CONSTRUCTION

Construction and finish materials for museum storage areas must meet conservation standards and security and fire prevention requirements. Except for certain cases of renovation or adaptive use, the basic building will probably be constructed essentially of concrete. The floor will be either a concrete slab on grade, a poured-in-place concrete floor structure, or a concrete topping poured over a precast concrete or steel structure. The walls will usually be of concrete block or brick, and the overhead structure will be either of concrete or fabricated from steel covered with a cement plaster fireproof coating.

Concrete is formed when cement, sand and gravel are mixed with water. Concrete block [sometimes erroneously referred to as cement block or cinder block] is made of these same ingredients in a manufacturing plant and shipped to the construction site as masonry units. Cement mortar is essentially concrete, using only sand and no gravel. Cement plaster is basically the same material. Bricks, on the other hand, are composed of fired clay, resulting in a basically inert material, but it also requires cement mortar in the construction proces.

The construction process depends upon the chemical reaction of cement hardening or curing in the presence of water to form concrete, mortar or cement plaster. This curing process goes on for several weeks, but only as long as the mixture is damp. After curing is completed, the material must dry. During both curing and drying, the atmosphere will be alkaline and humid. It is important for the conservator to be satisfied that curing and drying have been completed and that climate control equipment can maintain a neutral and properly humidity-controlled environment before museum objects are put in place. In a new building it may take up to two years for the alkalinity to drop to a safe level. If the concrete is sealed with a suitable paint or varnish, it may take less time. If a large amount of concrete construction is done in a renovation context, consideration must be given to special air-conditioning ventilation and dehumidifying equipment to speed the drying process and to protect museum objects elsewhere in the building.

Thoughtful consideration must be given to the construction of walls that separate storage areas from the corridors and from each other. Wood framing of the kind ordinarily used for house construction should generally be avoided in museum object storerooms because of the inherent fire hazard. If wood is used, however, the material should be fire-treated, either by a salt-curing process prior to delivery to the construction site, or by application of fire-resistant paint that foams up in the presence of intense heat to provide a protective insulating layer. Both processes are reasonably effective for fire protection, but the chemical composition, particularly of the salt treatment, may make them undesirable for conservation reasons. The high humidity maintained for many storage rooms can result in the salts leaching out of the wood and forming a crusty layer that can flake off, leaving actual salt deposits in the area. This can be counteracted by the use of certain sealants, but these should also be checked for their chemical content. Generally it is better to avoid large-scale use of plywood and wood framing in museum storage areas. Concrete block is generally superior to wood or drywall construction.

Security increases with the thickness of the walls, but thicker walls consume more space. Increased security can also be gained by the use of solid concrete blocks and steel reinforcing. All walls, regardless of thickness, should extend to the construction overhead and be tied structurally to it. A properly constructed wall system will not only increase security but will also help to maintain a constant temperature and relative humidity and will serve as a buffer in the event of fire.

Wall and door systems should be equally difficult to penetrate. There is no point in using a complicated security hardware system on an expensive metal door and then to use drywall construction or even lightweight concrete block for the walls.

Other materials commonly used in construction are steel and aluminium. Steel is frequently used for doors, door frames, sliding storage racks and shelving cabinets, and it should be painted to prevent rusting that may result from the high humidity levels maintained. The paint selected should be tested and approved by a conservator to assure that it does not emit harmful fumes. Aluminium is often used for smaller parts of equipment, storage racks and the like, and does not present any particular conservation problems.

The selection of finishing materials for storerooms must take into account conservation standards, detection of vermin, durability, 'cleanability', light reflectivity and acceptable appearance. Conservation standards should be strictly observed in the selection of all plastics, sealants, paints and coatings used in these areas. Close co-operation among the architect, contractor, vendor and conservator will be required to review the chemical make-up of each finish material.

Storerooms are generally viewed as utilitarian spaces, and the range of finishing materials is limited accordingly. The floor covering may be the concrete structure itself, either hardened and sealed or covered by a protective coating that may be painted or trowelled on like a thin coat of plaster. Another common choice is a premanufactured material in block, sheet or tile form. Other acceptable but less likely flooring materials include industrial endgrain wood block, oak or maple tongue-and-groove flooring, carpeting, brick, and ceramic or quarry tile pavers. By far the most commonly used material is vinyl asbestos tile, laid directly over the concrete and held in place by any of a number of different mastics currently on the market. Vinyl asbestos tile is manufactured using polyvinyl chloride (PVC), which can result in formation of small amounts of hydrochloric acid in the atmosphere. (The use of materials containing PVC, such as plastic wrap, for wrapping museum objects is generally considered bad conservation practice for this reason.) The amount of hydrochloric acid that can be formed in the air from the vinyl asbestos tile is generally considered to be harmless, particularly since the air in a new building tends to be somewhat alkaline as a result of the cement curing process. As a further precaution, the tile can be waxed with a mildly alkaline-based wax, which will both seal the surface and further neutralize any slight acidity. Attention should be paid to the chemical composition of the mastic used with tile or the sealers and hardeners used with concrete.

The walls and ceilings of storerooms, which are constructed of concrete or masonry, should be clean and dry before painting. Obviously it is important that the paint remain on the surface and not flake off and settle on the objects stored below. The chemical composition of all paints and sealers should also be checked with a knowledgeable conservator.

Although the materials described are the most common ones used in construction of museum object storerooms, other materials, such as wet plaster made of gypsum (as contrasted with cement plaster) and drywall (also known as gypsum board), may be used.

Colours should be selected for the floors, ceilings and walls in the storerooms and adjacent corridors on the basis of light reflectivity, durability and 'cleanability'. Architects are often asked to select materials that are easy to maintain and that hide dirt through the use of colour, pattern or texture, but the goal should not be to hide dirt or vermin, but to provide for easy detection so that the dirt or pests can be eliminated. Floors, walls and ceilings should be a light solid colour, without flecks or marbling. Plain white or off-white vinyl asbestos tile should be used, although it is more expensive.

White walls and ceilings reflect light well, which allows good visibility with a limited number of lighting fixtures. Light that is reflected off a white titanium oxide surface is almost entirely free of ultraviolet radiation. It is therefore both energy-efficient and good conservation practice to combine fewer lighting fixtures and a lower overall wattage with highly reflective floor, wall and ceiling surfaces. Consideration should be given, especially if fluorescent lighting is used, to directing the light upward to the ceiling so that all the light in the storeroom is reflected and essentially free of ultraviolet radiation. White floors, walls and ceilings also give a feeling of cleanliness that may encourage the staff to take better care of the space and objects.

Brightly coloured floors, walls and ceilings should be avoided because they distort the colour of objects. Designers of museum storage rooms should understand that these rooms are not only for storage, but for scholarly study and evaluation of the condition of the objects, comparison between objects, and other activities that require the ability to scrutinize them carefully. Light that most closely resembles natural light will be best for this purpose.

The durability of finish materials is not generally a problem, since traffic in and out of storerooms is small compared with traffic in other staff and public areas. Plain white flooring does, however, present some maintenance problems. Museum objects are generally transported on carts or dollies that have steel or rubber wheels. Steel tyres may scratch or abrade, and rubber tyres may mark the flooring material. Solid tyres of vinyl, neoprene, urethane or other plastics should be considered. Similarly, large storage screens that are floor-mounted and supported by wheels can make a permanent dent in the flooring. This makes the screens difficult to move and can cause conservation problems, since it is important to avoid vibrating or jarring the objects. It may be best to avoid the problem completely with a system of ceiling-mounted screens that glide from a track above.

Close attention must be paid throughout the design and construction phase to the selection of construction and finishing materials if the storage areas and corridor system are to meet the museum's needs.

CLIMATE

Proper climate controls regulate temperature and humidity, maintain air cleanliness and are essential to good museum object storage. Different objects have different temperature and humidity requirements. Since it is often difficult to anticipate exactly what each storeroom will house in the future, it is important to design both the construction of storage facilities and mechanical systems to permit flexibility of temperature and humidity standards. The question is not what temperature or humidity conditions will intially be maintained, but rather what standards and range of conditions the mechanical systems *will be capable of* maintaining. The museum staff would define this range and inform the architects and mechanical engineers of the museum's needs. This aspect of collections storage should be discussed carefully early in the design process when budgets are being established.

TEMPERATURE AND HUMIDITY

There is no such thing as an ideal temperature or humidity for storing all types of museum objects. Individual control of the conditions in each storeroom is highly desirable. This option is also expensive, and compromises may be necessary. For example, storerooms may be arranged so that one group is maintained at one temperature and humidity level and another group at a different level.

Designing facilities to provide proper climate control for object storerooms is not simply a matter of mechanical systems. The layout of the rooms in relation to one another will often be an important consideration, particularly in climates where winter temperatures fall well below zero degrees Fahrenheit. Maintaining high relative humidity (RH) when the outside air temperature is very low is one of the most difficult problems confronted by museums. This is a complex problem which is not well understood and appreciated by most architects and engineers. Although the relative humidity inside most public buildings is allowed to drop to approximately 20 per cent when the outside air temperature drops to 10 or 20 degrees below zero, RH levels in museums must generally be maintained between 45 and 55 per cent throughout the year. High humidity inside, coupled with low temperatures outside, is an extremely unusual standard in the construction industry. Museum professionals should realize that even well-trained, experienced architects and engineers may find it difficult to understand the implications of these requirements.

Under these circumstances, condensation tends to form on or within the exterior walls, and extraordinary precautions must be taken to prevent this. It is extremely difficult and costly to solve this problem after the building is constructed, so it must be dealt with from the outset. The solution involves the overall building design, the exterior walls and windows, and the insulation and vapour barriers, as well as the detailed engineering of the mechanical climate control systems.

Constancy is the most important criterion for a successful climate control system. Rapid changes in temperature and relative humidity are very destructive to museum objects. If the ideal RH for a group of objects is 50 per cent, it would be better to maintain the relative humidity at a constant 40 per cent than to permit the humidity to vary between 35 and 60 per cent RH from hour to hour or day to day. Exposure to such fluctuations can cause damage. Thus, the structure and mechanical systems must be capable not only of achieving certain conditions, but of maintaining them at constant levels. This requires sophisticated equipment and maintenance and is expensive. Judgements concerning acceptable tolerances should be carefully made early in the design process, since these judgements have important conservation and financial consequences. Although requirements may vary greatly from one type of museum to another and from one group of objects to another within a given museum, some basic guidelines may be established.

Temperature

Systems should maintain a constant temperature, regardless of outdoor weather conditions, at any desired setting between 17°C and 22°C. Fluctuations of plus or minus 2 degrees are generally considered acceptable.

Humidity

Decisions concerning proper relative humidity will depend upon the objects' composition and their past storage history. Ideally, mechanical systems should constantly maintain any desired humidity level – between 30 and 60 per cent – on a room-by-room basis. In general, metal objects that tend to rust or oxidize and unglazed ceramic objects or fossils that could leach salts need lower RH levels. Higher humidity levels are appropriate for wooden furniture, lacquers, furs or panel paintings that could dry out and crack.

In actual practice, room-by-room controls present a problem in that objects may not remain in the same room indefinitely. In addition, each time the storeroom door is opened and closed, temperature and humidity levels can change. An alternative would be to establish and maintain an acceptable median standard throughout the storage areas and all areas where objects are located. The development of microenvironment exhibition or storage cases permits museums to maintain general temperature and humidity levels throughout the building and provide special conditions for only those objects that require it. This general strategy will undoubtedly become increasingly common in the future.

Even if the desired temperature and humidity levels do not vary from room to room, individual room controls governing temperature and humidity levels are necessary. For example, one storeroom may be occupied, the door closed and the lights turned off, for days at a time. An adjacent storeroom may, during the same period, be the scene of considerable activity. New objects may be brought in, the collection reorganized, inventory taken, research or conservation activities carried out. This means that all the lights may be on and the door may be opened repeatedly during the day. After hours, this same room will become dark and unoccupied. In such a situation, if the two rooms were controlled by a single thermostat and humidistat, it would be impossible to maintain constant temperature and humidity levels in both rooms. Separate temperature and humidity controls for each individual storeroom are not a luxury – they are a necessity for good conservation practice.

AIR CLEANLINESS

Modern industry has polluted the environment, particularly in urban areas where many museums are located. Museum climate control systems must provide acceptably clean air as an environment for objects. The necessary corrective measures will vary greatly, depending upon the type and extent of pollution in a given locality. This is a fairly technical aspect of climate control, one that will require close co-operation between mechanical engineers and conservators. There are two basic types of pollution – particulates and contaminants. Particulates are fine particles or dust suspended in the air that may settle on the objects. Contaminants are gases contained in the atmosphere. These gaseous chemicals will not settle, but may react with and harm the objects.

To remove particulates one draws the air through filters, passes the air through an air washer to remove the particles in a kind of elaborate showerbath or electrically draws the particles towards a surface where an electrostatic precipitator removes them. Even though filters must be changed regularly, there are a number of automatic or semi-automatic devices that facilitate this process. These bags or continuous rolls of filtering material are the simplest acceptable devices for museum use, and are by far the most common. Air washers, probably the best method for very large, sophisticated systems, remove contaminants and control humidity in addition to removing particulates. These systems are more complicated and require knowledgeable, constant maintenance. Although electrostatic precipitators are effective, they create a destructive by-product, ozone. Therefore, they should never be used in museums unless they are coupled with activated carbon filters.

Contaminants generally cannot be removed by bag or roll filters and often require carbon filters or air washers. Although the need for filtering or washing devices may vary from museum to museum, considerable research has been done concerning the standards for acceptably clean air in museums.

Choose a climate control system that suits the institution's needs, and one that the staff can always maintain properly. All too often, sophisticated equipment is installed in museums and then not maintained, creating a worse situation than if less sophisticated systems had been installed in the first place.

Maintenance of these systems requires constant co-operation between the conservator and the building superintendent. The conservator must monitor temperature, humidity and air cleanliness levels constantly and report serious deviations to the building superintendent and the director. The building superintendent must routinely maintain, clean and repair all equipment and change filters properly. All of this requires time and money. If good maintenance procedures cannot be anticipated, the museum should install simpler, more foolproof systems.

One cannot discuss climate control in museums without mentioning energy conservation. Maintenance of constant temperature and humidity levels is essential, but it violates common energy conservation principles, which call for much higher room temperatures in the summer than in winter. One responsible compromise between the need to conserve energy and the need to preserve museum objects is to permit a slow, yearly fluctuation in temperature and humidity. For example, the temperature might be maintained at 18°C and 45 per cent RH in the winter, and 24°C and 55 per cent RH in summer. Then museum objects would be subjected to only one slow cycle of modest expansion and contraction throughout the year. For most objects, this is probably quite acceptable. Museums must not permit rapid hourly, daily or weekly fluctuations, their climate control systems must run 24 hours a day, 365 days a year. Administrative officials who are committed to energy conservation may not realize that museum air conditioning is not for the comfort of the director and staff, or even the public, but rather for the long-term well-being of the objects entrusted to the museum.

POTENTIAL WATER DAMAGE

Although equipment rarely malfunctions, and pipes rarely break or leak, such mishaps are an unacceptable risk in a museum setting. This must be explained clearly to your architects and engineers.

In general, pipes containing liquid or steam should run outside object storage areas and never overhead in a storeroom. Mechanical equipment should not be contained in the same area as collections storage. Not only is the potential risk of damage by water or continual vibration increased, but the security risk involved in making such an area accessible to engineers and repairmen is greater. Special precautions should be taken even if pipes or equipment are a level above object storage or in directly adjacent space. Ideally, pipes should run through corridor spaces, with the corridor on a slightly lower level than the storerooms.

To prevent water seepage, mechanical rooms should have a raised kerb at the doorway. Both corridors and mechanical rooms should have floor drains to carry away water that could result from a leak or malfunction. If it is necessary to run pipes through collections storage, consider sheathing them in sheet-metal that drains into the corridor or into a device that detects the presence of water on the floor. Regardless of the exact situation, store all objects on screens, shelves, racks, skids or cabinets at least 4 inches off the floor.

Sinks and running water are often located in collections storage. However, this convenience must be weighed against the inherent risks of leaky pipes or plugged drains.

Careful review of mechanical plans and insistence upon limiting the exposure of the collections to possible water damage may eliminate future disasters.

It is important to note that cold air ducts in storerooms can cause possible water damage in high humidity areas. Condensation on the sheet-metal ducts may drip onto the collections. With proper insulation, this problem can be avoided.

LIGHTING

The importance of proper lighting for collection storerooms cannot be stressed enough. Adequate lighting in corridors and storerooms prevents accidents during the handling of objects and exposes vermin, dust or dirt in the area. Storerooms are not merely repositories for inactive objects. They are often used for the study of collections and for comparison of objects. Routine cleaning or conservation examination and treatment of the objects may also occur there, as may basic photography. The storerooms may well be the site of scholarly research, inventory and reorganization of the collections.

Conflicting requirements make storeroom lighting difficult. From a conservation point of view, museum objects should be stored in complete darkness. When the staff works with the collections in storage the light sources should limit the most destructive forms of radiation. From a curatorial point of view, in order to see the objects most accurately, the light source should duplicate the visual spectrum of sunlight as far as possible. And from a maintenance point of view, lamps should not require complicated upkeep or frequent replacement and should be energy-efficient. In addition to these technical requirements, it is important to remember that lighting has a profound effect upon the aesthetic quality of space as a human environment and that even a basement storeroom can be made comfortable and attractive with proper lighting.

TECHNIQUES

Obviously, no one lighting system is optimal. Careful judgement and compromise are essential. Sunlight is not acceptable because it cannot be regulated adequately and carries destructive ultraviolet radiation and heat. Skylights and windows are a security threat and make climate control difficult.

Incandescent light bulbs offer one of the best solutions. Incandescent light is continuous across the visual spectrum and is stronger in the red range than in the blue. The human eye adapts readily to this situation and makes colour discriminations easily, and although incandescent light is not as good in this regard as sunlight, it is better than most other light sources. Incandescent light is free of ultraviolet components, an essential advantage from a conservation point of view. Incandescent bulbs, however, are energy-inefficient and have a short lamp life.

Fluorescent lamps are by far the most common light sources, although they too have definite disadvantages, some of which have been offset by recent technical developments. Fluorescent lamps are inexpensive, have a long life and are energy-efficient. Ordinary fluorescent lamps, however, have a high component of destructive ultraviolet radiation and have a very uneven energy distribution throughout the visible spectrum, making colour discriminations difficult. Nevertheless, there are now fluorescent tubes with very low UV radiation and a relatively even visible light spectrum distribution. Reflecting light off the walls and ceiling to create indirect light will soften the visual effect and provide an additional precaution against the damages of radiation, especially when the walls and ceiling are painted with titanium dioxide paint.

Fluorescent fixtures are manufactured with a number of different lenses which greatly reduce glare and improve the general visual ambiance. If lamps are used which are not free of UV radiation, plastic cylindrical filters can be slipped over the tube. These filters may have a limited life and should be checked periodically with a UV radiation meter.

No matter what form of lighting is used, plans should include an exterior switch so the storeroom can be illuminated before entry. Allowances must be made for an adequate number of interior electrical outlets for additional lighting and other equipment. Storerooms should also have battery-powered emergency lighting so that occupants, caught in a power failure, could vacate the room without damaging the objects.

TEMPORARY STORES

An institution involved in a special, temporary or travelling exhibition schedule, active loan programme or ongoing acquisition programme should assign separate areas for temporary or short-term storage. Objects, either crated or packed in protective material, generally arrive by truck. They may all arrive at one time if the exhibition is travelling from any other museum, or the museum may have to assemble them over a period of time from various sources. Regardless of the delivery schedule, the objects must be placed in a secure, temperature – and humidity – controlled storeroom immediately, even before they are removed from the crate or wrapping. Then the objects may be unpacked, the crates stored in one place and the objects stored in a staging area where they will be organized for exhibition.

Sometimes a museum is receiving a new exhibitions as it is dismantling another, and, in order to avoid confusion, these exhibits should be placed in separate storage areas. Ideally, two holding areas are needed to handle this situation. Each must be large enough to store comfortably an entire major exhibition, whether crated or not. In a small museum, it is possible to have only one holding area if the temporary exhibition schedule is light and the time between exhibitions is leisurely. None-the-less, a storage area separate from permanent collections storage is cetainly advisable.

Many museums have large numbers of incoming objects that are processed as loans, accessions or for study. The registrar or collections manager also may need storage space for outgoing loans and objects pending cataloguing and research or awaiting conservation. These objects are in the custody of the museum, but for one reason or another do not belong in permanent collections storage and are not part of an incoming or outgoing exhibition. Such objects are especially vulnerable to theft or accidental damage. The temptation to keep the object in limbo, until someone decides what the disposition should be, must not happen. Each object must be placed immediately in a special storage area under the direct supervision of the registrar or collections manager. This facility should be large enough to house a few museum objects of typical size. In a larger institution this may involve both a major storeroom and a high-security fireproof vault.

It may be advisable to have a separate storage room or vault, located in the office area, for the use of the director or curatorial staff. This area would be convenient and would provide security for temporary storage when other facilities are inaccessible.

Thought should also be given to the need for a storage area that can be used as a fumigation chamber and, if space and funds permit, for a large vault for extra security on a short-term basis. In addition to temporary storage, there should be separate space for crating and uncrating, shipping and receiving, carpentry and other related functions. Such activities should not take place in temporary holding storerooms.

Aside from size and location, temporary storage should meet the same requirements – climate control, security and lighting – as permanent object storerooms.

SECURITY

Electronic alarm systems are only one aspect of storage security. Equally important are the planning of the physical facilities and the development of appropriate staff and administrative procedures.

Storage rooms contain dense concentrations of valuable objects and in many ways are a less visible and, therefore, more tempting target for theft than public galleries. Security systems should force a burglar to make noise, take time and risk observation, and at the same time, restrict unlimited access to storerooms by museum personnel. Pay attention to obscure entry routes, such as mechanical duct shafts or grilles, as well as to small details such as locking systems.

Security and convenience are often in conflict. Good security procedures should prevent even the most trusted staff member from entering and leaving storerooms of his own free will. Curators, however, feel that collections storerooms are their personal turf and that it is not only an inconvenience but an affront to have any other staff member tell them whether and when they should enter the area. This is an understandable but dangerous attitude. Frustrating a burglar may frustrate legitimate staff to some degree. The physical design should, however, maximize the frustration of the burglar and minimize the inconvenience to the curator.

One of the most useful things museum planners can do to improve storeroom security is develop a basic layout that makes it difficult for anyone to approach the door of a storage room unobserved.

Valuable objects that are susceptible to theft should be stored in rooms located on a secure corridor. By requiring two staff members to co-operate to enter the corridor and then the storeroom itself, it immediately becomes impossible for a single individual to come and go unobserved. Since the safety codes will not allow storerooms to be locked behind the visitor, a checkout procedure should be established so that each entry is paired with an approved exit.

The specifics of security design involve wall construction, doors, hardware, electro-mechanical access control systems, closed-circuit television, and electronic detection, alarm and response systems. The selection of proper security hardware and the design of an electronic intrusion detection system are highly sophisticated and complex matters. Museum professionals and the architect must understand the principles involved in security, but only consultants trained and experienced in these fields should design in detail the locking or electronic detection systems. These consultants should be employed either directly by the museum or subcontracted by the architects.

Never allow a salesman to design a system. People operating in this capacity may be fully experienced and properly trained, but they represent a particular company and are motivated by the desire to sell and install the equipment manufactured by that company. Although engineering and design services from such a company are usually free, it is far better to engage a qualified specialist who is working for the museum. The consultant is then free to design the system that will work best for the museum, no matter what equipment is involved. The system should permit maximum competition among the suppliers so that the owner is not locked into a given company for parts replacement, modification or expansion of the system. A museum security specialist should be engaged at the outset of the project so that he can work closely with the architect and the museum staff as plans for the storage facilities develop.

FIRE PREVENTION

All storerooms, whether they contain museum objects or other materials such as pedestals and vitrines, lumber, paint or cleaning supplies, are likely places for fires to start. Although the building and storage equipment should be of non-flammable materials, the objects themselves may be flammable.

Because of the density of objects in storage, a storeroom fire can be far more devastating than one in a gallery. Such a fire can spread quickly and consume the entire collection in the room. Without an extinguishing system and well-constructed partitions to contain the fire, it can then spread to adjacent rooms as well. For security purposes, it is generally best to concentrate collections storerooms in one area where access is readily controllable. This tight grouping contributes to the possibility of major loss through fire, however, and requires special preventive measures and detection and suppression devices.

Fires are often started by faulty heating equipment. Open-flame furnaces, boilers and water heaters should be installed in a separate room equipped with a sprinkler system and isolated from the rest of the building by fire separations. This room and equipment must be rigorously maintained and all flammable material removed. Careless staff procedures in the handling of flammable liquid, poor housekeeping and faulty electrical wiring are other common causes of fire.

If a few basic procedures are followed, the chances of fire will be extremely low. Smoking should never be permitted in storage areas under any circumstances. Place all museum objects on non-flammable shelves or in non-combustible containers and never stack objects on the floor. Flammable liquids should be housed in an area removed from collections storage in non-breakable metal containers. Electrical wiring should be encased in standard conduits, checked carefully and replaced if it is faulty.

FIRE DETECTION

If a fire does start, however, there are a number of devices and systems that can greatly reduce the possible loss.

It is imperative to receive early warning of a fire. The design of a detection and alarm system is not a simple matter. Museum staff should work with a professional engineer to determine the requirements, design the system and prepare drawings and specifications for competitive bidding for installation, service and future modifications.

The museum professional should be acquainted with the fundamentals of these systems. Although technology is constantly evolving, there are three basic types of detection devices: heat, visible smoke and ionization. Selecting the proper device will require careful consideration. Each device works differently and costs can vary greatly.

A heat detector activates an alarm when the temperature surrounding it rises precipitously or above a certain level. This is a simple, inexpensive and reliable device, but does not provide the early warning that smoke or ionization detectors do. A fire frequently smoulders for some time before bursting into flame. As it smoulders, it may not generate sufficient heat to set off the alarm and the situation may go undetected until it is too late.

Photoelectric smoke detectors operate on a different principle. A small beam of light is transmitted through a short distance of air. If visible smoke particles break this beam of light, the alarm is activated.

Ionization detectors spot invisible products of combustion that carry an electric charge after combustion takes place. Upon detection of such ions, this device will activate an alarm. In most cases, the choice will be between ionization and photoelectric smoke detectors because of their greater sensitivity. Although this is a fairly complex and debatable subject, most engineers would recommend ionization detectors, even though they are considerably more expensive. Under many circumstances ionization devices detect fire somewhat earlier, giving museum staff or the fire department more time to act. Because of the high density and often high value present in object storerooms, it is wise to use a combination of both ionization and smoke detectors. Many smoke sensors contain a simple element that detects heat as well, so that it may be possible to install a system that will operate on all three principles of heat, smoke and ionization.

Monitoring the alarms and the museum's response system is equally important. This depends on staffing during closed hours and local police and fire response capabilities. These non-architectural, non-mechanical aspects should be given careful thought when the physical facilities are being planned, for they must all go hand in hand if the collections are to be kept safe from fire.

FIRE SUPPRESSION

As important as fire detection and alarm systems are, they only warn staff of a fire. Museum storage areas also need systems that will actually extinguish a fire. Automatic and manual fire suppression systems should be considered supplementary to one another.

There are three major types of automatic fire suppression systems: water sprinklers, carbon dioxide gas and halon gas. Conventional wisdom in museum circles has held that water sprinkler systems should not be used in collections storerooms or galleries because they could accidentally discharge, doing nearly as much damage as a fire. Surveys of institutions using water sprinkler systems indicate, however, that there is an extremely small incidence of accidental discharge. Sprinkler systems are definitely the most effective and inexpensive means of automatic fire suppression. They work quickly and positively, extinguishing the fire at its source and preventing its spread. Certainly water can cause considerable damage, not only to the objects located in the immediate area, but also on levels below. Although fires do not occur very often in museums, the damage can be devastating. Experts in the field ask the question, 'Which would you rather have: wet museum objects or ashes?'

There are two types of sprinkler systems. The simplest is a wet system in which the pipes contain water under pressure at all times. Sprinkler heads, activated individually by a material that melts at a predetermined temperature, allow water to flow freely, spraying in a circular pattern. The wet system carries with it the risk of a pipe leak and the possibility that a sprinkler head could discharge accidentally. Although such incidents have been extremely rare, the dry sprinkler system largely eliminates these risks. In this system the pipes do not contain water until an electronic detector in the room senses the presence of smoke or heat, releasing water into part of the system. At this point, it functions as a wet system, discharging water through a sprinkler head only if the heat has risen to a temperature that will melt the triggering material. This system is preferable as it provides a double protection. There is no danger of leaking or accidental discharge unless the electronic detector first senses the presence of heat or smoke.

The second type of suppression system discharges carbon dioxide gas, reducing the level of oxygen and thereby extinguishing fire. This does not present a hazard to museum collections, but it is lethal to human beings. Carbon dioxide systems should be used only when the protected areas are occupied by employees who are aware of the dangers and are carefully trained and rehearsed in evacuation procedures. In the case of museum objects storerooms, it is unreasonable to assume such consistent employee training. It is likely that fire suppression systems may be installed and never thought of again for several years. The risk to human life resulting from the discharge of such a system into an occupied room is too great to warrant its use in ordinary museum circumstances.

Halon gas systems appear to offer a nearly ideal solution for museum objects storerooms. When halon gas is released into the atmosphere it produces a complex chemical reaction that instantly and effectively extinguishes flame. There are advantages and disadvantages, however, which should be carefully considered. Low concentrations of halon gas are harmless to both museum objects and human beings. On the other hand, it is an expensive system and can only be used in isolated, contained areas. The system requires the installation of storage tanks and piping and a complex system of fire and smoke detection alarms, delayed discharge systems, automatic door closers and warning systems. This expense and complexity are a primary disadvantage.

In addition, halon will not extinguish a glowing or smouldering fire, although it will prevent the fire from bursting into flames. This permits museum or fire department personnel to deal with the situation before the fire can spread. If the halon system, which does not have a continuous discharge capability, discharges and the doors are open, reducing the halon gas content of the room, the fire may burst forth again and burn uncontrollably. Water sprinklers, on the other hand, continue to douse the area until they are turned off, leaving small chance that a fire could break out again. Although the relative harmlessness of halon systems is appealing for museum objects that could be damaged by water, museum fire protection experts are increasingly taking the position that properly designed water sprinkler systems may often be preferable, even in collections storerooms.

As a general rule, sprinklers are more appropriate for areas such as crate, pedestal or paint storage, and for objects that are highly flammable and would not be severely damaged by water discharge. Halon systems should be limited to small contained areas where there is an extraordinary density of objects that would be ruined by exposure to water.

In some cases it may be unwise or financially impossible to install automatic fire suppression systems. The decision may be made to rely upon a fire detection system, museum staff, the fire department and manual fire extinguishers. If this is the case, the museum staff should know how to use extinguishing equipment and the fire department should be briefed on the special problems of a museum.

Manual fire extinguishing equipment should be placed in all storage rooms and surrounding areas so that, if a fire is detected, the museum staff or fire department can extinguish the fire before the automatic system discharges. Timely use of the proper type of manual extinguisher will always be the most effective and least destructive extinguishing procedure.

Manual equipment includes water hoses, water and carbon dioxide, foam and dry carbon dioxide extinguishers.

When water and carbon dioxide extinguishers (the traditional metal cylinders) are inverted, they cause a chemical reaction that discharges the water. Such extinguishers are the least desirable because they produce water under pressure and contain chemicals that could be harmful to the objects. Foam extinguishers cover burning objects with a layer of insulating foam that snuffs out the fire. These extinguishers are especially effective for gasoline and electrical fires, but leave the objects and general vicinity covered with a foam that presents a conservation problem. Dry carbon dioxide extinguishers are a relatively harmless, quick way of smothering minor fires of all types. The fact that they are harmless encourages their immediate uninhibited use, which may result in a fire being stopped before it gets out of control. If the fire does grow to any sizeable proportions, such an extinguisher would not be adequate and a fire hose would be required. In most instances, the best combination would be a dry carbon dioxide extinguisher in each storeroom and adjacent corridors, with fire hoses in the corridors only.

Gaining entrance to storage is a particularly puzzling situation that will need careful thought. It would be a tragedy to have security and fire detection systems alert the staff and fire department to a fire, only to force them to stand helplessly outside the door able to take any action. Special alarmed key storage boxes are available to solve this problem.

CONSTRUCTION DURING RENOVATION

Too often the construction process is crude and expeditious and can place museum objects in serious jeopardy. Tradesmen are almost never called upon to be as fastidious and concerned as a museum curator or conservator. Still, somehow, the storerooms must be completed and the collection must remain intact in the process.

A carefully controlled construction process begins with complete and explicit specifications, prepared by the architect, detailing the procedures that the contractor must follow. Someone on the museum staff should assume responsibility for reading the specifications and for insisting upon additions or corrections if necessary. All of these special procedures will cost the museum money. Allowing the contractor to work without restriction is the least expensive avenue for the museum, but this may cost much more if a single object is destroyed or if the objects in a single storeroom are covered with plaster dust.

Selecting the right general contractor may not be easy. After the construction drawings and specifications are prepared, the project is put up for competitive bids. Publicly funded projects may have to accept the lowest bid, even if the company has a marginal reputation. If only private funds are involved, a list of bidders who have a reputation for doing exceptionally careful work should be prepared. This will be most helpful in the execution of the project, although there may be a cost premium.

When the construction contract is signed, the architect, members of the museum staff, the general contractor and the subcontractors should meet to discuss the particular concerns of the museum. Even though the general contractor carries the overall responsibility for executing the project, the subcontractors should be present at this meeting. It is necessary to know the key members of the construction team; impress upon each of them the importance of following proper procedures and of supervising their employees. Museum professionals must work closely with the architect. As the museum's representative, he is the most effective agent in monitoring and controlling the construction process and should be the only one giving instructions to the contractor. Close communication and co-operation are essential. Particular precautions should be taken during the construction process.

Access

In order to deliver materials and remove trash, construction workers must be able to move about freely. If object storerooms are being renovated, these workers may be moving through areas of the museum that present basic security problems. One misunderstanding can quickly result in tragedy, and although such mistakes usually occur without malice, they also illustrate how easily someone could steal a collection of gold coins during the construction period.

Every effort should be made to limit the access of the construction workers to an area where little harm can be done. This may be difficult. For example, electricians run wires and conduits in all kinds of places. It may be necessary to move objects from the construction site to temporary storage, but this, too, presents inherent dangers. More than likely extra guards will be required and should be worked into the budget.

There are no easy answers. The museum staff and the architects must work together diligently to protect the collection during the construction period.

Cleanliness

Dust and dirt are normal parts of the constructions process. Even though the construction area is cleaned regularly, special precautions must be taken to isolate it from the rest of the museum. Dust created by ordinary demolition outside a storeroom can pass under and around the door, requiring conservation cleaning for every object in the room. A simple dust barrier and careful taping of the door can prevent such mishaps. The following precautions should be taken to control dust:

- Remove trash daily.
- Sweep and vacuum the construction area frequently. Sprinkle sweeping compounds and other materials on the floor to control dust. The chemical contents of such materials should be inspected by conservators.
- Isolate construction areas with dust barriers.
- Tape doors of all storerooms containing objects. This will be a nuisance whenever the rooms are entered and there will be a strong tendency to let it go after a while. Special diligence will be required.
- Install a temporary air exhaust system. This will maintain a negative pressure in the construction area so that air leaks in, rather than out.
- Temporarily modify the air-conditioning system so that construction dust is not carried through the ducts to other parts of the museum.

Installation of mechanical and electrical systems

Someone on the museum staff should work with the architect and examine all the engineering drawings in detail to determine where all pipes, ducts, electrical conduits and devices will be installed, especially outside the immediate construction area. In order to do their work, tradesmen will have to be in various parts of the building and may not recognize an object or situation as presenting a special risk, consequently placing the collection in danger. This will be a special problem if pipes, ducts or conduits must run through occupied storerooms.

In order to run ducts, tradesmen first cut holes in existing walls. If a door is locked, workers may proceed anyway. In no time (approximately 20 minutes) a textile storeroom may have large, neat holes in several walls, with dust and broken concrete block strewn about, inside and out. Mishaps may occur, but if these high-risk operations are identified in advance and appropriate precautions taken, the risks can be minimized.

MONITORING THE USE OF CONSTRUCTION MATERIALS

All construction materials having contents that could affect museum objects should be approved by a knowledgeable conservator. The most frequent items of concern will be sealers, paints and coatings.

Some coatings will be applied on the job, but others will be applied in a shop, perhaps in another city, and the person mixing the paints will not question a routine process. Paint or varnish selections are often last-minute decisions. If a few days are taken at this critical point to check the paint's chemical makeup, the job will be delayed, costing the museum valuable time and possibly money for extending the contractor's overhead cost. Such extra costs are sometimes substantial and legitimate.

To avoid costly oversights, identify and test all materials that are of concern, in advance.

If possible, these items should be noted on the architect's specifications and discussed in initial and subsequent job meetings.

Job meetings and walk throughs

One of the most useful procedures is to have museum staff present at job meetings and walk through the project with the architect and contractor. This gives staff members the opportunity to ask questions, express concerns and stop some aspect of the work if necessary. Although there may be times when there is not much to discuss, meetings should be scheduled on a regular, businesslike basis.

Installation of storage equipment and movement of the collection

Designing and selecting shelves, cases, cabinets, racks, screens and other kinds of equipment is a complex and demanding process. This equipment is expensive and must be reflected properly in the budget.

Installing museum objects is clearly one of the most important curatorial and conservation operations in the museum. The key factor is to estimate properly the time involved in installing equipment and moving the collection, so that realistic project schedules can be established. As the construction process nears completion, a 'punch-list' of the activities that remain is prepared. Often the contractor comes back and tends to these minor items after the spaces are occupied. This, however, will not be possible in the case of museum storage, for security and conservation reasons. As a result, construction time may be considerably longer for the storerooms than for other parts of the museum, and other operations may be delayed accordingly.

Temperature- and humidity-control systems should operate properly and air pollutants should be reduced to acceptable levels before the objects are finally moved and installed.

CONCLUSION

Constructing good museum storage is not a simple matter. In many ways, it is the most difficult part of the museum to design correctly because the complexities are not readily apparent to architects or to museum professionals who have not gone through the process before. Museum objects storage is definitely not to be dealt with as an afterthought, as is so often the case.

Good storage facilities require intense concern from the very beginning of the planning process through design and construction to the final installation of the equipment and the museum objects themselves. These facilities are the core of good museum collections management. A museum's first responsibility is to protect and preserve the objects in its charge. The role of collections storage facilities is fundamental. In the end, nothing is as important.

This paper first appeared in Museum News *59(5) (1981), pp. 7–21; 59(6), pp 5–23; 59(7), pp. 49–60.*

20

Here's what to consider in selecting high-density storage
Abigail Terrones

Abigail Terrones gives a summary of what needs to be considered when installing mobile storage – now a popular storage option. Like many of the techniques used in the storage of objects, much here seems to be common sense. However, it is simply because of this assumption that storage projects commonly run into difficulties or do not meet their full potential.

Finding more space while retaining easy access to collections is a dual challenge every collections manager faces. At the National Museum of American Art in Washington, D.C., the graphic arts department found that a high-density storage system was the best solution to our specific set of problems. But the decision to install the high-density system was not made in haste; it was the result of a thorough assessment of collections management and curatorial needs. So before I address the details of our buying decision, let me explain a bit about the process we followed.

We began by taking a close look at our current situation. One obvious problem was the division of the collection among three separate rooms. Generally, catalogued prints and drawings were stored in one room, uncatalogued and framed items were stored in another, and photographs were stored in a third.

The department also faced severe overcrowding. Wooden storage shelves, which had been constructed years earlier, were filled; hundreds of prints, drawings and photographs, which ideally should have been stored in solander boxes, were kept in frames because of limited shelving space.

The logical solution, we determined, was to store the graphic arts and photography collections together in one room and permit those who work daily with the collection (the collections manager, cataloguers, matter/framers) to retain direct access to the collection. We also hoped to create an improved print study area for researchers and others wishing to examine artwork from the collection.

Because no expansion in actual floor space of the storage room was possible, the only alternative to consolidating the collection was to find some way of getting better use out of the space available through a different kind of storage system. We determined that a mobile, high-density system could work. Such a system eliminates several aisles in favour of a single 'floating' aisle. The number of aisles in the storage area can be reduced, then, because the steel framework (or carriages) on which the shelf sections are mounted moves laterally over floor tracks creating an aisle where one is needed rather than having fixed aisles between fixed storage sections. The reduction in aisle space dramatically increases the space for storage shelves.

Here are some of the factors we considered (and that you should investigate, too, before contemplating a similar setup) in choosing a high-density system:

The type of system selected will in some degree be dictated by the physical limitations of the building as well as the weight of the material to be stored. In the early planning stages, plan to conduct a floor-load study to determine whether the area selected for the storage system can support the increased weight.

In determining a maximum height for storage carriages, take all impediments into account. Be sure to allow adequate space to reach lighting, heating, cooling or sprinkler systems, for example. Such systems also should be reassessed in light of a new storage arrangement. Also consider the safety factor involved in reaching artwork from upper shelves.

Because floors often are not level and walls not squared, exercise care in selecting the maximum height and length of the mobile carriages. (Walls that are not squared could force installers to shift the entire system away from a wall by several inches.) In deciding on a carriage length, make sure you take into consideration the extra space for the handles at the end of each carriage.

In a department where the collection storage area is large or is used frequently, two or more floating aisles might be advisable so that more than one person may work in the space at one time. Also, in a museum using many carriages, an electrical system might be preferred over a mechanical-assist system (safety mechanisms then become an important consideration as well). In either case, carriages should be without torque and provide vibration-free movement over the tracks. Rubber bumpers will help prevent jarring as the carriages are moved together.

Determining the configuration of shelves or bins within the individual carriages depends on the range and scope of the collection. Inventorying the dimensions, types and volume of artwork to be stored will dictate the size, number and configuration of shelves and bins. And don't ignore the possibility of an expanded collection. By providing shelves and bins of various sizes, you can hope to accommodate atypical objects that might be collected in the future. The more pressing problem of storing oversized framed art may be accommodated to an extent by selecting vertical bins that extend the entire clearance height and depth of a carriage.

For our graphic arts department, we chose metal shelving over wood because of archival concerns; metal shelving also is somewhat flexible in permitting horizontal shelves to be rearranged with little effort. Conversely, we found vertical bins to be not as versatile, because they are custom-constructed.

The issue of flexibility in moving an entire system also is a factor in the selection process. A new track and raised floor would be required to relocate a storage system, but many of the components can be moved and reassembled with only the additional cost of shipping and labour.

Have all aspects of the plan diagrammed prior to purchase. It is fairly easy to misinterpret someone else's mental image of what the storage system's configuration will look like unless schematics are prepared. The museum staff person assigned to supervise the project should have a full understanding of all schematics to ensure that installers proceed according to instructions.

Workmanship also should be inspected as the job progresses. The project supervisor at our museum found it most effective to discuss any questions or problems with the person who sold us the system, who then spoke directly with the installers.

Finally, in the planning stages, imagine yourself actually using the storage system – moving framed artwork into vertical bins in the carriage, manoeuvring a ladder or cart around in the aisles, attempting to lift a solander box from an upper shelf. This will help in determining whether the anticipated configuration of the shelving and aisle space will be adequate.

Our recently installed high-density storage system has succeeded in meeting the graphic arts department's goals by nearly doubling the shelf capacity for solander boxes. Now, we have one room for all solander box storage; hundreds of works of art on paper have been unframed, stored in additional solander boxes, and shelved; and we have a new work space for researchers, members of the public, volunteers and interns who wish to examine prints and drawings in the collection.

The research, planning and monitoring that went into our project has resulted, then, in greatly improved and expanded storage. But not everything can be anticipated. For example, we experienced freight damage in shipment of the new storage system. Despite precautions taken to avoid damage in transit (an exclusive-use van direct from the factory), one upright panel arrived damaged and two others were defective. The delay in waiting for replacement parts from the manufacturer resulted in serious scheduling problems. And when the panels sent to replace the two defective panels arrived, it turned out they contained the same defect, thus causing further delays.

Overall, we are pleased with our new system and have found that the small sacrifice made in restricting aisle access with movable carriages is far outweighed by the benefits of increased storage capacity and ease of organization in having the collection housed in one room.

This paper first appeared in Museum News *67(5) (1989), pp. 80–1.*

21

A policy for collections access

Jeanette A. Richoux, Jill Serota-Braden and Nancy Demyttenaere

The 'reserve collection' is a term often applied to material in store. It begs the question 'Reserved for what?' Collections in store are a resource; they are there to be used. Jeanette Richoux, Jill Serota-Braden and Nancy Demyttenaere describe how access might be improved.

Access to the objects in museum storage areas has traditionally been limited. Now, however, museum collections are widely considered to be within the public domain, and many institutions have experienced pressure to allow the public to see and study objects with fewer restrictions. Greater emphasis on the museum's role in public education further indicates that it is no longer a question of why access for researchers should be allowed, but rather how and how much. In response, museums must now justify the restrictions they place on access to their collections and devise written access policies.

There are many advantages to allowing the public broad access to a museum's holdings. The increased use of the collections may be an asset to the museum's public education programmes. The research that is conducted will contribute to the body of knowledge about the collections. The museums's public exposure will grow, as may its chances of receiving financial support or donations of objects. Finally, greater access to storage areas will encourage the museum staff to plan collections management programmes that ensure the proper care and retrieval of artefacts and the information they provide.

Visitor access also entails certain disadvantages. Damage, theft and general wear of objects will occur, and greater funding for security and conservation will be required. The demands on facilities and staff may be considerable, detracting from other important museum functions.

Efficient and productive use of museum collections is possible, however, if a balance is struck among the needs of researchers, the collections and the staff. These needs are interrelated, and actions taken in one category may affect another. A researcher may feel that his work is essential, but his request must be weighed against the condition of the object he wants to study and the amount of staff assistance required. Co-operation among staff members, as well as between staff and individual researchers, is of paramount importance. The ultimate goal should be to make suitable objects available to the researcher in a safe environment with minimal interference in the staff's routine.

RESEARCHERS' NEEDS

Research requests come from many sources. A random survey of museums of all disciplines, followed by interviews with museum administrators, showed that these people consistently ask to see and study museum collections:

- *Research scholars*, such as independent professionals engaged in consulting work, visiting scholars from universities or other museums, industrial scientists, and museum staff doing research outside their own department
- *Undergraduate and graduate students* conducting research studies or working on their theses or dissertations
- *Elementary and secondary students and the general public.* The exhibits may stimulate their interest, and they may ask for further access to objects or information.
- *Commercial users* of collections – such as a fashion designers, architects and professional photographers – who may want to study the design or style of objects in museum collections for the purposes of their work
- *Dealers and collectors*
- *Amateurs and hobbyists*
- *Donors and their families*, who may want to ensure that their gifts are being cared for properly and that the stipulated restrictions are being enforced
- *Members of cultural groups*, especially Native Americans, who may want to see objects related to their heritage. Native American groups often want to use sacred objects and other items to revitalize and enrich aspects of their culture, or they may want to become familiar with a specific museum's Native American collections in order to have a better idea of objects they may wish repatriated.

THE PROBLEMS OF ACCESS

Our survey identified problems that can arise from visitor access and affect researchers' relationships with the staff and the collections. Researchers can abuse their privileges. They may not know what they want to see and may prefer to browse. Since they probably will be unfamiliar with the organization of the storage areas, this practice can impinge on staff time. Careless actions, such as the misplacement of specimens within storage trays or failure to close storage cases, are problems noted by many museums. Museum staff are also concerned about the unauthorized dissemination of data, which may occur when a visiting researcher uses or publishes information gathered by a staff member without the consent of the original researcher.

Museums present similar difficulties for researchers. Poor organization and management of storage can be frustrating. Overcrowded storage areas inhibit physical access to objects and attempts to examine objects may prove fruitless if the work or study areas are inadequate. Researchers are also frustrated by backlogs of uncatalogued objects which preclude complete investigation.

THE NEEDS OF THE COLLECTIONS

When researchers use museum collections, there are obvious dangers of damage, wear and theft. The staff must, therefore, decide which objects are sturdy enough to be handled and, as a preventive measure, show all visitors how to use and handle the collections properly.

Access to museum objects makes them more susceptible to changes in the environment, general wear and the possibility of a major damaging incident. These factors shorten the life span of the objects, especially the more popular ones. Theft and vandalism may also occur, so proper security precautions must be taken. These include deciding not only which researchers should be supervised, but what material should and should not be accessible to them.

STAFF NEEDS

Problems involving museum staff are not as clear-cut as those related to researchers and collections. Although the staff is responsible for the preservation and care of the collections, they are often unaware of how many researchers have access to storage areas or of the nature of their visits. A thorough, systematic screening process that applies to anyone requesting access will help eliminate these problems. Once access has been granted, museum personnel should realize that extra demands may be made on their time. Each researcher will have specific problems to solve and tasks to accomplish. Should visitors require prolonged assistance, their presence may interfere with the general operation of the museum. In such cases, charging for staff time may be warranted and should be considered.

GUIDELINES FOR A COLLECTIONS ACCESS POLICY

Many museum administrators are deceiving themselves in thinking that their institutions are prepared to handle an ever-increasing number of researchers. Most museums have only informal collections access policies or written procedures that were developed only after problems arose. But a well-thought-out policy can help resolve the major potential difficulties of collections access before the safety of a museum's collections is threatened.

The guidelines that follow are a synthesis of ideas rather than a working policy. They list the points that must be considered before formulating an individual museum's policy. Both administrative and protective guidelines are included. The administrative guidelines answer the major questions of who and how: Who will devise the policy? Who will implement it? How will it be executed? What are the legal considerations? This information encourages better management and ensures more efficient use of staff time and museum resources. The protective guidelines address problems of security and conservation. With increased handling and other demands on the objects, rules and regulations are needed to protect the collections and define the extent of use.

ADMINISTRATIVE GUIDELINES

Staff committee

The personnel who regularly assist researchers should be responsible for evaluating the institution's access problems and developing a written policy to be incorporated into the general collections policy, subject to the museum's established approval procedures.

Statement of policy and procedures

The statement should include detailed procedures for access to the collections and should be available to the public. Large museums may need additional departmental policies.

Access manager

One staff member should be responsible for scheduling visitor access to the collections and handling problems when they occur. Depending on the size of the museum, the registrar, a curator or the director would be the usual choice for this duty. The access manager should be familiar with the collections and their requirements for preservation. This person or another staff member should accompany the visitor into the storage areas. In the absence of the access manager, another designated staff member may authorize access, but the security and organization of the collections might be impaired if this occurs regularly. The access manager should develop an appointment procedure; only in unusual circumstances should a visitor be permitted to see and study the collections without advance notice.

Alternatives to access

Before researchers are allowed access to the collections, they should be shown other alternatives, such as public exhibits, photographs, catalogue information or other supplementary data. Computerized files that give a clear picture of the contents of the collections can be useful in enabling researchers to make better decisions about which objects they need to see. The museum staff must determine what records researchers may use and who, if anyone, may see confidential information about donors or the monetary value of objects.

Levels of access

To institute controls and ensure the preservation and general care of the collections, it may be useful to define the levels of visitor access. Two simple categories may suffice: *primary collections* (types, holotypes, and valuable and rare objects) and *secondary collections* (duplicates, objects of lesser value and reproductions). As a general policy, the museum might admit only qualified researchers, including some students, to the primary collections. Others, such as hobbyists, commercial users and collectors, might be allowed access only to objects in the secondary collections. The definition of 'qualified' should rest with the access manager. How a researcher progresses to a higher level of access must also be considered.

The museum might grant unsupervised access to some researchers. This is not an easy decision because there are risks involved, but a certain degree of flexibility should be maintained.

There are other ways to establish levels of access. Study-storage areas and visible storage, both innovative means of access control, can be easily maintained as well as accessible to visitors. Both may include reference catalogues for easy identification of storage material. The major difference between the two is that objects in study-storage may be touched or handled, while those in visible storage are available only for viewing. Both methods are ideal for amateurs, students and commercial users and, in many cases, may eliminate the need for staff supervision. Appropriate security, of course, should be employed in these areas.

Another option might be a learning centre where secondary collections, duplicates or cast-off specimens can be examined. This can be an ideal place for hobbyists and elementary and secondary students to satisfy their desire for access to certain museum collections.

Determining who may have access

Individual admittance should be decided by the access manager once the staff committee has established general procedures. He should evaluate the credentials and motives of the researcher, the length of stay, the demands on the staff and collections, and benefits the researcher may offer the museum. It may not be desirable to admit certain types of researchers to the collections at all. The committee should decide, for example, whether they have the time or the willingness to admit and supervise the curious visitor. The committee should also establish standard criteria for accreditation of qualified researchers, particularly the ones who are admitted to the most important collections.

Dissemination of data

Outside researchers may wish to publish information prepared by the museum's staff. Abuse of the research privilege may be discouraged if researchers sign a statement agreeing to the museum's policy regarding the dissemination of data. Such a statement should stipulate that an appropriate acknowledgement, footnote or credit be used in all cases where the museum has supplied information.

Budgetary needs

Good access is costly. The museum must budget time for staff members to assist researchers. A well-maintained and secured study area, other security measures, reproductions of artefacts, and the treatment of deteriorating objects all require added funds. Additional staff may be needed in order to fulfil the museum's responsibility for maintaining the collections.

Services and charges

The museum's administrators must decide what services can reasonably be offered, and whether there should or could be a charge for them. Photography, reproduction of documents and rent for use of facilities usually are chargeable expenses. Some museums are establishing fee schedules for processing loans, opening cases and even for staff time, especially when commercial users are involved. Scholarly researchers are less likely to be charged because they have fewer funds available and their studies can benefit the museum.

Many museums believe that they cannot charge for services if they receive federal funds, but there seems to be no legal basis for this belief, unless the particular grant specifies otherwise. The National Endowment for the Humanities has indicated that access costs would be a justifiable expense if a qualified researcher requested funds for it.

The museum should determine how the fees received should be used. The funds could support an additional staff position to deal with researchers or be applied to acquisitions, conservation or the museum's general fund.

Income from fees could be subject to taxation as unrelated business income. Staff services, for which the museum charges, must be related to the educational purpose of the museum, and charges for rent are also restricted. The museum should consult its attorney for advice about the tax implications of charging for access.

Evaluation of procedures

Periodic evaluation of the access procedures will ensure that they are effective and continue to suit the needs of the institution.

Legal considerations

The staff committee should be aware of the freedom of information or privacy laws that may apply in the museum's locality. If the institution is a public museum, receives government financial support or has a tax-exempt status, some researchers believe they have a right to access. The American Indian Religious Freedom Act may enable Indians to have access to anthropological collections in government museums. The museum must also consider its legal responsibility to hold the collections in trust for the future. Recent cases indicate that trustees or directors may be held liable for the condition of the collections in their institutions.

Attitudes towards researchers

In many instances, the museum benefits when researchers have greater access to the collections. Researchers help publicize the institution and may act, in effect, as unpaid consultants who add to the information about the collections.

Staff members should be willing to assist researchers when necessary, in accordance with the museum's access policy. Museums that do not include this statement in job descriptions should consider adding it.

PROTECTIVE GUIDELINES

Storage security

Keys and identification checks may be used to restrict the staff and other individuals who request access. Staff members should accompany every visitor into storage areas, unless the visitor has written approval for unsupervised access from a responsible official. This approval should not be given frequently.

Records of access

Each time a researcher or staff member enters a collection storage area, written records should show the person's name, address, the date, the time of entering and leaving, the purpose of the visit, the catalogue number(s) of the objects viewed and the name of the person accompanying the visitor. In addition to helping maintain security, this information provides a record of collection use. The condition of the objects that are used most often can be monitored more carefully.

Study area

There should be a supervised area, secured by perimeter controls, where researchers can study the objects brought out of storage. Microscopes and other equipment should be available for research use.

Screening researchers

Each museum needs to establish a systematic screening procedure, which may incorporate letters of introduction, an interview or a collections access request form. The information required should include the name of the researcher, institutional affiliation, purpose and duration of research and proposed use of research information. Students may be required to show that they are working on an approved academic project. Other researchers may be required to give references if they have no academic affiliation. Museums may ask researchers to sign a statement of responsibility for damages. Although enforcement might prove difficult, such statements serve to educate researchers to the degree of care expected of them.

Each museum will need to tailor the application form to its own collections and conditions. Such a form can screen out the researchers who do not know what they really want to see and give the administration an accurate picture of the kinds of researchers who use the facilities. Data on researchers help the museum justify additional staff or operating funds for access.

Handling

Every collection needs different written handling instructions. All researchers should be asked to review these instructions, for even experienced researchers can grow careless. The instructions should stipulate that only staff members may move objects from and to storage drawers and shelves. They should also describe any special condition problems and handling requirements. Researchers should realize the importance of keeping labels and fragments with an object.

Reproductions

Sometimes reproductions may be substituted for popular objects that cannot withstand additional stress. Copies of objects are acceptable for some types of research and satisfy the visitor's right to access. Only accurate reproductions of artefacts should be used, however, and with the full understanding of the researcher.

Inventory

An inventory of collections should be conducted periodically, with more frequent spot checks. Inventories are necessary to determine the condition of objects to be handled and to check on their location in the collections. The frequency of the inventory will depend on the size of the museum's collections and staff and the types of records that are kept.

Monitoring and maintenance

With increased attention and wear, the collections will need more intensive monitoring to prevent damage and to promote early treatment of conservation problems. Control of light levels, relative humidity, temperature, pollution levels and biological infestations will be complicated by increased access when objects are brought in and out of storage and exposed to different environmental conditions. Staff members should be aware of the potential conservation problems and work closely with a conservator to effect proper collections maintenance.

It is clear that requests for access to museum collections will be more numerous in the future. In anticipation of increased public use of museum objects and information, museum administrators must define the parameters of access to the objects that are entrusted to their care. Only then can researchers see and study museum collections with fewer restrictions and fewer risks.

This paper first appeared in Museum News *59(7) (1981), pp. 43–7.*

22

Visible storage for the small museum

Paul C. Thistle

Visible storage has been well tested in North America, and is now attracting interest elsewhere in the world. Paul Thistle's review of experience in Canada is essential reading for anyone considering the visible storage option.

The visible storage model of museum presentation has recently received an increasing amount of attention in Canada and elsewhere. Interest in it has arisen from the development in the 1960s and 1970s of an ideal based on the 'democratization' of museum collections.[1] According to that ideal, because the public is the true owner of the collections, it should have full access to all museum resources. In some quarters, a perception exists that museums have been 'hiding all the good stuff' in storage for the exclusive use of curators and scholars.[2] The visible storage concept is seen as a 'radical' departure from the contemporary museum model and is an attempt to open up all of the museum's resources to the public – to 'democratize' the whole enterprise. The philosophy has now been widely accepted in the museum community. Whether the visible storage approach is the best means of carrying out this philosophy remains to be determined.

Visible storage, sometimes referred to as 'open storage' or 'study storage', combines two functions that modern museology generally considers separate – storage *and* display.[3] In visible storage, collections are systematically presented in high-density arragements that lack interpretive labels but include access to the information available on each object.

At first glance, visible storage appears to be simple, straightforward, and close to what small institutions have always chosen or been forced to do – display all of their collections. As curator of a small museum that will be undertaking a major redevelopment project, this writer found the concept to be intriguing. The Sam Waller Little Northern Museum, originally a private collection, is now owned and operated by the Town of The Pas and has a varied collection of human and natural history objects numbering approximately 10,000. Although the approach may appear to be an attractive option for small museums, the concept is still on trial and has yet to receive the critical analysis necessary for widespread acceptance by small institutions that cannot afford the luxury of museological adventurism.

The information reported here is based on a summary of the available literature and inspection of a number of systems currently in use.[4] The study seeks to determine whether the system has been meeting the goals set for it, discover how to avoid the problems encountered, and how to make the most effective use of the system in the small museum setting.

ADVANTAGES OF VISIBLE STORAGE

Key benefits of the visible storage approach are listed here.

1 Visible storage closely approximates the ideal of effectively providing the public with extensive visual access and solving the problem of severely restricted access to collections held in a typical closed-storage format. Minority groups are reported to feel much more comfortable using visible storage without the need for supervision by the professional curator.[5]

2 Visible storage can accommodate a wide variety of interests and levels of participation and stimulate independent exploration and interaction with the objects.[6] The visitor becomes less a passive receptor and more an active learner. Especially in small community museums, visitors have participated in identifying objects and their uses and correcting erroneous catalogue data for the staff. Visitors in the visible storage gallery at the University of British Columbia Museum of Anthropology (UBCMOA) were found to be more at ease, animated, willing to engage in conversation with strangers, and less unsure of themselves[7] than visitors in exhibit galleries. Visitors, including children, were observed asking questions and taking particular interest in certain objects – all extremely desirable outcomes.

3 Visible storage can result in positive effects on the care of collections.[8] Conservation attains a high public profile, and visitors often bring problems to the attention of staff. In addition, the microclimates produced in visible storage units (often custom-made) protect objects from fluctuations in relative humidity and temperature as well as dust and other pollutants. Security is not compromised and may be enhanced.

4 Documentation improves.[9] Exchange of information about the collection between visitors and staff leads to the continual upgrading and expansion of the catalogue data.

5 Staff members are affected in a number of ways. They are placed in a much more prominent position with the public than in a typical museum model, where curators tend to be isolated.[10] Time required to change exhibits and supervise inspection of closed-storage collections is reduced.[11]

6 Visible storage reduces the need for separate storage areas and public galleries, thus making more efficient use of space and reducing the need for exhibit construction – especially important for the small museum. Visible storage may be cheaper to maintain than the traditional systems,[12] although there is some disagreement on this point.

7 Visible storage increases public support because visitors gain a better understanding of the museum's responsibilities, resources and true social utility. As the community begins to perceive the museum as its own, the institution becomes more fully integrated into community life. Proof of this effect is increase in donations of objects to the collections.[13]

DISADVANTAGES OF VISIBLE STORAGE

Significant problems have been identified; some believe that they greatly outweigh the system's advantages.

1 First among the concerns is conservation. Visible storage is potentially more damaging to the objects than traditional storage and display. The major concerns are: trauma to objects resulting from opening and closing of drawers in which they are contained; increase in light levels and prolonged exposure to light (as opposed to dark closed storage); temperature problems akin to those found in exhibits; dust;

increased security risk; increased handling (in mounting the objects). Some objects are deemed inappropriate for visible storage because of conservation risks.[14] The conservation department of the Glenbow-Alberta Institute has recommended the abandonment of visible storage largely because of the actual and potential damage to the objects.

2 The general public often tends to be confused and/or frustrated by the system.[15] A UBCMOA study found that 59 per cent of visitors reported a negative reaction.[16] Familiar with the traditional selective exhibit approach, many visitors are over-whelmed by the sheer numbers of objects on display, fail to understand how the collections are organized, and are frustrated by the lack of interpretive labels.[17] Access to the data is crucial since labels are absent – an abdication of a museum's responsibility to interpret in the view of some critics. In some systems, visitors have found access to the catalogue data too complicated and alien in format. Others are frustrated by the typically poor documentation of the objects once they have gone to the trouble of searching out the catalogue data.[18] In fact, few seem interested in acessing data. During the study at UBCMOA, only one visitor in four used the data books and then rarely for more than one or two objects. The Glenbow Museum found little or no purposeful use of its computerized system.[19] Visible storage is demanding. Visitors, lacking the specialized knowledge that provides context and meaning and would enable them to make sense of collections, can simply become confused and/or intimidated. In short, visible storage may not be appropriate for the general public and, as a result, it has been a seriously underused resource, according to some critics.[20]

3 No doubt resulting from the above difficulty is the misuse of the system. Some visitors have actually abused the drawer units, computer terminals and other elements of the system.[21] Frequent repairs have been required and, in some cases, there has been a need to replace the hardware. At the Glenbow Museum, the visible storage area was closed after two years because heavy drawer units were in danger of falling as a result of rough usage. Visitors often seem more interested in manipu-lating moving parts (drawers, lights, etc.) than in studying the objects. At the Glenbow Museum, informal evaluation found that, even after being instructed in the system's proper use, visitors showed little interest and soon moved on.[22] Many observations of visitor behaviour are not encouraging. The public tends to use the area more extensively (wandering up and down aisles as if in a supermarket) than intensively (studying the objects) as intended.[23] This lack of apparent interest is dis-appointing but may relate to the dearth of related programmes. Among children, the goal simply seems to be to open all the drawers, regardless of what is inside. They were also observed using large areas of visible storage at UBCMOA as a maze of hide-and-seek – exploratory behaviour, but not of the kind intended.

4 Visible storage inhibits the serious researcher, according to critics.[24] Duncan Cameron, director of the Glenbow Museum, maintains that the visible storage collection became inaccessible because retrieving specific objects for study was time-consuming and difficult. Some say that it has, in fact, been used to establish a barrier separating the public from staff and research collections.

5 Negative consequences for staff are also worrisome.[25] Because all the museum's errors, foibles, and insignificant kitsch are placed before the public, staff can be embarrassed more often than is the case with thoroughly researched exhibits. They are under pressure to upgrade and expand the catalogue data (although many regarded this as a positive consequence). They are forced into spending much more time dealing with visitors than would be the case with traditional systems. This may interfere with collections management and/or research. Some observers even make

the case that the position, authority and traditional responsibilities of curators may be undermined. Staff may also find working with a collection housed in a public area awkward and risky in security terms.

6 The initial costs and maintenance of visible storage are higher than the traditional model, some maintain.[26] There has been a tendency to 'overdesign' the cabinets, and visible storage is seen to be too elaborate to be a successful storage method. Additional costs also attach to the labour of mounting, providing security, installing individual locking systems, and providing public access to the documentation whether in text or computerized form. Of course, achieving the desired improvement in public accessibility will have attendant costs regardless of how it is accomplished.

7 Some argue that visible storage is inappropriate for small museums,[27] where collections tend to be unsystematic and poorly documented. Critics see a danger of creating a 'curio cabinet' full of unrelated objects with no underlying theme or apparent purpose.

SOLUTIONS

Unless squarely addressed and solved – or at least minimized – the problems outlined here clearly negate the advisability of implementing a visible storage system in any museum, much less a small one lacking the means to experiment.

Conservation, security and design

The most significant conservation difficulty is the damage caused to objects by drawer movement. Obviously, the solution requires mounting techniques involving deep slots in drawer liners, padding, and securing of objects.[28] At the Moncur Gallery of Pre-history, a simple and effective system has been installed to slow down the drawer motion and decrease the trauma to objects. Plastic electrical conduit tubing available at any hardware store has been used to develop a shock-absorbing system. Under each drawer, one tube is attached to the back of the case and another to the bottom of the drawer face to fit one inside the other. The air pressure and friction created within the tubes as the drawer is opened and closed slows the movement, thus reducing jarring. Such a system should be mandatory for any drawer units. Of course, the selection of suitable objects for drawer display is the primary defence; fragile items are better presented on shelves in glass-fronted cases. Better supervision, proper programming, and clearly labelling drawers would also serve to reduce the aimless opening of drawers.

Lighting is another conservation problem. Timed switches and exhibit-quality design help to minimize exposure. A drawer system that remains closed most of the time also protects light-sensitive objects. Rotation of collections to decrease cumulative exposure to light is practised by the Dugald Costume Museum.

Although fears have been voiced over security, current users report little or no difficulty.[29] Indeed, they claim that their security is improved over long-term closed storage because of the visibility of missing objects and the availability of location data. Visible storage systems for sensitive collections such as textiles have now been designed and tested by UBCMOA. The compromises achieved seem to be acceptable to all concerned.[30]

Visitor education and access to information

There has been a tendency to blame the system's failures on the visitor. However, orienting the general public to the visible storage concept, its use and potential value has been given insufficient attention.[31] This might be accomplished most effectively by traditional means, with the 'Mankind Discovering' introductory gallery at the Royal Ontario Museum as a model. Museums employing visible storage have been criticized for abdicating their responsibility to interpret their collections. By focusing didactic exhibit efforts on fostering an understanding of how to learn from objects, museums could be of great assistance to visitors by helping them use the resources housed in visible storage more effectively.[32]

Design of the information access system is also important. If visitors are alienated from or unable to use the information, intellectual access is denied and the whole system fails. Visitors have demonstrated *distaste* for the data book system. Small museum practitioners recommend keeping the catalogue information in relatively short, manageable books close to the related objects. The data must be accurate, complete (especially as to identification, date and provenance), presented in layman's language and delivered in a vehicle able to withstand intensive usage. Access must be simple and logical.[33] Short, readable interpretive essays spread throughout the data books have been suggested, to include the identification of uncertainities, gaps in the data, and areas where more research is required.[34] Whether such texts are more successful than similar labels in didactic exhibits (which tend to be ignored by visitors) remains to be seen. At any rate, the information would be available. The Alberni Valley Museum staff are convinced that photographs of objects on the data sheets are important; visitors quickly grasp the purpose of the data books and the system. The availability of staff is important in solving the access-to-information problem; curatorial offices are highly visible and open to the public at Port Alberni.

For some, computerization and interpretive video or laser disks are the only solution to providing access to information.[35] The use of computers is problematical, however. The Glenbow Museum found that computers became a plaything or the object of attention in competition with the objects on display.[36] Indeed, during the author's visit to UBC-MOA, an 'out-of-order' sign (unauthorized) was placed on the computer terminal when school groups were in the museum – evidence of serious unsolved problems with the computer strategy. Among them is logistics. If a small museum cannot afford numerous terminals, access to data is restricted to essentially one visitor at a time. Data books located throughout the exhibit are not so limited.

To combat misuse of facilities, increased stress on orientation is required.[37] Use of the system needs to be more highly structured by the museum, particularly for school groups. A major failing of the museums currently experimenting with visible storage is that they have neglected to provide adequate programming support. Few if any directly related educational activities have been devised to help visitors learn to use the system in a purposeful way.[38] Guided tours, task-oriented activities for families, and specific school programmes can help to provide a more structured approach to orienting the visitor to the resources available. Staffing the area with curators rather than security staff is another option; curator/visitor interaction provides both with the opportunity to give and receive information.

Maintaining research capabilities

Several strategies may be considered to solve the problem of inaccessibility of objects to serious research. Although the Glenbow Museum has concluded that visible storage collections become inaccessible, others would disagree.[39] Certain times can be provided for direct access during hours when the museum is closed to the public. Use of specially designed units that can be moved into a research lab, as is the case at UBCMOA,[40] is another solution. For many small museums, which may receive relatively few such requests, this type of availability is not a problem.

CONCLUSIONS

Although some observers feel that visible storage is not appropriate for the small museum, those visited during the course of this study all indicated general satisfaction with its suitability for them. Some maintain that the system in fact works better in small institutions, where the size of the collections to be displayed is not overwhelming[41] and the expectations of visitors, communities and trustees are different from those of large museums.

The major problems encountered by small museums seem to be solvable with attention to design of the system.[42] Recommendations include the use of solid wood (rather than particle board) for constructing drawer units, the use of heavy-duty hardware and locks, and the avoidance of large wide horizontal as well as vertical drawers, which are difficult for visitors to handle and which jam easily. Large uncovered walk-in cases such as those found at UBCMOA should be avoided because of wasted space needed for access corridors and because they are uncovered, which results in dust problems. The overall layout requires consideration of traffic flow and aisle width to accommodate circulation when the drawers are in use. In general, the design of visible storage systems assumes that the needs of the visitors are on a par with those of staff and conservation. This is a central tenet of the visible storage philosophy.

Staff commitment to the concept is crucial.[43] For curators (arguably the most threatened by the system), this commitment is especially important. Visible storage demands an uncommon level of user/visitor orientation on the part of the curator and a willingness to share his/her work with the public. Many argue that the increased contact (once accepted) has a positive consequence and solves some interpretive problems. Both curators and visitors gain through this closer interaction.

This investigation provided no clear answer as to whether the visible storage approach is more or less expensive to construct and operate than the exhibit and closed-storage model. Some savings may be realized from the combination of exhibit and storage systems. In the end, however, there may be additional costs for providing the fullest possible visual and intellectual access to the collections. Although important, cost should not become the sole determining factor in such fundamental questions as the best means of providing public access to the resources of the museum.

In making the decision to implement visible storage, a number of factors must be considered. The general philosophy, intended purposes, objectives, community role and desired image of the museum should be determined. Visible storage seems most suited to an institution primarily having intensive local usage, educational support purposes and research functions. It does not appear to be the most appropriate format for meeting the needs of the typical tourist visitor.

The nature of the collections must be evaluated. The Alberni Valley Museum found that the range, type and provenance of its collections were not suitable for properly depicting the community's development through traditional narrative exhibits.[44] The visible storage alternative was selected to portray the personal heritage and collecting interests that formed the basis of the museum.

Size of collections is also a factor. Many believe that the system works best with a small, narrowly defined collection that is of manageable size to install, maintain and comprehend.[45]

The average dimensions and form of object must also be taken into account. The Dugald Costume Museum, the Moncur Gallery, and the HMCS Chippewa Naval Museum selected visible storage because it handles varied small objects well. Fragmented or repetitively duplicated objects found in archaeological collections require close physical inspection and good interpretation and are not generally regarded as suitable for visible storage; however, the relatively small and homogeneous collection of the Moncur Gallery seems to be a satisfactory application. Systematic scientific collections can also be suitable for visible storage.[46] At The Sam Waller Little Northern Museum, visitors exhibit sustained interest in shelves of glass jars containing wet specimens and bird study skins on display in drawers – perhaps because few other museums exhibit such items.

The conservation requirements of the collections are also important considerations. Sturdy, easily mounted objects are the most suitable candidates for visible storage. Fragile or light-sensitive collections are not good candidates; however, effective compromises have been reached in a textile system developed at UBCMOA.[47]

Visitors' familiarity with the objects is another consideration. They tend to pay more close attention to and get more out of an inspection of objects whose context and function are familiar to them.[48] Collections of dolls, clothing or eating utensils, for example, are likely to be of greater interest than esoteric collections or general collections from exotic cultures. The least familiar collections are the least popular in visible storage.

The types and numbers of requests for physical access to the collections must be evaluated. The majority of requests come from students, commercial users, artists, photographers, collectors and hobbyists, ethnic groups, donors and other museums.[49] If most can be served through visual access, visible storage could reduce demands on staff. If requests require hands-on access, visible storage is less efficient than closed storage. If staff is limited and there are no plans to use the collections extensively for research or changing exhibits, visible storage may be an alternative worth considering.

Alternatives to visible storage should be evaluated. First is the traditional model of exhibits and closed storage. Given the desire for increased accessibility, this approach requires policies, procedures and facilities for providing the public with access to the museum's complete resource base. Many requests for access can also be met through photographic and laser disk imagery and catalogue records. Another approach is a stratified system which provides traditional exhibits and a study room for hands-on examination of selected reference collections. Traditional closed storage in conjunction with a research laboratory are provided to serve the needs of scholars. One potential alternative is the 'technological solution',[50] in which interactive computer and optical laser disk systems provide high-quality and varied visual records of the object while the computer provides the complete textual database. The technology to accomplish this has already been developed and tested, but the expense of such a system may be beyond the financial means of many small museums.

Utilizing visible storage for only part of the collection may also be considered. The Dugald Costume Museum rotates collections through its visible-storage system. This is a highly labour-intensive approach, but the cycle of rotation could be matched to staff resources.

Most museum workers have accepted the philosophy expounding increased public access to our institutional holdings. Visible storage has much to recommend it, yet there

193

are many potential problems involved in its application. For some purposes and for some collections, the difficulties identified are avoidable.

There are certain consequences of visible storage that must be kept in mind. The first is that – whether or not it is understood as such – visible storage is at one and the same time both a storage and a display system. Visitors need to be made aware that this is not the familiar type of thematic exhibit, and, particularly in light of the absence of interpretive labelling, they must be provided with some form of structured orientation and programming. Second, although the visible-storage approach puts collections at some conservation risk, every museum function creates a fundamental conflict between use and preservation. The challenge is to find the most effective compromises. In some limited cases, visible storage may indeed be the best middle ground. On the other hand, visible storage will never replace conceptually ordered didactic exhibits. If clearly differentiated for the visitor, the two formats may be ideal foils for one another.

As those who have examined this approach have pointed out, the visible-storage concept is rather museologically abstract. As we wrestle with our decisions and the problems of implementing our ideal of democratic access, we must not neglect to take into account the consequences for the museum's public. The visitor's experience with the collections housed in visible storage paralleling that of the curator may be so qualitatively valuable that we in the museum field will need to re-examine completely all our traditional approaches and, for the sake of truly engaging our visitors with the challenge of becoming their own curators and interpreters, learn to deal effectively with the costs involved.

This paper first appeared in Curator *33(1) (1990), pp. 49–62.*

ACKNOWLEDGEMENTS

Funding for this research was provided by the Foundation Fund of the Manitoba Museum of Man and Nature, the Town of The Pas, and the Bursary Programme of the Canadian Museums Association.

NOTES

1 Duncan F. Cameron (1983) 'Museums and public access', in Barry Lord and Gail Dexter Lord (eds) *Planning Our Museums*, Ottawa: National Museums of Canada, 85–6; Roland W. Force (1975) 'Museum collections – access, use, and control', *Curator* 18(4): 250–1, 254–5.

2 Michael M. Ames (1985) 'De-schooling the museum: a proposal to increase public access to museums and their resources', *Museum* 38(1): 27, 30; D. F. Cameron (1986) 'Creating visual and intellectual access to museum collections: a report to the Board of Governors', Calgary: Glenbow-Alberta Institute, 22.

3 Michael M. Ames (1977) 'Visible storage and public documentation', *Curator* 20(1): 69; Catherine Lee Blackbourn (1986) 'Visible storage: an overview of the advantages and pitfalls of this combined storage and display technique, with a look at four museums which use it', *Museum Quarterly* 15(3): 22; Cameron, 'Museums and public access'.

4 Institutions visited and staff interviewed were: Alberin Valley Museum: John Mitchell, director, Jean McIntosh, curator; Gordon Bailey, museum technician; the Dugald Costume Museum: Wyn Van Slyck, director; Glenbow-Alberta Institute: Duncan F. Cameron, director; Fred Greene, chief conservator; Brian King, preparator; H.M.C.S. Chippewa Naval Museum: Mike Shortridge, curator; Moncur Gallery of Prehistory; Anna Grace Diehl, director; University of British Columbia Museum of Anthropology: Michael M. Ames, director, Elizabeth Johnson, curator of collections, Len McFarlane, museum technician, Christopher Miller, head, Marketing and Development.

5 Ames, 'De-schooling the museum', 25–6; Elizabeth Johnson, interview, 3 June 1987.

6 Ames, 'Visible storage', 73, 78; Johnson, interview.

7 Len McFarlane, interview, 3 June 1987: Nathalie MacFarlane and Elena Parkins (1977) 'Museum evaluation and ethnography', unpublished paper, Anthropology 433, University of British Columbia Museum of Anthropology, 26–8, 35–7, 44.

8 Cameron, 'Museums and public access', 102; Michael M. Ames (1981) 'Preservation and access: a report on an experiment in visible storage', *Gazette* 14(3–4): 26, 27; Thomas S. Buechner (1962) 'The open study-storage gallery', *Museum News* 40(9): 34–5; Fred Greene and Brian King, interviews 2 June 1987; John Mitchell, interview, 5 June 1987.

9 John Fletcher Mitchell (1983) 'The community museum', in Barry Lord and Gail Dexter Lord (eds) *Planning Our Museums*, Ottawa: National Museums of Canada, 70; Nathalie Macfarlane (1984) 'Museums, collections, and their primary users in a community setting', *Museum Round-Up* 91: 20; Marjorie Halpin (1984) 'Access and the public imagination', audiotape of a paper presented at the Canadian Museums Association Annual Conference Session 'Rights of Intellectual Access in Museums', Quebec City, 23–25 May 1984, Ottawa: Canadian Museums Association.

10 Cameron, 'Museums and public access', 93; Buechner, 36; Ames, 'De-schooling the museum', 27.

11 Blackbourn, 'Visible storage', 26; Ames, 'Preservation and access', 26.

12 Mitchell, 70; Mitchell, interview.

13 Ames, 'De-schooling the museum', 29–30; Halpin, 'Access and the public imagination'; Macfarlane, 20; Johnson, interview; Bailey, interview, 5 June 1987.

14 Cameron, 'Creating visual and intellectual access', 46, 67; Force, 250; Elizabeth Jachimowicz (1977) 'Storage and access', *Museum News* 56(2): 33; Ames, 'De-schooling the museum', 26; Greene, interview; Johnson, interview; E. Verner Johnson and Joanne C. Horgan (1979) *Museum Collection Storage: Protection of the Cultural Heritage. Technical Handbooks for Museums and Monuments 2*, Paris: United Nations Educational, Scientific and Cultural Organization, 20, 32.

15 Blackbourn, 'Visible storage', 22–5; Macfarlane and Parkins, 50; Ames, 'Preservation and access', 24.

16 Macfarlane and Parkins, 37.

17 Johnson, interview; Cameron, 'Creating visual and intellectual access', 46.

18 Mitchell, 71.

19 Macfarlane and Parkins, 22–3, 53; Cameron, 'Creating visual and intellectual access', 44.

20 Johnson and Horgan, 20; Ames, 'De-schooling the museum', 26; Cameron, 'Creating visual and intellectual access', 32, 45.

21 Duncan F. Cameron, interview, 1 June 1987; King, interview; Wyn Van Slyck, interview, 8 June 1987.

22 Cameron, 'Creating visual and intellectual access', 65–7; Cameron, interview; Catherine Lee Blackbourn (1985) 'Access: visible storage and the museum visitor', unpublished final paper prepared for the Masters of Museum Studies Programme, University of Toronto, 64.

23 Blackbourn, 'Access', 64; Johnson and Horgan, 20.

24 Blackbourn, 'Visible storage', 24; Blackbourn, 'Access', 5; Cameron, 'Creating visual and intellectual access', 45, 54; Mitchell, interview; Van Slyck, interview.

25 Ames, 'Visible storage', 73, 77; N. Macfarlane, 27, 29; Johnson, interview; Mitchell, interview; Jean Mcintosh, interview, 5 June 1987.

26 Ames, 'Preservation and access', 27; Jachimowicz, 33; Blackbourn, 'Visible storage', 22; Johnson and Horgan, 20. Cf. opposite view by Ames, 'Visible storage', 73; and Mitchell, interview.

27 N. Macfarlane, 19; Blackbourn, 'Visible storage', 25.

28 L. MacFarlane, interview; Greene, interview. Materials used include ethafoam, surgical tubing, monofilament, Velcro and polyester netting. An alternative employed by the Alberni Valley Museum is acid-free museum board to which objects are secured with monofilament.

29 King, interview; L. MacFarlane, interview; Mitchell, interview.

30 Johnson and Lambert.

31 Blackbourn, 'Access', 33, 36, 52, 56, 85; Michael M. Ames, interview, 3 June 1987; Mitchell, interview.

32 Marshall McLuhan and H. Parker (1968) 'McLuhanism in the museum', *Museum News* 46(7): 11–18; Halpin, 'Access and the public imagination'.

33 Jachimowicz, 32; Blackbourn, 'Visible Storage', 26; Mitchell, 70.

34 Halpin, 'A new kind of museum', 306–7; Ames, 'Visible storage', 33; Blackbourn, 'Access', 75.

35 Cameron, 'Creating visual and intellectual access', 6, 9; Ames, interview; Margaret Stott, Curator of Ethnology and museum training coordinator, University of British Columbia Museum of Anthropology, letter to the author, 14 September 1987; Margaret Stott (1986) 'Videodiscs: museums and the future', *Muse* 3(4): 44–6; John Cash (1985) 'Spinning toward the future: the museum on laser videodisc', *Museum News* 63(6): 9–35; Fred Granger and Joan Mattie (n.d.) 'The Canadian Museum of Civilization's optical disc project', report, Ottawa: Canadian Museum of Civilization.

36 Cameron, 'Creating visual and intellectual access', 65; Blackbourn, 'Access', 54.

37 Blackbourn, 'Access', 36, 52, 56, 66, 85; Mitchell, interview; McIntosh, interview.
38 Ames, interview; Mitchell, interview; Stott, letter.
39 Cameron, interview is contradicted by McIntosh, interview.
40 Ames, 'Preservation and access', 26; Johnson, interview.
41 Mitchell, interview.
42 Derived from King, Greene, Mitchell, L. MacFarlane, Shortridge and Van Slyk interviews.
43 Ames, 'De-schooling the museum', 27; Halpin, 'Access and the public imagination'; Johnson, interview.
44 N. Macfarlane, 19.
45 Blackbourn, 'Access', 90; Johnson and Horgan, 20; Mitchell, interview.
46 Johnson and Horgan, 20. In fact, the majority of requests for information from museums are in the natural history field according to Blackbourn, 'Access', 14, 46.
47 Johnson and Lambert.
48 Blackbourn, 'Access', 64, 84; Mitchell, interview.
49 Blackbourn, 'Access', 14.
50 Cameron, 'Creating visual and intellectual access', 69; Granger and Mattie; Stott, 'Videodiscs'; Cash.

23

Curators' closet

Carrie Rebora

Carrie Rebora describes a major visible storage installation at the Metropolitan Museum of Art in New York.

Curators for years have vigorously debated whether open storage helps to 'demystify' museums or merely confuses visitors with its huge number of objects placed seemingly at random. The new open-storage facility at New York's Metropolitan Museum of Art features what has been described variously as 'a straightforward compromise' to the storage problem facing most art museums and 'the ultimate closet'. The Henry R. Luce Center for the Study of American Art, which opened in December 1988, is 16,000 square feet of open storage devoted to approximately 10,000 works of art. But it is more than merely open storage; it is the locus for the American art curators' cataloguing projects; the site of a computerized public access system; and the information centre of the Metropolitan's American Wing, providing facts on every work of art curated by this section of the museum.

Michael Ames, director of the Museum of Anthropology at the University of British Columbia, which has its own visible storage, once maintained that 'by hiding away their duplicates, copies, and "junk," museums can present themselves as "treasure houses" and their collections as "fine art," thus keeping from the public the wide range of style and quality that exist'. This charge echoed similar judgements from critics, academics and members of the general public who recognized that museums play a powerful role in setting forth chronologies and other arrangements of art and artefacts for students and the public. Exhibits, under such scrutiny, were too didactic or not didactic enough, too linear or nationalistic, included too many categories or too many mainstream artists, were overly designed or not designed properly.

Frustration with the so-called 'precious object' tradition – which enforces a selective, inherently qualitative hierarchy – often has been coupled with the opinion that public museum collections belong to members of the public, who have a right to see every object. The Glenbow Museum in Calgary, Alberta, Canada, for example, studied the selection process in museums (stored versus exhibited works of art) and projected a plan for open storage that 'would meet the needs and interests of all publics utilizing the museum's resources'. For museums with sizeable collections, such a democratic display requires not only ample space, but complete reorganization of fixtures, platforms, labels and other gallery devices.

In fact, so much reinstallation amounts to a logistical and theoretical ordeal that never can satisfy 'all publics'. Another study conducted in the mid-1980s found that putting a museum's entire collection on view actually abrogated the museum's responsibility to the public because it threatened viewers (who might be disoriented by so many works of art) as well as curators (whose job it is to arrange objects in a pleasing and art-historically sensible fashion).

The Luce Center can be accurately described as a product of its time, when building or installing open-storage facilities was a common and governmentally funded enterprise. But it is not a product of the museum demystification trend, nor does it 'threaten' viewers. As an alternative installation – forty-four regularly spaced, floor-to-ceiling glass cases containing objects arranged generally by medium or material and specifically by date, style, form, type or method of manufacture – the Luce Center required more, rather than less, arrangement and categorization. By default, because it allows the museum's American Wing to showcase a wider range of art than ever before, it responds to critics of curatorial selection. Moreover, because it reveals everything that was pre-viously stored, it might satisfy those who thought the museum had secreted important works of art from view (although curators always have escorted visitors into storage by appointment).

Open storage represents the third component in the American Wing's tripartite system of display: galleries, where selected objects of a particular time in history, theme or style are shown together; period rooms, where objects are displayed as they are believed to have been used at the time they were made; and comparative context, where similar objects or objects by a particular artist or craftsman are arranged side by side.

This system of varied display corresponds to the changes on the curating of American art at the Metropolitan that culminated in 1980, when the departments of American Painting and Sculpture and American Decorative Arts joined as the Departments of American Art to open the new American Wing, which houses the museum's collections of American art executed before the early twentieth century. Originally, American paintings hung with European paintings and American decorative arts were only repre-sented in period rooms. This presentation influenced installations in other museums and the way scholars and collectors looked at American art of the eighteenth and nineteenth centuries. But by the 1970s, it had become *retardataire* by most standards and was cer-tainly inefficient for showing the world's most comprehensive collection of American paintings, sculpture and decorative art.

The new wing integrates the potential for myriad changing exhibits and permanent installations, including large-scale architectural elements, stained-glass windows, sculp-ture and a special, elliptical gallery for John Vanderlyn's enormous *Panoramic View of the Palace and Gardens of Versailles*. Refurbished period rooms, along with several new rooms, complete a chronology of American interior design from the late seventeenth century through the early twentieth century.

The Luce Center, located on the American Wing's mezzanine, houses those American fine art and decorative art objects that are not on view in the permanent galleries and period rooms or on loan to other institutions. In general, the works of art in the Luce Center augment the selection of works on view throughout the American Wing. For example, visitors interested in John Frederick Kensett's last summer's work, a series of paintings given to the museum in 1874, can see all of the canvases by moving between the landscape painting gallery and the Luce Center. Those who come to the Metro-politan to see John Singer Sargent's notorious painting of *Madame X* will find out more about the artist by viewing many of his less famous paintings, which the museum received from his sister in 1950. The galleries focus attention on a selection of Pennsylvania German pottery, eighteen-century silver drinking vessels, and late nineteenth-century ceramics, for example, while the Luce Center shows hundreds of other objects that display similarities and differences.

The objects in the Luce Center, comprising nearly two-thirds of the collection of American art, are sometimes referred to as the reserve or study collection. The objects in the Luce Center represent a wide range of quality in terms of craftsmanship, technique and state of preservation; some are of questionable attribution or national origin awaiting further research; others are there because they duplicate, but nonetheless amplify, the works shown in the main galleries. Because the Luce Center is the American Wing's primary storage facility, it is not unusual to find highlights of the collection on view, awaiting reinstallation, conservation or shipping to borrowing institutions.

Designing and installing the Luce Center was a collaborative effort of curators and conservators, museum technicians, student interns, computer experts, architectural and graphic designers, lighting specialists and museum educators. Planning began with travel to institutions with open-storage facilities, research centres, and computerized public access systems. In 1985, six American Wing curators formed a working group to plan the open-storage facility with the aid of design consultants from George Sexton and Associates of Washington, D.C., and a museum computerization specialist, James L. Yarnall. For the next three years, these two aspects of preparation occurred simultaneously. While designers proposed various display solutions and floor plans and investigated appropriate vitrines, rapid data entry technicians filled the computerized database with information from the card catalogues. At times, as when thousands of objects were remeasured for case placement and for accuracy in the database, the two projects overlapped. Working group meetings served to check the progress of both activities, to discuss particular issues (for example, the arrangement of objects and the type of information that should be available in a public access system) and to ensure that the installation and the computer system would converge in late 1988.

The main design issue was the cases, which had to fit rigorous criteria of both curators and conservators. All-glass cases with large sliding doors satisfied the basic requirements: secure, but easily opened by museum technicians and curators with security clearance; heat-free and dust-free, but not airtight, so that the cases acclimatize to the controlled environment throughout the museum, rather than within each case, and adjustable shelving for objects and metal lattice screens for paintings.

Much of the working group's planning occurred before the cases were ordered to determine dimensions and the total number of cases. After ordering 21 cases for decorative arts, 15 narrower cases for paintings, and eight wall cases, curators turned their attention to more specific arrangements. A mock-up of one case module was constructed in the American Wing storeroom, and objects were placed, recorded and photographed by shelf. These photographs became the guide for the final installation.

The Luce Center computer network evolved from a single personal computer in 1984 to nearly fifty terminals by late 1988. Working with the basic data entered during 1985, a redocumentation team proofread, fact-checked and reconciled minute details. With only three years to recatalogue the entire American Wing collection, the team leaders confined research to sources available in the department archives, card catalogues and library. They standardized terminology ('tray', not 'salver', 'side chair', not 'chair, side') and wrote and rewrote data standards as the material presented itself during cataloguing. Interns were assigned to specific areas of the collection, and the data were eventually stored in three personal computers: one for furniture, silver and metalwork; another for natural substances, paintings and sculpture; and the third for ceramics and glass. Individualized information for every object in the collection (each spoon in a service, rather than one record for the entire set) was entered on a template with 58 essential fields, including title/description, date of execution, artist/maker name, life dates, medium, credit line, and so on.

In 1988, the various databases were joined in a network of IBM-compatible personal computers supported by two file servers, each with 330-megabyte hard disks and four megabytes of random access memory. One file server holds the active files for office use, the other supports the public access system in a secure, tamper-proof configuration. The database programs were updated periodically between 1985 and 1988; the current system is written in a program that provides menu-driven access to functions for adding and modifying information on each object. Curators continue to refine the data to reflect new research and recent acquisitions. The public access system, which goes by the acronym AWARE (American Wing Art Research), is a copy of the data that is updated once a week. Visitors are notified on the computer screens and in printed brochures that the data is copyrighted by the museum and subject to change.

As objects were placed in the Luce Center in 1988, interns posted locations in the computer for every object, whether it was in a gallery, the Luce Center, on loan, in conservation or in the photography studio. The computer, which can produce a variety of reports, printed case labels for furniture and paintings. To save space, smaller objects are identified by half-inch blocks silk-screened with accession numbers, the key to further information at the computers. The design and database projects came together in these final stages.

For three years, the Luce Center was the American Wing staff's major project. Since its opening, maintenance of the facility has been minimal. Having the entire collection on view has expedited curatorial research and has enhanced the wing's popularity with the public. School groups frequently visit to study and compare works of art. As for housekeeping, the cases require little care other than regular, exterior cleaning. When an object is removed, its place is marked with a 'temporarily removed' tag and its new location is recorded in the database. The tag is both a security measure and a space marker. Case lists, in holders at the end of most cases, describe the general contents of the case and direct visitors to the computers, where printed materials and the screens themselves lead visitors to further, detailed information. Volunteers and staff members make sure that the case holders are filled and that printed brochures, which provide a plan and description of the Luce Center, are amply supplied.

Major maintenance projects have been limited to replacing track light fixtures, because the first batch created intense glare, and additional alterations to increase the ventilation in the cabinets that house the computers.

In time, the public access computer system might be redesigned, because many museum visitors have found it difficult to use. Envisioning that the great majority of visitors would have some knowledge of computers and American art, the database was programmed to offer users a screen with 12 query fields and to respond to complicated searches. A visitor can, for example, search for mahogany chairs made in Boston between 1790 and 1800. Although many scholars and art history students make use of the computers for their research, most visitors are casual museum-goers who are confused by the multitude of query options.

The centre is, contrary to our expectations, most popular with people who notice that a particular work of art is related to something that they own, such as a glass dish, a porcelain vase or an upholstered chair. To serve the public better, a dictionary of terms commonly used to describe American art was recently added. Information on the museum's American miniatures, drawings and textiles – light-sensitive objects that are kept in closed storage – will be added soon.

Built into the Luce Center is an exhibition gallery designated for installations of the permanent collection that illuminate the results of new research and focus on works of art that are not usually shown in the galleries. Exhibitions of material related to Vanderlyn's panorama, American pastels, American period frames, and drawings by John Singleton Copley were well received and have laid the foundation for an active programme. Between special exhibitions, a history of the American Wing and collections of American art from the museum's founding through the present in text and photographs on wall-size panels is mounted in the Luce Center gallery. This installation turns the gallery into an orientation space that defines the Luce Center as a vital part of the American Wing's complete plan for viewers – and a useful and satisfying place to visit.

This paper first appeared in Museum News *69(7), pp. 50–4.*

24

Rules for handling works of art
Eric B. Rowlison

Poor handling is the greatest cause of object deterioration in museums. The principles, however, have changed little over the years. Eric Rowlison's list of rules, first written over twenty years ago, provide a useful basis for good practice.

A set of rules for handling works of art is only one of the ingredients necessary to ensure their safe movement within the museum. Demonstrations of correct techniques (preferably demonstrations in which staff can participate) are absolutely essential supplements to the printed word. Good equipment, in good working order, is another must. All the care in the world will not make a truck with a sticky wheel into a safe vehicle for the transport of paintings. Another necessity is a supervisory staff capable of adapting rules to unusual circumstances and of adjusting to emergencies of every sort. The most important requirement of all is a handling crew that work well together, are totally familiar with the correct procedures, and possess the ability to work in a careful and methodical manner. This is, perhaps, a tall order, but one deserving of the best efforts of all responsible institutions.

The moving of extremely large or heavy sculpture with cranes or rigging falls outside the realm of these rules. Such works present difficulties that the museum professional is not equipped to cope with: finding the correct balance point, attaching the ropes in such a way that they will neither slide off nor place undue strain on delicate projections, anticipating the movement of the ropes so as to cushion against abrasion, and so forth. Such efforts must be undertaken by specialists. The dangers involved in moving heavy sculpture (not only to the works themselves but to those handling them) turn the expense of hiring good riggers into an investment in safety.

In a similar way, the safe handling of works of art of any kind pays off in their increased well-being and in reduced premiums for the insurance that covers them. The following rules for handlers and supervisors and for the handling of specific kinds of museum objects are the product of observation and experience in art museums, but they should be useful for those responsible for moving many other kinds of valuable museum objects as well.

RULES FOR HANDLERS AND SUPERVISORS

Handlers

- Only one person directs any operation. Be sure you know who the supervisor is. Do not give directions unless you are in charge. Accept directions only from the supervisor, and address suggestions and comments only to that person.

- Look for existing damages before moving a work of art, and point them out to the supervisor. This protects you from blame and can save the object from further harm.
- Understand exactly where and how an object is to be moved before you move it. Be aware of any idiosyncrasies of the material involved. Ask questions freely.
- Ascertain whether a work contains loose or easily moving parts before handling it. If such parts are designed to be separated from the object (such as the pendulums of most clocks or heads of some marble sculptures), remove and transport them separately. If they are intended to remain attached to the object (such as portions of many modern sculptures and constructions or leaves of tables), secure them in such a way that they will not be harmed or cause damage during the move.
- Unless one person can easily and without hesitation manage both the size and weight of the object, two people must handle it. Never be reluctant to say that an object is too large or heavy for you to manage.
- Do not make any sudden or unnecessary movements while in the vicinity of works of art.
- Never walk backwards in the vicinity of works of art. Always be aware of what is behind you and how close you are to it.
- Do not smoke while handling works of art or while in the same room with them.
- Use clean cotton gloves to handle works of art at all times except when the objects you are moving are too smooth to grip safely through gloves. Keep your hands clean, even when using gloves; dirt and oil from fingers can cause serious damage.
- Handle only one object at a time, no matter how small. Use both hands in carrying.
- Handle works of art as little and as infrequently as possible. Carry them no farther than necessary; bring the vehicle to the works rather than the works to the vehicle.
- Never drag works of art.
- Take your time. Move slowly while carrying objects or pushing vehicles containing them.
- Never leave works of art sitting directly on the floor.
- Safely pad, pack or otherwise secure every object before moving it in a vehicle.
- Never put dissimilar works (such as sculpture and watercolours or ceramics and paintings) on the same vehicle. Never move objects of the same general type but of vastly different sizes, weights or materials together.
- Never overload any vehicle.
- Never discard packing materials before searching them thoroughly for fragments that may have dropped off in transit.
- Report all damages or possible damages to the supervisor immediately. Save all fragments. Remember that damages caused by careless handling frequently do not become visible for a considerable time. If the surface of a painting is bumped, it may be months or years before cracking and lifting of the paint surface appear.
- Make no distinctions as to supposed value or artistic merit. Treat every work of art as if it were the most important item in the collection.

Supervisors

- Only those totally familiar with correct handling should supervise an operation or train a new person.
- Supervisors who are not themselves conservators should consult with a conservator before undertaking moves of particularly fragile or unusual material. The supervisor should immediately report to the conservator any damage and should make a written

record of the circumstances under which it occurred.

- Be sure it is clear to everyone who the supervisor is.
- No person but the supervisor, whether a member of the work crew or an observer, must be allowed to issue instructions to the crew. See to it that all comments are directed to the supervisor.
- Check condition and note any special features of the material involved before making the move. If a work suffers from damage that may worsen in transit (such as lifting paint or a serious crack in a vase), ask a conservator to be present during the move.
- Always plan a move fully, transmit instructions to the crew clearly, and, once you have made a plan, follow it through. Be sure the crew understands precisely what is to be done.
- Refuse to undertake any move if you feel that you have too few handlers or that other considerations make the operation unduly hazardous. A good supervisor, however, can often devise an alternative method that can be safely undertaken with the existing group of handlers.
- Remember that too many hands are as dangerous as too few. It is up the supervisor to ensure that objects are moved by the appropriate number of handlers.
- The rules for handlers given above apply to everyone. Infractions are permitted *only* when the special nature of the material being moved dictates an exception. Only the supervisor can decide if such a situation exists. Should a supervisor break a rule for some reason, he should be sure to point out to the others involved why he has done so.
- When correcting someone for breaking a rule, always point out the reason for the rule. People are more inclined to do something right if it makes sense.
- Do not base cautionary instruction on value. In handling works of art, all are of equal value. The physical requirements of each object and the safety of the handlers must be the only considerations.
- Do not act nervous, no matter how delicate a handling operation may be. Do not make irrelevant comments or conversation during a move.
- Never urge haste.

RULES FOR HANDLING VARIOUS KINDS OF WORKS OF ART

Paintings and framed works

Handling paintings and framed works

- Before picking up a painting, be sure it is secure in its frame.
- Do not touch the front or back of a painting. Never allow *any* object to rest, however lightly, against either surface.
- Never apply tape or adhesive to either the front or the back of a painting or to the visible parts of its frame.
- Do not carry paintings by one side. Grip the painting with one hand beneath and one hand on the side of the frame, or with one hand on either side, whichever seems more stable.
- Hold paintings at points where the frame is strong, never on fragile gesso decoration.
- Never insert your fingers between the stretcher bar and the back of the canvas. This can do serious damage to the paint surface.
- Carry unframed paintings by grasping only the inner and outer *edges* of the stretcher

bar, not the broader sides parallel to the canvas. Your fingers must not touch the front or back of the painting or wrap around the stretcher bar.

- Always move paintings with their surfaces vertical unless instructed to the contrary by the supervisor.
- If you need to carry a painting through a closed door, be sure an extra handler is along to open *and hold* the door for you.
- Carry large paintings as close to the floor as possible without striking door sills or placing yourself in a clumsy position.
- Carry wrapped paintings with extra care. It is frequently impossible to recognize the problems of works that are covered, and often very hard to obtain a firm grip through the wrappings. Wrapped paintings should be moved on trucks or dollies whenever possible.
- Do not set paintings down balanced by one corner on the floor and one in your hand. Either hold the painting correctly or set it down completely.
- Always store paintings with their surfaces vertical unless instructed to the contrary by the supervisor. Works framed under glass should not be stored flat. Works whose paint is lifting or flaking, however, should be stored flat, paint surface up.
- Before hanging a painting, be sure its hanging devices are firm.
- Never hang paintings with their frames overlapping. Even in closely packed storage, allow enough room on all sides of the frame to grip and remove the painting without touching neighbouring works.

Stacking paintings and framed works

- Avoid stacking whenever possible. Paintings and framed works are frequently stacked, however, on painting trucks, and many of the rules given here apply to stacking both on trucks (see below) and in storage.
- Never stack unframed works or works whose frames do not extend beyond the surface of the painting.
- Never stack works with protruding hanging devices.
- Always stack on a non-skid surface such as rubber or cloth, never on tile or polished wood.
- Stack works of a similar size together. Put the largest work at the back tapering to the smallest at the front.
- Stand the inside work in as vertical a position as possible; it should hold easily without falling forward. Stand all succeeding works flush with this one. The natural tendency is to stack at too great an angle. This creates pressure harmful to works on the inside and may cause the stack to slide forward from the bottom. (See Fig. 24.1)
- Crisscross the works back to back and face to face so that they lie alternately vertically and horizontally. (See Fig. 24.2) This eliminates the danger of one frame slipping off another into the work next to it and protects the faces of the works from protruding objects on the backs of adjacent frames. Adjacent works must be large enough to crisscross each other completely.
- Keep stacks as shallow as possible. The weight of works at the front of a deep stack can damage frames at the back.
- Do not stack extremely large or heavy works directly against each other. Support each such work (or, in some cases, every other work) with a 2-by-4-inch beam angled out from the wall. (See Fig. 24.3) Keep such stacks very shallow; access to any work can be gained only by moving everything in front of it, and it is easy to damage the paintings in shifting the beams. Furthermore, because the beams all touch the wall, it is impossible to keep the stack lying flat, and after a few layers it begins to assume a dangerous angle.

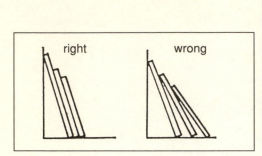

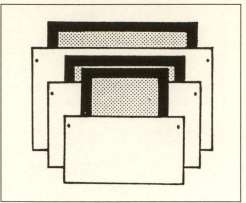

Fig. 24.1 Right and wrong way to stack paintings and other framed works

Fig. 24.2 In stacking, crisscross framed works back to back and face to face, vertically and horizontally

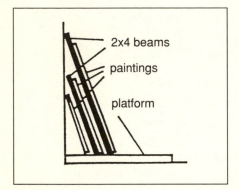

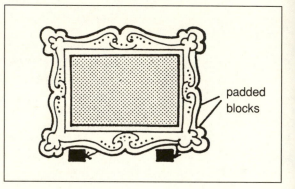

Fig. 24.3 When stacking large or heavy works, insert 2-by-4-inch beams for support

Fig. 24.4 Stack works with ornate frames on padded blocks

- Stack works with ornate frames only on padded blocks, which will spare fragile, extended corners from receiving the weight. (See Fig. 24.4) Place a sheet of cardboard larger than the outermost frame projection between each of the works.

Moving paintings on painting trucks

- In loading painting trucks, follow the rules for stacking given above.
- One handler should stay with the truck as it is loaded or unloaded to prevent its rolling as works are lifted on or off and to steady the works remaining on it.
- Do not allow the inside paintings on opposite sides of the truck to rest against each other above the truck's framework.
- Place unframed works on the outside of painting trucks, unless the works are protected by cardboard separation sheets.
- Do not load on a truck any painting so large that its frame or stretcher will not be firmly supported by the truck's framework. There must be no chance of a painting

slipping from this framework. For handling oversize paintings, see below.

- Do not overload trucks. The outside painting must not extend beyond the sides of the vehicle.
- Tie loaded trucks before moving them. Be careful that the rope does not come into contact with the surfaces of the paintings. Coil the rope neatly; do not allow it to drag on the floor.
- Two handlers, at least one of them experienced in handling works of art, should accompany each loaded truck.

Oversize paintings

- Handles screwed to the stretcher or frame of an extremely large or heavy work give a better grip. Extra handlers can steady the centre of the painting by means of handles attached to the crossbars of the stretcher.
- When carrying a very tall painting, the handler at each end should hold the sides only (rather than a side and the bottom). Lifting from underneath could raise the centre of gravity sufficiently to make the painting topple.
- Works too large for painting trucks can often be moved on sculpture dollies. This is hazardous but, if done carefully, less dangerous than carrying. At least three handlers are necessary. One handler supports each end of the painting. If the work is fairly light, these two can lift its edge onto the dolly, which is steadied by the third handler. If the work is heavy, one handler can raise the corner while the third handler slips the dolly under the centre of the work and holds it flush to the edge of the painting (See fig. 24.5). The painting and the dolly are then brought to the horizontal together and lowered to the floor. (If a heavy painting is angled onto a dolly set flat on the floor, the dolly might kick out when the painting is lowered.) The third handler steadies the dolly until the painting is securely set. Keep the painting *absolutely vertical* while it is being moved, as dollies have no fixed wheels and can kick out to one side if the painting is tilted. The third handler should steady the dolly over door sills and rough spots.

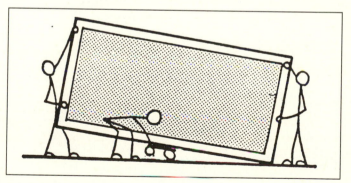

Fig. 24.5 When placing a large painting on a dolly for transport, lift the dolly to the edge of the painting and lower the two together

Taping glass on works of art

- Taping glass on works of art before packing them for travel affords protection against damage should the glass break during transit. Fragments of broken glass will adhere to the tape rather than fall onto the surface of the work. Never tape Plexiglas, as it is impossible to remove the adhesive marks from it.

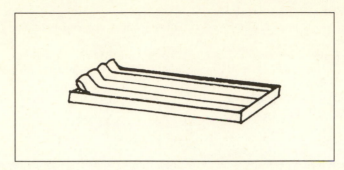

Fig. 24.6 When taping glass on works of art for protection during transit, double one end of the tape over against itself for ease of removing

- Use masking tape or a similar pressure-sensitive paper tape.
- Apply tape in parallel strips that overlap slightly or are at most 1/4 inch apart.
- Do not allow the tape to touch any part of the frame.
- Double the tape over against itself at one edge of each strip. (See Fig. 24.6) This makes the tape easier to remove. It is particularly advisable if the frame is gilt or has any surface susceptible to damage from adhesive.
- To remove the tape, pull each strip back slowly along its own length. Do not pull it at right angles to the surface, as the strain can break the glass. (See Fig. 24.7)
- To remove traces of adhesive from the glass, dampen a cloth and wipe with benzene if available, or with Windex, turpentine or rubbing alcohol. Do not pour the cleaning fluid directly on the glass. Do not allow the cleaning fluid to touch the frame or seep under the rabbet of the frame. Remove stubborn bits of adhesive with a razor blade.

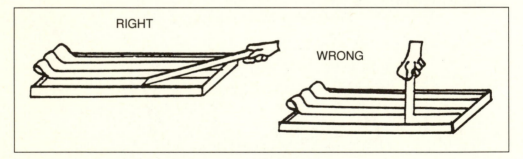

Fig. 24.7 Right and wrong way to remove tape from glass

Unframed works on paper

Handling mounted works

- Handle mounted works only by the mount; never touch the work of art itself.
- Keep mounts flat, face up.

Handling unmounted works

- Lift sheets by the upper corners so that they hang free without buckling. But do not carry them any distance in this manner, as air currents can cause creases.
- For carrying, lay unmounted sheets on clean cardboard. Keep works flat, face up.
- Lay works only on a clean, absolutely level surface.
- If rolling is unavoidable, roll the sheet face out with separation sheets lining the entire surface.
- Carry works that are on thin paper in a portfolio or Solander box or between sheets of cardboard.
- Take great care with charcoal, pencil and other easily smudged media. Carry each pastel separately, by itself, in a Solander box.

Piling mounted works

- Pile works face up.
- Pile only works of the same or similar sizes together, the largest at the bottom and the smallest at the top. If two adjacent edges of a pile are lined up, no mat opening should be visible.
- Keep piles shallow.
- Cover each pile with a large separation sheet to keep out dust.
- Do not rest objects on top of piles, not even weights to hold them down.
- Do not disturb piles. Shuffling through can cause creases and introduce dirt. If you must find something in a pile, search by creating a new pile.
- Move piles of mounted works on a tray truck or a flatbed truck.

Piling unmounted works

- Piling unmounted works is a *very* bad practice, but it is sometimes unavoidable. The following rules represent recognition of the existence of the custom, not an endorsement of it.
- Never pile works of easily smudged media. There is *no excuse* for piling pastel or chalk drawings.
- Place a separation sheet between each work. If the works are small, place each within a separation sheet folded in half. This helps to prevent the sheets and drawings from sliding apart.
- As with piling mounted works, keep the piles shallow, cover them with separation sheets, do not rest objects on top of them, and do not disturb them by shuffling through.
- Do not move piles of mounted works, unless the pile is contained in a Solander box, which will protect it from slipping or blowing apart. Keep the Solander box absolutely level while moving it.
- Do not allow piles to exist for longer than necessary.

Sculpture

General

- Never handle or lift sculpture by a projecting member such as an arm or head.
- Move and store sculpture in its most stable position. Some pieces are too top-heavy to stand upright without reinforcement; others can be damaged if laid flat. See, especially, the rules for marble and stone sculpture, below.
- Protect sculpture in transit with clean blankets, pads or cushions. Pad all ropes used

to tie the sculpture to the vehicle on which it is to be moved. Never allow sculpture to touch anything except padding, especially another work of art.

Metal sculpture

- Do not touch metal sculpture with bare hands, as fingerprints can leave dirt and oils that will eat into the metal. Touch metal sculpture only with gloves or soft cloth.

Marble and other stones sculpture

- Touch stone sculpture only with clean hands, as stone is porous and absorbs dirt and oil readily. Even better, wear gloves when handling stone sculpture.
- Support all protruding members of the sculpture with pads. Support all areas that do not rest on the body of the vehicle in a similar manner. Be sure the weight is distributed evenly; overpadding is as dangerous as inadequate padding.
- Move and store stone sculpture in the position in which it is installed unless this is not possible. Often the weight of a piece causes dangerous stresses if it lies at an unaccustomed angle. Stone can actually break under its own weight.

Small sculpture

- Always use two hands in carrying small pieces. Support the work with one hand under the base and steady the body of the piece with the other.
- Be sure a sculpture is firmly attached to its base before setting it down.

Large or heavy sculpture

- Moving heavy sculpture is a specialized field. Refuse to move any such work unless someone well versed in the subject is present and approves all arrangements. Each move is a unique problem. Do not assume you know everything about moving heavy sculpture; no one does.
- Do not carry heavy sculpture. Always transport it on properly padded trucks or dollies.
- Do not drag sculpture. Lift it onto the vehicle that will transport it.
- If a sculpture must be tilted to be placed on the dolly, one handler should lift the dolly and hold it flat against the underside of the work. Then tilt both the dolly and the sculpture back to the horizontal and lower them to the floor at the same time. This method offers maximum leverage and diminishes the danger of the dolly kicking out.
- Tie heavy sculpture down for transit, or otherwise completely secure it in position.
- Move even more slowly with heavy sculpture than with other material. These works can be dangerous and can seriously injure those handling them.
- Institutions that own hydraulic lift trucks can store and move heavy sculpture on skids or pallets, thus eliminating the need for physical contact with the work of art in transit.
- When circumstances warrant (for instance, when a heavy piece must be moved a short distance within an exhibition gallery), a work may be tilted onto a rug and the rug dragged slowly to the new location.
- Do not store heavy sculpture on the floor. This is the most difficult surface from which to pick it up, for there is no way to get under the piece. Store heavy sculpture on platforms or skids.

Decorative arts

Small objects

- Wear gloves when handling metal objects and unglazed ceramics, or handle them with tissue-paper. Slippery items (such as highly glazed ceramics) and objects whose surfaces are likely to catch on the threads of gloves (such as porcelain figures and some enamels) should be carried with *clean* bare hands.
- Life objects by sliding one hand underneath and steadying the body of the object with the other. Never lift by handles or edges; these are often the weakest parts, even if they were originally designed for carrying.
- Stand objects on their most stable surface for moving. Many bowls, for instance, are wider at the brim than the foot and should be transported in an inverted position.
- Always rest decorative art objects, especially glass and ceramics, on padded surfaces. Take care, however, that the surface is not so deeply cushioned that the objects cannot stand firmly.
- Pack objects in such a way that they cannot shift position in transit.
- As far as possible, move only objects of the same size together. Never move objects of different materials together.
- Do not overcrowd any vehicle. Objects should never be allowed to come into contact with each other or to protrude beyond the edge of the vehicle.

Furniture

- Remove marble or glass tops and similar material before handling furniture; transport these tops vertically.
- Tie down drawers, leaves and other loose or hinged parts of furniture with soft cord.
- Never drag furniture; always lift it. Lift from a point of structural strength; do not lift by arms or other protrusions. Lift chairs by the seat rail.
- Keep furniture in its intended position, never upside-down or on its side.

This paper first appeared in D. H. Dudley and I. B. Wilkinson (eds) (1979) Museum Registration Methods *(Washington, D.C.: American Association of Museums), pp. 355–66.*

25

Rentokil bubble: results of test

R. M. Entwistle and J. Pearson

The development of the Rentokil bubble has enabled the safer fumigation of collections using traditional chemicals but, as Entwistle and Pearson here explain, the bubble also provides an opportunity to explore safer alternatives.

This report follows the one in the November edition of *Conservation News*, in which we explained that we were fumigating parts of our collections with carbon dioxide and methyl bromide. We used the new inflatable Rentokil fumigation bubble and tested its efficiency by putting various life-stages of meal-worm beetle, *Tenebrio molitor*, blue-bottle fly, *Calliphora* sp., and carpet beetles, *Attagenus pellio* and *Anthrenus verbasci*, into the bubble with each fumigation, and keeping control samples of insects outside. Many museum conservators have encountered problems, and an objectionable smell when sulphur-containing materials have been fumigated with methyl bromide. As an experiment, materials specified as sensitive to methyl bromide were put into the bubble when this fumigant was ued.

Although carbon dioxide is probably a safer fumigant to use, there is very little information available as to its effectiveness under these conditions, and on this scale. We therefore considered it useful to describe our experiences using these two fumigants in the new bubble.

The dimensions of the bubble were 3 m × 3 m × 2.5 m. It consisted of a black base, upon which we constructed shelving, and a grey top which covers the objects and is sealed to the base once they are put inside. Before the fumigant is introduced, as much air as possible is extracted by a fan through a valve in the base. The fumigations were carried out in a secure outbuilding.

First to be fumigated with carbon dioxide was the natural history collection. The insects were placed into the bubble in their larval, pupal and adult stages, in suitable containers. The objects comprised birds and animal skins and birds' eggs. After the bubble was sealed, 70 kg of carbon dioxide was pumped in. Rentokil returned periodically over the next four weeks to top up the bubble, after which time the gas was vented off and the bubble opened. The insects were inspected and found to be still alive. Comparing the insects inside with those from the outside control, it was found that the carbon dioxide had only arrested their growth.

Rentokil called in their experts to see what had gone wrong. We also offered our suggestions to explain the failure. The problem was that the concentration of carbon dioxide had not been monitored, and it had not been high enough to kill the insects.

Rentokil's experts also found that the membrane of the bubble was permeable to carbon dioxide, and the method of introducing the gas was, in our view, unsatisfactory. No special coupling attachment exists in the present design for introducing carbon dioxide, only methyl bromide.

Rentokil hastened to make amends, and another fumigation was begun with fresh insects. This time the concentration of carbon dioxide within the bubble was measured, and Rentokil attempted by frequent refilling not to let this fall below 60 per cent at any time. Initially 70 kg of carbon dioxide were introduced into the bubble and over a three-week period a total of at least 259 kg of the gas used. A thermohygrograph was placed inside and the maximum temperature recorded was 17°C and the minimum 10°C. Temperature has a bearing on insect activity. An excessively low temperature means insect activity slows down and thus susceptibility to the fumigant is lessened.

After three weeks, the bubble was opened, and all the insect specimens, except one *Attagenus pellio* larva, were found to be dead. These have been subsequently kept under observation in a warm part of our laboratory. Since the fumigation, in early October, none of the test insects have revived, nor have any eggs that may have been present hatched.

After this, Rentokil raised its charges for further carbon dioxide fumigations with the bubble, and these were now prohibitive. A decision was made to fumigate the costume and ethnographic collections with methyl bromide. Some costume objects were kept out of the first fumigation, although test objects made of wool, fur, feathers, silk, cotton, tanned and untanned skins, in fact most materials reported as susceptible to methyl bromide, except rubber, were included. Another batch of fresh insects was put into the bubble, and a control of the same insects was placed outside.

The fumigation lasted three days, and 1 lb of methyl bromide was used. After the bubble was vented, the objects were left a further two days before removal. All the insects inside were carefully inspected and found to be dead, whilst those in the outside control remained alive. The insects from inside the bubble are still being observed, but so far none have revived, nor have any eggs hatched. With some trepidation we examined our test samples: none had changed their visible or physical appearance in any way, as far as we could tell. No lingering smell remained on any of the objects. We decided to fumigate the rest of the costume collection with methyl bromide, although caution dictated that we leave some very fragile susceptible objects out. The same results were obtained.

The ethnographic collection is composed mainly of basketry and wood, but also of untanned skins, furs, leather, cotton and wool. Again, fresh insects were used for the inside and outside control and the fumigation lasted three days. The results were the same as for the costume collection. All the insects inside were killed, and still show no signs of life, whilst the objects remained unchanged. They feel the same to handle afterwards, and none of the dyed or painted objects in any of the fumigations have faded.

All the objects will be monitored for any change in their condition or appearance. All the insects from the fumigations will be kept for a little longer, but none show any signs of life.

Carbon dioxide fumigation has no question marks about its safety and is obviously the most desirable. Although the second carbon dioxide fumigation was successful, it was not, however, a viable proposition with the bubble in its present form. Rentokil have already begun to design a bubble with a membrane impermeable to carbon dioxide. I look forward to seeing this with interest. A fumigation lasting three weeks may not suit many museums.

Methyl bromide is obviously quicker but how reactive is it with sulphur-containing materials, and is this reaction acceptable? We are not advocating its wholesale use, merely relating our experiences with it under a new fumigation method. None of our objects appears to have suffered from the methyl bromide fumigations. To all intents and purposes the objects are exactly the same now as before, except that they are pest-free. We suggest that the lingering smell reported could be due to using too great an amount of methyl bromide in too small an area. I would like to see properly controlled experiments using methyl bromide in museums, to find out exactly how it alters the chemical composition of sulphur-containing materials.

For museums that do not possess a fumigation chamber the Rentokil bubble is a useful alternative, although we would advise museums to check on prices for rental and fumigations. In our opinion, although the bubble is very efficient for the short-duration methyl bromide fumigation, it is less efficient in its present design for use with carbon dioxide.

We would like to acknowledge the complete co-operation of Rentokil, Norwich area, in the tests and fumigations.

'GREEN' FUMIGATION – RENTOKIL'S OWN STORY

A unique portable fumigation system capable of using carbon dioxide to disinfest collections within museum buildings is arousing considerable interest among curators.

The gas-proof fabric plastic chamber, sealed with a special gas-tight zip fastener and filled by means of a specially developed dispenser, is nicknamed 'the bubble' by Rentokil's Environmental Services Division, which has already used it to protect a wide variety of museum specimens, from stuffed birds to stuffed sofas and from documents to Daimlers.

Although the system can be used to make fumigation with the traditional gases methyl bromide or phosphine much more effective and safer, its ability to use carbon dioxide to eradicate fabric pests, booklice and other threats means it can be used in situations where the more toxic gases would be unwelcome or impracticable.

At Wells Museum, the entire natural history collection including mammals, birds, eggs and other material was successfully treated in this way. In this treatment the bubble was made of laminated aluminium, which further decreases any permeability so that all the gas is retained and the required fumigation period is reduced.

In the National Motor Museum at Beaulieu, the flexible bubble was used to eradicate woodworm and fabric pests from valuable motor cars and caravans but here methyl bromide and phosphine were used.

The Museum of the Order of St John of Jerusalem had valuable uniforms, fabrics and rare books saved and the technique was used with phosphine by Rentokil to preserve two ancient coracles in the Museum of Mankind that had cane worms on board. It has also been used to disinfest the wardrobe, some furniture and the 10,000 items in the costume collection at Glasgow's Citizen's Theatre – in that case five bubbles were used. The carbon dioxide facility proved the only possible way to kill cork moths in a cellar full of vintage champagne for a noble earl without tainting the bubbly.

In addition to using fumigant gases, the Rentokil bubble can be used with a dehumidifier to subject papers and documents to a sufficiently dry atmosphere for long enough to kill booklice and mites. The controlled humidity from ambient down to 5 per cent RH not only kills psocids but its bio-static effect will inhibit the growth of moulds.

For the first time, many collections can now be removed from cabinets, placed in the fumigation bubble, and while they are being treated, the cabinets and storage areas can be thoroughly cleaned, repaired and sprayed with insecticide without risk of tainting or otherwise affecting the specimens. The displays are thereby better protected than was previously possible.

Further research and development currently being undertaken by Rentokil's own scientists into the effectiveness of carbon dioxide at different temperatures on insect eggs and larvae indicates an increasing use of this material in future for conservation, within Rentokil's patented system.

Developed by the company's Project Development Unit, the major feature which makes the system unique is the special gas-proof, strong plastic or laminated aluminium fabric chamber which is fitted with a gas-tight zip, and a totally new method of dispensing fumigants. The system is compact, portable and versatile. All the equipment folds flat for easy transportation and can be used as a quarantine store, or a low humidity store as well as for fumigation.

The complete system comprises a base sheet of very durable hard-wearing flexible plastic, to which one-half of the zipper system is fixed. The item to be fumigated is placed on the base sheet and a top cover with the other half of the zip fitted to it is then unfolded and draped over. The two halves of the zip are then joined together using the unique closure device to make a gas-tight seal. Each unit has a predicted working life of at least five years.

If methyl bromide is the chosen fumigant, it is introduced from a special dispenser, through hoses and couplings fitted to the front of the system. The dispenser mixes the methyl bromide with air and ensures perfect fumigant distribution without layering so that the item or collection cannot be damaged by receiving an uneven dosage of gas. To enhance performance, the dispenser can also suck the air out of the sealed system prior to fumigation, thus forming a vacuum chamber which shortens fumigation times and increases efficiency.

If the chosen fumigant is phosphine, this gas will be released from a special phosphine dispenser which ensures good gas distribution and that no post-fumigation dust residues come into contact with the commodity.

The fumigation period will normally be less than for conventional *sheet* fumigation, due to the excellent gas retention of the system. This also reduces any residues. After the treatment, the fumigant is removed from the system by running the gas dispenser in reverse to suck it out. Hoses up to 100 metres in length can be connected to the system to disperse the fumigant into the atmosphere at any safe distance. When tests show that the fumigant has all been dispersed, the zips are opened and the items removed. Alternatively, a specially developed gas canister can be fitted to the suction side to absorb the fumigant, thus preventing any toxicant reaching the atmosphere. Valuable artefacts, fragile specimens or works of art can therefore be conveniently treated on site without being moved from the building in which they are stored or displayed.

The Rentokil system can also be used as a quarantine facility where specimens or artefacts can be kept isolated following fumigation. Exhibits which need to be kept in a controlled environment can be safely stored in the system until required. In buildings which are not pest-free or weatherproof, valuable items can be stored inside the system for unlimited periods, without the need for further fumigation.

Because the system holds gases for a long time, environmentally harmless fumigants such as carbon dioxide or nitrogen, which leave no residues, can be used. This makes possible the safe fumigation of delicate materials like silk or paintings, providing in effect an organic fumigation service and one which will not produce adverse chemical reaction with pigment or fibres.

Where conventional woodworm treatments cannot be used because of the inaccessibility of the affected area or the risk of damage to old frames, fumigation is a practical alternative. At Beaulieu, several cars, including a Prince Henry Vauxhall and one of the world's first caravans, have now been successfully preserved and their woodworm has been driven out.

Frank Ratcliffe, Rentokil's Service Development Manager, foresees a wide use for the system in museums, libraries, art galleries and archives throughout the world.

This paper first appeared in Conservation News *38 (1989), pp. 7–9.*

26

Carpet beetle: a pilot study in detection and control

Lynda Hillyer and Valerie Blyth

Lynda Hillyer and Valerie Blyth describe recent experiences of infestation at the Victoria and Albert Museum, London. Their paper discusses a strategy for monitoring and controlling insect pests, and, in particular, describes how freezing can be used as an alternative to fumigation.

INTRODUCTION

A series of hot summers and mild winters over the last few years has contributed to an increase in the activity of carpet beetle (*Anthrenus* spp.) particularly in the south of England.[1] Museum collections containing proteinaceous material such as wool, fur, feathers or mounted specimens provide potential food sources for the larvae (woolly bear) of carpet beetle which, unchecked, can cause widespread damage. Dramatic examples have been found in museums containing natural history specimens where entire entomological collections can be destroyed within months.[2,3]

South Kensington, where the Victoria and Albert Museum (V&A) is situated, is a recognized high-risk area for Guernsey carpet beetle (*Anthrenus sarnicus*).[4,5] It is a complex site of approximately 12 acres with 7 miles of galleries and stores, many of which contain material vulnerable to insect attack. Reserve collections of tapestries, carpets and theatre costume are stored at Blythe Road in West Kensington, 3 miles from the main museum site. Insects know no boundaries and what might appear to be a localized problem in one gallery or store is likely to occur in adjacent areas containing material from other collections. Evidence of insect activity, identified as Guernsey carpet beetle, was discovered in a textile gallery in the autumn of 1989 and resulted in the formation of a strategy for pest detection and control throughout the museum. Early on in the V&A project it became clear that successful detection and prevention of potential infestation could be achieved only with the collaboration of many different sections of the museum. One of the primary responsibilities of the team initiating the pest control strategy was to heighten awareness throughout the museum by distributing basic information in the form of guidelines (Appendix 1), backed up by training sessions to staff most actively involved with the handling of objects. A second key element of the strategy was the recognition that on a large and complex site there is the likelihood of some level of continuous insect activity. In order to maintain a threshold which is as low as possible, parts of the strategy have to be repeated annually. Inevitably this leads to a shift in museum priorities as a greater proportion of time is spent on preventive conservation. Some of the work can be incorporated into other essential operations such as surveys or store moves, but there remains a core of routine, systematic and labour-intensive work which has to be built into each year's work programme.

INSECT BEHAVIOUR AS THE KEY TO STRATEGIC PLANNING

Integrated pest control policies are established practice in some museums in the United States, for example in parts of the Smithsonian Institution such as the Museum Support Centre and the National Museum of Natural History, and some excellent publications are available on strategies.[6,7] The initial stages of planning, however, can be daunting, particularly on a large site. The advice and guidance of an entomologist with expertise in current detection and control methods was available throughout the V&A project.[8]

It is essential that conservators are familiar with the life cycle and habits of the insect that they are trying to control and are able to communicate relevant information to a wide cross-section of museum staff. The biology of the insect and particular aspects of the life cycle of *Anthrenus* spp. proved relevant in planning a monitoring and detection policy (Appendix 1). More detailed descriptions of *Anthrenus verbasci*, a similar, related species, can be found in Hinton,[9] Busvine,[10] and Pinniger:[11]

1 Insects are unable to regulate their body temperature. Their life cycles are dependent to a large extent on external (or seasonal) changes in temperature and relative humidity. However, a stable museum environment can provide conditions which may facilitate emergence of adult populations throughout the year[12] and an enclosed environment free of predators. Particularly favourable conditions may speed up the span of the life cycle of the carpet beetle, which can vary between ten months and two years.

2 Adult beetles are phototropic and are attracted to short wavelength ultraviolet radiation. They fly from the safety of a dark area where pupation has taken place towards the light in order to leave the building to mate. Thus adults may be found on window-sills, particularly of north-facing windows, during peak emergence months of June, July and August.

3 Female adults re-enter a building through chimneys, airvents and cracks in order to lay eggs. However, adults do not always have to leave the building to mate. Thus an infestation may become established and spread despite meticulous sealing of entry and exit points.

4 Eggs are laid in dark crevices, usually close to a food source for the newly emerging larvae. Breeding reservoirs inside buildings are usually associated with poor hygiene although it is not unknown for objects to be breeding reservoirs too. Typical external reservoirs are birds' nests, since feathers, bird droppings and broken birds' eggs provide a rich source of food for larvae. Nests can also be found inside a building under the eaves of the roof.

5 Because carpet beetle larvae are small and can exist on dust, hair, fibres from clothing and dead insects they do not have to move far for food. However, larvae are highly mobile although their migration patterns are not fully understood. There is evidence that they are attracted to some food sources. They can gain access to storerooms, display cases, vulnerable areas through cracks and crevices.

6 Within a major infestation, larvae may be found at several different developmental stages. A characteristic of new local infestations is the predominance of small larvae.

7 As the larvae grow, they shed their skins six to eight times and these skins or moults may be one of the first signs of infestation. In adverse conditions where there is an insufficient food supply the number of moults may be much higher. The insect pupates in the last larval skin which is left behind when the adult emerges. These large moults may be found in places which are some distance from infestation centres because the larvae have moved away to find a safe pupation site.

8 *Anthrenus* spp. are able to tolerate humidities as low as 20–30 per cent RH.[13]

DETECTION

The development of a monitoring programme

The monitoring programme in the museum developed in the initial stages as a response to larval moults found by chance in a textile gallery in the North-East quadrant of the museum when a case display was being dismantled. This kind of evidence can indicate that infestation has already reached damaging levels. A detailed inspection of surrounding galleries revealed this to be so. Larvae were found in typical habitat: protected from light under a wool-upholstered chaise longue; concealed between the underside of a chair and the metal supports of its legs and hidden inside a sofa bed. Clues were provided by large numbers of moults in surrounding areas. This particular series of galleries, which include the main Tapestry gallery, Textile Study Room, Far Eastern Study Room, part of the carpet collection and furniture galleries containing wool upholstery, was recognized as a high-risk area and a trapping programme was initiated. The routine established in this suite of galleries served as a model for other galleries and stores throughout the museum.

Traps

Three types of sticky traps are in current use in the museum and in off-site storage areas at Blythe Road. The window trap capitalizes on the known preference of larvae for enclosed spaces and crevices. It has a central sticky area surrounded with corrugated borders. It is useful for display cases where trapped insects can be seen without moving the trap. It is also recommended for dusty areas since the sticky area is protected by a transparent cover. The Lo Line Roach trap (a cockroach trap with a roach bait) was used in preliminary trials but has been superseded by the smaller and more discreet Detector or Trappit trap. Both offer an enclosed environment with a sticky base. The Detector trap can be placed in any high-risk area. It is used under objects or directly on floors of galleries and stores. Lasiotraps (originally designed for the detection of cigarette beetles) are used on window-sills at Blythe Road in the summer months to intercept adult beetles flying towards the light; sticky tape laid across sills can be equally effective.

The traps are placed in a grid formation (the recommended interval is from 2 to 6 metres), numbered, dated and entered on a floorplan of the area. Dark hidden locations, for example in corners or under furnishings, are likely to produce better results. Traps should be changed every six months or more frequently if they contain large numbers of insects since larvae can avoid the sticky surface, moult, and escape well-fed from the trap. Care must be taken to check that the more exposed sticky areas of the Lo Line Roach trap and the Detector trap have not become clogged with dust, which makes them ineffective. At the V&A, checking by both conservation and curatorial staff takes place weekly in the spring and summer months and fortnightly in the autumn and winter. All finds are recorded on forms which are collected centrally and the information is compiled onto a spreadsheet programme.

Monitoring

Monitoring has two functions. Its primary purpose is to detect and identify insect activity. Since there is no bait or pheromone (sex attractant)[14] in these traps, insects only enter them by random or investigative movement. Thus preliminary inspection may indicate that an area needs closer investigation. For example, the discovery of one larva in a trap in the Textile Study Room led to a supplementary search in the surrounding area and twenty live larvae were discovered in a nearby heating duct, an area already recognized as a likely breeding reservoir. Where an infestation has already been identified, traps can highlight clusters of activity, seasonal activity and to some extent indicate the scale of the infestation. By careful documentation of finds, some clues as to the stage that the infestation has reached may be given. Sizes of larvae, for example, can reveal whether the infestation is new or is well established. If more information is needed about the intensity of an infestation in a particular area, the grid of traps can be tightened and more intensive searches can be organized. Some museums use bait, e.g. wheatgerm or fishmeal in sticky traps.[15] Dead insects, particularly silverfish, are attractive bait for *Anthrenus* spp.

Valuable and often surprising information about types of insect activity can be obtained. A localized infestation of brown carpet beetle (*Attagenus smirnovi*), a comparatively unusual type of beetle, was discovered in one gallery of the museum through the use of traps. Meticulous recording is essential. All insects and all stages of insect life need to be identified. The advice of an entomologist is vital, particularly in the early stages of monitoring. With experience, staff can soon become familiar with a range of common pest species.

Monitoring in the period from autumn 1989 to the summer of 1991 has revealed a variety of species active on the main museum site and at Blythe Road. At the V&A site, Guernsey carpet beetle *Anthrenus sarnicus*, dermestid beetle *Anthrenocerus australis*, two spot carpet beetle *Attagenus pellio*, brown carpet beetle *Attagenus smirnovi*, hide beetle *Dermestes* sp. (probably *D. lardarius*) and wharf borer *Nacerdes melanura* were detected.

At the Blythe Road site, Guernsey carpet beetle *Anthrenus sarnicus*, varied carpet beetle *Anthrenus verbasci*, two spot carpet beetle *Attagenus pellio*, brown carpet beetle *Attagenus smirnovi*, plaster beetle *Cartodere filum*, Australian spider beetle *Ptinus tectus*, biscuit beetle *Stegobium paniceum*, common clothes moth *Tineola bisselliella*, brown clothes moth *Hofmannophila pseudospretella* and silverfish *Lepisma saccarhina* were found.

The second function of monitoring is to assess the broad picture of activity in the museum over several seasons. Migration patterns can be plotted. Monitoring has revealed levels of activity in what would normally be considered improbable areas. Moults have been found in cases containing metalwork and ceramics. Neither the case linings nor the adhesives used in the lining of the cases were a source of nutrition. Evidence of large moults suggested that the larvae had entered these cases in order to pupate. In a store containing theatre museum material, a disproportionate percentage of moults were collected from the calico cover of a dress rail which housed costume containing virtually no proteinaceous materials. Some live larvae were recovered but were very small. The larvae had been insufficiently nourished and had become progressively smaller. In such cases monitoring over a longer period may reveal whether there is a breeding reservoir still to be discovered in the vicinity or whether larvae have hatched in these areas by chance.

Monitoring allows the effectiveness of control methods to be evaluated. Data have now been collected for two years. At Blythe Road, where monitoring has been systematic and the site is easier to manage, levels of activity are much lower and have been eliminated from some areas. On the main museum site, activity of Guernsey carpet beetle *Anthrenus sarnicus* appears to be more widespread. However, the monitoring programme has been doubled since its start in the spring of 1990 and is now supported by regular routine inspections. Although the programme is well established, not enough consistent data has yet been accumulated to draw significant conclusions.

METHODS OF CONTROL

Elimination of the causes of infestation as the key to long-term pest control

Good housekeeping and hygiene

Carpet beetle infestation is almost always associated with poor hygiene. Initial inspections in the North-East quadrant of the museum revealed dust and debris in dark corners of galleries, areas which had been neglected because of their inaccessibility or because the necessary attachments for vacuum cleaners were not readily available. Given that larvae can survive on fibres from clothing, hair and dead insects, the importance of cleaning and the disturbance created by cleaning cannot be stressed enough. Training sessions have been organized both for cleaning staff and for specialist staff trained in object cleaning to inform them of the habits of carpet beetle and thus the need for vigilant and thorough cleaning. Vacuum cleaners can be transmitters of infestation if their bags are not changed after each cleaning session. The contents of a dust bag provide a virtual banquet for woolly bear larvae. Bags need to be sealed and destroyed to prevent transportation of infestation to other parts of the museum.

Deep cleaning of galleries and storage areas is essential to target possible breeding reservoirs and areas which are completely inaccessible for surface cleaning. Grilles covering cavities for heating pipes, where warm, dark and often very dirty conditions provide ideal breeding grounds, are one example. In two galleries it has been necessary to dismantle cases in order to gain access to covered heating pipes. Dead spaces under and behind cases are often neglected sources of infestation. Gaps between strips of parquet flooring can accumulate enough fibre and dirt to support growing larvae. Such crevices also provide attractive sites for egg-laying females. They need to be cleaned out thoroughly and sealed.

A new awareness of potential insect problems has been incorporated into the design of new galleries in the museum. Accessibility to all dead spaces for cleaning and/or treatment is now seen as an essential part of environmental planning.

The building

The South Kensington site is a particularly complex building. It was developed over a period of fifty years from 1857 'as a result of a tortuous and elaborate construction programme'.[16] This piecemeal development makes it extremely difficult to isolate the root causes of infestation. In summer months entry of adult beetles may be through open windows or doors. Museums surrounded by gardens or trees are particularly vulnerable. The most common entry points, however, are from the roof. Birds' nests, feathers, bird droppings and dead birds are typical habitats of *Anthrenus* spp. Entry is through chimneys, air vents, air-conditioning ducts and poorly fitting skylights. Regular inspections of the V&A roof and the roof area at Blythe Road have resulted in the removal of nests and the renewal of pigeon netting. Ducted airvents have been cleaned and blocked, fireplaces and chimneys sealed with fine-gauge metal mesh. Many windows in the museum are built over airbricks so standard prefilter mesh will be used to filter air flow necessary for the internal spaces.

Monitoring can often highlight a weakness in the building structure. The cause of infestation in a Blythe Road store was traced to redundant air vents which enabled adult beetles to enter. Findings in one basement area of the V&A could be related to a large number of sparrows' nests constructed into a nearby outside wall. The wall needs repointing and provides good anchorage for nests.

At least twice a month the museum site is inspected by a contract pest control company, Southern Pest Control, for dead rats and mice. *Dermestes* spp. (hide beetle) as well as *Anthrenus* spp. can thrive on rodent carcases.

Insecticides

Deep cleaning of suspect areas is augmented by a six-monthly programme of treatment with residual insecticides.

Coopex WP™ is a wettable power containing permethrin (3-phenoxybenzyl-3-(2,2-dichlorovinyl)-2,2 dimethylcyclopropanecarboxylate), a synthentic pyrethroid related to pyrethrin, a naturally occuring insecticidal compound which occurs in flowers of the single-flowered chrysanthemum (*C. cinerariifolium*).[17,18] It is not readily soluble and forms a suspension in water. When it is used as a surface spray it is deposited as a thin layer of particles on treated areas. These particles adhere to any insects which come into contact with them. The effects are rapid knockdown and subsequent kill. Where a wet application is inappropriate, an insecticidal dust containing the same formulation is used. Typical applications include crevices behind skirting-boards, dead spaces under cases, roof voids, cracks between wooden flooring, gaps between original flooring (as in a room setting) and the gallery floor and areas under heating grilles. Heat and ultra-violet radiation will reduce the effective life of this insecticide so areas near heating pipes may need to be retreated frequently.

The disturbance created by building works is a major inhibitor of infestation and treatment with insecticide in such cases is primarily a preventive measure to eliminate any survivors. For example, as building work proceeded on the ground-floor level of the North-East quadrant of the museum in preparation for the 'Visions of Japan' exhibition which opened in September 1991, the site was treated with Coopex WP™. This area has particularly complex ventilation systems[19] a common source of entry for *Anthrenus* spp. The recently opened Nehru Gallery of Indian Art and the Tsui Gallery of Chinese Art have also been treated.

Bendiocarb, 2.2 dimethyl-1,3-benzodioxol-4yl N-methylcarbamate, produced under the trade name Ficam™ (active ingredient – 80 per cent bendiocarb) has been used on the Blythe Road site. It is a wettable powder, although a dust formulation is also available. Areas treated have included air vents, window bays, floor ducts, fireplaces, water-tank lofts and cupboards under eaves. Application of both Coopex™ and Ficam™ has been undertaken by the consultant pest control company.

Dichlorvos (DDVP), 2.2 dimethyl dichlorovinyl phosphate, is a vapour phase insecticide which can be dispersed in PVC strips and is available commercially as Vapona™ (which contains 20 per cent DDVP). Dichlorvos is a knockdown insecticide which causes inactivity in insects and eventual death.[20,21] It works by slow sustained release. A Vapona™ strip used at the correct dosage in an enclosed space is effective for about three to four months. The length of its active life can be reduced by high temperatures, high humidities and the rate of ventilation in the enclosed space.

Dichlorvos readily hydrolyses in high humidities (above 65 per cent) to form dimethyl phosphoric acid and dichloroacetylaldehyde and presents a potential danger to objects with metal components. It is also easily absorbed at high humidities by plastics and resins. Polyvinyl chloride (PVC) is subject to oxidation and its breakdown products include hydrogen chloride. Breakdown products of the plasticizers used in Vapona strips also present a potential hazard as phthalic acid may be produced. In high humidities there is evidence of slight to moderate colour changes both on acid red dyes and on disperse red dyes. Many museums have discontinued the use of dichlorvos following research on the effect of breakdown products at high humidities.[22]

At normal RH and when used at the dosage recommended by the manufacturer, the quantities of these breakdown products are minute. Dichlorvos is the only vapour phase insecticide available for museum use. For these reasons it has a limited but valuable role in pest control and is still in use at the V&A in specific circumstances. It is mainly used in dead spaces, for example under cases or very occasionally in the display area of a showcase. It is not used to disperse vapour in public or working areas and its use is generally restricted to the more active period in the life cycle of the carpet beetle from late spring to mid-September. On very rare occasions it has been used with a bagged object if no immediate non-toxic control method is available.

Treatment of objects from suspect areas

Procedures have been established in the museum for action following the discovery of active insect infestation in or near objects. The underlying principle is that of confining the infestation by isolation. This may involve the isolation of an object by sealing it in polyethylene bags or sheeting or treating a particular space, for example a showcase, as a local isolation area.

Objects found to contain evidence of infestation are inspected by a conservator. Evidence in the form of larval moults may or may not be a sign of recent activity. Moults can survive intact for many years before finally disintegrating. In such cases the object is rigorously examined and particular attention is paid to those areas known to be typical habitats of larvae or attractive sites for egg-laying, for example inside folds, seam allowances and linings on garments. Good torches are essential and a magnifying glass is often useful since eggs can rarely be seen with the naked eye. After inspection the object is cleaned using a vacuum cleaner to remove the moults. Record-keeping is vital. If moults are left *in situ* it is impossible to determine at a later date whether infestation is recent or not. The object may be returned to its case or store depending on the picture presented by monitoring and inspection. If a store cannot be guaranteed free of infestation, the object must be protected and it is returned to the store in a sealed package. Where a gallery cannot be guaranteed free of infestation, the showcases may have to emptied for a prolonged period.

If the object presents positive evidence of insect activity it is sealed in polyethylene or Tyvek (a polyethylene material which permits air exchange through minute apertures) and placed in a quarantine area. Ideally this is a sealed room where isolated objects can be inspected, usually after a period of at least ten days to determine whether any eggs have hatched. Objects awaiting further treatment are stored and sealed in this quarantine area. Loan objects may be included in this category. Both incoming objects from other institutions and objects returned from loan requests are subject to scrupulous examination. Occasionally it may be appropriate to treat the display case as an isolation area. After inspecting, cleaning and recording the condition of the case, any dead space under the case is treated with an appropriate insecticide. The display area itself can be treated with slow-releasing dichlorvos strips. On one occasion it was found necessary to use dichlorvos with a bagged object when there was no immediate access to other forms of treatment. A large theatrical mask containing wool felt was found to contain a severe infestation of woolly bear larvae. A Vapona strip which would have been sufficient for a 3-cubic-metre volume was placed within its storage box while avoiding any direct contact with the object. The box was then sealed in polyethylene. The mask was inspected after a period of six months and no active sign of infestation could be detected.

Freezing as a method of control

Freezing at the appropriate temperature and exposure time is a simple and effective method of pest control and is particularly suitable for textile objects. Unlike alternative chemical means of control, for example fumigation by methyl bromide or sulfuryl fluoride, it is both environmentally safe and safe for operators. No residue can be left in the object. More work is needed on the effects of freezing on degraded organic materials but current research[23] does not indicate any damage to fibres as the result of exposure to low temperatures.

Two freezing projects have been carried out at the V&A. The first, in the summer of 1990, was organized in response to the preliminary findings of larval activity in textile galleries in the autumn of 1989. The second, carried out in the summer of 1991, was largely a preventive measure. Five hundred tapestries and carpets were moved from a suspect store on the main museum site to new storage at Blythe Road which monitoring had shown to be pest-free.

Insects have mechanisms which enable them to survive very cold temperatures. They can build up sugars and glycerols in the tissue of their cells which lower their freezing-point in preparation for the winter months. If an insect which has been acclimatized to warm temperatures or to the relatively stable environment of a museum is exposed to a sudden drop in temperature, it is generally unable to survive. The speed of the drop in temperature is critical, although it is not known what specific temperatures are needed to kill each development stage of particular species of museum pests. Pupae and eggs are known to be more resistant than adults and larvae and it has been noted that the feeding stages of insect life are the least resistant to freezing.[24] Much of the research carried out on freezing as a method of control for pest infestation has been carried out in the stored food industry. Mullen and Arbogast[25] found that survival times of the eggs of five common insect pests of stored food products decreased rapidly in direct relationship to the lowering of temperature or to the length of exposure time. Exposure to −20°C achieved 95 per cent mortality for all five species within a few hours.

Freezing is a well-established practice in some museums in the United States, Scandinavia and Australia. One of the first large-scale freezing projects to be undertaken was at the Beinecke Library at Yale University in 1977 to eradicate an infestation of *Gastrallus* sp. (Anobiidae).[26] Using a blast freezer (a food storage freezer which has fans behind the freezing coils which can move the cooled air very quickly around the chamber) a total of 37,000 books were treated over a period of thirteen months at a temperature of −29°C and an exposure time of seventy-two hours.

The most relevant information on the effect of using freezing as a control method for infested museum artefacts is contained in a Canadian publication.[27] It states:

> When living cells (90 per cent water content) are subjected to low temperatures, depending on the rate of cooling and thawing and the time at the final temperature reached, specific physical and chemical changes occur, some which may be lethal.

The actual cause of death is not known – whether a combination of events or a single factor is involved has not been conclusively shown.

The literature review on the lethal effects of freezing on living cells includes dehydration, osmotic swelling, loss of bound water and formation of ice crystals.

A common practice is double exposure of infested material to temperatures of −18°C or −20°C. Objects are frozen for a period of forty-eight hours, taken out of the freezer and left to return to ambient temperature for forty-eight hours. They are then replaced in the freezer unit for a further forty-eight hours. The effect of this freeze-thaw-freeze cycle ensures that any insect life not killed in the first exposure will be eradicated in the repeat exposure. It is thought that eggs respond to the interim rise in temperature and humidity and hatch. Few insects would be able to withstand the extreme fluctuation in temperatures used in this method. Most domestic freezers operate within these parameters. For small collections and as an emergency measure for larger collections this method is useful although the size of the objects that can be treated is necessarily limited.

This approach was considered when planning the first freezing programme at the V&A but the logistics of handling a large number of fragile tapestries twice were daunting and most of the textiles included in this first project were too large for a chest freezer. Recent research by the Danish entomologist, Toke Skytte, at the Museum of Natural History in Aarhus, Denmark, confirmed the effectiveness of the Yale method.[28] Skytte found that a temperature of −30°C was lethal to all stages of insect life tested. Freezing at −30°C has also been practised for several years at the Museum of Textile History in Boras, Sweden.[29]

The freezing programmes at the V&A were organized on this basis. A cold storage unit capable of reaching a temperature of −30°C was hired for both projects. Although not classified as a blast freezer, the unit is fitted with a fan which accelerates circulation of cold air. A defrost cycle operates for one hour every six hours, causing a rise in temperature to −18°C. This fluctuation is of immense benefit for the eradication of insects since it simulates a freeze-thaw-freeze cycle at very low temperatures. A temperature of −20°C can be reached within five hours and −29°C can be reached within ten hours. The total exposure time between the first drop to −29°C and the last recorded temperature of −30°C within a seventy-two-hour cycle averages at sixty hours.

The internal measurements of the cold storage unit are 2.20 m (height) 2.20 m (width) and 5.30 m (length), large enough to accommodate tapestries on 5 m length rollers. It was fitted with Dexion™ shelving in various arrangements according to sizes of objects being treated. Each shelf was covered with a layer of plastazote.

In order to work at low temperatures, staff were equipped with protective clothing: polar suits, balaclavas, gloves and freezer boots.

Exposure of common museum pests to low temperatures in the cold storage unit

Since so little published research exists on the exact temperature and time exposure needed to kill each stage of particular species of insect life, bioassays using live insects were carried out during both freezing projects. Where possible different developmental stages of insect life found in the museum were included in the experiments in order to establish the efficiency of using a single exposure treatment at a lower temperature.

In August 1990, ten treatment tubes containing mixed-age larvae of *Tineola bisselliella* (webbing clothes moth) were placed in sealed bags and placed in the cold storage unit.

They were exposed to temperatures of −30°C within a seventy-two hour period and then returned to the laboratory and incubated at 25°C. No adult moths emerged from any of the tubes. Seventy per cent emergence was observed from a control group of moth larvae.

In August 1991, during a seventy-hour exposure cycle to temperatures of −29.5°C, the following insects were placed in treatment tubes in the cold storage unit: webbing clothes moth *Tineola bisselliella* (larvae, adults), casemaking clothes moth *Tineola pellionella* (larvae), furniture carpet beetle *Anthrenus flavipes* (eggs, adults), Guernsey carpet beetle *Anthrenus sarnicus* (larvae), brown carpet beetle *Attagenus smirnovi* (larvae, adults), varied carpet beetle *Anthrenus verbasci* (larvae, adults) and two spot carpet beetle *Attagenus pellio* (adults).

All insects appeared to be dead on removal from the cold storage chamber. No recovery was apparent and inspection after seven days confirmed 100 per cent mortality.

Types of objects suitable for freezing

Many organic materials can be treated by freezing. Objects must be able to withstand minor changes in relative humidity and consequently minor dimensional changes which occur as the inevitable result of the decrease in temperature on cooling and the increase in temperature as conditions in the cold storage unit rise towards ambient levels.

Objects must be dry. Ice damage cannot occur when dry materials are subjected to low temperatures. None of the moisture content of the dry object including the intercellular bound water is frozen at low temperatures.[30]

It is not advisable or necessary to treat non-adsorbent materials (i.e. those that cannot take up moisture vapour) by freezing because of the danger of surface condensation. Such materials include metals, ceramics, glass. Textiles with metal attachments or metal-thread embroidery or with glass or ceramic components, however, can usually be exposed to low temperatures providing there is enough textile to act as the adsorber. A buffer material such as cotton-wool or thick acid-free paper can be included with the object. Silica gel can be included but it has not been used in this way in either freezing project.

Organic objects which are desiccated or very degraded and materials with a high water content such as gelatin may not be suitable for freezing. Objects with stratified layers, for example paintings on canvas and furniture with inlaid surfaces or veneers, are unsuitable for treatment by freezing. Many twentieth-century textiles may have plastic components. Polymers may be taken below their glass transition temperature (Tg) at low temperatures and become brittle. This is a reversible effect but care must be taken when handling objects which contain plastics at low temperatures. Empirical tests carried out in the cold storage unit using Mowilith DNC2 poly(vinylacetate), a copolymer of PVAC and dibutyl maleate, Beva ethylene-vinylacetate copolymer-Ketone resin N, and a silicone adhesive, FS2, showed no loss of flexibility or bond strength after exposure to low temperatures.

Procedures for the treatment of objects at low temperatures

The details of these procedures were worked out experientially during the course of the two projects but they closely followed those adopted by colleagues in the United States and Scandinavia. Objects are prepared for treatment by wrapping in medium-weight polyethylene to form a reasonably close-fitting bag. The purpose of the bag is to protect the object from condensation when it is removed from the cold storage unit. Where the polyethylene needs to be joined to create a bag, it should be folded over twice to form a secure and airtight seam. The seam can then be sealed with aluminium ducting tape. Care must be taken to ensure that there are no apertures in the bag.

A quarantine area must be created for this procedure in order to prevent the possible spread of infestation. For the first project which was carried out in an offsite storage area at Battersea, a polyethylene tent was erected containing two air-conditioning units. For the second, the bagging of objects was carried out in the main V&A site using the suspect storage area which was being vacated.

Objects are placed in the cold storage unit when it has reached a temperature of at least −10°C. Because of the defrost cycle of the unit it was not always possible to predict the exact temperature at the loading for each run. When the doors of the unit are opened there is an inevitable rise in temperature, usually to 0°C. Objects must be loaded at ambient temperature. It is essential that insects are not given an opportunity to acclimatize to a cooler temperature. Acclimatization can occur within the relatively short time span of eight to eighteen hours. Objects must remain in the cold storage unit for seventy-two hours.

The cold storage unit is switched off six hours before the objects are removed. One hour before the objects are removed the doors of the unit are opened to ensure that objects are brought back to ambient temperature slowly.

Objects are left in their sealed bags for at least forty-eight hours. There should be no condensate on the outside of the polyethylene bag when it is opened.

The object is inspected for any signs of insect life. Any moults or dead larvae must be removed using a vacuum cleaner. Left *in situ*, they provide misleading evidence for further inspections and a food source for future infestation. The object is repacked for storage in a safe area.

Changes of temperature and relative humidity during the cold storage cycle

The complexity of the relationship between temperature, relative humidity and the moisture content and moisture regain capacity of the object warrants greater study, which is beyond the scope of this paper. However, it is worth commenting on the observations of these complex relationships during this work.

A data logger capable of operating to a lower temperature limit of −50°C was used to monitor several cycles of temperature and humidity for several cycles of the cold storage unit during both projects.

Changes occur in the moisture equilibrium of objects when subjected to freezing. As the temperature is lowered during the cold storage cycle, the air in the sealed package containing the object is unable to retain its moisture content and excess moisture is adsorbed onto the object. Some conservators recommend partial evacuation of air from the package in an attempt to modify this effect. This was tried but found to be difficult to achieve. As objects are removed from the cold chamber, they experience an inevitable and sudden rise in relative humidity. Objects can be placed in an interim refrigerated unit to adjust the temperature more slowly or the unit can be switched off several hours in advance of removal.[31] Blast freezers are reputed to operate at constant temperature and humidity.[32]

Readings were taken at the core and on the surface of a dense object, an upholstered couch, in a short experimental cycle in the cold storage unit during the 1990 project. A time lag of one hour was observed before the core temperature started to drop. The total exposure time to temperatures lower than −28°C was longer (nine hours in a twenty-two hour run) at the core than at the surface (seven hours) due to the thermal mass of the object.

During the 1991 project the cold storage unit was unable to reach a temperature of −30°C with a full load of twenty tapestries. The project was carried out in hot summer months which undoubtedly affected the efficiency of the unit when it was fully loaded. The timing of the 1991 project was dependent on the store move which had been planned to take place from June to September. The unit reached a temperature of −29.5°C at its lowest point. It took eighteen hours to reach −20°C and forty hours to reach −28°C. External factors probably exacerbated the rise in RH as the objects encountered the warm ambient conditions on removal from the unit. The surface of the object will be most affected by these changes. In every case each object was protected by a covering of M tissue, a thick acid-free paper, which acts as a buffer to humidity fluctuations. There was no condensation at any time during either project.

More work needs to be done on controlling the final rate of the rise in relative humidity. The subjection of an object to temporary changes in humidity has to be weighed against the dangers of leaving objects exposed to potential insect damage.

CONCLUSION

The mechanics of an integrated pest control strategy are now well established in the museum but it is still too early to evaluate its long-term success. The pilot study has acted as a blueprint for future applications but has been recognized as a learning process. Key factors are the detection and monitoring programme and the collaboration of staff from different sections of the museum in implementing the policy. Future developments include plans to adapt the methyl bromide chamber in the museum for use with CO_2 gas so that objects not suitable for freezing can also be treated with a non-toxic method. Freezing projects will in the future be carried out in late spring so that external factors do not hinder either the workings of the unit or the return of objects to ambient temperature. The continuity of any of the aspects of the strategy is dependent on maintaining consistently high levels of communication, vigilance and co-operation. Some indication of the spread of responsibility across the museum is given in Appendix 1. The monitoring programme is to be expanded with the help of a wider section of museum staff to obtain a more comprehensive picture of insect activity.

The strategy is labour-intensive and can disrupt other work programmes. The combined store move and freezing programme in 1991, for example, employed twenty people on a rotation basis for three months. Detection of pests, however, is now recognized as a priority in collection management. This collaboration with the Conservation Department in a shift towards preventive conservation for at least a proportion of the year's work programme is a significant step for future success. One of the difficulties of monitoring a complex site is discovering what constitutes an acceptable level of insect activity. Despite numerous insect sitings the actual proportion of insect-damaged objects has been very small. Out of 600 objects selected for treatment by freezing, only 2–3 per cent showed positive signs of insect infestation and the rest were from suspect or high-risk areas.

SAFETY

Under the Control of Substances Hazardous to Health Regulations, institutions or companies must make a written assessment of the risks, precautions and emergency procedures associated with the work they will be undertaking.

The short-term exposure limit for a ten-minute reference period for dichlorvos is 3 mg/m^3. When used at the correct dosage dichlorvos strips maintain a concentration in air of 0.03 mg/m^3. Above 1 mg/m^3 in an eight-hour exposure period dichlorvos can cause headaches, nausea and blurred vision.[33]

The Vapona™ strip must be used in accordance with the manufacturer's recommended dosage and instructions. All contact with skin must be avoided. Vapona is approved for use in domestic situations by the Ministry of Agriculture, Fisheries and Food (MAFF) and by the Health and Safety Executive (HSE).[34]

Under the Control of Pesticides Regulations (1986)[35] it is now illegal for unskilled or untrained staff to use pesticides. Applications of Coopex™ and Ficam™ were undertaken by a contract pest control company.

Training sessions were organized for staff working in the freezer unit, and staff involved in loading and unloading the unit were issued with protective clothing. A written safe system of work, to comply with the Health and Safety at Work Act (1974),[36] was issued to staff working at low temperatures. The main points are:

1 Staff must be medically fit with no minor ailments and no heart or lung conditions. Staff taking prescribed medication should seek advice from their doctor on their suitability to undertake this work.
2 No member of staff must spend longer than twenty minutes in any thirty-minute period in the refrigerated area. A first-aider conversant with the identification and treatment of hypothermia and frostbite must be on hand at all times that cold temperatures are encountered.
3 Staff must not consume alcohol before or during the work cycle.
4 Staff must not work alone in the refrigerated area.
5 Protective clothing must be worn and must be kept dry.

In addition, caution must be taken in entering the freezer unit at low temperatures since the surface of the floor can be slippery. Caution must be taken when lifting heavy objects into or out of the freezer unit.

APPENDIX 1: VICTORIA AND ALBERT MUSEUM GUIDELINES

Woolly bear – carpet beetle infestation

The museum has a serious carpet beetle infestation. Detection, monitoring and control depend on the vigilance and co-operation of all staff involved in the care of collections and in the care of the building: conservation and curatorial staff, manual attendants, object cleaners and the Department of Building and Estates.

Textile objects constructed of wool are at risk throughout the building, also any museum object of which wool is a component. Wool-felt in display cases may also harbour larvae and eggs.

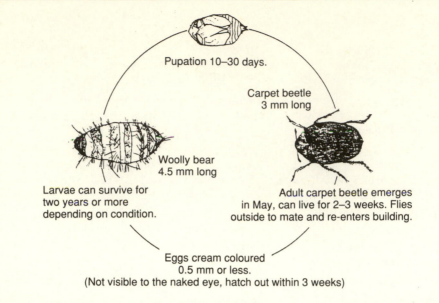

Pupation 10–30 days.

Carpet beetle
3 mm long

Woolly bear
4.5 mm long

Larvae can survive for
two years or more
depending on condition.

Adult carpet beetle emerges
in May, can live for 2–3 weeks. Flies
outside to mate and re-enters building.

Eggs cream coloured
0.5 mm or less.
(Not visible to the naked eye, hatch out within 3 weeks)

Fig. 26.1 Life-cycle of the woolly bear carpet beetle

Basic habits of the woolly bear carpet beetle

1 Adult carpet beetles enter the museum from May to September through:
   (a) open doors and windows;
   (b) ventilation shafts;
   (c) air-conditioning ducts;
   (d) 'dead' spaces in roof areas;
   (e) pot plants and cut flowers indoors;
   (f) shrubs and plants outdoors.

   The warmer the summer the greater is the risk. One fertilized female can lay enough eggs to begin an infestation. Birds' nests and dead pigeons on roof areas provide breeding grounds for pests.

2 Each adult lays from 20 to 100 eggs. Eggs and emerging larvae are very difficult to detect. Emerging larvae can penetrate crevices and tiny cracks.

3 Larvae are voracious feeders. They will attack wool, felt, fur, feathers, hide and silk. They will eat through other materials to reach these materials. They prefer:
   (a) gloomy, dusty and dirty conditions;
   (b) crevices and enclosed spaces, e.g. behind hangings, at the side of upholstery, under cushions, etc.;
   (c) soiled areas and soiled objects.

   They can survive for up to two years or more. Emergence as adults depends on conditions (e.g. food, temperature, disturbance). Warm summers and mild winters speed up development and can lead, if unchecked, to large-scale infestations.

As the larvae grow they leave moults, i.e., fine cast skins. One larva can deposit up to six or seven moults. Detection of moults may be the first sign of infestation.

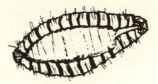

Fig 26.2 Larval moult of the woolly bear carpet beetle

CONTROL OF INFESTATION REQUIRES
CO-OPERATION AND VIGILANCE.

INSECTS DO NOT LIKE TO BE DISTURBED.

Inspection

This must be part of an on-going programme. A system must be worked into each year's cycle.

Where should one inspect?

'Dead' spaces, dark corners, areas of poor hygiene, storage areas, display cases and textile objects on open display should be inspected.

How should one look?

A methodical system should be established. A good torch should be used. Anything suspicious should be reported to the Textiles Conservation Department.

Vacuum cleaning is essential:

(a) to improve hygiene in galleries;
(b) to diminish the spread of infestation;
(c) to create disturbances in the life-cycle of carpet beetle by vacuum cleaning.

When using a vacuum cleaner:

(a) ensure all nozzles are thoroughly washed in hot water and detergent afterwards. Nozzles can pick up eggs and redeposit them elsewhere in the museum.
(b) make sure the bags used in the vacuum cleaners are sealed and disposed of after each cleaning session. Change the bag after each session.
(c) be vigilant about crevices, dark corners, areas with access to roof space.

Traps

Sticky insect traps have been distributed by Conservation to be placed in galleries, stores, display cases. These traps monitor the extent of the infestation. PLEASE LEAVE THEM *IN SITU*. It is very important that findings on traps (positive and negative) are recorded on the form devised by staff from the Textiles Conservation and Collections Departments.

Division of observation and cleaning

1 Conservation and curatorial staff, object cleaners, Buildings and Estates Department: To monitor insect traps using insect pest control form to record findings. Storage and gallery areas need to be observed regularly.

2 Manual attendants:

Please help by meticulous cleaning of galleries, particularly those containing woollen objects (e.g. upholstered furniture, carpets) on open display. Better hygiene and disturbance of these areas by cleaning is basic to pest control. Please observe guidelines regarding the cleaning of nozzles on vacuum cleaners and sealing and disposing of vacuum cleaning bags after each gallery session.

Please ensure that traps are retained in the galleries.

3 Object cleaners:

Please be meticulous about cleaning under and behind objects, and in crevices on upholstered furniture as outlined in gallery training. Please observe the guidelines regarding the cleaning of nozzles and disposing of vacuum cleaning bags after each gallery session.

4 Buildings and Estates:

Please make periodic checks of 'dead' roof spaces and areas with openings to the roof. Be alert to evidence of birds' nests.

THE MUSEUM IS A HUGE AND COMPLEX SITE.

THIS INFESTATION NEEDS THE CO-OPERATION OF
ALL SECTIONS INVOLVED.

This paper first appeared in The Conservator *16 (1992), pp. 65–77.*

NOTES AND REFERENCES

1 Shaw, M. R. (1991) 'New threats from museum beetles', *SSCR Journal* 2(3).
2 Armes, N. J. (1984) 'Aspects of the biology of the Guernsey carpet beetle, *Anthrenus sarnicus* and control of dermestid beetle pests in museums', *ICOM Committee for Conservation 7th Triennial Meeting*, Copenhagen 84.13.1.
3 Dr George McGavin, Head of Entomology Collection, Oxford University Museum, personal communication.
4 Armes, op cit., 1.
5 David Pinniger, consultant entomologist, personal communication.
6 Story, K. O. (1985) *Approaches to Pest Management in Museums*, Washington, D.C.: Conservation Analytical Laboratory, Smithsonian Institution.
7 Zycherman, L. A., Schrock, J. R. (eds) (1988) *A Guide to Museum Pest Control*, Washington, D.C.: Foundation of the American Institute for Conservation of Historic and Artistic Works and the Association of Systematics Collection (joint publication).
8 David Pinniger, consultant entomologist, MAFF Central Science Laboratory, London Road, Slough SL3 7HJ.
9 Hinton, H. E. (1945) *Monograph of the Beetles Associated with Stored Products*, London: British Museum (Natural History), 326–33.
10 Busvine, J. R. (1980) *Insects and Hygiene: The Biology and Control of Insect Pests of Medical and Domestic Importance*, London: Chapman & Hall, 409–14.
11 Pinniger, D. (1990) *Insect Pests in Museums*, Denbigh, Clwyd: Archetype Publications, 7–8.
12 Armes, op. cit.
13 Child, R. E. and Pinniger, D. B. (1987) 'Insect pest control in museums', in J. Black (ed.) *Recent Advances in the Conservation and Analysis of Artifacts*, London: Institute of Archaeology, University of London, 305.
14 Pheromones are specific to each insect species. The pheromone for varied carpet beetle (*Anthrenus verbasci*) has been identified but it is unlikely to be developed for specialized museum use. See Pinniger, D. (1991) 'New developments in the detection and control of insects which damage museum collections', *Biodeterioration Abstracts* 5(2): 126.
15 Zycherman and Schrock 'Trapping techniques for dermestid and anobiid beetles', op. cit., 109.
16 Physick, J. (1982) *The Victoria and Albert Museum: The History of the Building*, Oxford: Phaidon & Christies, 13.
17 Pinniger, op. cit., 34–5.

18 Linnie, M. J. (1990) 'Professional notes', *Museum Management and Curatorship* 9(4): 421.

19 Physick, op cit., Chapter IV.

20 Scudamore, K. A., Pinniger, D. B. and Hann, J. J. (n.d.) 'Study of Dichlorvos slow-release units used in museum cases for the protection of specimens against museum infestation', London: Ministry of Agriculture, Fisheries & Food, Pest Control Chemistry Department Report, no. 45.

21 Williams, S. L., Hawks, C. A. and Weber, S. G. (1984) 'Considerations in the use of DDVP resin strips for insect pest control in biological research collections', *Biodeterioration* 6: 349.

22 Zycherman and Schrock, 'Dichlorvos in museums, an investigation into its effects on various materials', op. cit., 159–67.

23 Florian, M. L. (1986) 'The freezing process, effects on insects and artifact materials', *Leather Conservation News* 3(1): 1.

24 Salt, R. W. (1970) 'Analysis of insect freezing temperature distributions', *Canadian Journal of Zoology* 48: 205–8.

25 Mullen, M. A. and Arbogast, R. T. (1978) 'Time-temperature-mortality relationships for various stored product insect eggs and chilling times for selected commodities', *Journal of Economic Entomology* 72(4): 476–8.

26 Nesheim, K. (1984) 'The Yale non-toxic method of eradicating book-eating insects by deep freezing', *Restaurator* 6: 147–64.

27 Florian, op. cit., 1.

28 Richter, J., Lecturer, Det Kongelige Danske Kunstakademi, Copenhagen, personal communication.

29 Haggren, A., Conservator, Textil Museet, Boras, Sweden, personal communication.

30 Florian, M. L. (1987) 'The effect of artifact materials of the fumigant ethylene oxide and freezing used in insect control', *ICOM Committee for Conservation 8th Triennial Meeting*, Sydney Working Group 3, 201.

31 Florian, 'The freezing process', 9.

32 Smith, R. D. (1984) 'Background, use and benefits of blast freezers in the prevention and extermination of insects', *Biodeterioration* 6, Papers presented at the 6th International Biodeterioration Symposium, Washington, D.C.

33 'Professional notes', *Museum Management and Curatorship* 9 (1990): 420.

34 The Ministry of Agriculture, Fisheries and Food. The Health and Safety Executive.

35 The Control of Pesticides Regulations (1986).

36 The Health and Safety at Work Act (1974).

27

Pest control in museums: the use of chemicals and associated health problems

Martyn J. Linnie

A wide range of substances has been used to repel insects or fumigate collections in museums. The overpowering odour of para-dichlorobenzene or naphthalene was, until a few years ago, the characteristic smell of the museum store. Today, few museums remain complacent about the use of these and other chemicals – Martyn Linnie's article is for those who do.

Museum collections containing natural history specimens, textiles or ethnographical material represent a potential food source for a variety of insect pest. Infestations, if not quickly eliminated, can result in serious and irreparable damage to collections (Dawson 1987; Stoate 1987; Zaitseva 1987). Current methods of protection against insect attack involve the use of a wide range of chemicals in display areas, cabinets, drawers and workplaces to deter pests from specific locations and to eliminate and control infestations.

Recent surveys (Edwards *et al.* 1980; Linnie 1987, 1990) have shown that many museum workers consider the use of chemicals to be a convenient, economic and effective means of insect control. However, accumulating evidence indicates that certain chemicals used to protect and preserve museum specimens may also damage and otherwise spoil their appearance (Dawson, 1987).

Although health hazards associated with chemical usage have been known for some time, recent publications have highlighted the problem and have raised concern over potential health risks to which museum workers may be exposed (Croat 1978; Peltz and Rossol 1983; Irwin 1987). Information is drawn specifically from recent surveys in which participants were requested to provide opinions on medical ailments and complaints which they associated with their particular occupational conditions and practices.

CHEMICALS, APPLICATIONS AND RELATED HEALTH PROBLEMS IN MUSEUMS

1 Para-dichlorobenzene (PDB)

Other names: p-dichlorobenzene, 1, 4-dichlorobenzene, Paracide, Paradow. Formulations include mothballs, flakes and crystals. It came into use as a fumigant in 1913 (Martin and Worthing 1977), and is now used widely in museums, generally as an insect repellent in drawers and storage cabinets, although recent information suggests that its use is being phased out by some museums (Linnie 1990).

The occupational exposure limits issued by the Health and Safety Executive (1985) recommend maximum long-term and short-term exposure limits for certain airborne substances in the workplace considered hazardous to human health. These are expressed as time-weighted average (TWA) concentrations and relate to airborne concentrations averaged over a specified period. The period for the long-term limit is 8 hours, and the short-term exposure is expressed as a 10-minute time-weighted average. Concentrations of gases and vapours are expressed as parts per million (ppm), a measure of concentration by volume, as well as in milligrams per cubic metre of air (mg m^{-3}) a measure of concentration by mass. For PDB the long-term exposure limit is set at 75 ppm (450 mg m^{-3}) while the short-term limit is 110 ppm (675 mg m^{-3}).

The strong odour of this substance, detectable between 15 ppm to 30 ppm (Dawson 1987), is an indication that these levels are often exceeded, and because of its volatile nature, loss of vapour from non-airtight cabinets and drawers may result in unacceptable concentrations in the museum atmosphere, particularly in unventilated areas.

PDB is rated for use with caution. Chronic effects of long-term exposure include liver and kidney damage, haemolytic anaemia, weight loss, profuse rhinitis and periorbital swelling. Individuals with pre-existing pathology (hepatic, renal, blood, central nervous system) or individuals on certain prescribed drugs are at an increased risk (Dawson 1987; Hall 1988).

Recent surveys (Linnie 1987, 1990) show that PDB has been associated with headaches, sore eyes and sore throat, dizziness, nasal irritation, breathing problems, chest pains and general body weakness. One case of vomiting caused by over-exposure to PDB was also reported. Croat (1978) in his survey of workers in American herbaria reported one case of hepatitis linked with prolonged use of PDB while Hall (1988) cites reports of kidney and liver damage in industrial workers associated with PDB. Two documented deaths of workers in a West German museum, the death of an American lepidopterist and a case of severe cirrhosis of the liver were traced to exposure to PDB (Irwin 1987).

2 Naphthalene

Common names: moth flakes, mothballs, white tar. Generally used in crystal form as an insect repellent in drawers and cabinets, although its effectiveness has been questioned (Peltz and Rossol 1983). Naphthalene is the most widely used chemical in museums in the British Isles and has also widespread use worldwide (Edwards *et al.* 1980; Linnie 1987, 1990). Maximum short-term exposure limit should not exceed 15 ppm (75 mg m^{-3}), and prolonged exposure over an 8-hour day should not average more than 10 ppm (50 mg m^{-3}) (Health and Safety Executive 1985). Odour is recognizable at 25 ppm (Dawson 1987). Health-related effects associated with this substance include profuse sweating, nausea, acute kidney failure, headaches and abdominal pain (Peltz and Rossol 1983). Inhalation of high concentrations may cause haemolysis of red blood-cells. Individuals with glucose-6-phosphate dehydrogenase deficiency – a genetic disorder found mainly in blacks and mediterraneans – are particularly susceptible to haemolytic anaemia, as are newborn infants (Dawson 1987). Direct eye-contact with dust has produced irritation and cataracts (Stanley and McCann 1980).

Tests on carcinogenic effects of naphthalene exposure indicated little risk of cancer (Purchase *et al.* 1978), although Wormersley (1981) states that naphthalene is carcinogenic. In a study of causes of death and cancer of the larynx in naphthalene workers, Wolf

(1976) reports a carcinogenic link associated with naphthalene while Irwin (1987) cites a case of naphthalene-induced toxic hepatitis in a museum curator at a South Australian museum. Linnie (1990) reported the loss of consciousness in one museum worker and a reported account of violent vomiting in another caused by overexposure to naphthalene. Headaches, sore throat, sore eyes, dizziness, dermatitis, increased salivation, chest pains and nausea were also associated with use of naphthalene.

3 Dichlorvos

Common names: DDVP, 2,2-dichlorovinyl dimethyl phosphate, A 120, Vaponite Nuvan, Vapona, No-pest strip, Herkol, Dedevap-71, Nogos-273, Insectigas. Formulations include impregnated polyvinyl chloride slow-release resin strips, emulsifiable compounds, dilute and concentrated solutions, baits and aerosol sprays. Generally used in resin strip form in cabinets and drawers. In popular use worldwide but uncommon in Asian and African museums (Linnie 1987, 1990). The maximum short-term exposure limit should not exceed 0.3 ppm (3 mg m^{-3}) and prolonged exposure over an 8-hour day should not exceed more than 0.1 ppm (1 mg m^{-3}).

Dichlorvos is a contact and stomach insecticide and apart from its application in museums it is widely used as a household and public health fumigant, especially against flies, for crop protection against certain insects and for the protection of commercially stored products (Martin and Worthing 1977). It has also been used in anti-flea dog-collars (Tinker 1972) and for the removal of parasites on farmed fish stocks (Ross and Horsman 1988).

Dichlorvos resin strips function by the sustained release of the active ingredient into a relatively enclosed air space. Above the stated threshold concentration damage to neuro-transmission in the human control nervous system has been reported (Hall 1988). Other health-related adverse effects include headaches, nausea, dizziness, tremor and muscular cramp, salivation, unconsciousness and chest discomfort (Peltz and Rossol 1983). In severe cases of overexposure signs and symptoms include fever, cyanosis, coma, heart-block, shock, respiratory failure and pulmonary oedema (Dawson 1987).

In 1972, Gillet *et al.* reported that, other than potential cholinesterase inhibition, dichlorvos resin strips possess no acute or imminent hazard and represent a significant improvement over other formulations containing dichlorvos. Slomka (1970) reports that dermal reactions to dichlorvos appear to be very rare, although dermatitis has been observed in children and animals associated with dichlorvos plastic flea collars (Gillet *et al.* 1972). Circumstantial reports from several countries of high individual sensitivity to dichlorvos have also been reported (Tinker 1972). Products containing dichlorvos were associated with a range of medical disorders among museum workers similar to those reported in previous literature (Linnie 1987) and include headaches, sore throat, dizziness, nausea, chest pains and digestive disorders. Carcinogenic tests by the National Cancer Institute (USA) have proved negative.

4 Natural pyrethrins and synthetic pyrethroids

Other names: Pyrethrum, Bioresmethrin, Tetramethrin, Cypermethrin, Permethrin, Deltamethrin. Pyrethrin is the trivial name given to the insecticidal compounds which occur naturally in the flowers of *Chrysanthemum cineraefolium* and *Chrysanthemum corrineum*. Natural pyrethrins are non-persistent and are rapidly broken down by ultra-violet light. They should be used with caution (Hall 1988) and are generally applied in aerosol form for their rapid 'knock-down' and kill effects but have also been used in some herbaria in powder form, known commercially as Drione, where satisfactory results were achieved for long-term protection against insect attack. Drione consists of a fine grade of silica gel combined with pyrethrins, a synergist and a solvent stabilizer. This combination allows the slow release of the active ingredients for as long as six months (Schofield and Crisafulli 1980).

Modern synthetic formulations include Bioresmethrin, Cypermethrin and Permethrin. The synthetic forms are divided into two categories, non-persistent pyrethroids and persistent pyrethroids. The non-persistent types, including Bioresmethrin, are degraded rapidly and are considered less toxic to man than natural pyrethrins. The persistent group, which includes Permethrin and Cypermethrin, are designed to achieve rapid knock-down effects and increased residual life. However, although relatively low concentrations are required to achieve desired results they are not considered as safe as either natural pyrethrins or non-persistent pyrethroids (Pinniger 1989).

Health-related effects include skin irritation and allergic dermatitis, headaches, nausea, vomiting and tinnitus (Dawson 1987). However, recent surveys indicated no specific adverse reactions associated with the use of these substances, while toxicity studies on industrial workers using refined pyrethrins showed no ill-effects (Casida 1973). Occupational exposure limits for pyrethrins (Health and Safety Executive 1985) are expressed as a measure of airborne concentration by mass. The maximum short-term exposure limit is given as 10 mg m^{-3} and the long-term exposure limit is set at 5 mg m^{-3}.

5 Methyl bromide

Other names: Bromomethane, Brozone, Brom-o-Gas, Methogas, MeBr. Because of its high toxicity, this fumigant is generally restricted for use by certified applicators only, using special monitoring and safety equipment and approved fumigation chambers (Peltz and Rossol 1983). The safe upper long-term exposure limit has been set at 15 ppm (60 mg m^{-3}), above which concentration respirators must be worn (Martin and Worthing 1977).

Symptoms of exposure to methyl bromide include irritation to skin, eyes and upper respiratory system. Acute effects usually appear between 30 minutes and 6 hours after exposure and include malaise, visual disturbances, nausea, headaches, vomiting, vertigo and hand tremor. In cases of high exposure tremor may become more severe and widespread, developing into epileptic-type convulsions followed by coma and death secondary to pulmonary and/or circulatory failure (Hall 1988; Peltz and Rossol 1983).

In a survey of seventy-two museums worldwide (Linnie, 1990), 15 per cent of respondents reported the use of methyl bromide, which was generally undertaken in fumigation chambers by specially trained museum personnel or commercial contractors. However, one museum worker reported a severe 'glandular throat reaction' after chamber fumigation using this chemical. In the survey of museums in the British Isles (Linnie 1987), one account of a range of medical ailments directly attributed to the use of methyl bromide was reported. These ailments included digestive disorders, headaches, sore eyes, sore throat, nausea and dizziness, and may have resulted from insufficient post-fumigation ventilation.

6 Other chemical substances used in museums

A wide range of pesticides and chemical substances is used in museums (Fig. 27.1). Apart from those already listed, other substances reported in recent surveys but in limited use include phosphine, carbon disulphide and DDT (Edwards *et al.* 1980; Linnie

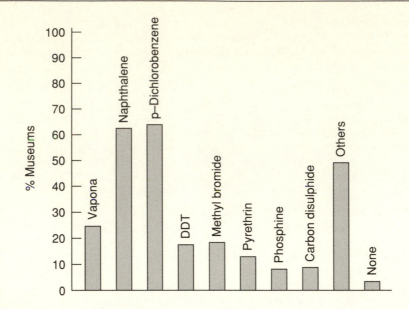

Fig. 27.1 Pesticides used to protect collections (World Survey: Linnie 1990)

1987, 1990). One account of hepatitis linked with general exposure to pesticides and chemicals was reported. Of major concern was a separate report of exposure to phosphine which induced vomiting and chest pain and subsequent development of immune system abnormalities (Linnie 1987, 1990).

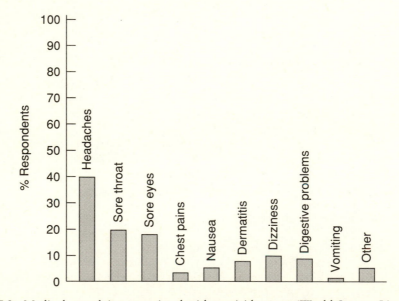

Fig. 27.2 Medical complaints associated with pesticide usage (World Survey: Linnie 1990)

CONCLUSIONS

Virtually all natural history museums use chemical methods for the protection of collections against insect attack. Use of these substances has in certain cases produced adverse health effects, ranging from mild acute symptoms (Fig. 27.2) to chronic illness and even death. The three most frequently used pesticides in museums – PDB, naphthalene and 'Vapona'-type products – because of their vapour phase activity represent potential health risks to museum workers and visitors. Poorly designed buildings, inadequate ventilation and non-airtight specimen containers contribute to the problem and may result in unacceptable levels of toxicant in the museum atmosphere. As safety threshold limits move downwards and more information becomes available on popularly used pesticides, a gradual reduction in chemical usage will be inevitable. Against this background, there is now an urgent need to assess the health implications of collection protection methods and to investigate fully new and alternative methods of chemical and non-chemical pest control feasible for use in museums.

This paper first appeared in Museum Management and Curatorship 9 *(1990), pp. 419–23.*

REFERENCES

Casida, J. E. (1973) *Pyrethrum, the Natural Insecticide*, New York: Academic Press.

Croat, T. B. (1978) 'Survey of herbarium problems', *Taxon* 27(2/3): 203–18.

Dawson, J. E. (1987) *Dealing with the Insect Problem in Museums: Chemical Control*, Technical Bulletin no. 15, Ottawa: Canadian Conservation Institute.

Edwards, S. R., Bell, B. M. and Stanley. E. M. (1980) *Pest Control in Museums: A Status Report*, Lawrence, Kans.: Association of Systematics Collections.

Gillet, J. W., Harr, J. R., Lindstrom, F. T., Mount, D. A., St Clair, A. D. and Webb, L. J. (1972) 'Evaluation of human health hazards on use of dichlorvos (DDVP), especially in resin strips', *Residue Review* 44: 115–59.

Hall, A. V. (1988) 'Pest control in herbaria', *Taxon* 37 (4): 885–907.

Health and Safety Executive (1985) *Occupational Exposure Limits*, Guidance note EH 40/85, London: HMSO.

Irwin, R. R. (1987) 'The hidden menace of PDB', *Amateur Entomological Society*, p. 1220.

Linnie, M. J. (1987) 'Pest control: a survey of natural history museums in Great Britain and Ireland', *International Journal of Museum Management and Curatorship* 6: 277–90.

—— (1990). 'Pest control in natural history museums: a world survey', *Journal of Biological Curatorship*.

Martin, H. and Worthing, C. R. (1977) *Pesticide Manual* (3rd edn), London: British Crop Protection Council.

Peltz, P. and Rossol, M. S. (1983) *Safe Pest Control Procedures for Museum Collections*, New York: Centre for Occupational Hazards.

Pinniger, D. (1989) *Insect Pests in Museums*; London: Institute of Archaeology Publications.

Purchase, I. F. H., Longstaff, E., and Ashby, J. (1978) 'An evaluation of six short-term tests for detecting carcinogenicity', *British Journal of Cancer* 37: 873–923.

Ross, A. and Horsman, P. (1988) *The Use of Nuvan 500 EC in the Salmon Farming Industry*, Marine Conservation Society Report, 1–24.

Schofield, E. K. and Crisafulli, S. (1980) 'A safer insecticide for herbarium use', *Brittonia* 32(1): 58–62.

Slomka, M. B. (1970) *Facts about 'No Pest' DDVP Strips*, Shell Chemical Co.

Stanley, E. M. and McCann, M. (1980) 'Appendix A: Technical reports on pesticides used in museums, 1981', in S. R. Edwards, B. M. Bell and M. E. King (eds) *Pest Control in Museums: A Status Report*, Lawrence: The Association of Systematics Collections, Universities of Kansas, A1–30.

Stoate, C. (1987) 'Beetles in Store', *Museums Journal* 86(4): 196–7.

Tinker, J. (1972) 'The Vapona dossier', *New Scientist* 53: 489–92.

Wolf, O. (1976) 'Cancer diseases in chemical workers in a former Naphthalene cleaning', *Deutsch Gesundheitswes* 31(21): 996–9.

Wormersley, J. S. (1981) *Plant Collecting and Herbarium Development*, Food and Agriculture Organization, Plant Protection and Production Paper 33.

Zaitseva, G. A. (1987) 'Protection of museum textiles and leather against the dermestid beetle (Col., Dermestidae) by means of antifeedents', *Studies in Conservation* 32: 176–80.

28

Experiencing loss

Barclay G. Jones

Barclay Jones's book is an invaluable source of information on natural disasters and their impact on buildings and collections. In this paper he cites some classic examples of the loss that can occur – which should encourage anyone who has not done so to formulate a disaster plan for their own museum.

PRESERVING THE WORLD CULTURAL HERITAGE

Since World War II interest in the cultural heritage represented by documents, artefacts and structures has increased enormously throughout the world. Accompanying this surge of interest has been a greater awareness of the irreplaceable value of objects which inform us about past cultures and societies and record their evolution to the present. Consequently, there has been a growing worldwide concern with surveying, documenting, recording, protecting, preserving and restoring architectural and engineering works and historic and cultural artefacts.

Enormous sums have been spent on projects as far removed as the restoration of the major historic structures in Leningrad from the depredations of the siege of that city in World War II, the rescue launched in 1963 of the temples of Abu Simbel from the rising waters of Lake Nasser behind the Aswan High Dam (Gerster 1969), and the painstaking reconstruction of the Stupa at Borobudur, neglected since the area was deserted following earthquakes and volcanic eruptions in 1006 (Morton 1983). The heroic efforts to protect Venice and London from subsidence and sea surges are remarkable (Judge 1972). The movable sea barrier erected between 1974 and 1982 across the Thames at Woolwich is an extraordinary engineering feat (Wholey 1982; Starbid 1983).

We have devised elaborate mechanisms for preserving and protecting the heritage. We have directed much attention to the threats of destruction by the natural elements such as decay, subsidence, air pollution and other forms of attrition. Many of the public efforts and much of the legislation that has been enacted is intended primarily to prevent destruction by human agents through neglect, demolition for replacement by more modern items, theft, vandalism and acts of war. We have excellent documents to assist us in these tasks (Tillotson 1977). In contrast, we have given relatively little attention to the threat of losses as the result of natural disasters, and only a few works on preservation deal specifically with this danger (Feilden 1982: pp. 117–29).

DESTRUCTION BY NATURAL DISASTERS

We are all quite aware, when we think about it, which apparently is not often enough, that natural disasters have been the cause of destruction that has obliterated many of the most valuable elements from our past. For example, we admire the torso as an art form and associate it with modern sculptors such as Rodin, Mailiol and Brancusi and with Greek and Roman works from antiquity. We seldom consciously acknowledge that the ancient works that provided the inspiration for modern efforts were not designed as torsos but are the major remains of complete figures, the limbs of which were undoubtedly snapped off in earthquakes or were broken when the statues were toppled.

We know that the seismic history of the civilized world has been active and violent. We acknowledge that disasters preserve and create as well as destroy: that some of the best preserved Roman artefacts, paintings and architecture we have were buried in Pompeii and Herculaneum in the devastating volcanic eruptions of 24, 25 August, AD 79; that the undisturbed ruins of the largest intact Roman provincial city, Jerash, are available to us because it was abandoned for 1,100 years after the violent earthquake in the Jordan Valley of 18 January 746; and that the handsome baroque centre of the city of Dubrovnik is a consequence of the rebuilding after the catastrophic earthquake of 6 April 1667, which killed two-thirds of the population (Judge 1982; Browning 1982; Carter 1972). We regret the losses, but we seldom think systematically about the enormity of the toll over the centuries.

RECENT LOSSES

Our ability to forget can be graphically illustrated simply by considering the losses from the major events of the last twenty years. The earthquake on 26 July 1963 that struck Skopje destroyed many historic buildings, damaged the Mosque of Mustapha Pasha, and did great damage to the Kursumli Han, an ancient caravanserai that housed the archaeological museum. Later that same year considerable damage was done to historic structures by the floods resulting from the collapse of the Vaiont Dam on the Piave river in northern Italy that was a consequence of earthslides on 10 October 1963.

Probably the most extensive devastation of historic structures, of works of art and museum collections in the recent past occurred three years later when the flood of the Arno river struck Florence on 4 and 5 November 1966 (Judge 1967; Klein 1969). The Ponte Vecchio was damaged, as were Ghiberti's bronze doors of the Baptistry of the Duomo and Andrea del Sarto's fresco in San Salvi, Cimabue's *Crucifixion* at San Croce, frescoes by Uccello, Botticelli, Lorenzetti and Martini. Archives and furniture were damaged or destroyed in the Strozzi Palace; ancient musical instruments were lost in the Bardini Museum, scientific instruments in the Museo delle Scienze, armour at the Bargello, and the Etruscan collection at the Museo Archeologico. A hundred and thirty thousand photographic negatives were among the losses of the Uffizi Gallery; and there was tremendous damage to the state archives, 6,000 volumes at the Opera di Duomo, 250,000 volumes at the Gabinello Vieusseux, 14,000 volumes at the Jewish Synagogue, 36,000 volumes at the Geography Academy, the entire collection at the Music Conservatory, and 1,300,000 volumes in the Biblioteca Nazionale (Horton 1967; Cornell 1976: 148). Salvage, cleaning, repair and restoration was a horrendous undertaking and provided invaluable experience to a generation of experts who devised many of our best current conservatorial methods.

241

Two years later, Hurricane Camille of 18 August 1969 did much damage to the Jefferson Davis Shrine in Biloxi, Mississippi, and the collections of documents, pictures, costumes, uniforms and other artefacts in the museum on the ground floor of the beachfront mansion (Organ and McMillan 1969). The subsequent Hurricane Frederick on 12 September 1969 damaged a number of historic structures in Mobile, Alabama. In the earthquake that struck Peru on 31 May 1970, the archaeological museum in Huaras was damaged. On 6 February 1971, an earthquake did enormous damage to the historic structures that composed the ancient hill town of Tuscania, north of Rome. Three days later in the United States the earthquake of 9 February 1971 in the San Fernando Valley in California severely damaged five rooms of the Villa Adobe on Olivera Street in Los Angeles, the oldest building in that city.

A year and a half later the floods produced by the rains resulting from Hurricane Agnes on 22 and 23 June 1972 severely damaged the collection of the Corning Glass Museum (Martin 1977), and many collections of historic furniture, archives and artefacts the full length of the Susquehanna river basin. These included extensive damage to the Heisey House, the headquarters and museum of the Clinton County Historical Society, at Lock Haven, Pa., and the Wyoming Historical and Geological Society at Wilkes Barre. Lesser damage was done to the Golden Plough Tavern and the General Gates House in York, Pa., and several other museums. While the Fort Pitt Museum was flooded and suffered much damage, the collections were saved (Whipkey 1973).

The same year many historic structures, including the cathedral and the Presidential Palace, were completely destroyed or severely damaged, along with their contents, in the devastating earthquake and subsequent fire in Managua, Nicaragua, on 24 December 1972. Less than a year later, on 28 August 1973, the earthquake that struck the states of Puebla, Veracruz and Oaxaca in Mexico damaged 200 important colonial churches, many beyond repair (Cornell 1976). The Xenia, Ohio, tornadoes that swept eleven states on 3 April 1974 destroyed historic homes and public structures in many communities (Boone 1974).

Large-scale devastations of historic structures and artefacts resulted from the severe earthquake of 6 May 1976 in the Friuli district in northeastern Italy (Pichard, Ambrayseys and Ziogas 1976; Schwartzbaum, Silver and Grissom 1977). Many cities, towns and villages suffered considerable damage, causing the effect on historic structures and artefacts to be extremely widespread. Subsequent earthquakes on 11 and 15 September further damaged structures weakened in the first shock and undid much of the salvage and repair work that had been initiated. On 4 March 1977, the earthquake in Romania, while it caused only moderate damage to the museum buildings in Bucharest, severely damaged the museum collections and contents, particularly the ethnographic collection. The museum contains the largest collection of works by Constantin Brancusi but fortunately none of these were lost. Historic structures in the countryside outside the capital city received substantial damage (Ambraseys 1977). Much less publicized is the fact that extensive damage was done to historic structures in northern Bulgaria that were affected by the same tremor (Brankov 1983). An ironic event was the July 1977 flood which destroyed the Johnstown Flood (31 May 1889) Museum in Johnstown, Pennsylvania.

A tornado on 10 April 1979 did extensive damage to the museum at Wichita Falls, Texas (Glass *et al.* 1980). The earthquake of 15 April 1979 that struck Montenegro damaged many historic buildings in Kotor, a city which had been severely struck by the same earthquake that devastated Dubrovnik in 1667 (Petrovski and Paskalov 1981). The moderate earthquake of 6 November 1979 in Greece produced no casualties and little damage but caused serious cracks in the Parthenon, the loss of a large number of amphorae in the Acropolis Museum and caused the National Museum in Athens to be closed for a number of months. The Campania Basilicata earthquake in southern Italy on 23 November 1980 did tremendous amounts of damage to the historic structures that gave the towns and villages of that countryside its character (Lagorio and Mader 1981). Much of the same area that had been devastated in the Naples–Bari earthquake of 23 July 1930 suffered again. It was the worst disaster in southern Italy since the tremors that levelled Messina and Reggia on 29 December 1908, and the Neapolitan earthquake of 1857.

While accounts can be found, it is necessary to dig rather deeply to determine the losses from many natural disasters. There are usually few reports in the press about the loss of cultural artefacts. Media coverage focuses on loss of life and the personal tragedies of the survivors (Scanlon and Alldred 1982). Few accounts of the crash on 1 March 1962 into Jamaica Bay of an American Airlines Boeing 707 bound from Kennedy Airport for Los Angeles that cost the lives of 95 people noted that 15 paintings and 5 drawings by Arshile Gorky bound for a West Coast exhibition were lost (Cornell 1976). The owners and proprietors of collections of artefacts and buildings are seldom inclined to publicize their losses. We do not have a really clear picture of the devastation to our cultural heritage through natural events in the recent, let alone the remote, past.

PREVENTIVE MEASURES IN RESPONSE TO LOSS

Indeed, it seems remarkable that anything at all has survived from the past. But there is clear evidence that at many times, in many places, people recognized the possibilities of natural disasters and took preventive measures to mitigate their effects. In particular, inhabitants of the earthquake-prone regions of the eastern Mediterranean appear to have developed aseismic building techniques as early as the Mycenean Age (Schaar 1974). Similar methods, called xylodesia, survive today in vernacular systems of construction (Porphyrios 1971). As is natural, we learn from experience, and disasters lead to devising new measures to safeguard lives, buildings and possessions. The great fire that destroyed most of London north of the Thames that raged for four days after it broke out on 1 September 1666 led to the banning of wooden construction and overhanging gables. The rebuilt city had wider thoroughfares to serve as fire-breaks. Among the losses in the fire were St Paul's Cathedral, 87 parish churches, 6 chapels, the Royal Exchange, the Customs House and the Guildhall (Cornell 1976). After the devastating earthquake in Sicily on 11 January 1693, the Spanish Viceregal government proposed reconstruction plans for cities that provided more open spaces for refuge and streets less likely to be impassable with rubble (Tobriner 1980). The earthquake and tidal wave that devastated Lisbon on 1 November 1755 led not only to reconstruction planning schemes to reduce the vulnerability of urban areas but also aseismic building designs and measures to reduce the spread of fire (Tobriner 1980). The Marquess de Pombal initiated the first scientific investigation of earthquakes, and the analysis of effects throughout Europe by the English physicist John Mitchell led to the first crude theory of wave motion (Cornell 1976). A generation later the series of extremely destructive earthquakes in Calabria led the government to the planning of towns less vulnerable to devastation and to the promotion of extremely sophisticated building methods (Tobriner 1983).

RENDERING EXPERIENCE INTO KNOWLEDGE

Perhaps we too will respond to the substantial number of disastrous events over the past twenty years by learning better how to protect, minimize damage, rescue, salvage and restore. But there is some urgency if we are to assimilate and transmit this knowledge. Many people have been involved in emergency measures during these events and in conservation and recovery operations after them and have acquired as a consequence tremendous funds of experience. Experts have gained knowledge at enormous expense not only in human time and effort but also in material losses. Important documents and source materials have been produced. But too frequently, there is little written record readily available of the actions that they took, the successes they had, and the methods and procedures that they learned. It is immensely important that this information not be lost but be collected and codified and made readily available. It should be extremely useful in helping people to anticipate the kinds of impacts disasters may have on them and their possessions and take appropriate preventive and preparatory measures to mitigate them. It will also provide a deep source of experience that will help experts and knowledgable people in the future to prepare themselves for the kinds of actions they will have to undertake in the event of finding themselves in a disaster. This exchange and dissemination of experience and information should be invaluable in protecting elements of the heritage from destruction and in facilitating their salvage, conservation and reconstruction. If less of our heritage is lost through catastrophic natural events in the next period, the exercise will have been rewarding.

This paper first appeared in B. G. Jones (1986) Protecting Historic Architecture and Museum Collections from Natural Disasters *(Oxford: Butterworth-Heinemann), pp. 3–13.*

REFERENCES

Ambraseys, Nicholas N. (1977) 'The Romanian earthquake of 4 March 1977', *Disasters* 1(3): 175–7.

Boone, C. F. (1974) *The Ohio Tornadoes April 3, 1974*, Lubbock, Tex.: C. F. Boone.

Brankov, Georgi Jordanov (1983) *Vrancea Earthquake in 1977. Its Aftereffects in the People's Republic of Bulgaria*, Sofia: Publishing House of the Bulgarian Academy of Sciences.

Browning, Iain (1982) *Jerash and the Decapolis*, London: Chatto & Windus.

Carter, Francis W. (1972) *Dubrovnik (Ragusa) A Classic City-State*, London: Seminar Press.

Cornell, James (1976) *The Great International Disaster Book*, New York: Charles Scribner's Sons.

Fielden, Bernard M. (1982) *Conservation of Historic Buildings*, London: Butterworth Scientific.

Gerster, Georg (1969) 'Abu Simbel's ancient temples reborn', *National Geographic* 135(5): 724–44.

Glass, Roger I., Craven, Robert B., Bregman, Dennis J., Stoll, Barbara J., Horowitz, Neil, Kerndt, Peter and Winkle, Joe, (1980) 'Injuries from the Wichita Falls Tornado: implications for prevention', *Science* 207(4432): 734–8.

Horton, Carolyn (1967) 'Saving the libraries of Florence', *Wilson Library Bulletin* 41: 1034–43.

Judge, Joseph (1967) 'Florence rises from the flood', *National Geographic* 132(1): 1–43.

— (1972) 'Venice fights for life', *National Geographic* 142(5): 591–631.

— (1982) 'On the slope of Vesuvius a buried Roman town gives up its dead', *National Geographic* 162(6): 686–93.

Klein, Richard M. (1969) 'The Florence floods', *Natural History* 78(7): 46–55.

Lagorio, Henry J. and Mader, George G. (1981) *Earthquake in Campagnia Basilicata, Italy, November 23, 1980*, Berkeley, Calif.: Earthquake Engineering Research Institute.

Martin, John H. (ed.) (1977) *The Corning Flood: Museum Under Water*, Corning, NY: The Corning Museum of Glass.

Morton, W. Brown III (1983) 'Indonesia rescues ancient Borobudur', *National Geographic* 163(1): 126–42.

Organ, Robert M. and McMillan, Eleanor (1969) 'Aid to a hurricane-damaged museum (Biloxi)', *Bulletin of the American Group-IIC* 10(1): 31–9.

Petrovski, Jakim and Paskalov, Trifun (eds) (1981) *The Montenegro, Yugoslavia, Earthquake of April*

15, 1979, Skopje, Yugoslavia: Publication no. 65 of the Institute of Earthquake Engineering and Engineering Seismology.

Pichard, Pierre, Ambraseys, Nicholas N. and Ziogas, G. N. (1976) *The Gemona di Friuli Earthquake of 6 May 1976*, Paris: UNESCO, UNESCO Serial No. FMR/CC/SC/ED/76/169, UNESCO Restricted Technical Report no. RP/1975/2,222,3.

Porphyrios, Demetrius Thomas Georgia (1971) 'Traditional earthquake-resistant construction on a Greek island', *Journal of the Society of Architectural Historians* 30(1): 31–9.

Scanlon, T. Joseph and Alldred, Suzanne, (1982) 'Media coverage of disasters: the same old story', Barclay G. Jones and Miha tomazevic (eds) *Social and Economic Aspects of Earthquakes*, Ithaca, NY: Program in Urban and Regional Studies, Cornell University.

Schaar, Kenneth W. (1974) 'Traditional earthquake-resistant construction: the Mycenaean aspect', *Journal of the Society of Architectural Historians* 23(1): 80–1.

Schwartzbaum, Paul M., Silver, Constance and Grissom, Carol A. (1977) 'Earthquake damage to works of art in Ariculi region of Italy', *Journal of the American Institute of Conservation* 17(1): 9–16.

Starbird, Ethel A. (1983) 'That noble river, the Thames', *National Geographic* 163 (6): 750–91.

Tillotson, Robert G. (1977) *Museum Security*, Paris: International Council of Museums and American Museums Association.

Tobriner, Stephen (1980) 'Earthquakes and planning in the 17th and 18th centuries', *Journal of Architectural Education* 33(4): 11–15.

— (1983) 'La Casa Baraccata: earthquake-resistant construction in 18th century Calabria', *Journal of the Society of Architectural Historians* 42(2): 131–8.

Whipkey, Harry E. (1973) *After Agnes: A Report on Flood Recovery Assistance by the Pennsylvania Historical and Museum Commission*, Harrisburg, P.: Pennsylvania Historical and Museum Commission.

Wholey, Jane (1982) 'Saving London from an impending threat of flood', *Smithsonian* 13(5): 78–87.

29

Museum disaster preparedness planning

John E. Hunter

John Hunter's article is the best succinct discussion of the disaster planning process for museums. It provides a structure for the planning and a great deal of useful practical information.

Why plan for disasters? Hilda Bohem of the University of California Library System provides the dictum that, 'A disaster is what happens only if you are not prepared for it' (Bohem 1978). Preparing for disasters may not prevent them but will lessen their impact. Preparing and following a disaster response plan can help to avoid costly or fatal damage and can prevent a disaster from becoming a tragedy.

Planning for museum emergencies and disasters is a four-phase process. The first phase requires identification of natural events that might threaten the institution, that is, conducting a multi-hazard vulnerability assessment, and determining what the effects of such hazards could be under varying circumstances. The second phase consists of designing and assessing strategies for coping with the identified events. Strategic goals should include disaster prevention where possible, minimization of damage during a disaster, mitigation of further damage or deterioration afterwards, and recovery and resumption of normal operations. The third phase entails writing a plan to guide the museum staff before, during and after a disaster. The fourth phase calls for regular reviews of the disaster plan to keep it current, training in the plan's execution, periodic drills to test the plan's effectiveness, and evaluation of the plan's performance after any disastrous occurrence.

Developing and implementing a disaster plan does not require a lot of technical knowledge. It does require the attention and dedication of at least one staff member. The planner must have the full management support and access to all relevant information on the museum's contents and operations. Developing a plan for a large or complex museum may take a year or more. Effective implementation of the plan – the training, testing and evaluation steps – will usually take longer than the design and production of a written plan.

The examination of the museum necessary to prepare a plan should make the museum's staff aware of the institution's vulnerabilities and may stimulate them to think about improvements that can be made in ordinary museum operations. For example, the survey required to identify the institution's most valuable assets can be carried out in conjunction with a conservation needs survey. The preventive actions that can be taken to prepare a museum for surviving an earthquake may also help protect it from burglary and vandalism and can enhance building maintenance and upkeep.

There are at least ten discrete steps or stages in the four-phase development, writing and evaluation of a disaster plan. The rest of this paper outlines what a disaster plan should contain and how an effective plan can be organized.

The first step in the preparation of a plan is designation of the person responsible for developing and writing the plan and the naming of an advisory committee. In a small institution, it is possible that everyone on the staff will play some role in developing the plan. In a large institution, a senior staff member will usually be in charge, assisted by individuals appointed from each department and perhaps from the museum's board. This planning team eventually may become the museum's Disaster Control Organization; its members would be the persons in charge of disaster mitigation and recovery efforts. Care in their selection is imperative.

Once the planning team has been selected, it should be given authority in writing and should enjoy the full support of management. Full support from the director, senior management, department heads and the board of trustees is vital to the success of the planning effort. Without enough support, the planning team may not get full co-operation from all departments and may not be able to implement any new policies or administrative changes needed to establish a disaster preparedness programme.

Once a team has been appointed and authorized to prepare a disaster plan, the second step is for them to locate sources of planning assistance and information. They should become familiar with disaster planning literature and should review plans developed by other museums. They should obtain as-built architectural drawings of the museum's building and, if possible, talk with the museum's architect and builder about its vulnerability to various disasters. They should find out what kinds of support local fire and building inspection offices can offer, not only in helping when disaster strikes but also in assessing the museum's vulnerability and helping with the planning effort. The team should contact other museums in the region to learn how they plan to deal with disasters and to explore the feasibility of mutual aid agreements. The team should also identify talents and capabilities possessed by the museum's own staff, trustees and volunteers. One of the museum's trustees or volunteers may have responsibility for corporate disaster planning in his or her business and could be invited to serve on the planning team.

The planning team must also contact state and local police, fire, and public health agencies, state and local civil defence agencies, the Red Cross, and state and regional museum organizations. Such contacts are advisable for two reasons. First, local organizations can provide planning assistance and technical advice and can explain the museum's place in existing community disaster plans. Second, local organizations must know of the museum's plans in order to incorporate disaster support for the museum into their own respective plans.

The third planning step is vulnerability assessment. I want to emphasize the importance of thoroughly assessing the total vulnerability of the museum *before* deciding how to protect it. Failure to consider the possibility of a particular disaster prevents planning for it. Faulty estimation of the damage that might result from a disaster will produce a disaster plan that falls short of affording full protection. Finally, inadequate vulnerability assessment may generate a false set of priorities for allocating the museum's resources to disaster prevention and mitigation.

The fourth step in the planning process is a survey to identify assets requiring protection against loss or damage from a disaster. This survey will produce an inventory or a summary of the museum's assets listed by importance to the museum and to its continued operation. Among the assets to be surveyed are: the collections and their catalogue and registration records; photograph and research files; the library and its card file; lab, shop and maintenance equipment and supplies; administrative files and records; the building and its operating systems; and sales shop merchandise. In conducting the survey, do not forget people, the museum's most important asset. Protection of visitors and staff must always come first in planning.

Evaluation of the museum's material assets will be based on the broad and somewhat subjective criteria of irreplaceability and value. The specific criteria used by a given museum will depend upon the nature of its assets, particularly the nature of the collections. Original works of art, natural history specimens, archaeological collections and most ethnographic specimens, are unique and irreplaceable. Books, prints, copies of sculpture and taxidermic specimens may be replaceable, but only at great cost. Library materials, tools, equipment and supplies may also be considered. The building itself may be replaceable or economically reparable. If it is an important historic structure, however, this may not be true.

Criteria for determining the value of assets can include the following considerations:

1 Intrinsic, sentimental or historic value
2 Aesthetic or scientific value
3 Legal and administrative value
4 Research and documentary value
5 Monetary value

Considerations of monetary value may be inapplicable to cultural materials or may be determined by the other considerations. Nonetheless, monetary value has an important bearing on the practicality of replacing damaged or destroyed assets and thus must be included in relative evaluations of the museum's property.

Evaluation will classify the museum's contents into at least three broad categories:

Priority 1: Assets of such importance that their safety must be guaranteed at all costs because their loss would be catastrophic.

Priority 2: Assets of relatively great importance, the loss of which would not be serious but not catastrophic.

Priority 3: Assets of relatively little importance, the loss of which would not be a handicap.

In general, assets in the first group will be limited in number and will receive the maximum possible protection. The second group will be somewhat larger and will receive special protection only within the constraints of personnel availability, facilities, reasonable expense and time. The third group will include the majority of the museum's assets. These assets will initially receive only the protection offered by the museum building. Only after assets in the first two groups have been protected appropriately will resources be devoted to protection of third-priority assets.

The importance of prioritizing the museum's assets cannot be overemphasized. Just as an earthquake vulnerability assessment can result in false assumptions about disaster risk, so too can inadequate setting of priorities result in misapplication of scarce resources during disaster recovery.

After the planning team has identified threats to the museum and established priorities for protecting its assets against those threats, it is ready to determine specific methods of protection. This phase of the planning process contains two steps, protection of assets in advance of disaster and recovery of assets after a disaster. These two steps are among the most difficult, time-consuming and crucial in the entire planning process. The decision made during these steps will determine the ultimate success and workability of the plan itself.

Step 5 is the design of protective measures. Selection of protective measures should be based on the following six considerations:

1 The degree of danger to which the museum's assets would be exposed during and after a disaster.
2 The level of protection currently afforded collections and other portable assets by the museum building and by the exhibit and storage cases in which they are kept.
3 The physical characteristics of the assets; that is, the fragility of their materials and their susceptibility to various kinds of damage.
4 How the assets are being used and whether such uses might contribute to risk. For example, objects on exhibition or left out for interpretive programmes may be at greater risk than objects in storage.
5 The values assigned earlier when assets were being prioritized.
6 The funds, personnel and other resources available for providing protection.

The sixth step in the planning process is formulation of recovery plans. In this step, the planning team determines how the museum is to recover from the unavoidable effects of disasters. When planning for earthquakes, floods, hurricanes and other major natural events, there are relatively few true *preventive* measures that can be taken. Planning aims to minimize the risk of asset losses to lessen the impact of losses that occur.

The kinds of measures selected by the planning team for incorporation into a recovery plan will depend upon the assets to be protected. More diversified collections will need a greater variety and complexity of recovery methods. Planning for recovery should provide for immediate and successful completion of certain tasks in the aftermath of disaster. Briefly, those tasks are:

1 Assessment of damage to determine what has been damaged and the location and extent of damage.
2 Assignment of specific priorities for recovery efforts, based on the general priorities established earlier in the planning process; these priorities will provide a basis for decisions about which assets to treat first.
3 Selection of specific recovery methods from among the methods identified in advance as those the museum must be prepared to execute.
4 Requesting assistance with recovery operations from outside the museum (e.g., other museums, outside conservators, local tradesmen and craftsmen, volunteers and local governmental authorities).

If the organization of recovery efforts has been well planned, recovery will be less difficult, less costly and more efficient. A critical part of the recovery plan will be providing for the protection of supplies and equipment that will be needed to begin the recovery effort. Such materials are much more valuable and much harder to obtain after a disaster than they might be under normal circumstances. Materials used for two primary purposes should be stockpiled: (1) materials for repair of the museum building, its operating equipment and protection systems and (2) supplies for emergency stabilization of the collections and collection records.

Stockpiled emergency materials must be given the same degree of protection from disaster as the collections themselves.

Emergency supplies and equipment can be classified into the following groups:

- Materials for removing dirt and debris
- Tools and equipment for demolition, repairs and rescue
- Construction materials
- Emergency lighting, communications and protection equipment
- Materials for protecting the health and safety of personnel
- Conservation supplies and equipment
- Miscellaneous supplies and equipment

A suggested list of supplies and equipment is included at the end of this paper. Most museums probably keep most of these materials on hand routinely. If so, it remains only for the disaster plan to ensure their protection during a disaster so that they will be ready for use afterwards. Subsequent papers will address the topic of specific recovery supplies and techniques.

In Step 7 the planning team brings the first two phases of the planning process to their logical conclusion by writing out the plans it has developed. There are many good reasons why the museum's disaster plan must be written. Perhaps the most important reason is that a written plan shortens response time when disaster strikes and will minimize the number of decisions that have to be made. In the absence of a written plan, everyone with responsibility for emergency action would have to confer on the division of recovery tasks.

A written plan will define the museum's emergency command structure and the scope of each person's authority and will identify staff responsibilities. A written plan will include assessment and inventory of the resources needed to support the museum during and after a disaster. Rapid access to emergency supplies, equipment and personnel will be vital to the success of the plan; the written plan will help locate these resources. Finally, a written plan can and should be used to train all employees in carrying out their disaster recovery responsibilities.

The act of writing a disaster plan will point out gaps in the planning and will ensure that planning objectives have been met. Writing the plan will also suggest needed improvements in the museum's day-to-day operations, such as the need for more extensive fire protection, a more efficient organizational structure or better internal communications. The written plan will describe the museum's Disaster Control Organization and will determine whether that organization is sufficient to control disaster and to recover from it. Finally, a written plan may be required by the museum's insurers or by persons from whom it has borrowed objects for exhibition. A plan may also be required if the museum is part of a larger organization, such as a university or a city or county government. In such a case, the museum's plan will probably be part of the plan for the entire organization and must be compatible with that plan.

The written plan should be characterized by flexibility, simplicity, detail and adaptability. The plan should be flexible enough to allow for changes in the staff, in the availability of outside help and recovery supplies, or in threats to which the museum may be vulnerable. The plan should also allow for reduced vulnerability assessment following the implementation of disaster preventive measures. The plan should be simple enough to be understood easily and executed quickly. Yet it must be detailed enough to minimize the number of decisions necessary during an emergency. The plan should be adaptable to situations it is not specifically designed to cover. It should be oriented to the effects of disasters, not their causes. For example, instead of including one plan for floods, a second for broken water-pipes, and a third for water damage due to fire fighting, it ought to include a single, multi-purpose plan for water damage in general. Similarly, a single plan for dealing with structural damage could be used for recovery from an earthquake, a tornado or an explosion.

There is no standard format for a museum disaster plan. Some authors have recommended seven to ten sections and I have seen plans with as many as thirty sections. I believe that most museums will find their needs met by a plan with six major sections and a series of appendices. The major sections would be: Introduction and Statement of Purpose, Authority, Scope of the Plan, Disaster Avoidance Procedures, Disaster Mitigation Procedures and Disaster Recovery Procedures.

Section 1, Introduction and Statement of Purpose, states why the plan has been developed and what it is intended to achieve. This is a good place to indicate how and by whom the plan was developed and how it is to be kept current.

Section 2, Authority, has three purposes. First, it documents the authority for preparation and implementation of the plan. Normally, the plan will be prepared under the authority of the museum's board of trustees or its director. Second, this section delegates responsibility for execution of the plan to a staff member designated Emergency Services Officer and placed in charge of the Disaster Control Organization. Third, this section establishes a Disaster Control Organization and indicates by name or title those responsible for co-ordinating all emergency activities.

Section 3, Scope of the Plan, identifies each of the emergencies and disasters the plan is intended to cover. It first lists and describes each of the events that could occur in the museum; these events will have been identified during the vulnerability assessment step of the planning process. Then this section indicates the probability of occurrence for each event, its expected frequency of occurrence, and the expected effects of the event on museum operations. The most likely events should be listed first. Vulnerability assessment must consider the 'trigger effect', wherein one event triggers others that create a more serious situation than that brought about by a single event. For example, in describing the potential impact of an earthquake, the plan should note that the losses may include not only structural damage to the building and its contents, but also death and injury, water damage, fire, contamination by chemicals and fuels, and looting. Planned responses to each of these events, including those 'triggered' by others, will be detailed subsequently in Sections 4 and 5.

A museum consisting of several buildings, particularly if they are widely scattered, may have an individual plan for each building or a single plan for the entire institution. If only one plan is written, Section 3 should describe its application to each building. This section should also describe how the disaster plan relates to any other emergency or operating plans that may exist, either within the institution or in the community (a medical emergency plan, a fire reaction plan or a general security plan). An explanation of how all plans relate to and complement each other and an indication of the circumstances under which they should be executed individually or simultaneously will enable a co-ordinated disaster response.

Sections 4, 5 and 6 are the heart of the disaster plan because they describe techniques for coping with every possible disaster. These sections will be based on the choices of protection and recovery methods made in Steps 5 and 6 of the planning process. They should assign responsibilities for implementing and executing each part of the overall plan, explain the circumstances dictating partial or complete execution of the plan, and detail necessary response procedures.

Section 4 will outline actions the museum can take to reduce disaster vulnerability such as structural modification to help withstand an earthquake or installation of fire protection systems. The actions outlined in the plan should be implemented as funds and other resources become available, ideally before the events whose effects they are to minimize.

Section 5 will treat disaster mitigation – response to unavoidable disasters normally preceded by a warning. Mitigation emphasizes reducing the impact of the events as they occur. For example, response to a hurricane warning will include weather-proofing buildings, relocating or evacuating artefacts and records to safer quarters, and covering objects that cannot be moved. The plan will also list procedures for recovering from the effects of the hurricane.

Recovery procedures may not have to be fully executed if predisaster mitigation is carried out successfully. Subsections should describe all activities to be carried out in response to each of the disaster events itemized in Section 3. If plans for the individual events share many features, a general subsection followed by a listing of the unique aspects of each event may suffice. The paramount goal is that the plans be accessible, understandable and workable.

Section 6 will cover disaster events for which there will normally be no warning. Plans in this section will place primary emphasis on recovery. For example, plans for recovering from major earthquake or flash flood damage will probably include: evacuating objects threatened by building collapse or looting; freezing water-soaked paper; drying metals subject to rusting; locating pieces of broken objects; securing the building against vandalism and theft; and, most importantly, evacuating and treating any injured people. The emphasis of this type of plan is not prevention of damage during the disaster event but protection from further damage afterwards.

These five sections will be the main part of the disaster plan. But these sections alone are not sufficient. They must be supplemented by appendices containing information necessary for execution of the plan but so subject to change that including it in the major sections of the plan would be impractical. The planning team will have to decide what kinds of information to include in the appendices. In most plans, the following appendices will be useful.

Appendix 1 should include an organization chart of the museum, showing all divisions and at least the key staff positions. If the museum is part of a larger organization, such as a university or a local government, the appendix should include a chart showing the museum's position within the larger organization. Reference to these charts during emergencies will facilitate communications and help to maintain the chain of command. The charts should be simple and clear. It will usually be sufficient to show only division and office names, functions, and the names and titles of their key personnel. Members of the Disaster Control Organization should be indicated on the organizational charts or perhaps on a separate chart. Coloured markers can be used to highlight the key personnel or activities.

Appendix 2 can consist of lists of key museum staff needed for execution of the plan. The list should include each person's name and title, home address and home telephone number. This list may also include a brief résumé of each person's responsibilities under the plan. The same appendix might well include a roster of the museum's entire staff in case there is an incident requiring a head count to determine whether everyone is safe.

Appendix 3 should list emergency contacts outside the museum. Such contacts would include: police and fire departments; the local Civil Defence organization; local utility companies, hospitals and ambulance companies; plumbers, electricians and glass companies; the museum's insurance agents; and any other organizations or persons the museum might have to contact in case of emergency. Both daytime and after-hours telephone numbers should be listed. Specific contacts in the listed agencies should be listed where appropriate.

Outside curators and conservators may be needed for advice and assistance. A list of various experts' addresses and specialities should be appended. If they must travel to the museum, transportation and compensation arrangements should be detailed. Previous arrangements may have been made to borrow personnel from nearby museums or sister organizations for assistance in evacuation or recovery operations. Record such arrangements and the appropriate contacts. List any volunteers you may need to call upon, along with their special skills. If anybody on the staff, including volunteers, has promised to bring certain equipment and supplies with him for personal or museum use, indicate what they are.

It is critical that this and all other call-up lists be kept current. They should be reviewed and revised at least once a month. Using a word processor can speed revisions.

Appendix 4 can be a description of the circumstances requiring a call to various outside agencies or persons and the kinds of services or assistance available from these outside sources. Appendices 3 and 4 might be combined if not too cumbersome.

Appendix 5 might include plans of the museum, its grounds and its immediate neighbourhood. Floor plans can indicate vulnerable parts of the museum or those containing the most valuable assets. They should show the locations of emergency exits and evacuation routes, gas and electric cutoffs, telephone closets, firefighting equipment, burglar and fire alarm devices and controls, emergency supplies and equipment stockpiles, and other such information.

Maps can show sidewalks, streets, driveways, gates, fences, buried and overhead utility lines, fire hydrants, manholes and other pertinent information. Certain floor plans might be posted at key locations around the non-public parts of the museum to facilitate movement during an emergency and to orient outside maintenance and service crews. Floor plans and maps will prove particularly useful if the museum depends upon volunteers or other non-staff personnel for help after a disaster. The inclusion of sensitive information in this appendix, like plans of the intrusion detection systems, may require restricting distribution of the museum's disaster plan or keeping the appendix in a sealed envelope or safe.

Appendix 6 might be an inventory of all collections, records and other valuable assets and the priority for their protection. With this record could be a floor plan that shows the location of each asset or group of assets on the inventory. A similar plan can be posted in museum storerooms and conservation labs to speed access to these assets by emergency evacuation personnel unfamiliar with your facility. Caution in including such details on a posted floor plan is prudent. It could become a shopping list for burglars. Some sort of private coding, such as with colours, might eliminate this problem.

Appendix 7 might be a summary of arrangements for evacuating and relocating the collections. This appendix would include packing and crating instructions and the location of available supplies and materials. This appendix would also indicate several possible sites for temporary storage in case the primary site suffers the same disaster that strikes the museum.

Appendix 8 could be instructions for emergency management of the building's utilities and for service and operation of vital building support systems. Such systems might include: burglar and fire alarm systems, fire suppression system, firefighting equipment, elevators and escalators, emergency lighting, emergency generator, heating and air-conditioning equipment, humidifiers and dehumidifiers. This appendix could either include information from manufacturers' instruction manuals or could refer to the manuals. If the vital information is only referenced, the cited manuals must be protected as well as the emergency plan itself.

Appendix 9 is one of the most important appendices; it contains an inventory of supplies, equipment and other local resources useful in time of disaster. Stockpiled emergency supplies and equipment should be described, as to purpose, quantity and location. Arrangements to borrow equipment like portable generators, power tools, fans and dehumidifiers should be recorded and delegated to certain staff for execution. Arrangements to procure supplies like plywood, nails, plastic sheeting, tissue-paper, cardboard boxes, tape and disinfectants should be in place and fully described. See the list of suggested materials at the end of this paper.

Appendix 10 might be a glossary of terms used in the disaster plan. A glossary will ensure that everyone using the plan will be speaking the same language.

An index would make a highly useful addition to the plan. However, because the plan will change fairly frequently, an index may be difficult to keep current. Nonetheless, an index should be considered and included if its usefulness would outweigh the effort required to keep it current.

Because the disaster plan will evolve, it can be kept most conveniently in a three-ring binder. The original should be stored in a secure, fire-resistant safe or vault. Each member of the Disaster Control Organization should have a copy of the plan. The Emergency Services Officer will be responsible for keeping the plan updated and should have a copy in which to make pen-and-ink changes. As he makes changes to his copy, a typist can revise the original. (This is another good application for a word processor.) If the museum occupies more than one building, at least one copy of the plan should be in each building. Additional copies should be placed at critical spots around the museum in disaster-resistant containers. Each copy of the plan should list the locations of all other copies. It is vital that the original and all copies be updated often. Changes should be posted as they occur, changed pages should be retyped, including the date of the change, and obsolete pages should be removed and destroyed.

At least one copy of the plan kept in the museum should be accompanied by selected publications for reference during emergency stabilization and conservation efforts following a disaster. For example, if you anticipate having to salvage and preserve wet paper, you would want to have Peter Waters's book *Procedures for Salvage of Water-Damaged Library Materials* published by the Library of Congress. If the museum has a staff conservator, he or she may prepare instructions tailored specifically for your collections, instead of using existing published instructions. If so, these special instructions would be kept with the plan or perhaps even made part of it.

The plan ought to be accompanied by a carefully selected assortment of blank forms, typing supplies and other materials needed for preparing purchase orders and reports during and after an emergency.

If the museum office is damaged during a disaster, these materials will permit the carrying out of vital administrative duties.

The disaster preparedness process does not end with preparation and distribution of a written disaster plan. The effectiveness of the plan during a disaster depends upon training all personnel who will execute the plan and upon regular testing of the plan under simulated conditions. The continued usefulness of the plan will depend upon how well it performs during actual emergencies, as determined by post-event evaluations.

The eighth step in the disaster preparedness process is training of the museum staff. Three purposes to training are:

1 to guarantee that every employee will react rapidly in an emergency;

2 to ensure that each person on whom execution of the plan depends will know his or her responsibility;

3 to ensure that each responsible person has acquired the skills and the confidence to do his or her job efficiently and without panic.

Two kinds of training are needed to achieve these purposes. The first is briefing everyone on the museum staff on the disaster plan's goals and on their individual roles and responsibilities in case of disaster. Such training can be held in conjunction with regular museum employee training and skills development programmes. New employees should be trained as soon as possible after joining the staff. Retraining should take place every time the plan changes enough to warrant it.

The second kind of training is for members of the Disaster Control Organization. They will need a higher level of training than the rest of the staff. They should probably take courses offered by local and state Civil Defence organizations; these courses are usually free and are excellent training opportunities. Major businesses and industries often have internal disaster preparedness courses and may be willing to train museum staff. Local public protection agencies, such as the fire department, offer training in such skills as fighting small fires with hand-held equipment and controlling crowds during an emergency. Reading as widely as possible on the subjects of emergency planning and disaster preparedness is also good practice. Particularly useful works are cited in the bibliography at the end of this paper.

The ninth step in disaster preparedness takes place after the plan is written and training of the museum's staff has begun. This step calls for testing the plan.

To ensure the plan's effectiveness under actual disaster conditions, the Disaster Control Organization must test it thoroughly under simulated disaster conditions. As Richard J. Healy warns, the effectiveness (or ineffectiveness) of the disaster plan should not be discovered first during an actual disaster (Healy 1969). Testing will reveal the plan's deficiencies and unrealistic features and may expose a need to add or revise procedures. In testing the plan, the Disaster Control Organization will receive valuable training in operation under emergency conditions.

Testing consists of holding periodic exercises covering the full range of expected emergency and disaster situations. The Disaster Control Organization can write test problems for each potential disaster event and present them for solution. Senior administrative and curatorial personnel should test the plan first, as soon as possible after the Disaster Control Organization itself is fully functioning. After they have participated in a series of exercises helping to improve the plan, the entire staff and the staffs of agencies supporting the museum in disaster can be tested. All exercises should be as realistic as possible and held with as little advance notice and preparation as feasible. Test exercises should be concerned with the full range of possible emergencies, from minor incidents to major disasters. Each exercise should conclude with a critique and suitable modification of the plan.

Constant evaluation of the disaster plan is essential to keeping it always up to date and fully capable of dealing with every event it is intended to. Evaluation is the tenth and last step in the disaster preparedness process. The most effective way to evaluate a plan is to examine how well it functions during actual disasters. For this reason, it is vital that the Disaster Control Organization keep records whenever any part of the plan must be executed. After the crisis has passed, all those involved in executing the plan should meet to discuss any problems they encountered. They should try to improve the plan so that similar problems do not arise in the future.

As part of the evaluation, it is very important to observe and record exactly what damage resulted from the disaster and why it occurred. Such records will enable the plan to be refined to focus on the kinds of damage that actually occur rather than on the kinds of damage predicted to occur. Analysing the causes of damage might permit the rebuilding or remodelling of the museum for greater resistance to the same kinds of damage in the future. Records of damage sustained may also be required by the museum's insurance carriers. Photographs are particularly useful as part of complete, graphic records. It is important that one or more cameras and accessories and a quantity of film be included in the museum's stockpile of protected emergency supplies.

CONCLUSION

Emergencies are a part of the life of a museum. You may never have been involved personally in a serious emergency, let alone a disaster. If so, count yourself lucky. On the other hand, you may already be prepared. If you are prepared, please keep vigilant and stay prepared.

The primary goal of emergency planning is to avoid or minimize loss of the museum's assets, and preparation is the key to achieving that goal. Reducing the impacts of a disaster and avoiding loss depend upon how well you have planned for meeting all possible emergencies and disasters, how well you and your staff react when a disaster occurs, and how much learning from experiences during actual disasters you apply to revising your plan and preparing for the future.

Some emergencies cannot be prevented. The impact of some disasters cannot be avoided. But, you *can* plan in advance. You *can* commit a plan to paper. You *can* keep the plan up to date, as you *can* train yourself and your staff to execute the plan. By taking these steps, you will be able to cope with any unavoidable emergency or disaster.

APPENDIX: SUGGESTED EMERGENCY SUPPLIES AND EQUIPMENT

The supplies and equipment listed here include a variety of items that may be needed to cope with emergencies or disasters; some items can be used to prevent or minimize damage and others can be used afterwards to clean up or recover from damage. Few museums will need to use all of these items. Each museum should acquire only those items that will be needed to cope with the range of emergencies and disasters that it can expect. On the other hand, this list is not all-inclusive; it is intended only as a guide. Any museum may find that it will require items not listed here.

Items listed here do not necessarily have to be obtained or stockpiled exclusively for use in an emergency. Some of the listed items will be found in all museums as a matter of routine. They can be diverted for use in cleanup and repair operations when they are needed. However, keep in mind that the items you may count on using in an emergency may be damaged or destroyed by the disaster. Therefore, those items that will be critical to the survival or recovery of the museum and that cannot be procured promptly from elsewhere after the disaster should be set aside or stockpiled in a safe place so they will be available if ever they are needed.

Remember, too, that some items – such as dry-cell batteries and certain first-aid supplies

– have a limited shelf-life. Plan on replacing such items periodically so that fresh stock is always on hand in your stockpile.

Finally, remember always to include operating manuals or instructions with items of mechanical and electrical equipment in case persons not experienced with their operation are required to use them.

Supplies and equipment for debris removal and cleanup

Low sudsing detergents
Bleaches
Sanitizers (such as chloride of lime or high-test hypochlorite)
Fungicides
Disinfectants
Ammonia
Scouring powders or other household cleaners
Rubber gloves
Brooms
Dust pans
Mops, mop buckets and wringers
Scoops and shovels
Scrub brushes
Sponges and rags or cloths
Buckets and tubs
Water hoses and nozzles
Throw-away containers or bags for trash
Wet/dry vacuum cleaner with accessories

Tools and equipment for demolition, repairs and rescue

Hammers (both claw and machinists)
Wrenches (pipe, channel-lock and Vise Grips in various sizes)
Pliers (adjustable, lineman's and needle-nose in various sizes)
Screwdrivers (straight blade and Philips in various sizes)
Wood saws
Hand drill with bits
(Power saw and drills may be selected if a source of electricity can be assured)
Metal saw with blades
Utility knife with extra blades
Wire cutters with insulated handles
Tin snips
Pipe cutters and possibly pipe threaders
Bolt cutter
Pry bar or crowbar
Axes, including fireman's axe
Rope
Dollies or handcarts
Folding rule or retractable tapemeasures
3-ton hydraulic jack
Sledgehammer
Block and tackle
Pit-cover hood (if applicable)

Hydrant and post indicator valve wrenches (if the museum has a sprinkle or hose and standpipe system)
Staple gun and staples
Ladder(s) and step-stool(s)

Construction materials

Plywood for covering or replacing windows
Dimensional lumber
Nails, screws, and assorted fasteners
Tapes of various kinds (masking, duct, electrician's, etc.)
Glue
Twine and cord
Plastic sheeting for protection against leaks and splashes
Binding wire

Emergency equipment

Emergency gasoline-powered electrical generator
Portable lights (to be powered from the generator if electricity unavailable)
Emergency lights with extra batteries
Flashlights or lanterns with extra batteries
Fire extinguishers (ABC type recommended)
Battery-operated AM/FM radio(s) with extra batteries
Walkie-talkie radios with extra batteries
CB radio with extra batteries
Portable public address system or bullhorn, electrical or battery-powered
Geiger counter and dosimeters
Gas-masks with extra canisters
Air breathers with extra oxygen tanks
Resuscitation equipment
Gasoline-powered water-pump (or pump that can be powered from the electrical generator) with hoses
Extension cords, preferably equipped with ground-fault interruptors

Personal equipment and supplies (some of these items may be provided by the individual employees and volunteers who are to use them)

Necessary protective clothing
Rubber boots or waders
Hard hats
Rubber lab aprons
Protective masks
First-aid kits and medical supplies
Food and food preparation equipment
Potable water
Sanitation facilities
Changes of clothing
Sleeping-bags and blankets

Conservation supplies and equipment

Polyester (Mylar) and polyethylene film (in rolls)
Newsprint (unprinted)
Polyethylene bags, various sizes (such as Zip-Lock and produce bags)
Plastic garbage bags
Thymol
Ethanol
Acetone
Industrial denatured alcohol
White blotter paper
Weights (such as shot bags)
Various sizes of thick glass or smooth masonite
Japanese tissue
Towels or clean rags
Clothes pins
Scissors
Sharp knives
Water displacement compound (such as WD-40)
Waxes and dressings (determined by nature of collection)
Other preservatives

Miscellaneous supplies

Boxes for packing and moving artefacts, records and equipment. (Record transfer boxes are the easiest to use, carry, and store. They come flat for storage and are set up as needed; they may be re-flattened for future use.)
Box sealing and strapping tapes
Tissue-paper, clean newsprint, plastic 'bubble pack', foam 'noodles' and other such materials for packing and padding artefacts for movement
Marking pens, preferably ones that are not water-soluble
Insecticides and rodenticides

Miscellaneous equipment

Fans
Space heaters, either electric or gas-operated
Portable dehumidifiers
Hygrometers
Photographic equipment (camera, lenses, flash, light meter, etc.)
Essential office equipment (manual typewriter, pocket calculator, pencil-sharpener, stapler, rulers, scissors, etc.)
Essential stationery and blank forms and other such supplies to ensure continuity of minimal administrative operations

This paper first appeared in B. G. Jones (1986) Protecting Historic Architecture and Museum Collections from Natural Disasters *(Oxford: Butterworth-Heinemann), pp. 211–30.*

REFERENCES

Part 1: Emergency and disaster preparedness and planning

American Society of Corporate Secretaries, Inc. (1970) *Continuity of Corporate Management in Event of Major Disaster,* Washington, D.C.: Office of Civil Defense, Department of Defense.

Association of Records Executives and Administrators (1966) *Protection of Vital Records*, Washington, D.C.: Office of Civil Defense, Department of Defense.

Bahme, Charles W. (1976), *Fire Officer's Guide to Emergency Action*, Boston, Mass.: National Fire Protection Association.

—— (1978) *Fire Officer's Guide to Disaster Control*, Boston, Mass.: National Fire Protection Association.

Bohem, Hilda (1978) *Disaster Prevention and Disaster Preparedness*, Berkeley, Calif.: Office of the Assistant Vice President for Library Plans and Policies, Systemwide Library Administration, University of California.

Committee on Conservation of Cultural Resources (1942) *The Protection of Cultural Resources Against the Hazards of War*, Washington, D.C.: National Resources Planning Board.

Cox, David L. (1972) 'Training for facility self-protection', *Security Management*, reprinted by Defense Civil Preparedness Agency.

Disaster Operations: A Handbook for Local Governments, Washington, D.C.: Defense Civil Preparedness Agency, Publication no. CPG 1–6.

Disaster Planning Guide for Business and Industry (1974) Washington, D.C.: Defense Civil Preparedness Agency, Publication no. CPG 25.

Disaster Response and Recovery Program Guide (1980) Washington, D.C.: Federal Emergency Management Agency.

Fennelly, Lawrence J. (ed.) (1982) *Museum, Archive, and Library Security*, Woburn, Mass.: Butterworth Publishers.

Healy, Richard J. (1969) *Emergency and Disaster Planning*, New York: John Wiley & Sons.

Local Government Emergency Planning (1978) Washington, D.C.: Federal Emergency Management Agency, Publication no. CPG 1–8.

Myers, James N. and Bedford, Denise D. (1981) *Disasters: Prevention and Coping*, Stanford, Calif.: Stanford University Libraries.

Noblecourt, Andre F. (1958) *Protection of Cultural Property in the Event of Armed Conflict*, Paris: UNESCO, Museums and Monument Series VIII.

Tillotson, Robert G. and the International Committee on Museum Security (1977) *Museum Security/La Sécurité dans les musées*, Paris: International Council of Museums.

Upton, M. S. and Pearson, C. (1978) *Disaster Planning and Emergency Treatments in Museums, Art Galleries, Libraries, Archives, and Allied Institutions*, Belconnen, A. C. T. Australia: Institute for the Conservation of Cultural Materials, Canberra College of Advanced Education.

Part 2: Salvage and recovery

Agricultural Research Service (1971) *How to Prevent and Remove Mildew: Home Methods*. Washington, D.C.: US Department of Agriculture, Home and Garden Bulletin no. 68 (Rev.).

Cohen, William (1975) 'Halon 1301: library fires and post-fire procedures', *Library Security Newsletter* (May) 5–7.

First Aid for Flooded Homes and Farms (1972) Washington, D.C.: US Department of Agriculture, Agriculture Handbook no. 38.

Fischer, David J. (1975) 'Problems encountered, hurricane Agnes flood, June 23, 1972 at Corning, NY and the Corning Museum of Glass', in George M. Cunha, *Conservation Administration*, North Andover, Mass.: New England Document Conservation Center, 170–87.

Fischer, David J. and Duncan, Thomas (1975) 'Conservation research: flood-damaged library materials', *AIC Bulletin* 15(2): 27–48.

Haas, J. Eugene *et al.* (eds) (1977) *Reconstruction Following Disaster*, Cambridge, Mass.: MIT Press.

Keck, Caroline K. (1972) 'On conservation: instructions for emergency treatment of water damage', *Museum News* 50(10): 13.

Koesterer, Martin G. and Getting, John A. (1976) 'Restoring water-soaked papers and textiles: applying freeze-drying methods to books and art objects', *Technology and Conservation* (Fall) 20–2.

McGregor, L. and Bruce, J. (1974) 'Recovery of flood damaged documents by the Queensland state archives', *Archives and Manuscripts* 5(8): 193–9.

Martin, John H. (1975) 'Resuscitating a waterlogged library', *Wilson Library Bulletin* 241–3.

—— (1977) *The Corning Flood: Museum Under Water*, Corning, N.Y.: Corning Museum of Glass.

Minoque, Adelaide (1946) 'Treatment of fire and water damaged records', *American Archivist* 9(1): 17–25.

Montuori, Theodore (1973) 'Lesson learned from Agnes', *Journal of Micrographics* 6(3): 133–6.

Morris, John (1979) *Managing the Library Fire Risk* (2nd edn), Berkeley, Calif.: Office of Risk Management and Safety, University of California. (Available only from author at 333 Nutmeg Lane, Walnut Creek, Calif. 94598.)

Sellers, David Y. and Strassberg, Richard (1973) 'Anatomy of a library emergency', *Library Journal* 98 (17): 2824–7.

Spawn, Wilman (1973) 'After the water comes', *Bulletin* [of the Pennsylvania Library Association] 28 (6): 243–51.

Surrency, Erwin C. (1973) 'Guarding against disaster', *Law Library Journal* 66(4): 419–28.

Walston, S. (1976) 'Emergency conservation following the Darwin cyclone', *ICCM Bulletin* 2(1): 21–5.

Waters, Peter (1975) *Procedures for Salvage of Water-Damaged Library Materials*, Washington, D.C.: Library of Congress.

Whipkey, Harold E. (1973) *After Agnes: A Report on Flood Recovery Assistance by the Pennsylvania Historical and Museum Commission*, Harrisburg, Pa.: Pennsylvania Historical and Museum Commission.

30

Emergency treatment of materials
M. S. Upton and C. Pearson

Effective recovery from disasters will require the involvement of specialist conservators who can advise on and undertake the treatments necessary. Upton and Pearson give a useful introductory list of the actions which might be employed during and immediately following a disaster.

THE PROBLEM

Disasters which strike museums, art galleries, libraries and archives such as floods or cyclones can sometimes be predicted, but more usually (as with fires and earthquakes) they strike without warning.

Damage to the various collections and materials housed in these institutions is usually caused by water, fire, mechanical agencies, flood debris, burst oil pipes or a combination of these. However, water is the major cause of damage, whether due to rain, the result of a flood, or from fire-fighting procedures.

The incorrect use of fire extinguishers, especially where a small fire is concerned, may cause more damage than the fire. Powder extinguishers leave an alkaline residue which is difficult to remove, and soda-acid extinguishers produce an alkaline foam which can cause serious damage to paintings. It is therefore advisable *not* to have either of these types in a museum, art gallery, library or archive, but supply instead CO_2, BCF, or Halon extinguishers. For this reason liaison with the local fire authorities is important to determine the most suitable small- and large-scale fire-fighting systems for the particular materials in question.

One form of damage often overlooked by those planning to combat disasters is the steady *deterioration* of materials. Because of its very nature the problem is seldom recognized until it is a disaster. However, it can be overcome by sound conservation methods.

The Institute for the Conservation of Cultural Material Incorporated (ICCM), the conservation organization in Australia, can assist in providing technical expertise following a disaster and may be contacted through any of the major museums, art galleries, libraries or archives. It should be stressed that all institutions housing collections referred to in this publication should become members of the ICCM, and thereby benefit from mutual aid programmes.

It is most important following a disaster that emergency treatment of the damaged material can be carried out as soon as possible. This ideally should be done by trained personnel. Failing their availability, however, immediate steps have to be taken to treat the material in a manner that will cause the least damage and ensure its greatest possible survival while preventing further deterioration, pending the arrival of expert help. The specialized conservation and restoration work can then commence at a later date.

SUSCEPTIBLE MATERIALS AND PREPARATION FOR DISASTER

The materials most susceptible to damage by fire and water are paper, textiles, costumes, wood, leather, paintings, film and tapes. Fire damage is irreversible but a great deal of water damage can be treated and the damaged material restored close to its original condition, provided the material can be examined and treated quickly (e.g. by freezing) after the damage has occurred.

The major types of damage caused to these materials by water (including moisture and humidity) are:

(a) Mould growth and mildew with subsequent staining and deterioration of the material.
(b) Dimensional changes as items dry out, causing shrinkage, warping and splitting in textiles, parchment, wood and other hygroscopic materials.
(c) Loss or damage to surface films such as the blanching of varnish and paint, and the loosening, buckling and flaking of paint and veneer.
(d) Disfigurement and stains from mud suspension and oil slicks.

Ceramics, glass, stone and metal objects (excluding iron) are more resistant to water damage; they should therefore be segregated from material receiving priority treatment following a disaster. Iron objects will deteriorate in the presence of water and, although their treatment is not so urgent as paper and textiles, etc., they should be carefully dried and also segregated to avoid staining other materials. The corrosion products from copper-based alloys can also cause stains.

Materials stored on the floor are the most susceptible to damage in the event of flooding. They may also prevent drainage of water from the area after a disaster. It is therefore advisable to have all material stored at least 10 cm above floor level. Materials which are particularly water-sensitive should be stored in watertight containers which should, if practicable, constitute the permanent storage for such material.

Procedures for protecting various items and materials from a foreseeable disaster such as a flood or cyclone should be included in a disaster plan. These procedures will be determined by the type of institution and the material to be protected. As examples, the card catalogue of the average library or archive probably contains material which has the most expensive replacement ratio per cubic centimetre; it should therefore be securely protected when danger is imminent; fine screens placed over drains in a building containing musical instruments would catch most of the pieces floating free in flood waters. This preplanning can save a lot of valuable material.

All items should be securely labelled using a material that will not become detached when affected by moisture and preferably with some fireproof identification attached by means of a fireproof adhesive or fastening.

Routine inspection of the buildings should be included in a disaster plan. This will prevent, or help to reduce, minor disasters such as those caused by faulty plumbing, blocked drains or hazardous placement of material.

Names and addresses of conservation experts should be compiled so that their advice can be readily sought.

A supply of the correct chemicals and equipment should be available for carrying out emergency treatment of materials following a disaster. If this is not possible, a list and details of these materials and their suppliers should be compiled, after consultation with an expert, and distributed to various responsible persons as part of a disaster plan.

Although it may not be possible to store all the materials required, those which may not be readily available following a disaster should be acquired and held in readiness. This will reduce delays in waiting for them to arrive, especially when transport and communication services may be disrupted.

Even though the majority of these materials have a long shelf-life they should be checked at least annually and, in order that they are not all lost in a disaster, duplication of storage facilities should be arranged.

Generally speaking, a source of clean hot and cold water will be required, also drying facilities and air-circulating fans. As the biggest threat after water damage will be from fungus growth, a fungicide such a thymol or sodium pentachlorophenate with an appropriate solvent such as ethyl alcohol or industrial methylated spirits, is an essential item. (Note: Ethyl alcohol comes under the control of the Department of Customs and Excise and may be more difficult to obtain than industrial methylated spirits (denatured ethyl alcohol). Ordinary household 'methylated spirits' must never be used as it contains a purple dye; isopropyl alcohol, on the other hand, may be used.) Clean non-printed newsprint will be required if books and paper require drying, and racks and hangers for textiles and costumes. Polythene gauze and sheet will also be useful commodities, as will be plastic bins and trays, etc.

Freezing facilities are also an important aid following water damage to material and investigations into the availability of local freezing facilities and transportable refrigerated containers should be carried out in advance so that they may be called upon immediately when required. These facilities could be available from ice works and frozen food manufacturers.

In preparation for an emergency it is most important to have a well prepared and practiced disaster plan available and experience has shown that, following a disaster, shock and the personal losses by staff often delay or prevent the necessary remedial action being taken in time. Advance preparation for a disaster is therefore the best way to reduce its effects.

ASSESSMENT OF NEEDS FOLLOWING A DISASTER

One of the critical factors immediately after a disaster is the weather conditions which follow. The formation of mould, a major problem, commences within three to eight days depending on the temperature and humidity with values above 25°C and 70 per cent relative humidity providing ideal conditions for mould growth. If the weather is hot and humid, action is required more urgently than in cold, dry conditions. For example, the Florence flood in 1966 occurred in cold weather and so mould growth was inhibited. However, the fire and subsequent flooding at the Jewish Theological Seminary in April 1966 occurred during a heat wave, with high humidity, and even with hundreds of assistants, many books suffered mould damage.

It is therefore important that a rapid and accurate assessment of the damage is made so that priorities can be established for treating the damaged material. Consideration should be given not only to the importance or value of the items in a collection but also to their susceptibility to further damage and/or deterioration.

It is important, when possible, for the curator or person responsible for the material being salvaged, to examine the damaged items and determine the priorities. Items requiring priority treatment should be sorted, labelled and treated as soon as possible.

A record should be kept of the items treated, together with all labels and identification markings, whether or not attached to the items. Care should be taken to ensure the labels, and also the marking medium, used on the items being treated are not susceptible to water. Pencil is a safe marking medium; ink should not be used unless it is a special waterproof ink.

Sorting and determination of priorities can be expedited if it is known which are the most important items in a collection and also their location within the building (to be detailed in any disaster plan). This will ensure that time is not wasted sorting through general material looking for special items.

The types of facilities required for rescue operations will depend on the nature of the material to be treated. A work area adjacent to, but not in the centre of, the damaged material is required. This must be serviced with hot and cold water, and also electricity. It is advisable never to use the water direct from a tap following a disaster. With broken pipelines and polluted reservoirs, the water is very likely to change suddenly from being clear and clean to dirty and contaminated. The water should be run into a tank and either syphoned out or collected with buckets. If mains electricity is not available, a portable generator can be used, but care must be taken with the use of electrical gear in wet areas.

To prevent mould formation the temperature and humidity in the area containing the damaged material must be kept as low as possible, certainly not greater than 20°C and 50 per cent relative humidity. This can be achieved by the use of air-conditioning, dehumidifiers and air-circulating fans to prevent local pockets of high humidity. Instruments for measuring and/or recording temperature and relative humidity are essential. Rooms set aside for drying waterlogged material should be supplied with fans and dryers. Suitable drying conditions are 30–35 per cent relative humidity with a temperature of 50–60°C. Whatever type of equipment is used for controlling the temperature and humidity it should be left running 24 hours a day. It should not be switched off overnight.

If air-conditioning is available it should be used with caution. The majority of air-conditioners are not designed to cope with the large excess of water which would be present in a building following a flood. Some air-conditioning systems reduce the temperature by spraying water into the atmosphere, i.e. evaporative cooling. These systems are not recommended as they will increase the relative humidity. With the usual air-conditioning temperature in Australia of 20–22°C, the addition of the high humidity would create ideal conditions for mould growth. In these circumstances, dehumidifiers must be used in conjunction with the air-conditioner, and the temperature control of the latter must be adjusted to below 20°C. If dehumidifiers are used they should initially be set to just below the level of relative humidity in the local environment and then gradually reduced to 60 per cent. This will ensure that there is not a rapid decrease in relative humidity, which could damage some materials.

A further precaution concerns the use of vacuum drying or vacuum fumigation facilities. These should not be used for waterlogged material as the water would be extracted too rigorously, causing damage to the fibres of the material. Slow, controlled drying is required to cause the least damage to these materials.

If possible, only trained personnel should be used to carry out the emergency treatment of damaged items; however, the immediate availability of such personnel is uncommon. If local volunteers are used, care must be taken to select the right sort of persons. They must be reliable, and must be made fully aware of their responsibilities and the problems they are likely to encounter. Over enthusiasm should be treated with firmness. For example, a great deal of damage can be caused by the rough handling of waterlogged material. The size of the working party should be carefully controlled and will be determined by the size of the task and the treatment facilities and work space available. These are very often rather limited following a disaster and overcrowding might cause additional problems.

A routine should be established for the rescue and treatment of damaged material. This will improve efficiency and ensure that all items receive the required treatment. Each member of a work party should be given a specific task and responsibility.

Inspection, assessment and treatment of material should be carried out as a continuous process. Do not wait until everything has been sorted and its priority determined before commencing the emergency treatments; these should be commenced immediately they have been assessed.

In general, the reduction or prevention of further damage to material can be accomplished by:

(a) freezing all items, except paintings, to a temperature of $-7°C$ to prevent immediate deterioration;
(b) storage of damaged material at a low temperature and humidity (less than 20°C and 50 per cent relative humidity);
(c) air drying of all organic material such as paper, textiles and books, etc. This, however, does not apply to coated papers which must be separated before drying out.

These are interim measures pending the arrival of expert assistance. The more specific treatments recommended for particular types of material are detailed in the following sections.

EMERGENCY TREATMENT OF LIBRARY AND ARCHIVE MATERIALS

These include paper, prints and books, many of which will also be found in museums, art galleries, libraries and archives. Following a disaster, every effort must be made to lower the temperature of the area to reduce the rate of deterioration of the material.

Freezing is universally accepted as the best way of stabilizing water-soaked paper against further deterioration. This is especially important where there are large volumes of material to be treated. In this case, instead of wasting time sorting through the material in the wet state, it would be advisable to freeze everything immediately. Priorities can then be made for the specialized treatment (to be carried out by or under the direction of experts) of the frozen material.

Although it cannot be said with certainty that freezing will not damage some types of material, any damage so caused will be minimal compared with that occurring if freezing is not carried out. Materials can be left frozen for several months; some large collections have in fact been kept frozen for several years and then dried with little or no permanent damage.

If freezing space is limited, apart from valuable items priorities should be given to:

(a) items which have already developed mould;
(b) leather- and vellum-bound materials;
(c) artefacts, manuscripts, prints, drawings, maps and books with water-soluble components (inks, water-colour, tempera, dyes, etc.).

Although it is sometimes preferable to remove mud and dirt before freezing an item, this must only be carried out under expert guidance as it can be time-consuming and also, if mishandled, can cause further damage. For example, materials with water-soluble components such as inks, water-colours and certain dyes should never be washed. They should be frozen and then handed over to an expert for restoration.

The items should be individually wrapped in freezer paper and labelled, if possible with an indication of priority. They should then be placed in the freezer within 12 hours. The size and type of freezer will be determined by the volume of material to be frozen. A few items could be handled in a home freezer. Large collections require either mobile refrigerated units (trucks or railway wagons) or rapid transportation to an ice works or frozen food plant. Temperatures between -10 and -7°C for both initial freezing and storing are required. Slightly lower temperatures can be tolerated but they must never be allowed to drop as low as -40°C (used by some frozen food plants) as this will cause permanent damage to the material. Dry ice is a useful commodity in achieving initial lowering of the temperature of material subsequent to its being frozen.

The material should later be defrosted under expert guidance and only in quantities that can be conveniently handled and dried with the facilities available.

Occasions arise when there are no freezing facilities available and alternative procedures such as air drying must be carried out.

The moisture content and the temperature of items requiring treatment by air drying must be kept as low as possible. This can be achieved with ice or dry ice as the cooling agent, contained in polythene bags. Good air circulation will help to reduce the level of humidity.

Items must be sorted into priorities and the treatment routines established.

Dirt and mud can be removed from items such as books and papers provided that they contain no water-soluble material. This should be carried out by washing in clean, cool running water using a gentle dabbing action with a sponge. Do not use hot water. No rubbing or brushing of the items should be attempted. Cloth- or paper-bound books can be left soaking in water for a few days to facilitate dirt removal. After washing, the water should be squeezed from the books with the hands only. Do not use mechanical means.

No attempt should be made at this stage to remove oil stains or persistent areas of dirt: this treatment must be carried out by, or under the direction of, experts. Books must never be stacked on top of each other when wet. Care must be maintained to watch out for books with coated papers because these items will require special drying.

The next stage of the procedure is to dry the washed items. This will require a drying-room set apart from the washing area and also from the rooms housing the material being treated. All surfaces, especially those of wood, should be covered with polythene sheeting. Ample air circulation facilities, dehumidifiers and heating units are required, and also instruments for measuring the temperature and relative humidity of the drying area. Ideal drying conditions are 50–60°C and a relative humidity of 30–35 per cent and dryers should be kept running 24 hours a day. Do not use talcum-powder for drying books and paper. Useful drying racks can be made with aluminium-framed nylon or fibreglass flyscreens. These should be supported on bricks or a metal stand to allow free air circulation.

To prevent the formation of mould during drying, fungicide-impregnated papers are required in large quantities. The most widely used fungicide is thymol, obtainable in the form of crystals. Clean non-printed newsprint is cut into suitable sizes for spreading on the drying surfaces and also for interleaving books. These can be obtained ready cut to size from the supplier. The sheets are dipped into a 10 per cent solution of thymol in ethyl alcohol or industrial methylated spirits (do not use the household methylated spirits as this contains a purple dye which may be transferred to books or papers being dried) and then allowed to dry. As the thymol is volatile, the sheets are then stored in polythene bags until required. An alternative is sodium pentachlorophenate which is made up as a 10 per cent solution in acetone for the impregnantion of the newsprint. Ten per cent chlorocresol in ethyl alcohol or industrial methylated spirits is another common fungicide which can be used for this purpose. Thymol can also be applied as a vapour, the material to be treated being placed in a cabinet or under a polythene tent which has facilities to hold a tray of crystals with a 60 or 100 watt light bulb underneath. The heat of the bulb vaporizes the thymol crystals where the material remains for 24 hours. Sixty grams of thymol crystals are required for every cubic metre of space. Crystals of chlorocresol placed in a container or distributed on the bottom of cupboards will create an environment which will prevent mould growth.

Thymol and sodium pentachlorophenate crystals are toxic and the recommended solvents flammable, therefore precautions should be taken during the preparation of these impregnated papers. Rubber gloves and an aspirator of the type used by painters should be worn.

No attempt should be made to remove mould from wet books; this will only force the mould into the paper and also increase the risk of staining. The mould on dried or partly dried books or paper can be removed by careful brushing in the open air well away from the work areas and buildings housing the damaged material.

It is preferable to dry books by carefully opening them and standing them on their ends. This is relatively simple with hardback books whose covers are still intact, and the books should be stood upside-down on their head ends as this will compensate for the accumulated sag a book acquires in normal upright storage. It can also be done with damaged or softback books by propping several against each other or by the use of supporting techniques adapted for this purpose. The covers or spines of the books should not be removed as they provide support for the leaves of the book. If water-logged, the books should not be forced open but allowed to dry until the pages and covers separate naturally. However, if it appears that the pages are going to stick (common with some forms of paper, particularly coated papers) they must be separated before drying.

As soon as possible, drying should be assisted by placing thymol-impregnated sheets between the fly leaves and covers (the covers usually contain most moisture). If the latter are very thick, then isolation with polythene sheet may be advisable to prevent them from rewetting the interior leaves. When the leaves start to dry out, interleaving with the drying sheets should be carefully commenced, initially about every twenty five pages. The sheets should be changed as often as is necessary to increase the drying efficiency.

At a later stage the book may be placed flat on its spine and interleaved at more frequent intervals. The interleaving, however, must not exceed one-third the total thickness of the book. All interleaving must be removed if any forced hot-air drying is to be used.

If the spine of a book warps during drying, then provided that most of the moisture has been removed from the book the warp can be taken out by suspending the book horizontally by its spine on nylon threads. The number of threads, which are passed along the spine, will be determined by the thickness of the book.

Final drying can be achieved by laying the book flat on thymol-impregnated papers with light weights on the surface to retain the correct shape of the book.

Framed prints, drawings and water-colours should be unframed but this should be carried out by a person experienced in the handling of waterlogged paper.

Separate sheets such as prints and manuscripts should not be handled, especially if found in masses. Ideally they should be frozen and left to an expert, but failing this they can be separated, washed and dried with the aid of polyester-type non-woven fabric which will not adhere permanently to the paper. Great care is required in using this technique, which involves backing both sides of a sheet with the polyester fabric. Thin polyester or polyethylene sheet is used for picking up and separating masses of individual sheets which are then backed with the polyester fabric. The sheets are then allowed to dry away from forced ventilation on thymol-impregnated paper to prevent mould formation. No pressure should be used during the drying of these individual sheets.

The weighing of books and papers before, during and after drying is a useful technique to determine the rate and efficiency of the drying technique used. However, this can only be carried out easily when there is a relatively small number of items to be dried.

Industrial microwave ovens (not regular ovens) have been used successfully to dry water-damaged books. The high-frequency energy in these ovens safely bakes out the moisture because uniform temperature gradients are created through the wet masses by radiant heat. The drying facilities which were initially designed to dry such products as bricks, ceramics, glue, rice, straw, textiles and tobacco can be used providing care is taken that the correct drying environment is maintained, and that drying is carried out slowly.

EMERGENCY TREATMENT OF PHOTOGRAPHIC MATERIALS, TAPES AND PHONORECORD DISCS

Photographic materials, although normally held in libraries or archives, are considered separately from paper and books.

It is not advisable to freeze any type of film, as permanent damage may be caused to the emulsion layer. Items can be cold-stored for a few days, however, without the gelatine swelling or spoiling.

Kodak (Australasia) Pty Ltd provide an emergency service for cleaning and drying photographic materials, and the following information has been compiled with their assistance.

If the water-damaged films are still wet, do not allow them to dry, but keep the films wet and take them to the nearest appropriate processing laboratory for proper handling as soon as possible. This is most importan with film in rolls or on reels, such as movie films, and also for negatives in glassine envelopes.

If water-damaged film has completely dried, take it to the nearest appropriate processing laboratory for proper handling. Many films that are not reels or in rolls can be salvaged even after they have dried.

Exposed films that have not been processed and have suffered water damage should be handled in the same way, although they are generally much more difficult to salvage. If the subject matter is valuable, the cost of having a processing laboratory attempt to salvage the film may be warranted. If the film is of little value, it may be less expensive to discard the damaged film, purchase new film and photograph the subject at a later date.

Bacterial slimes and algae seem to develop very quickly in tanks containing photographic films, especially if they are exposed to the light. Therefore, any film that is stored in water should be kept in the dark, inside a sealed container.

Water-damaged prints should be stored flat in a tray in water at room temperature. Try to get them to a professional photographer or photofinisher within 24 to 48 hours for proper washing and drying. Generally speaking, try to salvage only those prints for which negatives are not available or those prints that are not badly stained.

If outside professional facilities are not immediately available, or if it is decided to carry out treatment on the premises, then the following procedures should be carried out:

(a) Black-and-white prints should be placed flat in a tray and the tray filled with cold water. Change the water several times within 30 minutes while agitating the tray. Dry by placing paper towels underneath and on top of the prints, place them on a flat table, and apply weight evenly to the prints until they are dry.

(b) The same procedure should be followed for colour print. However, the wash time may be reduced. Lacking the proper chemicals, however, colour prints are likely to fade.

(c) Do not use hot water for washing films, or emulsions will swell and separate from the base film. If possible, always wear rubber gloves to avoid damage to photographic emulsions.

(d) Black-and-white films should be washed in clean, cold water for half an hour. Gently swab the film to remove grit. Dip the films in photoflo solution and then dry without heat. If you do not have photoflo solution, you may dip them in a mild detergent solution, rinse thoroughly and then dry without heat. Nylon clothes-dryers are suitable for drying sheet negatives and short film rolls. Do not lay sheet film on paper to dry.

(e) Colour transparencies and negatives should be washed in clean water that is about the same temperature as the flood water for half an hour. Rinse Kodacolour negatives and Kodachrome slides in a photoflo solution, if available. Ektachrome slides must go through an E-3 or E-4 stabilizer bath; if this is not available, it is highly recommended that you take them to a processing laboratory. Slides on Eastman colour film should also be handled by a processing laboratory. Once washed, dry the films at room temperature. If slide mounts are warped, you may carefully remove the slides for remounting; however, it is recommended that you have a processing laboratory remove the mounts and remount the slides.

(f) Motion picture films and movie films on a reel which has been allowed to dry may very well never be salvaged. Store the film in cool or cold clean water by total immersion in any container available, excluding light. Take them to a processing laboratory as soon as possible for proper cleaning and handling.

(g) Microfilm and radiographic films should be kept wet if possible. Because of the specialized nature of these films it is advisable to get them to the nearest appropriate processing laboratory for proper handling as soon as possible. Special care should be taken if film has been exposed to contaminants, especially acids, alkalis and sulphur-containing compounds. They should be washed and neutralized as soon as possible before image 'bleaching' begins. Hydrogen sulphide-polluted waters would be particularly hazardous for photographic materials.

Contamination to magnetic, video and computer tapes should be confined to the exposed edges as a tape is wound in layers. This should be washed off with clean water and the tape left to dry without heating. After drying, the tape should be fast-wound against a felt pad (without the tape contacting the heads) to remove any dried extraneous matter from both the oxide and base surfaces.

With cassettes and cartridges, the possibility of reclamation depends on the degree of contamination. Anything but the most minor ingress of mud will seriously increase the frictional forces applied to the tape, destroying the correct operation of the mechanism. The possibility of opening the cassette or cartridge case for cleaning purposes is limited because many designs are irreversibly sealed during manufacture.

Phonorecord discs which have been deformed or abraded cannot be treated: however, with undamaged records any foreign matter deposited on the surface should be removed without adding clogging cleaning agents to it.

The records should be cleaned with distilled water containing 1 per cent of a non-ionic wetting agent, such as Lissapol TN 450. A soft brush may be used with this solution to lightly dislodge particles in the grooves. This is followed by thorough rinsing in distilled water.

Finally, the records should be left to dry slowly at ambient temperature, suitably protected from further contamination or heat.

EMERGENCY TREATMENT OF TEXTILES

Textiles can be frozen in a similar fashion to the method used for paper. If this is not possible they should be stored cool to prevent mould formation. Also, unnecessary exposure to direct sunlight should be avoided.

Textiles should be separated from all other forms of material such as card supports, metal fittings and, if part of furniture, be separated from the wood, although this should only be carried out by an expert upholsterer. All items should be clearly labelled and recorded. If they are in a fragile state they will need to be supported. The supports can be made from wooden frames (polythene or varnish-coated) with fibreglass fly netting stretched across (do not use iron nails, etc., to make the frames as they will rust during the treatment and stain the textiles). Alternatively, aluminium-framed flyscreens can be used.

Dirt and mud can be removed from wet textiles by either hosing with a fine spray of water or rinsing in distilled or clear warm water containing 1–2 per cent calgon. Gentle brushing can be used if the fabric permits. Any mould will be removed during the washing and subsequent drying process. However, fabrics can be treated for mould if necessary with thymol or chlorocresol in the form of a vapour. The frames mentioned previously are ideal for supporting textiles during washing and they will allow the mud and dirt to be removed relatively easily. Do not work with hot water and do not wash textiles which show evidence of unstable colours and dyes; these should be allowed to dry (detailed later) and left to experts.

Soiled but dried textiles can be cleaned by gentle brushing with a fine brush or with a vacuum cleaner and screen (do not vacuum direct onto the textile; place a screen over the vacuum hose). These textiles will need to be cleaned properly at a later date.

After washing, the excess water is removed by gentle squeezing or preferably by the use of clean cotton mattress pads or cotton towelling. Do not wring out items. Heavy and thick items such as rugs and tapestries should have as much water removed as possible before being hung to dry otherwise mechanical damage may occur due to the weight of the item.

The air drying should then be carried out as carefully as possible with the textiles being dried in a single layer avoiding folding or stacking. They should also be formed to their appropriate shape before drying.

Fragile items should be dried on their support screens. Strong, large and heavy items may be dried over coated wooden poles or nylon wires placed close together. Good air circulation and dehumidifiers will accelerate the rate of removal of moisture (a moderate temperature and 30–50 per cent relative humidity are required). Do not use hot drying temperatures, especially for wool. If there are no racks available, then the textiles can be dried on the ground or on tables on thick cotton mattress pads, towelling or sheeting. Frequent changing of the water-absorbent cotton is required in this process.

After drying, the textiles should be returned to their normal storage environment and position (e.g. on dummies in an air-conditioned and darkened room) with care being taken to carry out regular inspections for mould formation, shrinking and splitting of the textiles.

EMERGENCY TREATMENT OF LEATHER

Leather can be treated in a similar way to textiles. However, great care must be taken with the drying procedure. This should be carried out slowly and at room temperature (21°C). Weights must not be placed over the whole surface during drying but merely at the outer edges to provide restraint against distortion. Before the leather has finally dried out, a conservator should be consulted concerning the treatments required to restore the leather fully.

EMERGENCY TREATMENT OF WOODEN OBJECTS (INCLUDING FURNITURE, MUSICAL INSTRUMENTS AND WOODEN PANEL PAINTINGS)

Remove all iron or steel fittings for separate treatment, taking care to record their position on the wooden item. Open all drawers and lids with care; do not force pieces. Raise large items off the floor to allow good air circulation. When moving these items, use only the weight-bearing members: do not lift tops, lids, handles, knobs or carvings. Do not lift chairs by the back or arms. Label all broken pieces of wood and, if loosely attached to an item, carefully remove, using a wooden implement.

The textile coverings on furniture should be removed as they will shrink, split and stain. This should be carried out by an upholsterer. The padding need not be removed, but metal tacks should be, to avoid staining.

Dirt and mud can be removed from wooden surfaces by gentle sponging with a 1–2 per cent solution of calgon in cold water. If water is not available, excess mud can be removed with a wooden blade.

In drying wood it is very important to avoid rapid and sudden drying out as shrinkage and cracking will occur. Any unpainted wooden object which has only superficial wetting can be dried by blotting the surface with a suitable absorbent material. However, objects that are thoroughly wet should be allowed to dry out slowly at a relative humidity of 50 per cent with good but not direct air circulation. Small items can be placed in polythene bags containing a few holes to allow slow drying to take place. Large items can be slowly dried under a polythene tent or envelope. The humidity (which must be monitored) is maintained with either dishes of water placed around the objects or if necessary a fine spray from a water hose. A dish of thymol crystals (which will slowly vaporize) placed under the tent will help reduce mould formation. While drying, the objects should be kept away from heat or direct sunlight.

Painted wooden objects such as polychrome sculpture and panel paintings and also veneered objects pose difficult problems and expert advice should be sought as soon as possible.

EMERGENCY TREATMENT OF OIL-PAINTINGS

Oil-paintings must not be frozen as this may cause extensive damage. If they have shrunk and warped with resultant buckling and flaking of the paint no attempt should be made to treat them; this is a job for the expert.

In general, with water-soaked oil-paintings on either cardboard or fabric supports, the object of the treatment is to dry protectively under pressure as soon as possible to prevent distortion and loss of paint adhesion.

Oil-paintings on cardboard must not be unframed and they should be dried face upwards. Protect the painting with Japan tissue or failing this clean non-printed newsprint paper. Then apply sheets of thymol-impregnated paper to both sides of the paper. On the top side place a sheet of masonite or glass which is kept weighted down. Initially, change the thymol sheets every few minutes, slowly extending to a few hours until the painting is dry. If the tissue or paper in contact with the paint surface adheres to it, do not attempt to remove. This provides protection against accidental removal of the paint and can be removed at a later date by an expert. If the painting has impasto, this will be flattened by glass or masonite, in which case a protective layer of sponge rubber should be placed between the painting/tissue-paper and the glass or masonite.

Oil-paintings on fabric should be unframed but not removed from their stretcher. They are dried face downwards on a flat surface. Again, protect the face of the painting with tissue or paper and place the whole on thymol sheets. More sheets and the weighted masonite or glass are positioned on the reverse of the painting. As previously, the sheets are changed until the painting is dry. Care must be taken when changing the sheets to ensure that no creases are impressed into the paint film (difficult to see as on the underside). The thickness of the layer of sheets underneath the painting on the face side will be determined by the surface relief of the painting. For the treatment of water-colour paintings refer to p. 269.

EMERGENCY TREATMENT OF CERAMICS, GLASS, METALS AND STONE

In general, these are not greatly affected by the action of water. However, if painted, they can cause serious problems due to flaking paint, etc., for which expert advice must be sought. Following a disaster, it is important to separate these materials from those such as paper, wood and textiles which require urgent treatment.

Ceramics, glass and stone, if completely waterlogged with relatively clean water (such as from a burst main or rainwater) can be allowed to dry out naturally. However, if impregnated with salt water or coated with mud or oil they are best kept wet until expert help arrives. If allowed to dry out, salt for example can cause mechanical damage to the object as it crystallizes out.

With the exception of iron and steel, most metals will not deteriorate rapidly after a short immersion in water. They can easily be wiped dry with absorbent cloth. Iron will rust quite quickly in water, especially if it contains salts, and although this will probably not be enough to cause any conservation problem, iron can badly stain materials in contact with it. This is particularly the case with costumes and uniforms which consist of a number of different materials in close proximity. Care must be taken to isolate the iron components as soon as possible. These are then wiped dry and coated with a protective oil or wax.

Copper (and its alloys) can also cause staining if left in contact with moisture for any length of time.

EMERGENCY TREATMENT OF BIOLOGICAL MATERIALS

Biological materials can be divided into two categories: dry specimens such as skins, furs, feathers, pinned insects and herbarium material, and wet specimens which are normally stored in 60–95 per cent ethyl alcohol.

Large dry vertebrate specimens which have been saturated with water should first be allowed to dry out. This is continued until a relative humidity of 60 per cent is achieved, which is the correct environment for these materials.

The dry specimens should then be cleaned using fine-haired paint brushes, or a vacuum cleaner with a cloth baffle over the hose, to remove dirt and mould.

To prevent the growth of mould, the specimens are treated in a cabinet with thymol or chlorocresol crystals. For large specimens a 10 per cent solution of either sodium pentachlorophenate or sodium orthophenylphenate in ethyl alcohol or industrial methylated spirits (NOT household 'methylated spirits') can be applied as a spray using a garden spray-gun. A spirit-soluble fungicide must be used so that the relative humidity of the environment is not increased.

Pinned insects that have become wet should be dried fairly rapidly at a temperature no greater than 40°C. In this way they can be dried before any mould growth can occur. Should there be any hold-up in the drying due to the amount of material that is wet, the bulk of the material should be held in a freezer. Either thymol or chlorocresol may be used to prevent mould growth where immediate drying or freezer space is not available.

Should mould have developed on specimens it may be readily removed, after drying, by immersing the specimen for a short time in chloroform and then cleaning off the remaining mycelia with a fine camel-hair brush as the specimen dries.

Dried herbarium material, usually in paper folders, should be treated in the same manner as library materials.

The majority of wet specimens are stored in ethyl alcohol contained in glass jars or tubes. If these containers are broken, care must first be taken to retain all identification labels with the correct specimens if this is possible. Provided the specimens have not dried or shrivelled, they should be washed, first in clean water, then in a fresh mixture of the preservative in which they were stored. They may then be stored, in preservative, in a new jar or tube.

Should the specimens have become dried or shrivelled, more especially the exoskeletons of invertebrates, they can be completely restored by soaking them in Decon 90 (a surface active agent) for about 16 hours. Following this they should be thoroughly rinsed and immersed in water until restoration is complete. They may then be stored.

EMERGENCY TREATMENT OF ETHNOGRAPHIC MATERIALS

Ethnographic materials are considered separately here because there are so many collections of this material in Australia. In addition, objects invariably consist of a number of different materials, some of which are very susceptible to water damage.

Objects which consist of a single material, for example wooden spears, boomerangs and utensils, also hair and feather objects, can be treated according to the procedures detailed in the earlier sections. Care, however, must be taken with painted and decorated objects with regard to their paints and binding media. The cleaning operations will depend on whether the object has been painted with an unbound pigment or whether it has been painted during the post-contact period with the use of synthetic paints, binding media or consolidants. In the latter case the pigments are likely to be more stable and careful washing with water can be used. However, great care must be taken with unbound pigments and specialist help should be called in.

The same applies to the use of fungicides for treating ethnographic materials which are in fact very prone to fungal growth. Natural resins and gums are used extensively in the fabrication of ethnographic objects and therefore solvent-based fungicides such as thymol, chlorocresol and sodium pentachlorophenate in acetone or methylated spirits must not be used. The same applies to 'modern' ethnographic objects where synthetic resins have been used for painting and sealing purposes, these will also be damaged by the solvents. In addition, the vapour of thymol crystals will soften gums and resins.

In the case of objects which have a well-consolidated surface or those containing gums and resins, it would be advisable to wipe or gently brush on a solution of 10 per cent sodium pentachlorophenate in distilled water as a fungicide. (Available as a 50 per cent solution of sodium pentachlorophenate – Santobrite from ICI.) This should be the final stage of the cleaning process before allowing the object to dry out.

Experience has shown that most collections contain a wide variety of paint types and surface coatings and each object must be individually tested before being cleaned. Many objects which at first appear to be coated with unbound ochre may in fact contain organic binding media such as emu fat or egg white and therefore extreme care must be taken with this material and should be left for expert attention.

This paper first appeared in M. S. Upton and C. Pearson (1978), Disaster Planning and Emergency Treatments in Museums, Art Galleries, Libraries, Archives and Allied Institutions *(Institute for the Conservation of Cultural Material Inc., Canberra).*

31

Protecting museums from threat of fire

H. L. Lein

Fire is potentially the most destructive disaster likely to affect a musuem. However, actions can be taken in advance which can limit the likely damage to the building and collections. Lein considers some of the options available to curators.

INTRODUCTION

Museum collections, libraries and historical buildings are terribly vulnerable to damage by fire, smoke and water. Museum visitors thronging to view the collections add to the problem: not only do they increase the risk of fire but at the same time they must be safeguarded from threat of fire.

These problems increasingly occupy the thoughts of museum managers. How can the responsibility for preserving irreplaceable treasures best be discharged? How should the museum protect itself from risk of fire? And if fire does occur, how can it be extinguished as early as possible to ensure the least possible damage and threat to life?

Museums occupy buildings that range from ultramodern steel-and-glass structures to historic landmarks. Some were designed to accommodate a constant flow of visitors, but many were originally designed for entirely different purposes. Museum buildings, too, serve many functions. In addition to exhibition halls, laboratories, offices, vaults and libraries, museums may house auditoriums, classrooms, restaurants, cafeterias and shops.

ORIGINS OF FIRE

Because of the varied nature and uses of a museum, there are many types of fire hazards. Careless smoking is always a danger. Electrical wiring can be a hazard, particularly during renovation work or preparation of new exhibits, as can the presence of various equipment involved in alterations – movable partitions, temporary materials, blowtorches, soldering irons and paint cans. Fires have begun through furnace malfunction, poor housekeeping practices, careless storage of maintenance supplies, vandalism – emphasizing the point that there is no way to *guarantee* against the threat of fire.

Fortunately, modern technology has addressed itself to these problems. The world has come a long way since the days when a fire system involved a manual pull station, used to ring a bell and let everyone know a fire was in progress. Fire protection systems of great sophistication are available that operate early enough so that damage can often be avoided or held to a minimum.

THE FOUR STAGES OF FIRE

To see how fire protection works, it is first necessary to understand the nature of a fire. The typical fire develops in four distinct stages:

1 *Incipient stage*. In the incipient stage, although no visible smoke, flame or significant heat has developed, a condition exists which generates a significant amount of combustion particles. These particles are created by chemical decomposition. Too small to be visible to the human eye, they behave like a gas, rising to the ceiling.

This first stage of fire usually develops over a long period of time: minutes, hours, even days. If the incipient fire can be detected at this stage, extinguishing it is a fairly simple matter, and damage is minimal.

2 *Smouldering stage*. If the fire condition continues to develop, the quantity of combustion particles increases to the point where their collective mass becomes visible: this is commonly called smoke. There is still no flame or much heat, and little irreparable damage.
3 *Flame stage*. As the fire condition develops further, the point of ignition occurs. Flames appear and heat increases.
4 *Heat stage*. At this point, large amounts of heat, flames, smoke and toxic gases are produced, and a full-scale fire rages. This stage usually develops very quickly from the third, often in seconds.

Most fires begin in a small way and, in the initial phase, develop very slowly. Obviously, the faster action is taken, the more quickly the fire can be brought under control, and the less likelihood of damage from flames, smoke or water.

POSSIBLE RESPONSES TO FIRE

Most museums have a good-sized staff of guards and watchmen on hand, so human response with portable extinguishers is often the best solution to a fire caught early. Dry chemical extinguishers leave a slight residue, but this can be cleaned up. Extinguishers containing Halon 1211 are also quite effective since they leave no residue, but they should be used with care in enclosed spaces or on extremely hot flames. The main problem is the loss of time in attempting to fight a fire by hand methods when it is already out of control.

Sprinkler systems

In the typical building, water sprinkles may be considered adequate provision for property safety. At the best of times, though, sprinklers are a compromise. They are activated by heat detectors, which aren't likely to react until a sizeable fire is raging. By this time the fire has a head start and smoke and toxic gases may have imperilled lives.

The museum has a more specific problem with sprinkler systems: water damage to vulnerable artefacts, particularly in storerooms, libraries and galleries.

Attempting to avoid problems with water, some museums use an automatically controlled 'dry' sprinkler system. With this method, an alarm will automatically energize the water valve for the appropriate sprinkler zone. The pipes then fill with water to the sprinkler heads, but no water is released until the temperature at the sprinkler head reaches its rating – usually 165°F. Only the heads that reach that high temperature will release water. In this way, water discharge is limited to the immediate area of fire threat, decreasing potential water damage. The problem is, of course, that by the time the heat reaches 165°F at the sprinkler heads in the ceiling, a considerable fire may be in progress down at floor level.

Flooding with halon

Halon 1301 is a halogenated gaseous compound, much denser than air, which can be liquefied by compression and stored for use. Released into a fire area, Halon 1301 interferes with the chemical chain reaction during combustion, thereby extinguishing the fire.

While occasionally used in hand extinguishers for local application, the prime value of Halon is in total flooding of an area. For this use, the museum must be divided into zones with doors that automatically close and ventilation that stops on receiving a fire-alarm signal. Within a few seconds of detection, the Halon 1301 gas is released and floods the area, effectively quenching the fire.

Colourless, odourless, and electrically non-conductive, Halon 1301 can be breathed and is considered safe at concentrations of up to 7 per cent, but prolonged inhalation is not recommended. Provisions must be made to evacuate all occupants of a Halon-flooded area as quickly as possible. For this reasons – and because it is a relatively expensive fire-extinguishing agent – Halon protection is more often provided in vaults and areas smaller than public galleries.

Carbon dioxide extinguishing is another common method of smothering a fire with gas. It is not suitable for occupied areas, except after a personnel evacuation. Dry chemicals, high-expansion foam and other extinguishing agents are also available for areas such as vaults and storerooms that house valuables that could be damaged by water.

The fire suppresion methods outlined here have one point in common: they can't begin to work until the fire has been detected. The best possible detection system is the key to any method of fire protection, and fortunately a variety of modern detection systems is available. These detectors provide the early warning necessary to evacuate the museum and begin extinguishing the fire while it is still small.

The factor of early warning becomes particularly important at night, when the building is deserted or much more lightly manned. Automatic fire detectors monitor the building and sound the alarm at the first traces of smoke – long before flames appear – to give fire-fighters that vital head start that can make all the difference between a small incident and a disaster involving loss of irreplaceable treasures and perhaps lives as well.

The type of detection depends on the use of the area. Most useful for early detection of a fire is the ionization-type smoke detector, defined as 'a device which detects the visible or invisible particles of combustion' generated by incipient (stage I) fire conditions.

Most common types of smoke detection devices are ionization and photoelectric detectors. Ionization detectors react to both visible smoke and invisible aerosols too small to be seen. Photoelectric detectors respond only to visible smoke – they do not detect invisible particles.

In general, the ionization detector is regarded as the best all-purpose early-warning device, since the release of invisible combustion products usually precedes any visible evidence of fire. In addition, invisible aerosols are released throughout all stages of fire development, so the ionization detector is always viable.

A useful feature for public galleries is that both ionization and photoelectric detectors may have adjustable levels of sensitivity, which can be set higher if some transient condition (such as cooking) tends to set off unwanted alarms.

Thermal devices, which detect a certain temperature or rate of increase, are also valuable for applications such as furnace rooms, garages and cafeterias, where particles of combustion from normal activities would unnecessarily set off smoke detectors.

In addition to these most commonly applied types, there are a number of highly specialized designs such as heat-sensing wires and flame detectors which may be recommended for certain specific situations.

Detectors pinpointing the location of fire or smoke are every museum's first line of defence. Reaction to this warning may be varied, according to assessment of the nature of the hazards involved.

Simplest is the human response with fire extinguisher. Most certain is an automatic signal to a central station or direct to the fire department, combined with automatic release of fire-suppression agents.

To avoid the more drastic suppression means while at the same time assuring backup protection if portable extinguishers prove inadequate, many museums provide a dual system.

One arrangement, with a built-in degree of protection from false alarm, involves early-warning smoke detection plus independent heat detectors. An early-warning system is used to alert building personnel, who respond with portable extinguishers. Should the fire continue to develop, heat detectors then activate automatic suppression systems and signal the fire department.

Another arrangement designed to avoid setting off the system except when necessary involves 'cross-zoning'. Activation of one detector sounds the alarm, but two detectors must be activated to operate the extinguishing system or signal the fire department. This arrangement uses no more detectors than normal, but a minimum of two zones is necessary in this design. One very effective method of utilizing cross-zoning is to equip one zone with ionization detectors and the other with photoelectric detectors.

Since each system should be carefully designed to suit the special contents and utilization of one particular museum, there is no way to predict the cost of fire detection and protection short of an actual estimate by an authority. Economics is another story; should a detection system be used just one time, it may have paid for itself many times over.

CONCLUSION

This article is intended to give a general overview of many of the types of fire protection suitable for museums and historic buildings. Fire protection is a highly specialized field, so much so that the architect, contractor or consulting engineer will probably wish to specify an integrated protection system to be designed, installed and maintained by a company specializing in fire protection.

After the special vulnerabilities and needs of a particular situation are pointed out and reviewed, the fire protection specialist will recommend a system that, in his experience, will best meet the situation.

This paper first appeared in Curator 25(2) (1982), pp. 91–6.

Further reading

Anderson, H. and McIntyre, J. E. (1985) *Planning Manual for Disaster Control in Scottish Libraries and Record Offices,* Edinburgh: National Library of Scotland.

Bachmann, K. (1992) *Conservation Concerns: A Guide for Collectors and Curators,* Washington, DC: Smithsonian Institution Press and Cooper Hewitt.

Child, R. E. (1993) *Electronic Environmental Monitoring for Museums*, Denbigh: National Museum of Wales and Archetype Books.

Dudley, D. H. and Wilkinson, I. B. (eds) (1979) *Museum Registration Methods*, Washington, DC: AAM.

Jones, Barclay G. (ed.) (1986) *Protecting Historic Architecture and Museum Collections from Natural Disasters*, Oxford: Butterworth-Heinemann.

Martin, J. H. (1987) *The Corning Flood: Museum under Water*, Corning Museum of Glass.

Mecklenburg, M. F. (1991) *Art in Transit: Studies in the Transport of Paintings*, Washington, DC: National Gallery of Art.

Museums Association (1987) *Lighting*, a conference on lighting in museums, galleries and historic houses, London: The Museums Association.

Oddy, A. (1992) *The Art of the Conservator*, British Museum Press.

Pinniger, D. (1989) *Insect Pests in Museums*, London: Institute of Archaeology.

Richard, M., Mecklenburg, M. F. and Merrill, R. M. (1991) *Art in Transit: Handbook for Packing and Transporting Paintings,* Washington, DC: National Gallery of Art.

Stolow, N. (1987) *Conservation and Exhibitions: Packing, Transport, Storage and Environmental Considerations*, London: Butterworth.

Thompson, J. M. A. (1992) *Manual of Curatorship* (2nd edn), Oxford: Butterworth-Heinemann.

Thomson, G. (1986) The Museum Environment, Oxford: Butterworth-Heinemann.

Upton, M. S. and Pearson, C. (1978) *Disaster Planning and Emergency Treatments in Museums, Art Galleries, Libraries, Archives and Allied Institutions*, Canberra: Institute for the Conservation of Cultural Material Inc.

Various (1993) 'Disaster planning' (special issue), *Museum News* 69(3).

Various (1993) 'Emergency preparedness' (special issue), *History News*, 48(1).

Index

acetic acid 85, 130, 140
acetone 32–3
acid free card 134
activated alumina 134, 136, 139
activated carbon 107–8, 136, 139, 142, 165
adhesives 16, 129
air conditioning 7, 57, 85–6, 107–16, 120, 124, 136–8, 165
alkaline wash 136, 139, 165
American Institute for Conservation 14, 19, 86
archaeology collections 3, 5, 51–3, 193
art market 2, 28

bendiocarb 222
biology collections 3, 83, 149, 193, 274–5
biscuit beetle 220
booklice 214–15
books 266–7
British Antique Furniture Restoration Association 13
British Museum 56–8

Cairo Museum 85
carpet beetle 212–13, 217–33
cellulose nitrate 138
ceramic collections 52, 55, 57, 130, 263, 274
cleaning 16–17, 30–4
clothes moth 220, 226
collection access 179–86
collection condition surveys 6, 54, 60–82
collection management 1, 2
collection managers 4
collections access policies 181
computers 7, 101–6, 115, 126–7, 147–50, 199–201
concrete 136, 142, 160
condensation 7, 111, 149
conservation 5, 47–50, 51; cleaning 5, 21–9; construction materials 160–2, 174–5; documentation 19; ethics 4, 5, 11–34; materials 5, 18; research 84; scientific examination 16
conservators 4–5, 11–20, 30–4, 47–50, 54
Coopex 222
corrosion inhibitors 112, 138
costume collections 6, 193
Courtauld Institute 32
Crafts Council 13

databases 199–201
dataloggers 7, 101–4, 126
demonstrations 35
Dichlorvos 222–3, 236
disasters 6, 40, 42, 240–5; asset evaluation 248; cleaning 27–9, 267; emergency supplies 249–50, 256–9; emergency treatments 262–75; freezing 264, 266, 269; planning 10, 246–51; planning team 247; plans 251–4, 263; prevention 243; protection 249
discovery centres 9
display 88–92, 123–8
distressing 18–19
Drione 236–7
Dugald Costume Museum 190, 193

earthquakes 241–2
electrostatic precipitators 165
environmental surveys 6–7
epoxy resin 16
equilibrium moisture content 93–100
ethnographic collections 56–7, 83, 213, 275
ethylene oxide 138

fakes 19
Ficam 222
fire 103, 242, 276–9; alarms 170; BCF 262; causes 169–70, 277; carbon dioxide 171, 262; detection 170, 278, Halon 171–2, 262, 277, 278; manual extinguishers 172; powder extinguishers 262, 277; prevention 169–70; protection 149; retardants 133; sprinklers 149, 153, 171–2, 277–8
flood 109, 156–7, 166, 212, 242, 263–75
Florence flood 241, 264
formaldehyde 85, 129–34, 136; control 107, 112
formic acid 85, 130, 140
fragility 215
fumigation 10, 138, 168
fungicide 264
furniture collections 6, 11–20, 164, 211

geology collections 3, 48, 83, 158, 164
Getty Conservation Institute 62, 83–7, 102
glass 55, 130, 134, 263, 274
glaze 25, 31, 34, 218
Glenbow Museum 191, 197

handling 6, 9, 53, 56, 85, 202–11, 213; large objects 207; taping glass 207–8
historic houses 117–22
history collections 3
hurricanes 242
hydrogen sulphide 140

industrial collections 3
insecticides 222–3
interactive technologies 9
Israel Museum 85

leather 52, 137, 141, 143, 213, 267, 272
Library of Congress 136
light 55, 57–8, 113, 117, 141, 162, 166–7, 190, 212; control 6, 118–20, 123–8; fibre optics 7; louvres 124, 126; monitoring 6, 102, 104, 118, 125, 127; natural 7, 118–20, 123–8

lining 26–7, 28, 48
Louvre, the 22, 23

magnetic media 271
meal worm beetle 212
medical collections 3
metal storage materials 133–4
metals 8, 52, 54–5, 57–8, 85,
    129–30, 134, 137, 140, 143,
    164, 263, 274
methyl bromide 214, 212–13, 237–8
Metropolitan Museum of Art 22,
    24, 30, 197–201
microenvironments 7, 85, 88–100,
    164
mothballs 236–8
mould 263–5, 268, 274
Museum Registration Scheme 3
museum policy 2
Museums and Galleries Commis-
    sion 3
musical instrument collections 3

naphthalene 235–9
National Gallery 22, 27, 29–34,
    123–8
National Museum of American Art
    176
National Trust 62, 117–22
natural science collections 5
neglect 3, 8
nitrogen oxides 136–43

object condition 65–9
object condition reports 6, 15
object life 2
object stability 4–5, 51–9, 84
open days 9
oxygen-free environments 7, 57–8
ozone 85, 136–43, 165

packing and packaging 9–10, 53,
    89, 167–8
paintings 21–9, 48, 52, 88–92,
    117, 120, 123–8, 137, 142, 158,
    164, 204–9, 273; stacking
    205–6, 209
paper 56–7, 117, 137, 141, 143,
    266–9
para-dichlorobenzene (PDB) 234–5,
    239
particulate filters 107, 139, 165
particulates 136, 142, 165
patina 16, 24–6
pests 6, 10, 52, 57, 212, 212–33;
    behaviour 218–21, 230; carbon
    dioxide 10, 212–13, 215–16,

228; control 149, 221–28;
    control strategies 10, 153, 217;
    freezing 10, 224–30; isolation
    223–4; monitoring 219–20, 231;
    nitrogen 10, 216; safety 229,
    236–9; sources 218, 221–2
phosphine 214–15, 237–8
photographic collections 137–8,
    141, 143, 176, 269–71
plaster beetle 220
plastics 56
pollutants 6, 8, 57, 85, 135–6,
    164–5; from construction
    materials 85–6, 107, 129–34,
    136–40
potassium permanganate filters
    108, 112, 134
Prado, the 136
preventative/preventive conserva-
    tion 6, 9–10, 28, 83–7, 102, 117
pyrethrin 236–8

registrars 4
relative humidity 7, 15, 53–4, 117,
    120, 130, 141, 157, 163–5,
    269–81; control 6, 84, 86,
    88–92, 93–100, 107–16, 121,
    149; electronic monitors 105–6,
    120; monitoring 6, 101–4, 111,
    120, 127; see also computers;
    dataloggers
Rentokil bubble 212–16
replacement parts 5, 16–17, 36,
    41–2
reproductions 37, 39, 58
restoration 5, 17–18, 21, 23, 35
retouching 18, 21, 23, 27, 30
reversibility 5, 15–16, 22, 26–7
rubber 52, 56, 137

safety 152
salt efflorescence 55
saturated salt solutions 7, 97
science collections 5, 35–46
Science Museum 35–46
sculpture 202–3, 209–10
sectioning 9, 36–44
security 53, 103, 152, 157,
    159–61, 168–9, 179, 180,
    184–5, 190
shock 10
showcases 88–92
silica gel 7, 88–100; conditioning
    90, 95–100
silverfish 220
Smithsonian Institution 149–54
smoke 8, 135

smoking 140–3
solvents 16, 31–4
space 8
space audit 147–54
specialist curators 3, 4, 47–50
specialist groups 3
standards of care 3
sticky traps 219–20, 231
stone 57, 130, 263, 274
storage 6, 8, 85, 151, 154–75;
    access 158, 179–86; construction
    173–5; high density 176–8; off-
    site 8, 158; organisation 180;
    temporary 167–8; users 180;
    visible 9, 187–201
study areas 184
sugar 56, 58
sulphur oxides 8, 135–7, 139–43

Tate Gallery 7, 123–8
temperature 54, 104–6, 117, 120,
    130, 141, 163–5; control
    107–16, 121; monitoring 127
textiles 52, 55, 58, 117, 120, 137,
    141–2, 266, 271–2
thermohygrographs 102, 120
training 9, 49, 86, 254–5
transport collections 35, 36–8, 52
transportation 6, 9–10, 53, 89

ultraviolet radiation 7, 55, 57, 167;
    control 162; monitoring 106,
    118–19
United Kingdom Institute for
    Conservation 11, 13, 14, 19, 47,
    49
University of British Columbia
    Museum of Anthropology 188–9,
    192–3, 197

vacuum drying 265–6
vacuum hot table 27
Vapona 222–3, 236, 238–9
vapour barriers 110, 113
varnish 23–4, 30–4
vibration 10, 53
Victoria and Albert Museum 11,
    105–6, 217–33

water damage 263–4
whirling hygrometers 120
wooden construction materials 55,
    129–33, 140
wooden objects 52, 272
woodworm 216
working exhibits 5, 6, 35–46